9.23.77

GREAT DEBATES IN ECONOMICS

A Special Note from the Publisher

Because the subject categories of these debates fall so logically into two main divisions (I, History, Development, and Growth; and II, Analysis and Policy), we anticipated that some readers would want to deal with each of those divisions individually, and for your convenience this book is also available in two separate volumes.

Volume I is subtitled History, Development, and Growth and contains all of the material which is in Part I of this book.

Volume II is subtitled Analysis and Policy and contains all of the material which is in Part II of this book.

GREAT
DEBATES
IN
ECONOMICS

RICHARD T. GILL

Goodyear Publishing Company, Inc.
Pacific Palisades, California

Library of Congress Cataloging in Publication Data
Main entry under title:
Great debates in economics.
    1. Economics — Addresses, essays, lectures.
I. Gill, Richard T.
HB34.G67 1976b   330   75-46180
ISBN 0-87620-370-5

Copyright © 1976 by
Goodyear Publishing Company, Inc.
Pacific Palisades, California

Current printing (last digit):
10 9 8 7 6 5 4 3 2 1

Y-3705-4
ISBN: 0-87620-370-5

Printed in the United States of America

1993701

For Thomas

Preface

THIS book of readings focuses on differences of opinion about the fundamental principles of economics. In Part I, the debates center on issues of history, development, and growth; in Part II, attention is given to more short-term, but nevertheless deep, problems of economic analysis and policy.* In total, the nine debates cover the most prominent areas of economics where experts have differed, and still differ, quite sharply. The book is meant to stand as a supplement to a standard textbook in a principles of economics course at the college level.

This project is an offshoot of my earlier book: *Economics: A Text with Readings, 2nd ed.* That book contains debates in economics as well as standard textual material on the theory that economics can be properly conveyed to the student only when its controversial aspects are related to its basic structure. By separating off some of the material included in that book, I have been able to expand each of the Great Debates, to include several additional debates, and, of course, to make the debates available to those who were not using that very large text. In view of the importance of the controversies considered here, it seemed desirable that they be made available to the largest possible audience. Historians, political scientists, and philosophers, for example, may easily find these materials as interesting as do students of economics.

My debts in the preparation of this book are great, especially to the authors, past and present, of the readings included here. Without them, there would, of course, be no book at all. I also thank my publisher, Al Goodyear, who, in the course of seven books now, has taken an unusually helpful and creative attitude to my work. I would further like to acknowledge the help of Dr. Roger Nelson, Myrtle Nelson,

---

*Part I and Part II have also been published as two individual books: *Great Debates in Economics I: History, Development, and Growth* and *Great Debates in Economics, II: Analysis and Policy.*

David G. Gill, and Professor Herbert Geyer for their assistance in collecting some of the materials included here. The preparation of the book was possible only through the helpful work of Colette Conboy, Patrice Sobin, Jane Hellesoe-Henon, and especially Gerald P. Rafferty.

Always at the end, in the place of special honor, is my wife. My debt this time is even greater than usual. It was her frequently repeated question — "When are you going to do that interesting debates book?" — that kept *my* interest alive, and actually got me down to work. Usually, one accepts sole responsibility for the final product. In this case, I have to ask that she accept a share as well.

Richard T. Gill

Contents

GREAT
DEBATES
IN
ECONOMICS

Introduction

ECONOMISTS sometimes agree. It seems necessary to stress this fact in a decade when disagreement among economists seems more apparent. Of course, agreement is not necessarily virtuous. Later generations of economists have frequently been particularly harsh with the agreed upon "truths" of earlier generations. Still, economists do often agree, and part of their agreement is that the field has developed enormously over the past two centuries: in its scope, in the refinement of its concepts, and in the sophistication of its statistical and other techniques.

This is the good news. It is not, however, the news that this book will emphasize. We are concerned precisely with those areas where economists have disagreed, both in the past and especially in the present. The disagreements recorded here are not superficial. They are profound, passionate, and often seemingly irreconcilable. Finding such areas is not very difficult. In fact, they loom so large in the contours of our subject that no serious student can avoid them.

Why do economists disagree? Commonly, three reasons are cited. First, there is the possibility of logical error on the part of one or both parties to a dispute. Human beings — even mathematicians — are fallible and, as techniques and problems become more and more complex, the likelihood of logical error increases. Machines may protect us from some of our simpler errors, but basically machines tell us only what we have programmed them to tell us, and logical error may easily be present in the structure of our thinking.

Second, there is the possibility of disagreement about the facts of the case. Economists cannot usually perform controlled experiments. They must wait for history to generate their data. But the economic data that this history generates are sometimes crude and unreliable, seldom in the exact form that economic theoreticians would like, and almost always distorted by social, political, and other "exogenous" factors, making the economic components of the data virtually impossible to separate out. An appeal to the "facts" can sometimes be the end of a debate in economics; more often, it is at the core of the dispute.

Finally, economists may disagree because they have different views of what should be, as opposed to what is. Their values may be different. Here we are dealing with different concepts of the good individual or the good society. The Bible says that it is easier for a camel to get through the eye of a needle than for a rich man to enter the kingdom of heaven. If you accept this philosophy, you will find yourself opposed to the advice of most economists on virtually every economic issue because most of this advice will be based on the premise that "more" is "better." There may be no disagreement at all on logic or fact; it is solely a difference of ideals — the ascetic monk versus the epicurean.

Although it has certain virtues, however, this threefold division of sources of disagreement is somewhat artificial. For one thing, as you will see in reading this book, most debates in economics involve all three differences simultaneously. Thus, in the Galbraith-Solow-Marris debate about the Industrial State (Great Debate Six), there are clearly many disagreements on matters of fact — the degree of dominance of the large corporation, the behavior patterns of corporate management, the persuadability of consumers by advertising, and the like. But there is also a dispute about logic: Solow accuses Galbraith of making a "sophomore error," to which Galbraith replies that "alas, the error is again Professor Solow's." And differences of value judgments abound: witness Marris' comments about capitalism that he suspects will be "disliked" by both Galbraith and Solow. In no case in this book, does a debate fall neatly within one or even two of our three compartments.

More seriously, however, is the problem of the interaction among logic, empirical issues, and general philosophies. Thus, Schumpeter notes in his analysis of the Marxian critique of capitalism (Great Debate Two) that Marxism contains a vital religious element and that this caused Marx to shade or alter his logic from time to time to conform to his values. Schumpeter also notes that the follower of Marx tends to regard dissent from the master as evidence not only of error but of "sin." Similarly, in the contemporary debate over monetarism (Great Debate Eight): a frequent criticism of Milton Friedman and his followers is that they have a certain ideology which blinds them to evident economic realities. Running through all these debates, indeed, is the notion that one's opponents are very likely missing the truth because of underlying bias. The implication is that the particular economist knows how he wants the evidence to come out; and that, in one way or another, he will cut corners to make sure it does come out that way.

Interaction can even be carried a step further. Economic theories, if they are influential enough, can actually affect subsequent economic events, and thus the "facts" that later emerge. In the debate over democracy and economic development (Great Debate Three), Professor Wrong suggests that Heilbroner's views on the need for strong central governments, most likely communist governments, to promote development in the poor countries of the world could actually help bring about that outcome. It is widely accepted that one of the reasons for the success of Marxism in the world generally is the Marxian view that the triumph of communism is "inevitable." If people think a certain outcome is inevitable, they may work harder (not less hard) to help achieve it.

In sum, our theories and values may actually help shape the factual world of the future. At a minimum, they will influence the problems we find interesting to analyze, the particular areas of knowledge we seek out, and the facts that loom up as important to us. Particularly if our values are largely implicit or unconsciously held, we may feel we are only being objective when, in fact, we persistently fail to cope with parts of the evidence that seem obvious to an outsider.

The word "outsider" suggests the nature of the problem. In the field of economics we are essentially all "insiders." It might seem that when it came to an historical debate, like Ricardo versus Malthus (Great Debate One), we could be quite objective. But actually, one's evaluation of that particular debate is likely to hinge greatly on one's view of the Keynesian Revolution more than a century later, and that Revolution is, of course, still a matter of passionate concern and dispute in many respects. When it comes to more clearly contemporary problems — should we place limits on growth, on energy consumption, on high personal incomes, on wages-and-prices, and so on? — then everyone of us is affected by prior views of what he wishes the answer would turn out to be. We are deeply, unavoidably involved in the final outcome.

This personal stake is what makes debates in economics difficult to judge, but also fascinating to study. And, of course, it poses a special problem for the author. In the introductory essays, I have tried to place each debate in its context within the field of economics at large. I have also tried to bring out certain of the central issues that separate the participants. This is important because, in several cases, the readings were not written in direct response to a particular book or article, but simply express a point of view that is in contrast to that of the book or article. In either event — and here is the difficult point — I have tried not to take sides in introducing the debates. Because of the problems we have been discussing, it is unlikely that I have been completely successful in muting the prejudices I do hold with respect to many of these questions. By definition, I could not hope to avoid the personal prejudices of which I am unaware.

Hence, it is necessary to begin this book with a warning. Don't accept things at face value; inspect the arguments closely; use your own judgment. Or, to put it in terms of one of the most ancient phrases in economics: *caveat emptor*. Let the buyer — in this case, the reader — beware!

PART I

HISTORY, DEVELOPMENT, AND GROWTH

GREAT DEBATE ONE

RICARDO VERSUS MALTHUS ON "GENERAL GLUTS"

RICARDO VERSUS MALTHUS ON "GENERAL GLUTS"

NO DEBATE in the history of economics has had more distinguished participants nor more interesting later repercussions than the one with which we begin this book. Such is the nature of the Ricardo-Malthus controversy over the possibility of "general gluts."

Both men were among the great economists of all time. Thomas Robert Malthus (1766–1834) achieved fame with his first major publication and has been a household name ever since. Indeed, his theory of population pressure and scarce food supplies—the well-known Malthusian "geometric" and "arithmetic" ratios—may well have more relevance today (especially in Asia) than it did in his own time. David Ricardo (1782–1823) was equally renowned in his day and had enormous influence on all economists (including Karl Marx) who followed after him. In a technical and professional sense, Ricardo's work dominated nineteenth century economics more profoundly than did that of his contemporary, Malthus. Ricardo was a superbly logical and controlled thinker. Malthus was less consistent, but, by the same token, less rigid and often more insightful. The constant discussions between these two men—carried on in visits together, at meetings of the Political Economy Club, in correspondence, in notes on each other's writings, and, in one instance, by Ricardo's writing the equivalent of a book in criticism of Malthus' work[1]—represent the interaction of the finest minds coping with the very basics of economic thought.

We will be discussing and presenting their disagreement over the possibility of universal gluts, or what we today would call depressions—periods of mass unemployment where there is a lack of demand for (a "glut" of) all commodities in general. Ricardo said that there could be an oversupply of particular goods but not

[1] The work in question was Malthus's *Principles of Political Economy*. We shall be quoting from this book and from Ricardo's elaborate notes on it at the very beginning of the debate that follows (see pp. 14–28).

of all goods in general. Malthus said that there could be such a general oversupply and that, in fact, there *was* this condition in Britain at that very time. And here we come to the great later significance of this debate. For Malthus was actually foreshadowing what was to be the most important single development in twentieth century economics: the Keynesian Revolution. Malthus's theory of gluts was not fully developed and its impact at the time was small—in part because of Ricardo's impressive rebuttal—but the insight was definitely there. What we witness in this debate then is an early encounter with one of the major ideas that has shaped modern economics.

THE THEORETICAL BACKGROUND OF THE DEBATE

What was Malthus' particular version of this important idea? Equally interesting, how was it that Ricardo, a truly brilliant man, failed to see any real virtue in his friend's argument?

In order to understand their disagreement, one has to appreciate one or two points about the general theoretical framework within which the discussion was carried on. Both men dealt with an economic world composed of three classes: landlords, capitalists and laborers. They had some differences of opinion about the functions and merits of these various classes, but on two points they were largely agreed. First, they both accepted the same general theory of the response of population to economic change. Or, to put it in terms of economic classes, they believed that increases in the wages and the standard of living of the laborers of the society would cause an increase in the supply of labor. This increase could be a product of lower death rates or earlier marriages and higher birth rates, and it might take a greater or lesser number of years to take place, but, in principle, they were agreed that high wages would bring more workers, fairly quickly.

Second, they agreed about the function of the capitalist and the general nature of the process of capital accumulation. Their mental picture of this process was somewhat different from ours today, in part at least because their society was still predominantly agricultural. We think of capital accumulation today in terms of added machines, factories, buildings and the like. They tended to think of the process in terms of what they sometimes called "advances to labor." In order to produce corn (our wheat) next year, someone has to support and provide tools for the laborer who will be working in the fields in advance of the harvest. The person who provides this support is the capitalist. The form of the support is the food, other necessaries and tools that the capitalist already has in his possession at the beginning of the year (that is, in the case of corn, from the previous harvest). The sacrifice that the capitalist makes is in terms of his own consumption foregone. Had he not made these "advances" to his laborers, he could have consumed more goods himself today. Why then does he make this sacrifice? Ultimately because of profits. By not consuming today, he puts laborers to work who will return him a greater product at the end of the year than he advanced to them at the beginning of the year. In other words, the advanced wages are less than the final product.

(and the difference is the capitalist's profit.[2] Of course, the higher these wages are, other things equal, the lower the profits will be. If profits get too low, the capitalist might lose interest in accumulating any further capital.

All this is agreed between Malthus and Ricardo and, further, they both assume an additional feature of the process of capital accumulation: namely, that it involves the advancing of food, clothing, and so on, to *productive* as opposed to *unproductive* laborers. This is an important distinction in Classical thought, which we need only mention and will not develop here. Essentially, Ricardo and Malthus (and Adam Smith before them) divided laborers into two groups: productive laborers (for example, farm or factory laborers) who produce tangible goods, and unproductive laborers (for example, household servants, government employees) who produce services. When the capitalist or the landlord hires more servants for his estate, he is acting in a way economically indistinguishable from consuming more goods himself. In other words, the consumption of the well-to-do can take the form either of consuming more goods or of consuming the services of unproductive labor. By contrast, when the capitalist advances the necessaries of life to an added laborer in the field he receives a tangible good (say, corn) at the end of the production process. This is capital accumulation. Although the Classical distinction between productive and unproductive labor has merit in some contexts, it is doubtful that it will stand quite the burden of argument they rested on it. However, this need not be a major difficulty for us because the distinction does not form a point of contention between our two debaters.

THE MAIN POINT OF CONTROVERSY

We can now summarize the main point of contention rather succinctly. Malthus argues that there can be such a rapid accumulation of capital under certain circumstances that there will be no market for the flood of goods that all these productive laborers will produce (pp. 14–15).[3] There will then occur a general glut. There will be insufficient effective demand for all goods at once, and also for labor. The result will be stagnation in business and unemployment for many workers. Imagine, Malthus says, a situation in which all capitalists (and even landlords) decide to cut their consumption to the bone so that they can advance more and more capital to productive laborers. A great flood of goods will come forth. But who will consume these goods? Not the capitalists or landlords, answers Malthus, because, by hypothesis, they are interested only in saving, not in consumption (p. 14). How about the workers? Well, no capitalist in his right mind would want to keep accumulating capital simply to enrich his workers. No, claims Malthus, there will be a general lack of demand for these goods. And the capitalists (and any

[2] This is not quite accurate because there is the landlord's land rent to be paid out of the final product. We are largely setting aside the question of rent payments here because they do not materially affect the point at issue between Ricardo and Malthus on the matter of gluts.
[3] Unless otherwise specified, page references will be to pages in this book. This will be our practice throughout all the Great Debates.

landlords who are operating like capitalists) will quickly cut back on production. The net result—a general glut and mass unemployment.

Ricardo's basic answer to Malthus' contention can also be put rather succinctly. According to Ricardo, the rapid accumulation of capital that Malthus envisages may lead to one of two results. If the capitalists and landlords have accumulated too rapidly, the consequence will be very high wages for labor and very low profits on the advanced capital (pp. 15–16). This reflects the fact that the demand for productive labor has gone up and the immediate supply of labor is given. There will be no trouble marketing the goods that the laborers have produced because high wages mean precisely that the laborers will be demanding and consuming more goods than before. Hence there will be no "glut." However, because profits are so low, the capitalists and landlords will doubtless cut back on their rate of accumulation. The next year, they themselves will consume more, advance less capital and thereby cause a reduction of wages and a return of the rate of profit to an appropriate level.

In the long run, moreover, if wages stay high for a time, population will increase (p. 16). In this case, the added supply of laborers will bid down wages per workers (though, of course, there will be more workers), and profits will be at least partially restored.[4] The added goods in this case will be demanded and consumed partly by the added labor force and partly by the capitalists and landowners. As in the first case, there will be no oversupply of goods in general.

The reason Ricardo can be so sure of his position is that he is envisioning a picture of the economic process in which general gluts are virtually impossible. Malthus (on p. 18) makes a critical reference to M. Say (the French economist, J. B. Say, 1767–1832), and it is, indeed, what we call Say's Law that is in the back of Ricardo's mind. This law states that because "supply creates its own demand," it is impossible to have a general excess of supply or general deficiency of demand in the economy as a whole. If I produce another bushel of corn (added supply), I either consume it myself (added demand) or give it to my servants (added demand) or put it out in advances to productive laborers (added demand in the form of capital accumulation). In each case, the added supply creates an exactly equivalent amount of added demand (p. 17). Of course, we may have too much corn *relative to, say,* clothing, but this is simply saying that we have too little clothing—particular excesses and deficiencies will always balance out.

INTUITION VERSUS RIGOR

In the twentieth century, John Maynard Keynes assaulted Say's Law head on, and the result, even critics would agree, was a basic rethinking of the structure of economic analysis. Malthus tried the same thing more than a century earlier and,

---

[4] Only partially restored, because as population increases in the Classical world, diminishing returns in agriculture puts both profits and wages together in an ever tighter squeeze. Indeed, eventually this squeeze gets so tight that both further capital accumulation and further population growth must cease.

for this reason, earns the great tribute paid to him by Keynes in the excerpt that concludes our debate (p. 37). However, to say that he deserves credit for his insight is not to say that he proved his case in the actual discussion with Ricardo. In fact, in terms of debating points, most unprejudiced observers would probably award the prize to Ricardo (as, in fact, the nineteenth and early twentieth century did by ignoring this aspect of Malthusian thought). Ricardo has a quite consistent theory, which, moreover, he has fully in his grasp, while Malthus is struggling to express a new concept and one which seems to shift ground slightly every time he tries to express it.

Ultimately, to make the case he wanted to make, Malthus would have had to move away from the real-commodity world of Say's Law to the monetary world in which actual economic transactions take place. He never quite did this, although he did show a remarkable awareness that money might somehow be at the root of this particular evil (see, for example, his footnote on page 24). Also, he has a much more vivid view of certain decisions, particularly consumption decisions, than did Ricardo. Ricardo lives in a world in which a decision not to invest or accumulate capital is more or less automatically a decision *to* consume. Malthus, by contrast, emphasizes the fact that it is often a rather complicated matter to increase economic wants and to insure that consumption demand in the economy as a whole will be sufficient. He never makes the sharp distinction that Keynes was later to make between investment decisions and saving (or not consuming) decisions, but his argument tends that way, and at times it almost seems that he understands the matter quite firmly.

Thus, we have a clear contrast in this debate between an imperfectly expressed, but substantial, intuition and a quite clearly expressed, but rather limited, formal economic theory. And this brings out an important feature of the evolution of economics: the more consistent and intellectually compelling argument is not always the better one. In the world of hindsight, winners and losers are not always what they seemed earlier on. Fruitful errors can sometimes be more significant than apparently air-tight arguments. These lessons, drawn from the Malthus-Ricardo confrontation, may be useful to keep in mind as we proceed in this book from the past to the great economic debates of our own time.

"Of Accumulation, or the Saving From Revenue to Add to Capital, Considered as a Stimulus to the Increase of Wealth."

Thomas Robert Malthus

Thomas Robert Malthus (1766–1834), a British parson but also a professor of political economy, is known today primarily for his pessimistic theory of population; his theory of "general gluts," however, was what especially attracted Keynes' attention.

Those who reject mere population as an adequate stimulus to the increase of wealth, are generally disposed to make every thing depend upon accumulation. It is certainly true that no permanent and continued increase of wealth can take place without a continued increase of capital. . . . But we have yet to inquire what is the state of things which generally disposes a nation to accumulate; and further, *what is the state of things which tends to make that accumulation the most effective, and lead to a further and continued increase of capital and wealth.*

It is undoubtedly possible by parsimony to devote at once a much larger share than usual of the produce of any country to the maintenance of productive labour; and it is quite true that the labourers so employed are consumers as well as unproductive labourers; and as far as the labourers are concerned, there would be no diminution of consumption or demand. But it has already been shewn that the consumption and demand occasioned by the persons employed in productive labour can never alone furnish a motive to the accumulation and employment of capital; and with regard to the capitalists themselves, together with the landlords and other rich persons, they have, by the supposition, agreed to be parsimonious, and by depriving themselves of their usual conveniences and luxuries to save from their revenue and add to their capital. Under these circumstances, I would ask, how it is possible to suppose that the increased

Excerpted from Thomas Robert Malthus, *Principles of Political Economy,* in Piero Sraffa, ed., *The Works and Correspondence of David Ricardo,* Vol. II (New York: Cambridge University Press, 1951), pp. 301–31. Reprinted by permission.

[Note: This debate has been set up to show both views of the Ricardo-Malthus controversy. The phrases within the Malthus text to which Ricardo's comments refer are italicized.]

Ricardo's Notes on Malthus
David Ricardo

David Ricardo (1782–1823) entered economics late and died young, but produced in the *Principles of Political Economy and Taxation* (1817), one of the great classics of economics.

Ricardo   *But it has already been shewn &c.*

The consumption and demand, occasioned by the persons employed in producing any particular quantity of wealth, can never be a sufficient motive for producing it, if they are to have the whole of the commodities produced, and are to give for it only the labour which produced it; but suppose they take seven eighths of it, and their employer retains one eighth, with which he can again employ 5 or 10 additional men, who again take seven eighths of the commodities they produce, leaving the employer the power to employ additional labour the following year; cannot such accumulations go on while the land last cultivated will yield more food than is consumed by the cultivators?—when it will not do that, there is an end on every system to all accumulation. But if a society consisted of nothing but landowners, farmers, manufacturers of necessaries, and labourers, accumulation could go on to this point, provided only that population increased fast enough. If capital increased too rapidly for the population, instead of commanding seven-eighths of the produce, they might command ninety-nine hundredths, and thus there would be no motive for further accumulation. If every man were disposed to accumulate every portion of his revenue but what was necessary to his urgent wants such a state of things would be produced; for the principle of population is not strong enough to supply a demand for labourers so great as would then exist. But the condition of the labourer would then be most happy, for what

Excerpted from Malthus-Ricardo correspondence, from Piero Sraffa, ed., *The Works and Correspondence of David Ricardo*, Vol. IX (New York: Cambridge University Press, 1951), pp. 9–11, 14–27. Reprinted by permission.

Malthus quantity of commodities, obtained by the increased number of productive labourers, should find purchasers, without such a fall of price as would probably sink their value below the costs of production, or, at least, very greatly diminish both the power and the will to save.

Ricardo can be more prosperous than the condition of him who has a commodity to sell for which there is an almost unlimited demand, while the supply is limited, and increases at a comparatively slow rate. All this is conformable to the general principle which has been often mentioned. Profits would be low because wages would be high, and would only continue so till population increased and labour again fell.

Mr. Malthus asks "how is it possible to suppose that the increased quantity of commodities, obtained by the increased number of productive labourers should find purchasers, without such a fall of price as would probably sink their value below the cost of production, or, at least, very greatly diminish both the power and the will to save?["] To which I answer that the power and the will to save will be very greatly diminished, for that must depend upon the share of the produce allotted to the farmer or manufacturer. But with respect to the other question where would the commodities find purchasers? If they were suited to the wants of those who would have the power to purchase them, they could not fail to find purchasers, and that without any fall of price.

If a thousand hats, a thousand pairs of shoes, a thousand coats, a thousand ounces of gold, were produced, they would all have a relative value to each other, and that relative value would be preserved, if they were suited to the wants of the society, whether the greatest portion went to the labourers or to their employers.

If wages are low, only one-half may perhaps be given to the labourers. If high three-fourths—but whether in the hands of the masters or of the men they would not have a different value.

If £500 in money were in the hands of the masters, and 500 hats, 500 qrs. of corn &c. &c. and the remaining quantity in the hands of the workmen, they would have the same relative value, as if £600 money were in the hands of the masters and 600 of every other commodity, and the remaining quantity in the hands of the workmen. Which of these distributions shall take place depends on the proportions between capital and labour, but whichever it may be, no effect can be produced on price, if the commodities be suited to the wants of those who can command them. If they are not it is the interest of the producers to make them so. It follows then, from what I have here said, that if the commodities produced be suited to

Ricardo the wants of the purchasers, they cannot exist in such abundance as not to find a market.

Mistakes may be made, and commodities not suited to the demand may be produced—of these there may be a glut; they may not sell at their usual price; but then this is owing to the mistake, and not to the want of demand for productions. For every thing produced there must be a proprietor. Either it is the master, the landlord, or the labourer. Whoever is possessed of a commodity is necessarily a demander, either he wishes to consume the commodity himself, and then no purchaser is wanted; or he wishes to sell it, and purchase some other thing with the money, which shall either be consumed by him, or be made instrumental to future production. The commodity he possesses will obtain him this or it will not. If it will, the object is accomplished, and his commodity has found a market. If it will not what does it prove? that he has not adapted his means well to his end, he has miscalculated. He wants for example cotton goods, and he has produced cloth with a view to obtain them. Either there are cotton goods in the market or there are not—if there are, the proprietor wishes to sell then only with a view to purchase some other commodity—he does not want cloth, but he does want silks, linen or wine—this at once indicates that the proprietor of cloth has mistaken the means by which to possess himself of cotton goods, he ought to have produced silks, linen or wine; if he had, there would not have been a glut of any commodity, as it is there is certainly a glut of one, namely cloth; and perhaps of two, because the cotton goods may not be required by any other person. But there may be no cotton goods in the market, what then should the person wanting them have produced to obtain them. Why, if there be no commodity with which he can purchase them, which is the most extravagant supposition, he can instead of producing cloth which he does not want, produce himself cotton goods which he does want. What I wish to impress on the readers mind is that it is at all times the bad adaptation of the commodities produced to the wants of mankind which is the specific evil, and not the abundance of commodities. Demand is only limited by the will and power to purchase.

Whoever has commodities has the power to consume, and as it suits mankind to divide their employments, individuals will produce one commodity with a view to purchase another;—these exchanges are mutually beneficial, but they are not absolutely necessary, for every man might employ his funds, and the labour at his command, in producing the very commodities he and his workmen intended to consume; in which case, there would be no market, and consequently there could be no glut. The division of the produce between master and men, is one thing;—the exchanges made between those to whom they are finally awarded, is another.

Ricardo   I have been thus particular in examining this question as it forms by far the most important topic of discussion in Mr. Malthus' work. If his views on this question be correct—if commodities can be so multiplied that there is no disposition to purchase and consume them, then undoubtedly the cure which he hesitatingly recommends is a very proper one. If the people entitled to consume will not consume the commodities produced, themselves, nor cause them to be consumed by others, with a view to reproduction; if, of the two things necessary to demand, the will and the power to purchase the will be wanting, and consequently a general stagnation of trade has ensued, we cannot do better than follow the advice of Mr. Malthus, and oblige the government to supply the deficiency of the people. We ought in that case to petition the King to dismiss his present economical ministers, and to replace them by others, who would more effectually promote the best interests of the country by promoting public extravagance and expenditure. We are it seems a nation of producers and have few consumers amongst us, and the evil has at last become of that magnitude that we shall be irretrievably miserable if the parliament or the ministers do not immediately adopt an efficient plan of expenditure.

Malthus   It has been thought by some very able writers, that although there may easily be a glut of particular commodities, there cannot possibly be a glut of commodities in general; because, according to their view of the subject, commodities being always exchanged for commodities, one half will furnish a market for the other half, and (production being thus the sole source of demand) an excess in the supply of one article merely proves a deficiency in the supply of some other, and a general excess is impossible. M. Say, in his distinguished work on political economy, had indeed gone so far as to state that the consumption of a commodity by taking it out of the market diminishes demand, and the production of a commodity proportionably increases it.

This doctrine, however, to the extent in which it has been applied, appears to me to be utterly unfounded, and completely to contradict the great principles which regulate supply and demand.

It is by no means true, as a matter of fact, that commodities are always exchanged for commodities. The great mass of commodities is exchanged directly for labour, either productive or unproductive; and it is quite obvious that this mass of commodities, compared with the labour with which it is to be exchanged, may fall in value from a glut just as any one commodity falls in value from an excess of supply, compared either with labour or money.

Ricardo   *The great mass of commodities*

It is quite true that commodities may exist in such abundance, compared with labour, as to make their value so to fall, estimated in labour, as not to afford any inducement to their further production. In that case labour will command a great quantity of commodities. It is this that Mr. Malthus subsequently denies. If Mr. Malthus means that (there may be such a glut of commodities as to make them ruinously cheap in labour) I agree with him, but this is only saying that (labour is so high that it absorbs all that fund which ought to belong to profits) and therefore the capitalist will have no interest in continuing to accumulate. But what will be the situation of the labourer? will that be miserable?

Malthus   In the case supposed there would evidently be an unusual quantity of commodities of all kinds in the market, owing to the unproductive labourers of the country having been converted, by the accumulation of capital, into productive labourers; (while the number of labourers altogether being the same, and the power and will to purchase for consumption among landlords and capitalists being by supposition diminished, commodities would necessarily fall in value, compared with labour, so as to lower profits almost to nothing, and to check for a time further production. But this is precisely what is meant by the term *glut*, which, in this case, is evidently general not partial.

Ricardo   *In the case*

No one denies this. They would fall in labour value, but not in money value.

Malthus   M. Say, Mr. Mill, and Mr. Ricardo, the principal authors of the new doctrines on profits, appear to me to have fallen into some fundamental errors in the view which they have taken of this subject.

In the first place, they have considered commodities as if they were so many mathematical figures, or arithmetical characters, the relations of which were to be compared, instead of articles of consumption, which must of course be referred to the number and wants of the consumers.

If commodities were only to be compared and exchanged with each other, then indeed it would be true that, if they were all increased in their proper proportions to any extent, they would continue to bear among themselves the same relative value; but, if we compare them, as we certainly ought to do, with the numbers and wants of the consumers, then a great increase of produce with comparatively stationary numbers and

Malthus with wants diminished by parsimony, must necessarily occasion a great fall of value estimated in labour, so that the same produce, though it might have *cost* the same quantity of labour as before, would no longer *command* the same quantity; and both the power of accumulation and the motive to accumulate would be strongly checked.⟩

Ricardo *If commodities were only*

I deny that the wants of the consumers generally are diminished by parsimony—they are transferred with the power to consume to another set of consumers. I acknowledge that the power and motive of the capitalist to accumulate would be checked.

Note. I deny and admit as above on the supposition that population does not increase with the same rapidity as the funds which are to employ it.

Malthus It is asserted that effectual demand is nothing more than the offering of one commodity in exchange for another. But is this all that is necessary to effectual demand? Though each commodity may have cost the same quantity of labour and capital in its production, and they may be exactly equivalent to each other in exchange, yet why may not both be so plentiful as not to command more labour, or but very little more than they have cost; and in this case, would the demand for them be effectual? Would it be such as to encourage their continued production? Unquestionably not. Their relation to each other may not have changed; but their relation to the wants of the society, their relation to bullion, and their relation to domestic and foreign labour, may have experienced a most important change.

Ricardo *It is asserted that effectual demand*

If I give an ounce of gold for a quarter of corn these commodities Mr. Malthus allows are equivalent to each other in exchange.

But he asks "may they not both be so plentiful as not to command more labour, or but very little more than they have cost? Would the demand for them be effectual? Would it be such as to encourage their continued production?["] I answer with Mr. Malthus, Unquestionably not. But is this the subject in dispute? This is merely saying that when labour is exceedingly dear as compared with commodities, profits will be so low as to afford no inducement to accumulate. Who denies this proposition? Mr.

Ricardo Malthus original question was this, If capital is accumulated and a great quantity of commodities produced they will not exchange freely for each other in the market; there will be no demand for them. Can any two propositions be more different than these two(Because commodities are so plentiful as not to command much labour, would taxing the people and increasing the expenditure of government raise profits, the only thing wanted to ensure the continued production of commodities?)

Malthus . . . Another fundamental error into which the writers above-mentioned and their followers appear to have fallen is, the not taking into consideration the influence of so general and important a principle in human nature, as indolence or the love of ease.

It has been supposed that, if a certain number of farmers and a certain number of manufacturers had been exchanging their surplus food and clothing with each other, and their powers of production were suddenly so increased that both parties could, with the same labour, produce luxuries in addition to what they had before obtained, there could be no sort of difficulty with regard to demand, as part of the luxuries which the farmer produced would be exchanged against part of the luxuries produced by the manufacturer; and the only result would be, the happy one of both parties being better supplied and having more enjoyments.

But in this intercourse of mutual gratifications, two things are taken for granted, which are the very points in dispute. It is taken for granted that luxuries are always preferred to indolence, and that the profits of each party are consumed as revenue. What would be the effect of a desire to save under such circumstances, shall be considered presently. The effect of a preference of indolence to luxuries would evidently be to occasion a want of demand for the returns of the increased powers of production supposed, and to throw labourers out of employment. The cultivator, being now enabled to obtain the necessaries and conveniences to which he had been accustomed, with less toil and trouble, and his tastes for ribands, lace and velvet not being fully formed, might be very likely to indulge himself in indolence, and employ less labour on the land; while the manufacturer, finding his velvets rather heavy of sale, would be led to discontinue their manufacture, and to fall almost necessarily into the same indolent system as the farmer. That an efficient taste for luxuries, that is, such a taste as will properly stimulate industry, instead of being ready to appear at the moment it is required, is a plant of slow growth, the history of human society sufficiently shews; and that it is a most im-

Malthus portant error to take for granted, that mankind will produce and consume all that they have the power to produce and consume, and will never prefer indolence to the rewards of industry, will sufficiently appear from a slight review of some of the nations with which we are acquainted. . . .

Ricardo

But in this intercourse &c.

Here again Mr. Malthus changes the proposition. We do not say that indolence may not be preferred to luxuries. I think it may and therefore if the question was respecting the motives to produce, there would be no difference between us. But Mr. Malthus supposes the motive strong enough to produce the commodities, and then contends there would be no market for them after they were produced, as there would be no demand for them.

It is this proposition we deny. We do not say the commodities will under all circumstances be produced, but if (they are produced we contend that there will always be some who will have the will and power to consume them, or in other words there will be a demand for them) Mr. Malthus brings forward a case of a society not accumulating, preferring indolence to luxuries, not demanding labour, not cultivating their land as a proof of the evil effects which would result from the very opposite course; where capital would be accumulated, where activity would take place of indolence, where there would be the greatest demand for labour,—and where lands would be made the most productive; for all these are included in the meaning of the word *accumulation*. Men will prefer indolence to luxuries! luxuries will not then be produced, because they cannot be produced without labour, the opposite of indolence. If not produced they cannot want a market, there can be no glut of them.

Malthus   A third very serious error of the writers above referred to, and practically the most important of the three, consists in supposing that accumulation ensures demand; or that the consumption of the labourers employed by those whose object is to save, will create such an effectual demand for commodities as to encourage a continued increase of produce.

Mr. Ricardo observes, that "If £10,000. were given to a man having £100,000. per annum, he would not lock it up in a chest, but would either increase his expenses by £10,000., employ it himself productively, or lend it to some other person for that purpose; in either case demand would be increased, although it would be for different objects. If he increased his expenses, his effectual demand might probably be for buildings, furniture, or some such enjoyment. If he employed his £10,000. productively, his effectual demand would be for food, clothing, and raw materials, which might set new labourers to work. But still it would be *demand*."

Malthus   Upon this principle it is supposed that if the richer portion of society were to forego their accustomed conveniences and luxuries with a view to accumulation, the only effect would be a direction of nearly the whole capital of the country to the production of necessaries, which would lead to a great increase of cultivation and population. But, without supposing an entire change in the usual motives to accumulation, this could not possibly happen. The usual motives for accumulation are, I conceive, either the future wealth and enjoyment of the individual who accumulates, or of those to whom he means to leave his property. And with these motives it could never answer to the possessor of land to employ nearly all the labour which the soil could support in cultivation; as by so doing he would necessarily destroy his neat rent, and render it impossible for him, without subsequently dismissing the greatest part of his workmen and occasioning the most dreadful distress, either to give himself the means of greater enjoyment at a future distant period, or to transmit such means to his posterity.

Ricardo   *Upon this principle it is supposed*

The question discussed here is as to the motives for accumulation—that is not the question in dispute, we have spoken only of the effects of accumulation. There is a very marked distinction between these two questions.

Malthus   The very definition of fertile land is, land that will support a much greater number of persons than are necessary to cultivate it; and if the landlord, instead of spending this surplus in conveniences, luxuries and unproductive consumers, were to employ it in setting to work on the land as many labourers as his savings could support, it is quite obvious that, instead of being enriched, he would be impoverished by such a proceeding, both at first and in future. Nothing could justify such a conduct but a different motive for accumulation; that is, a desire to increase the population—not the love of wealth and enjoyment; and till such a change takes place in the passions and propensities of mankind, we may be quite sure that the landlords and cultivators will not go on employing labourers in this way.

Ricardo   *The very definition*

In all this I agree but it is foreign to the question.

Malthus   What then would happen? As soon as the landlords and cultivators found that they could not realize their increasing produce in some way which would give them a command of wealth in future, they would cease to employ more labour upon the land;[1] and if the business of that part of the society which was not engaged in raising raw produce, consisted merely in preparing the other simple necessaries of life, the number required for this purpose being inconsiderable, the rest of those whom the soil could support would be thrown out of work. Having no means of legally demanding a portion of the raw produce, however plentiful it might be at first, they would gradually decrease in numbers; and the failure of effective demand for the produce of the soil would necessarily diminish cultivation, and throw a still greater number of persons out of employment. This action and reaction would thus go on till the balance of produce and consumption was restored in reference to the new tastes and habits which were established; and it is obvious that without an expenditure which will encourage commerce, manufactures, and unproductive consumers, or an Agrarian law calculated to change the usual motives for accumulation, the possessors of land would have no sufficient stimulus to cultivate well; and a country such as our own, which had been rich and populous, would, with such parsimonious habits, infallibly become poor, and comparatively unpeopled.

Ricardo   *And a country such as our own which had been rich and populous*

That is to say there being no motive to parsimony and accumulation, with such limited wants, there would be no parsimony and accumulation, and therefore a country with such parsimonious habits, would become poor and comparatively unpeopled.

---

[1] Theoretical writers in Political Economy, from the fear of appearing to attach too much importance to money, have perhaps been too apt to throw it out of their consideration in their reasonings. It is an abstract truth that we want commodities, not money. But, in reality, no commodity for which it is possible to sell our goods at once, can be an adequate substitute for a circulating medium, and enable us in the same manner to provide for children, to purchase an estate, or to command labour and provisions a year or two hence. A circulating medium is absolutely necessary to any considerable saving; and even the manufacturer would get on but slowly, if he were obliged to accumulate in kind all the wages of his workmen. We cannot therefore be surprized at his wanting money rather than other goods; and, in civilized countries, we may be quite sure that if the farmer or manufacturer cannot sell his products so as to give him a profit estimated in money, his industry will immediately slacken. The circulating medium bears so important a part in the distribution of wealth, and the encouragement of industry, that to set it aside in our reasonings may often lead us wrong.

Malthus   The same kind of reasoning will obviously apply to the case noticed before. While the farmers were disposed to consume the luxuries produced by the manufacturers, and the manufacturers those produced by the farmers, all would go on smoothly; but if either one or both of the parties were disposed to save with a view of bettering their condition, and providing for their families in future, the state of things would be very different. The farmer, instead of indulging himself in ribands, lace and velvets, would be disposed to be satisfied with more simple clothing, but by this economy he would disable the manufacturer from purchasing the same amount of his produce; and for the returns of so much labour employed upon the land, and all greatly increased in productive power, there would evidently be no market. The manufacturer, in like manner, instead of indulging himself in sugar, grapes and tobacco, might be disposed to save with a view to the future, but would be totally unable to do so, owing to the parsimony of the farmers and the want of demand for manufactures.

Ricardo   *But by this economy he would disable the manufacturer*
            from purchasing the same amount of his produce

True, but would not the manufacturer's labourers purchase it, or something that would be made instead of it?

Malthus   An accumulation, to a certain extent, of common food and common clothing might take place on both sides; but the amount must necessarily be extremely confined. It would be of no sort of use to the farmer to go on cultivating his land with a view merely to give food and clothing to his labourers. He would be doing nothing either for himself or family, if he neither consumed the surplus of what they produced himself, nor could realize it in a shape that might be transmitted to his descendants. If he were a tenant, such additional care and labour would be entirely thrown away; and if he were a landlord, and were determined, without reference to markets, to cultivate his estate in such a way as to make it yield the greatest neat surplus with a view to the future, it is quite certain that the large portion of this surplus which was not required either for his own consumption, or to purchase clothing for himself and his labourers, would be absolutely wasted. If he did not choose to use it in the purchase of luxuries or the maintenance of unproductive labourers, it might as well be thrown into the sea. To save it, that is to use it in employing more

Malthus labourers upon the land would, as I said before, be to impoverish both himself and his family.

It would be still more useless to the manufacturers to go on producing clothing beyond what was wanted by the agriculturists and themselves. Their numbers indeed would entirely depend upon the demands of the agriculturists, as they would have no means of purchasing subsistence, but in proportion as there was a reciprocal want of their manufactures. The population required to provide simple clothing for such a society with the assistance of good machinery would be inconsiderable, and would absorb but a small portion of the proper surplus of rich and well cultivated land. There would evidently therefore be a general want of demand, both for produce and population; and while it is quite certain that an adequate passion for consumption may fully keep up the proper proportion between supply and demand, whatever may be the powers of production, it appears to be quite as certain that a passion for accumulation must inevitably lead to a supply of commodities beyond what the structure and habits of such a society will permit to be consumed.

Ricardo

There would evidently therefore be a general want of demand, both for produce and population.

The specific want would be for population. "It would be of no sort of use," says Mr. Malthus, "to the farmer to go on cultivating his land with a view merely to give food and clothing to his labourers, if he neither consumed the surplus of what they produced himself, *nor could realize it in a shape that might be transmitted to his descendants.*" What but a deficiency of population could prevent him from realizing it in a shape that might be transmitted to his descendants. I am a farmer possessed of a thousand quarters of corn, and my object is to accumulate a fortune for my family. With this corn I can employ a certain number of men on the land, which I rent, and after paying my rent the first year, realize 1300 qrs., or 300 qrs. profits. The next year if there be plenty of labour in the market, I can employ a greater quantity than before, and my 1300 quarters will become 1700, and so from year to year I go on increasing the quantity till I have made it 10,000 quarters, and if labour be at the same price can command ten times the quantity of it that I could when I commenced my operations.[1]

---

[1] Note. When I had the 1000 quarters the whole was consumed within the year, and so at every subsequent period—it is always consumed and reproduced. The word accumulation misleads many persons and sometimes I think it misleads Mr. Malthus. It is by many supposed that the corn is accumulated, whereas to make such a capital productive and to increase wealth it must be constantly consumed and reproduced.

Ricardo   Have I not then accumulated a fortune for my family? have I not given them the power of employing labour in any way they please, and of enjoying the fruits of it? And what is to prevent me doing so but an increase in the price of labour, or a diminution in the productive powers of the land? Of the latter we have already spoken; that necessarily limits all accumulation. Of the increase of the price of labour I have also spoken; if population did not keep pace with capital, labour would rise, and the quantity of corn which I should annually obtain, instead of increasing in the proportions of 1000, 1300, 1700 and so on, might, by the sacrifices I should be obliged to make to obtain the labour required, increase my capital only in the proportions 1000, 1200, 1300 &c. &c. The precise reason then that my accumulation goes on at a slow pace, is that there is a scarcity of labour; how then can Mr. Malthus make it appear that "there will be a general want of demand both for produce, and population." Mr. Malthus may indeed say that my operations will increase the quantity of corn faster than it will be required to feed the actual population.

I grant it, but if my object be accumulation why should I produce corn particularly, why not any other commodity which may be in demand?

Malthus   But if this be so, surely it is a most important error to couple the passion for expenditure and the passion for accumulation together, as if they were of the same nature; and to consider the demand for the food and clothing of the labourer, who is to be employed productively, as securing such a general demand for commodities and such a rate of profits for the capital employed in producing them, as will adequately call forth the powers of the soil, and the ingenuity of man in procuring the greatest quantity both of raw and manufactured produce. . . . It is not, of course, meant to be stated that parsimony, or even a temporary diminution of consumption, is not often in the highest degree useful, and sometimes absolutely necessary to the progress of wealth. A state may certainly be ruined by extravagance; and a diminution of the actual expenditure may not only be necessary on this account, but when the capital of a country is deficient, compared with the demand for its products, a temporary economy of consumption is required, in order to provide that supply of capital which can alone furnish the means of an increased consumption in future. All that I mean to say is, that no nation can *possibly* grow rich by an accumulation of capital, arising from a permanent diminution of consumption; because, such accumulation being greatly beyond what is wanted, in order to supply the effective demand for produce, a part of it would very soon lose both its use and its value, and cease to possess the character of wealth.

Ricardo   *All that I mean to say is*

By accumulation of capital from revenue is meant an increase of consumption by productive labourers instead of by unproductive labourers. Consumption is as certain in one case as in the other, the difference is only in the quantity of productions returned.

Malthus   On the supposition indeed of a *given* consumption, the accumulation of capital beyond a certain point must appear at once to be perfectly futile. But, even taking into consideration the increased consumption likely to arise among the labouring classes from the abundance and cheapness of commodities, yet as this cheapness must be at the expense of profits, it is obvious that the limits to such an increase of capital from parsimony, as shall not be attended by a very rapid diminution of the motive to accumulate, are very narrow, and may very easily be passed. . . .

Though it may be allowed therefore that the laws which regulate the increase of capital are not quite so distinct as those which regulate the increase of population, yet they are certainly just of the same kind; and it is equally vain, with a view to the permanent increase of wealth, to continue converting revenue into capital, when there is no adequate demand for the products of such capital, as to continue encouraging marriage and the birth of children without a demand for labour and an increase of the funds for its maintenance.

Ricardo   *Though it may be allowed*

The temptation to increase capital does not arise from the demand for its products, for that never fails; but from the profits arising from the sale of the products.—High wages may totally destroy those profits.

What Mr. Malthus calls a demand for capital I call high profits—capital is not bought and sold, it is borrowed at interest, and a great interest is given when profits are high. Mr. Malthus' language appears to me in this instance *"new and unusual."*

Malthus-Ricardo Correspondence

MALTHUS TO RICARDO

St. Catherine's July [7th, 1821]

My dear Ricardo

... I fear I must have expressed myself very clumsily throughout the whole of my long final chapter in my last work, as both in your notes and conversation you appear quite to have misunderstood me. You constantly say that it is not a question about the motives to produce. Now I have certainly intended to make it almost entirely a question about motives. We see in almost every part of the world vast powers of production which are not put into action, and I explain this phenomenon by saying that from the want of a proper distribution of the actual produce adequate motives are not furnished to continued production. By inquiring into the immediate causes of the progress of wealth I clearly mean to inquire mainly into motives. I dont at all wish to deny that some persons or others are entitled to consume all that is produced; but the grand question is whether it is distributed in such a manner between the different parties concerned as to occasion the most effective demand for future produce: and I distinctly maintain that an attempt to accumulate very rapidly which necessarily implies a considerable diminution of unproductive consumption, by greatly impairing the usual motives to production must prematurely check the progress of wealth. This surely is the great *practical* question, and not whether we ought to call the sort of stagnation which would be thus occasioned a glut. That I hold to be a matter of very subordinate importance.

"Malthus-Ricardo Correspondence," excerpted from Piero Sraffa, ed., *Works & Correspondence of David Ricardo,* Vol. IX, op. cit., pp. 9–11; 14–27.

But if it be true that an attempt to accumulate very rapidly will occasion such a division between labour and profits as almost to destroy both the motive and the power of future accumulation and consequently the power of maintaining and employing an increasing population, must it not be acknowledged that such an attempt to accumulate, or that saving too much, may be really prejudicial to a country. Do look at my chapter again after this explanation. . . .

Ever truly Yours
T R MALTHUS

RICARDO TO MALTHUS

Gatcomb Park Minchinhampton
9 July 1821

My Dear Malthus

. . . You are right in supposing that I have understood you in your book not to profess to enquire into the motives for producing, but into the effects which would result from abundant production. You say in your letter "We see in almost every part of the world vast powers of production which are not put into action and I explain this phenomenon by saying that from the want of the proper distribution of the actual produce adequate motives are not furnished to continued production." If this had been what I conceived you to have said I should not have a word to say against you, but I have rather understood you to say that vast powers of production are put into action and the result is unfavourable to the interest of mankind, and you have suggested as a remedy either that less should be produced, or more should be unproductively consumed. If you had said, "after arriving at a certain limit there will in the actual circumstances be no use to try to produce more—the end cannot be accomplished, and if it could instead of more less would belong to the class which provided the capital", I should have agreed with you—yet in that case I should say the real cause of this faulty distribution would be to be found in the inadequate quantity of labour in the market, and would be effectually cured by an additional supply of it. But I say with you, there could be no adequate motive to push production to this length, and therefore it would never go so far. I do not know whether I am correct in my observation, that "I say so with you," for you often appear to me to contend not only that production can go on so far without an adequate motive, but that it actually has done so lately, and that we are now suffering the consequences of it in stagnation of trade, in a want of employment for our labourers &c. &c., and the remedy you propose is an increase of consumption. It is against this latter doctrine that I protest and give my decided opposition. I acknowledge there may not be adequate motives for production, and therefore things will not be produced, but I cannot allow, first that with these inadequate motives commodities will be produced, and secondly that, if their production is attended with loss to the producer, it is for any other reason than because too great a proportion is given to the labourers employed. Increase their number, and the evil is remedied. Let the employer consume more himself, and there will be no diminution of demand for labour, but the pay of the labourer, which was before extravagantly high, will be reduced. . . .

Ever Yours
DAVID RICARDO

MALTHUS TO RICARDO

St Catherine's Bath
July 16th 1821

My dear Ricardo,

. . . With regard to our present subject of discussion it seems as if we should never thoroughly understand each other, and I almost despair of being ever able to explain myself, if you could read the two first paragraphs of the first section of my last chapter, and yet "understand me to say that vast powers of production are put into action, and the result is unfavourable to the interests of mankind."

I expressly say that it is my object to shew what are the causes which call forth the powers of production; and if I recommend a certain proportion of unproductive consumption, it is obviously and expressly with the sole view of furnishing the necessary motive to the greatest continued production. And I think still that this certain proportion of unproductive consumption varying according to the fertility of the soil &c: is absolutely and indispensably necessary to call forth the resources of a country. Is it not almost a contradiction, to quote with approbation that passage of Adam Smith which says that the demand for food is limited by the narrow capacity of the human stomach, but that the demand for luxuries and conveniences has no limits, and yet to say that parsimony, or the saving of expenditure in luxuries and conveniences and increasing the production of necessaries cannot be unfavourable to wealth.

Surely I have no where said, as you seem to intimate, that people will continue to produce without a motive; because I expressly give as the reason for the scanty produce of the world, the want of sufficient motives to produce. Now among the motives to produce, one of the most essential certainly is that an adequate share of what is produced should belong to those who set all industry in motion. But you yourself allow that a great temporary saving, commencing when profits were sufficient to encourage it, might occasion such a division of the produce as would leave no motive to a further increase of production. And if a state of things in which for a time there is no motive to a further increase of production be not properly denominated a stagnation, I do not know what can be so called; particularly as this stagnation must inevitably throw the rising generation out of employment. We know from repeated experience that the money price of labour never falls till many workmen have been for some time out of work. And the question is, whether this stagnation of capital, and subsequent stagnation in the demand for labour arising from increased production without an adequate proportion of unproductive consumption on the part of the landlords and capitalists, could take place without prejudice to the country, without occasioning a less degree both of happiness and wealth than would have occurred if the unproductive consumption of the landlords and capitalists had been so proportioned to the natural surplus of the society as to have continued uninterrupted the motives to production, and prevented first an unnatural demand for labour, and then a necessary and sudden diminiution of such demand. But if this be so, how can it be said with truth that parsimony, though it may be prejudicial to the producers cannot be prejudicial to the state; or that an increase of unproductive consumption among landlords and capitalists may not sometimes be the proper remedy for a state of things in which the motives to production fail. . . .

Ever truly Yours
T R Malthus

RICARDO TO MALTHUS

Gatcomb Park
21 July 1821

My Dear Malthus

. . . With respect to the particular subject of discussion between us you seem to be surprised that I should understand you to say in your book "that vast powers of production are put into action, and the result is unfavorable to the interests of mankind." Have you not said so? Is it not your objection to machinery that it often produces a quantity of commodities for which there is no demand, and that it is the glut which is the consequence of quantity which is unfavorable to the interests of mankind. Even as you state your proposition in your present letter, I have a right to conclude that you see great evils in great powers of production, from the quantity of commodities which will be the result, and the low price to which they will fall. Saving, you would say, would first lead to great production—then to low prices, which would necessarily be followed by low profits. With very low profits the motives for saving would cease, and therefore the motives for increased production would also cease. Do you not then say that increased production is often attended with evil consequences to mankind, because it destroys the motives to industry, and to the keeping up of the increased production? Now in much of this I cannot agree with you. I indeed allow that the case is possible to conceive of saving being so universal that no profit will arise from the employment of capital, but then I contend that the specific reason is, because all that fund which should, and in ordinary cases, does, constitute profit, goes to wages, and immoderately swells that fund which is destined to the support of labour. The labourers are immoderately paid for their labour, and they necessarily become the unproductive consumers of the country. I agree too that the capitalists being in such a case without a sufficient motive for saving from revenue, to add to capital, will cease doing so —will, if you please, even expend a part of their capital; but I ask what evil will result from this? none to the capitalist, you will allow, for his enjoyments and his profits will be thereby increased, or he would continue to save. None to the labourers, for which we should repine; because their situation was so exceedingly favorable that they could bear a deduction from their wages and yet be in a most prosperous condition. Here it is where we most differ. You think that the capitalist could not cease saving, on account of the lowness of his profits, without a cessation, in some degree, of employment to the people. I on the contrary think that with all the abatements from the fund destined to the payment of labour, which I acknowledge would be the consequence of the new course of the capitalists, enough would remain to employ all the labour that could be obtained, and to pay it liberally, so that in fact there would be little diminution in the quantity of commodities produced,—the distribution only would be different; more would go [to] the capitalists, and less to the labourers.

I do not think that stagnation is a proper term to apply to a state of things in which for a time there is no motive to a further increase of production. When in the course of things profits shall be so low, from a great accumulation of capital, and a want of means of providing food for an increasing population, all motive for further savings will cease, but there will be no stagnation—all that is produced will be at its fair relative price and will be freely exchanged.—Surely the word stagnation is improperly applied to such a state of things, for there will not be a general glut, nor will any particular commodity be necessarily produced in greater abundance than the demand shall warrant.

You say "we know from repeated experience that the money price of labour never falls till many workmen have been for some time out of work." I know no such thing, and if wages were previously high, I can see no reason whatever why they should not fall before many labourers are thrown out of work. All general reasoning I apprehend is in favor of my view of this question, for why should some agree to go without any wages while others were most liberally rewarded. Once more I must say that a sudden and diminished demand for labour in this case must mean a diminished reward to the labourer, and not a diminished employment of him—he will work at least as much as before, but will have a less proportion of the produce of his work, and this will be so in order that his employer may have an adequate motive for employing him at all, which he certainly would not have if his share of the produce were reduced so low as to make increased production an evil rather than a benefit to him. . . .

Ever truly Yours
DAVID RICARDO

Keynes' Comments on Malthus and Ricardo

John Maynard Keynes

John Maynard Keynes (1883–1946), probably the single
most influential economist of the twentieth century, found
Malthus' ideas quite helpful when he wrote his classic
General Theory of Employment, Interest, and Money
(1936).

... Malthus had continued his economic studies with a pamphlet, published anonymously in 1800, entitled *An Investigation of the Cause of the
Present High Price of Provisions*. This pamphlet has importance both in
itself and as showing that Malthus was already disposed to a certain line of
approach in handling practical economic problems which he was to develop later on in his correspondence with Ricardo,—a method which to
me is most sympathetic, and, as I think, more likely to lead to right
conclusions than the alternative approach of Ricardo. But it was Ricardo's
more fascinating intellectual construction which was victorious, and
Ricardo who, by turning his back so completely on Malthus' ideas, constrained the subject for a full hundred years in an artificial groove.

According to Malthus' good common-sense notion prices and profits
are primarily determined by something which he described, though none
too clearly, as "effective demand." Ricardo favored a much more rigid
approach, went behind "effective demand" to the underlying conditions
of money on the one hand and real costs and the real division of the
product on the other hand, conceived these fundamental factors as automatically working themselves out in a unique and unequivocal way, and
looked on Malthus' method as very superficial. But Ricardo, in the
course of simplifying the many successive stages of his highly abstract
argument, departed, necessarily and more than he himself was aware,
away from the actual facts; whereas Malthus, by taking up the tale much
nearer its conclusion, had a firmer hold on what may be expected to

happen in the real world. Ricardo is the father of such things as the Quantity Theory of Money and the Purchasing Power Parity of the Exchanges. When one has painfully escaped from the intellectual domination of these pseudo-arithmetical doctrines, one is able, perhaps for the first time for a hundred years, to comprehend the real significance of the vaguer intuitions of Malthus. . . .

[The] friendship [between Malthus and Ricardo] will live in history on account of its having given rise to the most important literary correspondence in the whole development of Political Economy. . . . Here, indeed, are to be found the seeds of economic theory, and also the divergent lines—so divergent at the outset that the destination can scarcely be recognized as the same until it is reached—along which the subject can be developed. Ricardo is investigating the theory of the *distribution* of the product in conditions of equilibrium, and Malthus is concerned with what determines the *volume* of output day by day in the real world. Malthus is dealing with the monetary economy in which we happen to live; Ricardo with the abstraction of a neutral money economy. They largely recognized the real source of their differences. In a letter of January 24, 1817, Ricardo wrote:

It appears to me that one great cause of our difference in opinion on the subjects which we have so often discussed is that you have always in your mind the immediate and temporary effects of particular changes, whereas I put these immediate and temporary effects quite aside, and fix my whole attention on the permanent state of things which will result from them. Perhaps you estimate these temporary effects too highly, whilst I am too much disposed to undervalue them. To manage the subject quite right, they should be carefully distinguished and mentioned, and the due effects ascribed to each.

To which Malthus replied with considerable effect on January 26, 1817:

I agree with you that one cause of our difference in opinion is that which you mention. I certainly am disposed to refer frequently to things as they are, as the only way of making one's writings practically useful to society, and I think also the only way of being secure from falling into the errors of the taylors of Laputa, and by a slight mistake at the outset arrive at conclusions the most distant from the truth. Besides I really think that the progress of society consists of irregular movements, and that to omit the consideration of causes which for eight or ten years will give a great stimulus to production and population, or a great check to them, is to omit the causes of the wealth and poverty of nations—the grand object of all enquiries in Political Economy. A writer may, to be sure, make any hypothesis he pleases; but if he supposes what is not at all true practically, he precludes himself from drawing any practical inferences from his hypotheses. In your essay on profits you suppose the real wages of labour constant; but as they vary with every alteration in the prices of commodities (while they remain nominally the same) and are in reality as variable as profits, there is no chance of your inferences being just as applied to the actual state of things. We see in all the countries around us, and in our own particularly, periods of greater and less prosperity and sometimes of adversity, but never *the uniform progress which you seem alone to contemplate.*

But to come to a still more specific and fundamental cause of our difference, I think it is this. You seem to think that the wants and tastes of mankind are always ready for the supply; while I am most decidedly of opinion that few things are more difficult than to inspire new tastes and wants, particularly out of old materials; that one of the great elements of demand is the value that people set upon commodities, and that the more completely the supply is suited to the demand the higher will this value be, and the more days' labour will it exchange for, or give the power of commanding. . . . I am quite of opinion that practically *the actual check to produce and population arises more from want of stimulus than want of power to produce.*

One cannot rise from a perusal of this correspondence without a feeling that the almost total obliteration of Malthus' line of approach and the complete domination of Ricardo's for a period of a hundred years has been a disaster to the progress of economics. Time after time in these letters Malthus is talking plain sense, the force of which Ricardo with his head in the clouds wholly fails to comprehend. Time after time a crushing refutation by Malthus is met by a mind so completely closed that Ricardo does not even see what Malthus is saying. . . .

If only Malthus, instead of Ricardo, had been the parent stem from which nineteenth-century economics proceeded, what a much wiser and richer place the world would be today! We have laboriously to rediscover and force through the obscuring envelopes of our misguided education what should never have ceased to be obvious. . . .

GREAT DEBATE TWO

THE MARXIAN CRITIQUE OF CAPITALISM

THE MARXIAN CRITIQUE OF CAPITALISM

IN JUNE, 1971, Paul A. Samuelson, Nobel-prize-winning economist from the Massachusetts Institute of Technology, published a highly technical article on Marx in the *Journal of Economic Literature.* Its complex title was, "Understanding the Marxian Notion of Exploitation: A Summary of the So-Called Transformation Problem Between Marxian Values and Competitive Prices." Not the kind of article, one would think, that would make people sound the alarums and man the battle stations. But it did. Few articles in the history of that journal have stirred such controversy. A flood of comments and rebuttals poured forth. As late as March, 1974, the journal was carrying these articles: a critique of Samuelson's views by William J. Baumol of Princeton, a reply by Samuelson to Baumol, a reply to Samuelson by Michio Morishima of the London School of Economics, a comment by Baumol on Samuelson's reply, and a rejoinder by Samuelson to both Baumol and Morishima.

This episode is important to us for two reasons. First, it shows that beneath its technical veneer, economics is still a subject pulsing with potential and very lively disagreements among its practitioners. We do not have to go back to the days of Ricardo and Malthus to find divisions, and deep ones, within this field.

Second, this incident proves again what most of us already know: the special controversiality of Karl Marx (1818–1883). No aspect of his theory is fully agreed upon. The issue at dispute in the journal was the "transformation problem"— essentially, how does Marx get to a proper theory of prices when he begins with a creaky vehicle called the *labor theory of value.*[1] If economists will flail at each other over such an issue, how much more vigorous might their arguments be when it comes to such Marxian ideas as the necessity of revolution and the ultimate victory of communism!

[1] We'll discuss this theory briefly on pages 45–46.

Actually, we shall not spend much time in the discussion of communism in this Great Debate. The fact is that Marx spent far more of his life and writings in "proving" the downfall of capitalism than in outlining the communist society to come. We shall come to the issue of communism in the following Great Debate: Economic Development versus Democracy? (pp. 85–127). It is ironic but true that Marx's greatest appeal has come not in the societies in which he would have expected it—the mature capitalistic economies, the United States, England, Germany—but in the less-developed parts of the world—Russia in 1917, present-day China, Vietnam. In some ways communist revolutions have actually refuted rather than vindicated Marx's own analysis!

Our concern here, however, will be with his vision of the decline, inevitable as he believed, of the capitalistic system. Marx felt that all previous socialist thinkers were "Utopian"; he, in contrast, was "scientific." He would show not only that capitalism might fail, but that it must fail, inexorably, with the ironclad guarantee of historical necessity. This was one of the most influential ideas to have emerged from the whole of the nineteenth century, and it has been subject to sharp debate ever since.

SOME BASIC TENETS OF MARXIAN THOUGHT

Marx saw the economic system of his time as in a process of evolution and change, not as a "given," and this sense of historical relativity distinguishes his theory from that of many economists who preceded him, and, indeed, from that of many who have followed after. In broad scope, his theory rested on the following hypotheses:

1. *The social and political history of a society is largely determined by the evolution of economic forces.* This view is often called "economic determinism." The notion is that the politics, form of government and social and intellectual life of a nation are largely determined by the economic system, and that this economic system has a certain evolution of its own. Marxists have always been skeptical of the possibilities of reform, as, for example, through the "welfare state." Why? Because they see the agent of reform—the government—as simply a tool of the ruling economic classes—the rich monopoly capitalists. Marx looked beneath the surface structure and ideology of a society to find inner meanings and motives. In his particular view, economic interests seemed the dominant underlying force behind the more overt political and social forms. His "guiding principle," as he put it, was that "the mode of production of material life conditions the general process of social, political and intellectual life. It is not the consciousness of men that determines their existence, but their social existence that determines their consciousness" (p. 58).

Furthermore, this underlying mode of material production is constantly changing over time; and, in due course, the productive forces of the society come into conflict with the social and legal institutions within which they are housed. These "changes in the economic foundation lead sooner or later to the transformation of the whole immense superstructure" (p. 58).

2. *History is a long succession of class struggles.* The form that historical evolution takes in Marxian theory is the class struggle. The famous opening line of the *Communist Manifesto* is: "The history of all hitherto existing society is the history of class struggles" (p. 50). Marxian theory here is in sharp contrast with the prevailing mood of the classical economics that emerged in the late eighteenth-century world of Adam Smith. Smith sought to show that there could be (within limits) a harmony in economic life, as private self-interest was led, as if by an "invisible hand," to promote the well-being of society. This notion of a basically harmonious society was challenged to some degree by our friend, David Ricardo, who saw that there might be a basic conflict between certain classes in society. He thought that a serious conflict could arise between the landlords of the society, who were interested in high land rents and expensive food, and the capitalists and laborers, who would both be squeezed if land and agricultural produce were dear. Marx carried this germ much further. He saw the basic conflict as between those who owned or controlled the means of production of society and those who did not, and this conflict was the dominating social fact, far more so than any surface harmony of interests that might seem to exist. In the case of capitalism, the conflict was between the capitalists, or bourgeoisie, and the laborers, or proletariat. This was a struggle to the death, and no hand, visible or invisible, would be able to stay the bloody outcome.

3. *Economic classes become more and more polarized in the course of capitalist evolution.* The class struggle becomes ever sharper under capitalism and it becomes simplified (p. 50). There are two related aspects to this process. First of all, the little capitalists gradually get driven out of business by their bigger rivals; this leaves no real "middle" class between the capitalists and the proletariat. Second, the big capitalists get bigger and bigger. Means of production are "centralized," property is concentrated "in a few hands," little workshops are supplanted by "great factories," labor is concentrated "in greater masses," machinery "obliterates all distinctions," and so on (p. 50). In other words, we enter into the world of large-scale, modern enterprise. The self-sufficient individual, the professional man, the independent artisan—all these are basically swept away. We have, on the one hand, the great factory-owners, rich, powerful, hard taskmasters, and, on the other hand, the great masses of factory labor, men working at machines, with only the most superficial differences in their ranks and stations. This polarization of classes helps set the stage for the revolution that will ultimately mark the end of capitalism in Marxian theory. Workers, forced together in large industrial concentrations, will not be long in understanding what their common interest is: namely, the overthrow of the system that is exploiting them.

4. *The working classes are increasingly immiserized.* This sense of exploitation and the further polarization of workers and capitalists are abetted by the increasing misery of the proletariat. There is some dispute among the experts as to whether Marx did or did not predict a decline of the real wages of the average worker in the course of capitalist development. At a minimum, he clearly expected no great

increase in real wages. Thus, he writes: "The various interests and conditions of life within the ranks of the proletariat are more and more equalized . . . and nearly everywhere reduces wages to the same low level." And even more strongly: "The modern laborer, on the contrary, instead of rising with the progress of industry, sinks deeper and deeper below the conditions of existence of his own class. He becomes a pauper, and pauperism develops more rapidly than population and wealth" (p. 56). It might seem that what Marx is saying is simply that the poor get poorer and poorer and the rich get richer and richer. However, the matter is a bit more complicated than this. Marx never seems to doubt the enormous productive powers of capitalism. However, in his theoretical structure the capitalists as well as the laborers are under a certain kind of economic pressure. He believes that there is a long-run tendency for the rate of profits to fall. This is a proposition much emphasized in his major theoretical work, *Capital*.[2] But, if capitalism is so enormously productive, and if the workers are getting poorer and poorer, and if the rate of profits is also falling, exactly where is all this productive power going to?

5. *Capitalism is filled with internal contradictions, as, for example, its tendency to out-produce its markets.* The foregoing question is no easy one, but, in response, a good Marxist would doubtless say that capitalism is filled with internal contradictions. Economic evolution takes place essentially as the means and methods of production come to outlive the institutions that originally gave them expression. In the case of capitalism, its enormous productive powers expand beyond the capability of the capitalistic system to absorb them. Capitalism produces the goods, but then cannot find the markets for selling those goods. "The need of a constantly expanding market for its products chases the bourgeoisie over the whole surface of the globe. It must nestle everywhere, settle everywhere, establish connections everywhere" (p. 51). In other words, Marx, like Malthus, saw the possibility of universal gluts. Indeed, it is because these business crises and depressions get worse and worse over time that the revolution becomes increasingly inevitable as capitalism advances. In its mature stages, capitalism displays such deep internal contradictions that there is really no alternative but for the whole structure to be dismantled.

The ultimate heir, of course, is communism and the "classless" society. Historical evolution thenceforth takes on a new, and presumably more beneficent, character.

AN INTERNAL CONTRADICTION IN ACTION

Still, we cannot leave the matter of these "internal contradictions" without at least some further comment. Marx really faced a very difficult problem in terms of what he wanted to prove. He acknowledges, even stresses, the enormous productive capacity unleashed by the capitalistic system. At the same time, he wants to show

[2] Thus, Marx writes of the "law" of a falling rate of profit: "Since this law is of great importance for capitalist production, it may be said to be that mystery whose solution has been the goal of the entire political economy since Adam Smith."

that the laborers do not benefit from this capacity but are in fact exploited by their capitalist taskmasters. Furthermore, he wants to show that this exploitation is not simply a result of the crudity and avarice of the bourgeoisie but is an historically necessary process. To do this, he must find some way of putting the screws on the capitalist class. There must be enough pressure on them to force them to continue, preferably to increase, their exploitation of labor over time. They are not pushing down wages because they are mean men (though Marx thought they were very mean indeed), but because they are caught up in a social process such that, if they fail to exploit labor to the maximum degree, they themselves will not survive. In this world, the paradox and internal contradiction are very clear: they must exploit the proletariat harder and harder in order to survive, but this very process of increasing exploitation helps create the polarization of classes and the revolutionary consciousness that will ultimately bring their overthrow. In sum, to avoid destruction, they undertake actions which, in the long run, will ensure their destruction.

But why all this pressure on the capitalists? In the Marxian world, the ultimate answer to this question involves the labor theory of value, which we have mentioned earlier. In theoretical terms, Marx was much indebted to the economic writings of Ricardo, and Ricardo accepted a modified version of the labor theory. In its simplest form, this theory states that the relative prices of commodities are proportional to the quantities of labor employed in their production. Why does a pair of shoes cost, say, ten times a loaf of bread? The labor theory answers: Because it takes ten times as many man-hours of labor to make a pair of shoes as it does to make a loaf of bread.

Now Ricardo had modified this theory in several ways to try to cope with a number of obvious problems—how about natural resources, how about capital goods, how about different qualities of labor? and so on. In Marx, however, the theory emerges at times with an almost mystical quality. Labor is not only the source of the relative values of commodities but of their absolute values. In fact, labor power—or, as he sometimes puts it, "socially necessary labor"—seems to be virtually equivalent in meaning to the term "value."

We cannot pursue the numerous problems of interpretation that arise here. Our interest, in any event, is simply to show how a specific internal contradiction in capitalism can arise in practice. In particular, we wish to show how the capitalist is put under increasing pressure by economic forces not under his control, and how this increasing pressure forces him to ever harsher exploitation of labor. The way it works is as follows:

Labor is the source of all economic value. Labor is also the source of the value of labor itself. By this we mean that, in equilibrium, the capitalist will pay the laborer an equivalent of the amount of labor it takes to bear, rear and educate the laborer and bring him into the work force. A certain amount of labor goes into "producing" a laborer. This is basically what the capitalist will pay the laborer.

But labor produces a "surplus." It takes, on the average, say, six hours of work a day for the laborer to pay the cost of producing a laborer. *But*—a huge "but"—the laborer works not six hours a day, but, say, twelve hours a day. Half the laborer's time is devoted to producing his sustenance (his "subsistence wage"); the other half is a surplus. This so-called "surplus value" is the source of all the capitalist's profits and represents the way in which capitalism "exploits" the laborer. The laborer produces everything; he only gets what is necessary to produce him; the surplus value is the exploitational consequence of the fact that the capitalist owns the means of production in the society and can turn this surplus into profits for himself.

Now the trouble with surplus value for the capitalist is that it is too attractive. He wants more. The obvious way to get more is to hire more laborers. But if all capitalists try to do this—as they do—they will start bidding against each other for laborers, hence bidding up the wage of labor above the subsistence level, hence cutting into the very surplus value they are trying to increase. The way the capitalists will try to avoid this is by introducing machinery to replace labor. The introduction of machinery causes technological unemployment. In fact, it creates what Marx called "the industrial reserve army of the unemployed." And this army is an indispensable feature of capitalism. Why? Because it keeps wages down. Normally, wages would go up as capitalists try to get more and more surplus value. But, instead, machinery increasingly replaces labor in production, and the existence of a large body of unemployed workers serves to keep wages low. If the worker asks for a raise, the capitalist simply takes him to the factory window and shows him the lines of unemployed outside. Wages are kept at the subsistence level, and a high rate of exploitation can be maintained.

But, alas for the capitalist, he has avoided one problem only to create another. By replacing labor with machinery, he is giving up part of the very source of his surplus value. Machinery produces no surplus value, only labor does. To increase the proportion of machinery in production is ultimately to reduce the rate of profits. And, in fact, this is what happens over time under capitalism, according to Marx. Capitalists keep introducing more and more machinery into production, staving off in this way rising wages, but creating a smaller and smaller relative base for the extraction of surplus value. Hence, over time, the rate of profits will fall, and capitalists, like the immiserized laborers, will be under economic pressure. This is an internal contradiction of the system, because there is no way this pressure can be avoided. If the capitalists do *not* introduce machinery, the surplus value will be eaten away by higher wages. If they do, they are replacing value-fertile workers with value-sterile machines. Either way, they are doomed.

Thus, Marx's picture of the inner workings of capitalism.

CRITIQUE OF MARX

In a sense, it seems almost beside the point to try to determine the degree of literal truth in these Marxian assertions. As Schumpeter notes (p. 59): "Purely scientific achievement, had it even been much more perfect that it was in the case of Marx, would never have won the immortality in the historical sense which is his." Marx was a prophet as well as an economist, and his followers, whether individuals or nations, have often given his writings a religious veneration. His appeal is emotional; his disciples are usually quite intolerant of differences of opinion.

Still, for the more mundane of us, such differences of opinion do exist and, in fact, they apply to each of the tenets of his thought we have just outlined. In brief:

1. *Weaknesses of economic determinism.* Marx was ahead of his time in understanding the evolutionary possibilities of social systems. Joan Robinson notes (p. 63) that he had a much keener sense of the historical relativity of capitalism than did the more orthodox economists who preceded and followed him. On the other hand, he surely overstated the degree to which economic factors dominate social and political factors in the course of that evolution. Is the state under capitalism simply the agent of the ruling capitalist classes? Berle argues that Marx thoroughly failed to foresee the evolution of the role of the state such as we have witnessed in the United States. This state, far from being a tool of capitalists, has increasingly come to regulate the capitalists and to work toward "a socially directed commonwealth" (p. 71). Clark Kerr notes that in many countries, "political parties with worker support came to rule governments" and that often "the state turned to welfare" (p. 82). The welfare state is not a myth but a reality in most of Western Europe. In the United States, federal expenditures on human resources were estimated for 1976 at $177 billion, or approximately half the federal budget. This is no tokenism or window-dressing; and it is very difficult for the true Marxist to accept.

2. *Class conflict or common stakes?* Perhaps the Classical Economists overstated the degree of harmony in society, but is class conflict the really central social fact under mature capitalism? Berle pictures a society in which common interests increasingly tend to dominate conflicting interests. Thus, the state, as suggested above, acts on behalf of all classes in the United States to some degree. Also there is widespread public ownership of the large corporations. Writes Berle (p. 70); "Probably 50,000,000 Americans who do not even know they derive income from stocks receive a share of these profits" through the holdings of such institutions as pension trusts, mutual funds, life insurance companies, and the like. Furthermore, workers have not wanted to fight management but simply to increase their share in national income. The prevailing union philosophy in the United States has from the beginning been not "revolution," but simply "more." This attitude gives labor—like business—an important stake in the growth of total output. Indeed, in the inflationary 1970s, many commentators have felt that a kind of implicit collusion between labor and management—labor demanding higher wages, management passing on these increased costs in the form of higher prices to the consumer—has been more common (and perhaps more alarming) than class conflict.

3. *Failure of the classes to polarize.* Nor have the classes polarized along the lines of Marx's prediction. Again, Marx was ahead of his time in understanding the role of large-scale industry under capitalism. Indeed, Baran and Sweezy feel that

Marx could have gone even further along this line; to them, "the prevalence of large-scale enterprise and monopoly" (p. 74) is a dominating feature of latter-day capitalism and explains, among other things, the constant tendency for capitalism to produce more goods than it can dispose of properly.

However, the Marxian prediction of increased polarization fails historically on numerous counts. Berle again stresses the widespread dispersal of ownership of the large corporations and the role of the government in regulating industry. Also, one should note the great recent growth in the service industries, and especially in professional workers (lawyers, doctors, teachers and so on) and public employees. How do these workers, employed by the state, or often self-employed, fit into the Marxian scheme of polarized classes? Most important of all, perhaps, is Kerr's point that our "evolution is leading to an all-pervasive middle class" (p. 79. There is conflict in our society, but it is not really class conflict because instead of a sharper and sharper division developing between capitalists and proletariat we have had the emergence of an increasingly large and dominating middle class. Indeed, when the radicals of our period wish to criticize society, it is often precisely in terms of its middle class goals, standards, morality and the like. This simply does not jibe with the Marxian notion of a few rich and innumerable poor.

4. *Comfort rather than immiserization for the working classes.* Nor have the poor been getting poorer under capitalism by any conceivable standard. The striking fact over the past century or more has been the rise in the real wages of the average worker. "The net result," Berle writes (p. 70), "has been that American labor now has the highest standard of living in the world." Nor is this rise in living standards confined to the American worker; similar developments, though not always quite so dramatic, have occurred in the mixed capitalistic economies of Western Europe and Japan. It would not be intellectually fair to compare the living standards of the average worker in the United States or Western Europe with those of a similar worker in the Communist bloc countries: the latter nations started their industrial revolutions rather later on the average than in the West. However, if the Marxian prediction were really accurate, then the workers should be the worse off the more developed and mature the capitalist economy in which they worked. Clearly, this prediction has missed the basic direction of historical trends over the past century.

5. *Internal contradictions: depressions or recessions?* We spoke of the internal contradictions of capitalism in Marxian theory, especially the tendency to overproduce the available markets. Both Robinson and Baran and Sweezy speak favorably of Marx's analysis in this regard. Again, Baran and Sweezy would go even further than Marx: "Only under monopoly capitalism does 'too much' appear as a pervasive problem affecting everyone at all times" (p. 70).

But if Marx—like Malthus before him—is to be given credit for understanding the possibility of crises and depressions in a capitalistic society, he should also have to take responsibility for his view that these crises would get worse and worse over time. This aspect of Marxism actually had great appeal to many intellectuals in the

Great Depression of the 1930s. It did, indeed, seem that the United States and other industrial countries were simply incapable of distributing and consuming the goods which they were technically capable of producing. Indeed, many economists feared that, at the end of the second World War, we would face another depression that would make even the 1930s look relatively mild.

But it has not happened. Although there have been many, and serious, economic problems in the West in recent years, the fact is that four decades have now passed without anything like a repetition of the Great Depression experience. Recessions, yes. Inflation, urban problems, energy crises, pollution. Again, yes. But simply no overwhelming economic crisis to unite the proletariat, force the revolution, and bring an end to the whole social, political and economic framework as we have known it.

DOES MARX STILL LIVE?

Does the above rebuttal fairly well dispose of the theories of Karl Marx? Hardly. No more than an evolutionist's critique of Adam and Eve and the Garden of Eden would dispose of the Bible. A Marxist can readily admit that Marx made some historical errors: after all, he was writing in the mid-nineteenth century, at the same time as John Stuart Mill, before the automobile, the airplane, radio, television, nuclear power, before, indeed, many of the most characteristic features of our modern civilization had yet emerged. It is always possible to believe that a central truth is being expressed in a particular doctrine, even though changed circumstances continually alter the manner in which that central truth must be applied.

The purpose of this book is not to settle the issues in these debates but to present them. In this sense, the following readings with their varied points of view will give the reader the raw material for coming to some of his own, if still tentative, opinions on the question: Does Marx still live? Do his theories still have something to tell us, or have they been so outmoded by subsequent experience that they are merely an historical curiosity?

Perhaps the most fundamental level at which this question can be framed is in terms of the expected future pattern of historical evolution. If you see the economic systems of the Western world as likely to become both more rigid and more hard-pressed as time goes on, so that the only way release can occur is through violent change, then you are, if not a Marxist, at least in the Marxist tradition. If, however, you foresee a world in which imperfection, compromise, amelioration, reform, coexistence, convergence are characteristic—indeed, are characteristic on *both* sides of the Iron Curtain—then it is unlikely that you will find Marxism a particularly helpful guide. Then, indeed, you are likely to conclude that man's consciousness is not wholly determined by his social existence, but may often work, in small ways and large, to guide and even to improve that existence.

Manifesto of the Communist Party

Karl Marx

Karl Marx wrote the Communist Manifesto jointly with
Friedrich Engels in 1848. Engels later attributed its
"fundamental proposition" to Marx.

The history of all hitherto existing society is the history of class struggles.

Freeman and slave, patrician and plebeian, lord and serf, guild-master and journeyman, in a word, oppressor and opppressed, stood in constant opposition to one another, carried on uninterrupted, now hidden, now open fight, a fight that each time ended, either in a revolutionary re-constitution of society at large, or in the common ruin of the contend-ing classes.

In the earlier epochs of history we find almost everywhere a compli-cated arrangement of society into various orders, a manifold gradation of social rank. In ancient Rome we have patricians, knights, plebeians, slaves; in the middle ages, feudal lords, vassals, guild-masters, jour-neymen, apprentices, serfs; in almost all of these classes, again, subordi-nate gradations.

The modern bourgeois society that has sprouted from the ruins of feudal society has not done away with class antagonisms. It has but established new classes, new conditions of oppression, new forms of struggle in place of the old ones.

Our epoch, the epoch of the bourgeoisie, possesses, however, this dis-tinctive feature: it has simplified the class antagonisms. Society as a whole is more and more splitting up into two great hostile camps, into two great classes directly facing each other: Bourgeoisie and Proletariat.

The bourgeoisie, historically, has played a most revolutionary part.

The bourgeoisie, wherever it has got the upper hand, has put an end to all feudal, patriarchal, idyllic relations. It has pitilessly torn asunder the

Excerpted from Karl Marx, "Manifesto of the Communist Party," reprinted in *Capital and Other Writings of Karl Marx*, edited by Max Eastman (New York: Modern Library, Random House, 1932), pp. 321–34.

motley feudal ties that bound man to his "natural superiors," and has left no other nexus between man and man than naked self-interest, than callous "cash payment." It has drowned the most heavenly ecstasies of religious fervor, of chivalrous enthusiasm, of Philistine sentimentalism, in the icy water of egotistical calculation. It has resolved personal worth into exchange value, and in place of the numberless indefeasible chartered freedoms, has set up that single, unconscionable freedom—Free Trade. In one word, for exploitation, veiled by religious and political illusions, it has substituted naked, shameless, direct, brutal exploitation.

The bourgeoisie has stripped of its halo every occupation hitherto honored and looked up to with reverent awe. It has converted the physician, the lawyer, the priest, the poet, the man of science, into its paid wage laborers.

The bourgeoisie has torn away from the family its sentimental veil, and has reduced the family relation to a mere money relation.

The bourgeoisie has disclosed how it came to pass that the brutal display of vigor in the Middle Ages, which reactionists so much admire, found its fitting complement in the most slothful indolence. It has been the first to show what man's activity can bring about. It has accomplished wonders far surpassing Egyptian pyramids, Roman aqueducts and Gothic cathedrals; it has conducted expeditions that put in the shade all former Exoduses of nations and crusades.

The bourgeoisie cannot exist without constantly revolutionizing the instruments of production, and thereby the relations of production, and with them the whole relations of society. Conservation of the old modes of production in unaltered form was, on the contrary, the first condition of existence for all earlier industrial classes. Constant revolutionizing of production, uninterrupted disturbance of all social conditions, everlasting uncertainty and agitation distinguish the bourgeois epoch from all earlier ones. All fixed, fast frozen relations, with their train of ancient and venerable prejudices and opinions, are swept away, all new formed ones become antiquated before they can ossify. All that is solid melts into the air, all that is holy is profaned, and man is at last compelled to face with sober senses, his real conditions of life, and his relations with his kind.

The need of a constantly expanding market for its products chases the bourgeoisie over the whole surface of the globe. It must nestle everywhere, settle everywhere, establish connections everywhere.

The bourgeoisie has through its exploitation of the world market given a cosmopolitan character to production and consumption in every country. To the great chagrin of reactionists, it has drawn from under the feet of industry the national ground on which it stood. All old-established national industries have been destroyed or are daily being destroyed.

They are dislodged by new industries, whose introduction becomes a life and death question for all civilized nations, by industries that no longer work up indigenous raw material, but raw material drawn from the remotest zones; industries whose products are consumed, not only at home, but in every quarter of the globe. In place of the old wants, satisfied by the productions of the country, we find new wants, requiring for their satisfaction the products of distant lands and climes. In place of the old local and national seclusion and self-sufficiency, we have intercourse in every direction, universal interdependence of nations. And as in material, so also in intellectual production. The intellectual creations of individual nations become common property. National onesidedness and narrowmindedness become more and more impossible, and from the numerous national and local literatures, there arises a world literature.

The bourgeoisie, by the rapid improvement of all instruments of production, by the immensely facilitated means of communication, draws all, even the most barbarian nations into civilization. The cheap prices of its commodities are the heavy artillery with which it batters down all Chinese walls, with which it forces the barbarians' intensely obstinate hatred of foreigners to capitulate. It compels all nations, on pain of extinction, to adopt the bourgeoisie mode of production; it compels them to introduce what it calls civilization into their midst, i.e., to become bourgeois themselves. In a word, it creates a world after its own image.

The bourgeoisie has subjected the country to the rule of the towns. It has created enormous cities, has greatly increased the urban population as compared with the rural, and has thus rescued a considerable part of the population from the idiocy of rural life. Just as it has made the country dependent on the towns, so it has made barbarian and semibarbarian countries dependent on civilized ones, nations of peasants on nations of bourgeois, the East on the West.

The bourgeoisie keeps more and more doing away with the scattered state of the population, of the means of production, and of property. It has agglomerated population, centralized means of production, and has concentrated property in a few hands. The necessary consequence of this was political centralization. Independent, or but loosely connected provinces, with separate interests, laws, governments, and systems of taxation, became lumped together in one nation, with one government, one code of laws, one national class interest, one frontier, and one customs tariff.

The bourgeoisie, during its rule of scarce one hundred years, has created more massive and more colossal productive forces than have all preceding generations together. Subjection of Nature's forces to man, machinery, application of chemistry to industry and agriculture, steam navigation, railways, electric telegraphs, clearing of whole continents for cultivation, canalization of rivers, whole populations conjured out of the ground—what earlier century had even a presentiment that such productive forces slumbered in the lap of social labor?

We see then: the means of production and of exchange on whose foundation the bourgeoisie built itself up, were generated in feudal society. At a certain stage in the development of these means of production and of exchange, the conditions under which feudal society produced and exchanged, the feudal organization of agriculture and manufacturing industry, in one word, the feudal relations of property became no longer compatible with the already developed productive forces; they became so many fetters. They had to burst asunder; they were burst asunder.

Into their places stepped free competition, accompanied by social and political constitution adapted to it, and by economical and political sway of the bourgeois class.

A similar movement is going on before our own eyes. Modern bourgeois society with its relations of production, of exchange and of property, a society that has conjured up such gigantic means of production and of exchange, is like the sorcerer, who is no longer able to control the powers of the nether world whom he has called up by his spells. For many a decade past, the history of industry and commerce is but the history of the revolt of modern productive forces against modern conditions of production, against the property relations that are the conditions for the existence of the bourgeoisie and of its rule. It is enough to mention the commercial crises that by their periodical return put on its trial, each time more threateningly, the existence of the entire bourgeois society. In these crises a great part not only of the existing products, but also of the previously created productive forces, are periodically destroyed. In these crises there breaks out an epidemic that, in all earlier epochs, would have seemed an absurdity—the epidemic of overproduction. Society suddenly finds itself put back into a state of momentary barbarism; it appears as if a famine, a universal war of devastation, had cut off the supply of every means of subsistence; industry and commerce seem to be destroyed; and why? Because there is too much civilization, too much means of subsistence, too much industry, too much commerce. The productive forces at the disposal of society no longer tend to further the development of the conditions of the bourgeois property; on the contrary, they have become too powerful for these conditions by which they are fettered, and as soon as they overcome these fetters they bring disorder into the whole of bourgeois society, endanger the existence of bourgeois property. The conditions of bourgeois society are too narrow to comprise the wealth created by them. And how does the bourgeoisie get over these crises? On the one hand by enforced destruction of a mass of productive forces; on the other, by the conquest of new markets, and by the more thorough exploitation of the old ones. That is to say, by paving the way for more extensive and more destructive crises, and by diminishing the means whereby crises are prevented.

The weapons with which the bourgeoisie felled feudalism to the ground are now turned against the bourgeoisie itself.

But not only has the bourgeoisie forged the weapons that bring death to itself; it has also called into existence the men who are to wield those weapons—the modern working class—the proletarians.

Modern industry has converted the little workshop of the patriarchal master into the great factory of the industrial capitalist. Masses of laborers, crowded into factories, are organized like soldiers. As privates of the industrial army they are placed under the command of a perfect hierarchy of officers and sergeants. Not only are they the slaves of the bourgeois class and of the bourgeois state, they are daily and hourly enslaved by the machine, by the overlooker, and, above all, by the individual bourgeois manufacturer himself. The more openly this despotism proclaims gain to be its end and aim, the more petty, the more hateful, and the more embittering it is.

The lower strata of the middle class—the small tradespeople, shopkeepers and retired tradesmen generally, the handicraftsmen and peasants—all these sink gradually into the proletariat, partly because their diminutive capital does not suffice for the scale on which Modern Industry is carried on, and is swamped in the competition with the large capitalists, partly because their specialized skill is rendered worthless by new methods of production. Thus the proletariat is recruited from all classes of the population.

The proletariat goes through various stages of development. With its birth begins its struggle with the bourgeoisie. At first the contest is carried on by individual laborers, then by the workpeople of a factory, then by the operatives of one trade, in one locality, against the individual bourgeois who directly exploits them. They direct their attacks not against the bourgeois conditions of production, but against the instruments of production themselves; they destroy imported wares that compete with their labor, they smash to pieces machinery, they set factories ablaze, they seek to restore by force the vanished status of the workman of the Middle Ages.

At this stage the laborers still form an incoherent mass scattered over the whole country, and broken up by their mutual competition. If anywhere they unite to form more compact bodies, this is not yet the consequence of their own active union, but of the union of the bourgeoisie, which class, in order to attain its own political ends, is compelled to set the whole proletariat in motion, and is moreover yet, for a time, able to do so. At this stage, therefore, the proletarians do not fight their enemies, but the enemies of their enemies, the remnants of absolute monarchy, the landowners, the non-industrial bourgeois, the petty bourgeoisie. Thus the whole historical movement is concentrated in the hands of the bourgeoisie, every victory so obtained is a victory for the bourgeoisie.

But with the development of industry the proletariat not only increases in number; it becomes concentrated in greater masses, its strength grows and it feels that strength more. The various interests and conditions of life within the ranks of the proletariat are more and more equalized, in proportion as machinery obliterates all distinctions of labor, and nearly everywhere reduces wages to the same low level. The growing competition among the bourgeois, and the resulting commercial crisis, make the wages of the workers even more fluctuating. The unceasing improvement of machinery, ever more rapidly developing, makes their livelihood more and more precarious; the collisions between individual workmen and individual bourgeois take more and more the character of collisions between two classes. Thereupon the workers begin to form combinations (Trades' Unions) against the bourgeois; they club together in order to keep up the rate of wages; they found permanent associations in order to make provision beforehand for these occasional revolts. Here and there the contest breaks out into riots.

Further, as we have already seen, entire sections of the ruling classes are, by the advance of industry, precipitated into the proletariat, or are at least threatened in their conditions of existence. These also supply the proletariat with fresh elements of enlightenment and progress.

Finally, in times when the class struggle nears the decisive hour, the process of dissolution going on within the ruling class—in fact, within the whole range of an old society—assumes such a violent, glaring character that a small section of the ruling class cuts itself adrift and joins the revolutionary class, the class that holds the future in its hands. Just as, therefore, at an earlier period, a section of the nobility went over to the bourgeoisie, so now a portion of the bourgeoisie goes over to the proletariat, and in particular, a portion of the bourgeois ideologists, who have raised themselves to the level of comprehending theoretically the historical movements as a whole.

Of all the classes that stand face to face with the bourgeoisie today the proletariat alone is a really revolutionary class. The other classes decay and finally disappear in the face of modern industry; the proletariat is its special and essential product.

Hitherto every form of society has been based, as we have already seen, on the antagonism of oppressing and oppressed classes. But in order to oppress a class, certain conditions must be assured to it under which it can, at least, continue its slavish existence. The serf, in the period of serfdom, raised himself to membership in the commune, just as the petty bourgeois, under the yoke of feudal absolutism, managed to develop into a bourgeois. The modern laborer, on the contrary, instead of rising with the progress of industry, sinks deeper and deeper below the conditions of existence of his own class. He becomes a pauper, and pauperism develops more rapidly than population and wealth. And here it becomes evident that the bourgeoisie is unfit any longer to be the ruling class in society, and to impose its conditions of existence upon society as an overriding law. It is unfit to rule, because it is incompetent to assure an existence to its slave within his slavery, because it cannot help letting him sink into such a state that it has to feed him, instead of being fed by him. Society can no longer live under this bourgeoisie; in other words, its existence is no longer compatible with society.

The essential condition for the existence, and for the sway of the bourgeois class, is the formation and augmentation of capital; the condition for capital is wage labor. Wage labor rests exclusively on competition between the laborers. The advance of industry, whose involuntary promoter is the bourgeoisie, replaces the isolation of the laborers, due to competition, by their involuntary combination, due to association. The development of Modern Industry, therefore, cuts from under its feet the very foundation on which the bourgeoisie produces and appropriates products. What the bourgeoisie therefore produces, above all, are its own grave diggers. Its fall and the victory of the proletariat are equally inevitable.

The Guiding Principle of Marxian Analysis

Karl Marx

A few brief remarks regarding the course of my study of political economy may, however, be appropriate here. . . .

The first work which I undertook to dispel the doubts assailing me was a critical re-examination of the Hegelian philosophy of law; the introduction to this work being published in the *Deutsch-Französische Jahrbücher* issued in Paris in 1844. My inquiry led me to the conclusion that neither legal relations nor political forms could be comprehended whether by themselves or on the basis of a so-called general development of the human mind, but that on the contrary they originate in the material conditions of life, the totality of which Hegel, following the example of English and French thinkers of the eighteenth century, embraces within the term "civil society"; that the anatomy of this civil society, however, has to be sought in political economy. The study of this, which I began in Paris, I continued in Brussels, where I moved owing to an expulsion order issued by M. Guizot. The general conclusion at which I arrived and which, once reached, became the guiding principle of my studies can be summarized as follows. In the social production of their existence, men inevitably enter into definite relations, which are independent of their will, namely relations of production appropriate to a given stage in the development of their material forces of production. The totality of these relations of production constitutes the economic structure of society, the real foundation, on which arises a legal and political superstructure and

Excerpted from "Preface," in *The Guiding Principle of Marxian Analysis*, by Karl Marx (Moscow: Progress Publishers, 1970; distributed by Collet's Holdings, Ltd., England), pp. 19–23.

production of material life conditions the general process of social, political and intellectual life. It is not the consciousness of men that determines their existence, but their social existence that determines their consciousness. At a certain stage of development, the material productive forces of society come into conflict with the existing relations of production or —this merely expresses the same thing in legal terms—with the property relations within the framework of which they have operated hitherto. From forms of development of the productive forces these relations turn into their fetters. Then begins an era of social revolution. The changes in the economic foundation lead sooner or later to the transformation of the whole immense superstructure. In studying such transformations it is always necessary to distinguish between the material transformation of the economic conditions of production, which can be determined with the precision of natural science, and the legal, political, religious, artistic or philosophic—in short, ideological forms in which men become conscious of this conflict and fight it out. Just as one does not judge an individual by what he thinks about himself, so one cannot judge such a period of transformation by its consciousness, but, on the contrary, this consciousness must be explained from the contradictions of material life, from the conflict existing between the social forces of production and the relations of production. No social order is ever destroyed before all the productive forces for which it is sufficient have been developed, and new superior relations of production never replace older ones before the material conditions for their existence have matured within the framework of the old society. Mankind thus inevitably sets itself only such tasks as it is able to solve, since closer examination will always show that the problem itself arises only when the material conditions for its solution are already present or at least in the course of formation. In broad outline, the Asiatic, ancient, feudal and modern bourgeois modes of production may be designated as epochs marking progress in the economic development of society. The bourgeois mode of production is the last antagonistic form of the social process of production—antagonistic not in the sense of individual antagonism but of an antagonism that emanates from the individuals' social conditions of existence—but the productive forces developing within bourgeois society create also the material conditions for a solution of this antagonism. The prehistory of human society accordingly closes with this social formation. . . .

Karl Marx

London, January 1859

Marx the Prophet

Joseph A. Schumpeter

Joseph A. Schumpeter (1883–1950), one of the great
economists of this century, was born in Austria and later
became professor of economics at Harvard.

It was not by a slip that an analogy from the world of religion was
permitted to intrude into the title of this chapter. There is more than
analogy. In one important sense, Marxism *is* a religion. To the believer it
presents, first, a system of ultimate ends that embody the meaning of life
and are absolute standards by which to judge events and actions; and,
secondly, a guide to those ends which implies a plan of salvation and the
indication of the evil from which mankind, or a chosen section of mankind, is to be saved. We may specify still further: Marxist socialism also
belongs to that subgroup which promises paradise on this side of the
grave. I believe that a formulation of these characteristics by an
hierologist would give opportunities for classification and comment which
might possibly lead much deeper into the sociological essence of Marxism
than anything a mere economist can say.

The least important point about this is that it explains the success of
Marxism.[1] Purely scientific achievement, had it even been much more
perfect than it was in the case of Marx, would never have won the
immortality in the historical sense which is his. Nor would his arsenal of
party slogans have done it. Part of his success, although a very minor part,
is indeed attributable to the barrelful of white-hot phrases, of impas-

---

[1] The religious quality of Marxism also explains a characteristic attitude of the orthodox
Marxist toward opponents. To him, as to any believer in a Faith, the opponent is not merely
in error but in sin. Dissent is disapproved of not only intellectually but also morally. There
cannot be any excuse for it once the Message has been revealed.

Excerpted from Joseph A. Schumpeter, *Capitalism, Socialism and Democracy*, 3rd ed. (New York: Harper
& Row Publishers, 1950), pp. 5–8. Reprinted by permission of the publishers, Harper and Row, and George
Allen & Unwin, Ltd.

sioned accusations and wrathful gesticulations, ready for use on any platform, that he put at the disposal of his flock. All that needs to be said about this aspect of the matter is that this ammunition has served and is serving its purpose very well, but that the production of it carried a disadvantage: in order to forge such weapons for the arena of social strife Marx had occasionally to bend, or to deviate from, the opinions that would logically follow from his system. However, if Marx had not been more than a purveyor of phraseology, he would be dead by now. Mankind is not grateful for that sort of service and forgets quickly the names of the people who write the librettos for its political operas.

But he was a prophet, and in order to understand the nature of this achievement we must visualize it in the setting of his own time. It was the zenith of bourgeois realization and the nadir of bourgeois civilization, the time of mechanistic materialism, of a cultural milieu which had as yet betrayed no sign that a new art and a new mode of life were in its womb, and which rioted in most repulsive banality. Faith in any real sense was rapidly falling away from all classes of society, and with it the only ray of light (apart from what may have been derived from Rochdale attitudes and saving banks) died from the workman's world, while intellectuals professed themselves highly satisfied with Mill's *Logic* and the Poor Law.

Now, to millions of human hearts the Marxian message of the terrestrial paradise of socialism meant a new ray of light and a new meaning of life. Call Marxist religion a counterfeit if you like, or a caricature of faith—there is plenty to be said for this view—but do not overlook or fail to admire the greatness of the achievement. Never mind that nearly all of those millions were unable to understand and appreciate the message in its true significance. That is the fate of all messages. The important thing is that the message was framed and conveyed in such a way as to be acceptable to the positivistic mind of its time—which was essentially bourgeois no doubt, but there is no paradox in saying that Marxism is essentially a product of the bourgeois mind. This was done, on the one hand, by formulating with unsurpassed force that feeling of being thwarted and ill treated which is the auto-therapeutic attitude of the unsuccessful many, and, on the other hand, by proclaiming that socialistic deliverance from those ills was a certainty amenable to rational proof.

Observe how supreme art here succeeds in weaving together those extra-rational cravings which receding religion had left running about like masterless dogs, and the rationalistic and materialistic tendencies of the time, ineluctable for the moment, which would not tolerate any creed that had no scientific or pseudo-scientific connotation. Preaching the goal would have been ineffectual; analyzing a social process would have interested only a few hundred specialists. But preaching in the garb of analysis and analyzing with a view to heartfelt needs, this is what conquered passionate allegiance and gave to the Marxist that supreme boon which consists in the conviction that what one is and stands for can never be defeated but must conquer victoriously in the end. This, of course, does not exhaust the achievement. Personal force and the flash of prophecy work independently of the contents of the creed. No new life and no new meaning of life can be effectively revealed without. But this does not concern us here.

Something will have to be said about the cogency and correctness of Marx's attempt to prove the inevitability of the socialist goal. One remark, however, suffices as to what has been called above his formulation of the feelings of the unsuccessful many. It was, of course, not a true formulation of actual feelings, conscious or subconscious. Rather we could call it an attempt at replacing actual feelings by a true or false revelation of the logic of social evolution. By doing this and by attributing—quite unrealistically—to the masses his own shibboleth of "class consciousness," he undoubtedly falsified the true psychology of the workman (which centers in the wish to become a small bourgeois and to be helped to that status by political force), but in so far as his teaching took effect he also expanded and ennobled it. He did not weep any sentimental tears about the beauty of the socialist idea. This is one of his claims to superiority over what he called the Utopian Socialists. Nor did he glorify the workmen into heroes of daily toil as bourgeois love to do when trembling for their dividends. He was perfectly free from any tendency, so conspicuous in some of his weaker followers, toward licking the workman's boots. He had probably a clear perception of what the masses are and he looked far above their heads toward social goals altogether beyond what they thought or wanted. Also, he never taught any ideals as set by himself. Such vanity was quite foreign to him. As every true prophet styles himself the humble mouthpiece of his deity, so Marx pretended no more than to speak the logic of the dialectic process of history. There is dignity in all this which compensates for many pettinesses and vulgarities with which, in his work and in his life, this dignity formed so strange an alliance.

Another point, finally, should not go unmentioned. Marx was personally much too civilized to fall in with those vulgar professors of socialism who do not recognize a temple when they see it. He was perfectly able to understand a civilization and the "relatively absolute" value of its values, however far removed from it he may have felt himself to be. In this respect no better testimony to his broad-mindedness can be offered than the *Communist Manifesto* which is an account nothing short of glowing[2] of the achievements of capitalism; and even in pronouncing *pro futuro* death sentence on it, he never failed to recognize its historical necessity. This attitude, of course, implies quite a lot of things Marx himself would have been unwilling to accept. But he was undoubtedly strengthened in it, and it was made more easy for him to take, because of that perception of the organic logic of things to which his theory of history gives one particular expression. Things social fell into order for him, and however much of a coffeehouse conspirator he may have been at some junctures of his life, his true self despised that sort of thing. Socialism for him was no obsession which blots out all other colors of life and creates an unhealthy and stupid hatred or contempt for other civilizations. And there is, in more senses than one, justification for the title claimed for his type of socialist thought and of socialist volition which are welded together by virtue of his fundamental position: Scientific Socialism.

[2] This may seem to be an exaggeration. But let us quote from the authorized English translation: "The bourgeoisie . . . has been the first to show what man's activity can bring about. It has accomplished wonders far surpassing Egyptian pyramids, Roman aqueducts and Gothic cathedrals. . . . The bourgeosie . . . draws all nations . . . into civilization. . . . It has created enormous cities . . . and thus rescued a considerable part of the population from the idiocy [sic!] of rural life. . . . The bourgeosie, during its rule of scarce one hundred years, has created more massive and more colossal productive forces than have all preceding generations together." Observe that all the achievements referred to are attributed *to the bourgeoisie alone* which is more than many thoroughly bourgeois economists would claim. This is all I meant by the above passage—and strikingly different from the views of the vulgarized Marxism of today or from the Veblenite stuff of the modern non-Marxist radical.

Essay on Marxian Economics
Joan Robinson

Joan Robinson, of Cambridge University, England, is the
author of the classic *Economics of Imperfect
Competition,* and of countless other important books
and articles.

The fundamental differences between Marxian and traditional orthodox
economics are, first, that the orthodox economists accept the capitalist
system as part of the eternal order of Nature, while Marx regards it as a
passing phase in the transition from the feudal economy of the past to the
socialist economy of the future. And, second, that the orthodox
economists argue in terms of a harmony of interests between the various
sections of the community, while Marx conceives of economic life in terms
of a conflict of interests between owners of property who do no work and
workers who own no property. These two points of difference are not
unconnected—for if the system is taken for granted and the shares of the
various classes in the social product are determined by inexorable
natural law, all interests unite in requiring an increase in the total to be
divided. But if the possibility of changing the system is once admitted,
those who hope to gain and those who fear to lose by the change are
immediately ranged in opposite camps.

The orthodox economists, on the whole, identified themselves with the
system and assumed the role of its apologists, while Marx set himself to
understand the working of capitalism in order to hasten its overthrow.
Marx was conscious of his purposes. The economists were in general
unconscious. They wrote as they did because it seemed to them the only
possible way to write, and they believed themselves to be endowed with
scientific impartiality. Their preconceptions emerge rather in the prob-

Excerpted from Joan Robinson, *An Essay on Marxian Economics* (London: Macmillan & Co., 1942), pp.
1–8, 115. Reprinted by permission of the author, St. Martin's Press, Inc., and Macmillan, London and
Basingstoke.

lems which they chose to study and the assumptions on which they worked than in overt political doctrine.

Since they believed themselves to be in search of eternal principles they paid little attention to the special historical features of actual situations, and, in particular, they were apt to project the economics of a community of small equal proprietors into the analysis of advanced capitalism. Thus the orthodox conception of competition entails that each commodity in each market is supplied by a large number of producers, acting individualistically, bound together neither by open collusion nor by unconscious class loyalty; and entails that any individual is free to enter any line of activity he pleases. And the laws derived from such a society are applied to modern industry and finance.

Again, the orthodox conception of wages, which has its origin in the picture of a peasant farmer leaning on his hoe in the evening and deciding whether the extra product of another hour's work will repay the extra backache, is projected into the modern labor market, where the individual worker has no opportunity to decide anything except whether it is better to work or to starve.

The orthodox economists have been much preoccupied with elegant elaborations of minor problems, which distract the attention of their pupils from the uncongenial realities of the modern world, and the development of abstract argument has run far ahead of any possibility of empirical verification. Marx's intellectual tools are far cruder, but his sense of reality is far stronger, and his argument towers above their intricate constructions in rough and gloomy grandeur.

He sees the capitalist system as fulfilling a historic mission to draw out the productive power of combined and specialized labor. From its birthplace in Europe it stretches out tentacles over the world to find its nourishment. It forces the accumulation of capital, and develops productive technique, and by these means raises the wealth of mankind to heights undreamed of in the peasant, feudal or slave economies.

But the workers, who, under the compulsion of capitalism, produce the wealth, obtain no benefit from the increase in their productive power. All the benefit accrues to the class of capitalists, for the efficiency of large-scale enterprise breaks down the competition of the peasant and the craftsman, and reduces all who have not property enough to join the ranks of the capitalists to selling their labor for the mere means of existence. Any concession which the capitalist makes to the worker is the concession which the farmer makes to his beasts—to feed them better that they may work the more.

The struggle for life binds the workers together and sets them in opposition to the propertied class, while the concentration of capital in ever larger concerns, forced on by the development of technique, turns the capitalists towards the antisocial practices of monopoly.

But the condemnation of the system does not only depend upon its moral repugnance, and the inevitability of its final overthrow does not only depend upon the determination of the workers to secure their rightful share in the product of their labor. The system contains contradictions within itself which must lead to its disruption. Marx sees the periodic crises of the trade cycle as symptoms of a deep-seated and progressive malady in the vitals of the system.

Developments in economic analysis which have taken place since Marx's day enable us to detect three distinct strands of thought in Marx's treatment of crises. There is, first, the theory of the reserve army of unemployed labor, which shows how unemployment tends to fluctuate with the relationship between the stock of capital offering employment to labor and the supply of labor available to be employed. Second, there is the theory of the falling rate of profit, which shows how the capitalists' greed for accumulation stultifies itself by reducing the average rate of return on capital. And thirdly, there is the theory of the relationship of capital-good to consumption-good industries, which shows the ever-growing productive power of society knocking against the limitation upon the power to consume which is set by the poverty of the workers.

In Marx's mind these three theories are not distinct, and are fused together in a single picture of the system, racked by its own inherent contradictions, generating the conditions for its own disintegration.

Meanwhile, the academic economists, without paying much attention to Marx, have been forced by the experiences of modern times to question much of the orthodox apologetic, and recent developments in academic theory have led them to a position which in some respects resembles the position of Marx far more closely than the position of their own intellectual forebears. The modern theory of imperfect competition, though formally quite different from Marx's theory of exploitation, has a close affinity with it. The modern theory of crises has many points of contact with the third line of argument, distinguished above, in Marx's treatment of the subject, and allows room for something resembling the first. Only the second line of argument—the falling rate of profit—appears confused and redundant.

In general, the nightmare quality of Marx's thought gives it, in this bedevilled age, an air of greater reality than the gentle complacency of the orthodox academics. Yet he, at the same time, is more encouraging than they, for he releases hope as well as terror from Pandora's box, while they preach only the gloomy doctrine that all is for the best in the best of all possible worlds.

But though Marx is more sympathetic, in many ways, to a modern mind, than the orthodox economists, there is no need to turn him, as many seek to do, into an inspired prophet. He regarded himself as a serious thinker, and it is as a serious thinker that I have endeavoured to treat him.

Marx, however imperfectly he worked out the details, set himself the task of discovering the law of motion of capitalism, and if there is any hope of progress in economics at all, it must be in using academic methods to solve the problems posed by Marx.

Marx was Wrong and so is Khrushchev

Adolf A. Berle, Jr.

Adolf A. Berle has been making important contributions
to economics since 1934, when he collaborated with
Gardner C. Means on the path-breaking study, *The
Modern Corporation and Private Property.*

"Your grandchildren will live under socialism," says Khrushchev to us. "We will bury you (capitalists)," he predicted to an American visitor in Moscow. Both comments capsule a major ingredient of communist propaganda the world over: capitalism is doomed. It is self-destructive. Fate and history make communism the inevitably victorious system. Clever men had best get on the bandwagon now.

The line is not new. Westwardbound empire builders from Eurasia have always used it. Attila, Genghis Khan, Tamerlane, all urged their opponents to collapse gracefully because fate had written them off. But they did not base their claim on economics, or attempt a reasoned argument, as do present-day communists.

But, in Moscow, doubts are arising. The American system, classified by Marxians as monopoly-capitalist and therefore due for death, gives surprisingly few signs of dying, or even of illness. Subtly, the communist line is emphasizing a quite different note: "We can overtake and out-produce you; we can do everything you can faster and better."

One outspoken Soviet economist, Eugene Varga, ten years ago risked his career by predicting that the American system would not then destroy itself by a post-war economic crisis. After a period of disgrace, he was restored to favor. True, Karl Marx had asserted nearly a century earlier that capitalist industrial societies would create the conditions for their own self-destruction. But something had happened to delay the calculation, and careful communist analysts knew it.

What had happened, certainly in the American case, was an evolution within the capitalist frame, knocking out the basis of Marx's prophecy and, incidentally, of the current communist propaganda line. Briefly, the United States, without revolution, changed from a nineteenth-century "property system" to a social system. It did this in a way no communist could have forecast, and it created what is, in essence, a different system; so different that one French scholar, Jacques Maritain, insists that it is a new and fluid system, still in the making, "which renders both capitalism and socialism things of the past."

Another scholar, Father Bruckberger, has recently written a book to prove it. It may not be an accident that both are French; the clearest estimates of America have come from France—witness Alexis de Tocqueville in the nineteenth century and André Siegfried in the twentieth.

This American system has not yet received a distinctive name. It has been called "people's capitalism." A new book about to come out, by Dr. Paul Harbrecht, calls it "paraproprietal society" (a society beyond property). When Khrushchev and his associates talk about capitalism, they describe a system which perhaps did exist a century ago. But in America it stopped existing somewhere between 1920 and 1930. It is important both for the Soviet Union and for America to know this. Kremlin communists are fighting a ghost, and their more sophisticated analysts know it. Americans are just coming to realize that they are operators of a system more advanced and, in its way, more revolutionary than the Marxian.

Predictions of a short life for capitalist society, as it functioned about 1900, had, I think, a reasonable basis at the time. Marx thought private ownership of factories, plants and industry inevitably would cause the rich to grow richer as their profits accumulated. Meanwhile the workers and the poor would stay at subsistence level. The small owner class, he insisted, would own and operate the government, the courts and all social organization. These would be used to defend the growing accumulations of this class. As the poor stayed poor (or grew poorer) markets for manufactured goods would not increase as fast as production—the masses would not have the buying power.

So, markets would have to be extended by military conquest and every capitalist state must become a built-in "imperialism," always seizing more territory to increase markets for its owner class. There would be recurrent crises of growing severity, as production outran markets and the going got harder. Eventually an insuperable crisis would blow up the whole system. Then the communist dictatorship of the proletariat representing the masses would take over. So ran the argument.

If we had looked at Europe in 1870—or at America from 1890 to

1900—circumstances would have lent color to the idea. At that time, individual owners of private capitalist enterprise were in fact accumulating, high, wide and handsome. In America we were having the "age of the moguls"—proprietor-tycoons piling up fabulous fortunes from the profits of railroads and mines, steel, copper and oil. In England, Charles Dickens had described the plight of the masses in "Bleak House" and "Oliver Twist." In the United States, Upton Sinclair and his friends were telling a similar story, American-style.

Marx was right in one respect: it could not (and in fact, did not) last. But he was completely wrong in his guess as to how it would change.

In the United States three new elements (among other less powerful factors) emerged and changed both the direction and structure of affairs, though none of them involved or contemplated blowing up the system.

The first development was the American corporation. This operated surprisingly. In one generation it replaced the individual or family-owners. In a second period, it displaced the tycoons and moguls, substituting professional mnagement. It did not behave at all like a personal fortune-builder.

The second was the rise of American labor unions. These refused to try to seize the ownership position or take over government. Instead, they insisted only on representing workmen.

The third, and probably the most important, was the position of the American democratic government. This simply declined to be owned and operated by and in the interest of the tycoon (or any other) class. It intervened from time to time to steer the economic system toward social goals. None of these possibilities had figured in Marx's calculation, and Russian commentators today find difficulty in explaining them.

First, the corporations. These organizations became and now are, the titular "owners" of American industry. But corporations are not individuals or families and do not behave like them. As productive organizations they can and do pile up huge aggregations of property. But simultaneously they must distribute much of their profit to a continuously growing proportion of the population of the United States. Corporations whose stock is listed on the New York Stock Exchange carry on at least three-fourths of all American industry; the 500 largest of them probably carry on about two-thirds of it. Were these 500 families, the results might have justified Marx's predictions and produced the foreseen catastrophe.

Actually, according to the New York Stock Exchange, they have about 12,500,000 direct stockholders. Even more important, a large and growing amount of their stock is held by institutions—notably pension trusts, mutual funds and, increasingly, life insurance companies. These in turn distribute the industrial profits. Probably 50,000,000 Americans who do not even know they derive income from stocks receive a share of these profits through the holdings of such institutions. This number will grow. Their proportionate take of industrial profits will also grow—both factors are expanding just now with considerable rapidity.

Nor are the managers and groups controlling corporations owners. They are almost always salaried officials. They are becoming a kind of non-statist civil service. The corporate system at present is thus in effect operating to "socialize" American industry but without intervention of the political state. No Marxist could ever have thought up that possibility.

Then there is the phenomenon of the American labor movement. For practical purposes, organized labor became a substantial economic factor after World War I. It gained full recognition through the Wagner Act. It has now become a vast, permanent and powerful element in the American economic system.

But it refused to behave like its European ancestors. It did not wish to own and manage the plants. In fact, it has steadily declined to enter management. Instead, it aimed only to represent the workers and to get for them, through wages, pensions and fringe benefits, the largest practicable share of national income.

In the past 30 years it has succeeded in steadily raising the "real" wage of workers about 3 percent annually, or 30 percent in each decade —though workers do not receive this only in cash but also in shorter working hours, vacations and more leisure. The net result has been that American labor now has the highest workers' standard of living in the world. The workman himself lives, thinks and feels not as an oppressed proletarian seeking to be saved by revolution but as a member of the middle class to whose children any position is possible. It is, in fact, increasingly hard to find a "proletariat" in the United States except in a few isolated areas.

Still less has the labor movement followed European patterns in forming a political party or seeking to assume government; still less to overturn the existing system. It does get into politics very effectively to defend its own interests, dealing more or less impartially with both political parties. But it declines to become a Socialist party itself and shows no desire whatever to attempt creation of a "labor" government.

Finally, and certainly most important, the American government most obstinately refused to be merely an expression of the "ownership class." According to Marx, such refusal could not happen—but it did. Surprisingly to European thought, many of the "ownership" group were outspoken in opposing that conception of government. President Theodore

Roosevelt intervened violently against one ownership sector in the Mogul Age when he forced regulation of railroads and set a conservative party to control "malefactors of great wealth."

President Woodrow Wilson moved effectively against the financial ownership class, proclaiming the doctrines of the "New Freedom" and compelling passage of the Federal Reserve Act of 1913. With even more effect, he sponsored income and inheritance tax legislation about the same time.

In 1933, President Franklin Roosevelt and the New Deal undertook the larger task of hauling the whole system toward a socially directed commonwealth. Social Security legislation was one great instrument. Systematic direction of a larger share of national income toward farmers and agriculture was another. Development of public works and state-directed production when unemployment threatens was a third. Use of the credit system to assure housing, electricity and land reclamation was a fourth. And there were many more.

Thus, in mid-century, Americans are operating a so-called "capitalist system" in which all the elements dominant in the nineteenth century have changed. What is left of the old system is its form of organization and, in general, its separation from the political government.

That organization has achieved a per capita level of production beyond older dreams—so much so that equaling it is the present expressed dream of the Soviet Union and of communist China. In terms of distribution it has done better than communist systems because it had more to distribute. And its methods of distribution have been on the whole less arbitrary and infinitely less oppressive. The results have been more satisfactory to 175,000,000 Americans than those of socialist distribution to the 210,000,000 citizens of the Soviet Union.

This American system is miles from being perfect. All kinds of things turn up in it that should not be there. All kinds of inequities have to be dealt with. Our methods for keeping production and distribution in balance are still unsystematic and crude; better means still need to be worked out. Steering an adequate amount of the national income into necessary noncommercial activities, notably education and the arts, remains a problem.

But, by comparative standards, our system is far out ahead. As a single example, during 40 years of the Soviet system, Russia at all times has had more political prisoners in concentration camps behind barbed wire than the United States has ever had unemployed men—though Khrushchev is credited with having reduced the number materially in the past few years.

The vitality and rapid evolution of the American system—and it has not stopped growing and has not stopped evolving—has worried the Russian theoreticians. At the Twentieth Communist Congress in Moscow, a then favorite communist doctrinaire, Dmitri Shepilov (later Foreign Minister), was put up as a principal speaker to explain true doctrine to the comrades. He did not ignore the fact that the United States and its system had evolved and was going great guns, but he had to prove nevertheless that "capitalism is doomed."

Taking account of the newer studies of the American system, he singled out for attention (along with John Foster Dulles) the work of Prof. J. Kenneth Galbraith of Harvard ("American Capitalism: The Concept of Countervailing Power") and a current book of mine. He made no attempt to meet the modern American facts. "It can't happen," he proclaimed. Socially directed capitalism, freed from the vices Marx had observed, must be like hot ice: it couldn't exist.

Sophisticated communist scholars know better. A more serious explanation was attempted this summer, again by Eugene Varga, ablest of the Soviet economists. In the official "Problems of Peace and Socialism" last August, he published an article. He renewed the statement that "under capitalism crises of overproduction are inevitable," but he said we were now in a system of "state monopoly capitalism" and this system made it easier for "monopolies" to weather these crises.

Specifically, the state moved to support the "monopolies" (he means the big corporations) through government orders, chiefly military, and thus assure a minimum of production even during crises. Further, we slowly inflated the currency, reducing real wages without direct wage cuts.

The fact that the corporations are not monopolies and neither control, nor are controlled by, the state, he ignored, and he omitted the fact that they now distribute profits as well as wages to a huge sector of the United States. Nor had he discovered that the real wage of the American workman steadily rises.

Still less, of course, had he noted that "government orders" include nonmilitary items such as huge road systems, municipal improvements, housing, power, scientific development and other activities whose amount exceeds military expenditures. (If the armament burden were lifted tomorrow, that same machinery could be used with general approval from the American public to increase production and markets alike.) But he continues hopefully to assert that "the cyclic movement inherent in the capitalist mode of production will, we believe, resume its normal course with a world economic crisis occurring every six years or so."

Well, his reasoning does not take account of facts. It ignores the structural change in the property system achieved during the past fifty years, and the astonishing capacity of the American system to make new adaptations.

Its crises (there will be some) can be handled on a humane basis. They will be infinitely less dangerous than the recurrent bloody crises inescapable in the political power monopoly built into the Soviet dictatorship. The American system continues to evolve successfully, and is keeping right on.

Monopoly Capital

Paul A. Baran and Paul M. Sweezy

Two highly influential American Marxist economists are
Paul M. Sweezy, currently coeditor of the *Monthly
Review,* and the late Professor Paul A. Baran.

Like the classical economists before him, Marx treated monopolies not as essential elements of capitalism but rather as remnants of the feudal and mercantilist past which had to be abstracted from in order to attain the clearest possible view of the basic structure and tendencies of capitalism. It is true that, unlike the classicists, Marx fully recognized the powerful trend toward the concentration and centralization of capital inherent in a competitive economy: his vision of the future of capitalism certainly included new and purely capitalist forms of monopoly. But he never attempted to investigate what would at the time have been a hypothetical system characterized by the prevalence of large-scale enterprise and monopoly. Partly the explanation is no doubt that the empirical material on which such an investigation would have had to be based was too scanty to permit reliable generalization. But perhaps even more important, Marx anticipated the overthrow of capitalism long before the unfolding of all its potentialities, well within the system's competitive phase.

Engels, in some of his own writings after Marx's death and in editorial additions to the second and third volumes of *Capital* which he prepared for the printer, commented on the rapid growth of monopolies during the 1880s and 1890s, but he did not try to incorporate monopoly into the body of Marxian economic theory. The first to do this was Rudolf Hilferding in his important work, *Das Finanzkapital,* published in 1910. But for all his emphasis on monopoly, Hilferding did not treat it as a qualitatively new element in the capitalist economy; rather he saw it as effecting essentially quantitative modifications of the basic Marxian laws of capitalism. Lenin, who was strongly influenced by Hilferding's analysis of the origins and diffusion of monopoly, based his theory of imperialism squarely on the predominance of monopoly in the developed capitalist countries. But neither he nor his followers pursued the matter into the fundamentals of Marxian economic theory. There, paradoxically enough, in what might have been thought the area most immediately involved, the growth of monopoly made the least impression.

We believe that the time has come to remedy this situation and to do so in an explicit and indeed radical fashion.

MONOPOLY CAPITALISM IS SELF-CONTRADICTORY

Twist and turn as one will, there is no way to avoid the conclusion that monopoly capitalism is a self-contradictory system. It tends to generate ever more surplus, yet it fails to provide the consumption and investment outlets required for the absorption of a rising surplus and hence for the smooth working of the system. Since surplus which cannot be absorbed will not be produced, it follows that the normal state of the monopoly capitalist economy is stagnation. With a given stock of capital and a given cost and price structure, the system's operating rate cannot rise above the point at which the amount of surplus produced can find the necessary outlets. And this means chronic underutilization of available human and material resources. Or, to put the point in slightly different terms, the system must operate at a point low enough on its profitability schedule not to generate more surplus than can be absorbed. Since the profitability schedule is always moving upward, there is a corresponding downdrift of the "equilibrium" operating rate. Left to itself—that is to say, in the absence of counteracting forces which are no part of what may be called the "elementary logic" of the system—monopoly capitalism would sink deeper and deeper into a bog of chronic depression.

Counteracting forces do exist. If they did not, the system would indeed long since have fallen of its own weight. It therefore becomes a matter of the greatest importance to understand the nature and implications of these counteracting forces. Here we confine ourselves to a few preliminary remarks.

The self-contradictory character of monopoly capitalism—its chronic inability to absorb as much surplus as it is capable of producing —impresses itself on the ordinary citizen in a characteristic way. To him, the economic problem appears to be the very opposite of what the textbooks say it is: not how best to utilize scarce resources but how to dispose of the products of superabundant resources. And this holds regardless of his wealth or position in society. If he is a worker, the ubiquitous fact of unemployment teaches him that the supply of labor is always greater than the demand. If he is a farmer, he struggles to stay afloat in a sea of surpluses. If he is a businessman, his sales persistently fall short of what he could profitably produce. Always too much, never too little.

This condition of affairs is peculiar to monopoly capitalism. The very notion of "too much" would have been inconceivable to all precapitalist forms of society; and even in the competitive stage of capitalism, it described a temporary derangement, not a normal condition. In a rationally ordered socialist society, no matter how richly endowed it might be with natural resources and technology and human skills, "too much" could only be a welcome signal to shift attention to an area of "too little." Only under monopoly capitalism does "too much" appear as a pervasive problem affecting everyone at all times.

From this source stem a whole series of attitudes and interests of crucial importance for the character and functioning of monopoly capitalist society. On the one hand, there is a stubborn spirit of restrictionism which pervades the institutional structure. Union featherbedding and Henry Wallace's plowing under of little pigs are only the best publicized examples of practices which are all but universal in business and government: the most primitive reaction to an excess of supply is simply to cut back. During the 1930s, when "too much" took on the dimensions of a universal disaster, primitive restrictionism acquired, in the National Industrial Recovery Act and the National Recovery Administration, the dignity and sanction of official national policy.

But cutting back as a remedy for "too much," even if beneficial to particular groups or individuals, only aggravates the situation as a whole. A secondary and more sophisticated set of attitudes and policies therefore emerges, gropingly and slowly at first but with increasing purposefulness and momentum as monopoly capitalism develops. Their rationale derives from the simple fact that the obverse of "too much" on the supply side is "too little" on the demand side; instead of cutting back supply they aim at stimulating demand.

The stimulation of demand—the creation and expansion of markets —thus becomes to an ever greater degree the leitmotif of business and government policies under monopoly capitalism. But this statement, true as it is, can easily be misleading. There are many conceivable ways of stimulating demand. If a socialist society, for example, should find that through some planning error more consumer goods were being produced than could be sold, given the existing structure of prices and incomes, the simplest and most direct remedy would clearly be to cut prices. This would reduce the amount of surplus at the disposal of the planning authorities and correspondingly raise the purchasing power of consumers. The threatened glut could be quickly and painlessly averted: everyone would be better off, no one worse off. Such a course of action is obviously not open to a monopoly capitalist society, in which the determination of prices is the jealously guarded prerogative of the giant corporations. Each makes its own decisions with a view to maximizing its own private profit. Except for short periods of all-out war, when inflationary pressures threaten the entire economic and social fabric, there is no agency charged with controlling prices. Moreover, every attempt to maintain or establish such an agency in peacetime has resulted either in ignominious failure (witness the fiasco of price control after the Second World War) or in the thinly disguised legalization of monopoly pricing practices in "regulated" industries. The plain fact is that the pricing process is controlled by the most powerful vested interests in monopoly capitalist society. To imagine that it could possibly be regulated in the public interest would be to imagine away the very characteristics of that society which make it what it is.

If stimulation of demand through price reduction is impossible within the framework of monopoly capitalism, this cannot be said of other possible methods. Take, for example, advertising and related forms of salesmanship. Every giant corporation is driven by the logic of its situation to devote more and more attention and resources to the sales effort. And monopoly capitalist society as a whole has every interest in promoting rather than restricting and controlling this method of creating new markets and expanding old ones.

Just as with price cutting and salesmanship, other forms of stimulating demand either are or are not compatible with the pattern of interests, the structure of power, the web of ideology that constitute the essence of monopoly capitalist society. Those which are compatible will be fostered and promoted; those which are incompatible will be ignored or inhibited. The question for monopoly capitalism is not whether to stimulate demand. It must, on pain of death.

THE IRRATIONAL SYSTEM

It is of the essence of capitalism that both goods and labor power are typically bought and sold on the market. In such a society relations among individuals are dominated by the principle of the exchange of equivalents, of *quid pro quo*, not only in economic matters but in all other aspects of life as well.

Not that the principle of equivalent exchange is or ever has been universally practiced in capitalist society. As Marx showed so convincingly in the closing chapters of the first volume of *Capital,* the primary accumulation of capital was effected through violence and plunder, and the same methods continue in daily use throughout capitalism's dependent colonies and semi-colonies. Nevertheless the ideological sway of *quid pro quo* became all but absolute. In their relations with each other and in what they teach those over whom they rule, capitalists are fully committed to the principle of *quid pro quo,* both as a guide to action and as a standard of morality.

This commitment reflected an important step forward in the development of the forces of production and in the evolution of human consciousness. Only on the basis of equivalent exchange was it possible to realize the more rational utilization of human and material resources which has been the central achievement of capitalism. At the same time, it must never be forgotten that the rationality of *quid pro quo* is specifically capitalist rationality which at a certain stage of development becomes incompatible with the underlying forces and relations of production. To ignore this and to treat *quid pro quo* as a universal maxim of rational conduct is in itself an aspect of bourgeois ideology, just as the radical-sounding assertion that under socialism exchange of equivalents can be immediately dispensed with betrays a utopian view of the nature of the economic problems faced by a socialist society.[1]

But even during the life span of capitalism itself, *quid pro quo* breaks down as a rational principle of economic and social organization. The giant corporation withdraws from the sphere of the market large segments of economic activity and subjects them to scientifically designed administration. This change represents a continuous increase in the rationality of the parts of the system, but it is not accompanied by any rationalization of the whole. On the contrary, with commodities being priced not according to their costs of production but to yield the max-

---

[1] Marx emphasized in his *Critique of the Gotha Program* that the principle of equivalent exchange must survive in a socialist society for a considerable period as a guide to the efficient allocation and utilization of human and material resources. By the same token, however, the evolution of socialism into communism requires an unremitting struggle **against** the principle, with a view to its ultimate replacement by the ideal "From each according to his ability, to each according to his need." In a fully developed communist society, in which social production would be organized as in one vast economic enterprise and in which scarcity would be largely overcome, equivalent exchange would no more serve as the organizing principle of economic activity than at the present time the removal of a chair from one's bedroom to one's sitting room requires charging the sitting room and crediting the bedroom with the value of the furniture. This is obviously not to imply that the communist society of the future can dispense with rational calculation; what it does indicate is that the nature of the rationality involved in economic calculation undergoes a profound change. And this change in turn is but one manifestation of a thoroughgoing transformation of human needs and of the relations among men in society.

imum possible profit, the principle of *quid pro quo* turns into the opposite of a promoter of rational economic organization and instead becomes a formula for maintaining scarcity in the midst of potential plenty. Human and material resources remain idle because there is in the market no *quid* to exchange against the *quo* of their potential output. And this is true even though the real cost of such output would be nil. In the most advanced capitalist country a large part of the population lives in abysmal poverty while in the underdeveloped countries hundreds of millions suffer from disease and starvation because there is no mechanism for effecting an exchange of what they could produce for what they so desperately need. Insistence on the inviolability of equivalent exchange when what is to be exchanged costs nothing, strict economizing of resources when a large proportion of them goes to waste—these are obviously the very denial of the rationality which the concept of value and the principle of *quid pro quo* originally expressed.

The obsolescence of such central categories of bourgeois thought is but one symptom of the profoundly contradictory nature of monopoly capitalism, of the ever sharpening conflict between the rapidly advancing rationalization of the actual processes of production and the undiminished *elementality* of the system as a whole. This conflict affects all aspects of society. While rationality has been conquering ever new areas of consciousness, the inability of bourgeois thought to comprehend the development of society as a whole has remained essentially unchanged, a faithful mirror of the continuing elementality and irrationality of the capitalist order itself.

Social reality is therefore conceived in outlived, topsy-turvy and fetishistic terms. Powerless to justify an irrational and inhuman social order and unable to answer the increasingly urgent questions which it poses, bourgeois ideology clings to concepts that are anachronistic and moribund. Its bankruptcy manifests itself not so much in the generation of new fetishes and half-truths as in the stubborn upholding of old fetishes and half-truths which now turn into blatant lies. And the more these old fetishes and half-truths lose whatever truth content they once possessed, the more insistently they are hammered, like advertising slogans, into the popular consciousness.

The claim that the United States economy is a "free enterprise" system is a case in point. At no time was enterprise really free in the sense that anyone who wanted to could start a business of his own. Still the concept conveyed an important aspect of the truth by pointing up the difference between the relative freedom of competitive capitalism on the one hand and the restrictions imposed by the guild system and the mercantilist state on the other. Having long ago lost this limited claim to truthfulness and referring as it now does to the freedom of giant corporations to exercise undisturbed their vast monopoly powers, "free enterprise" has turned into a shibboleth devoid of all descriptive or explanatory validity.

Bourgeois ideology is no longer a world outlook, a *Weltanschauung,* which attempts to discern order in the existing chaos and to discover a meaning in life. It has turned into a sort of box of assorted tools and gimmicks for attaining the central goal of bourgeois policies. And this goal—which in its younger days the bourgeoisie defined in terms of material progress and individual freedom—is more and more explicitly limited to one thing only: preservation of the status quo, alias the "free world," with all its manifest evils, absurdities and irrationalities.

It is of course impossible to advance a reasoned defense of this status quo, and indeed the effort is seldom made any more. Instead of taking the form of a demonstration of the rationality and desirability of monopoly capitalism, the defense increasingly focuses on the repudiation of socialism which is the only real alternative to monopoly capitalism, and on the denunciation of revolution which is the only possible means of achieving socialism. All striving for a better, more humane, more rational society is held to be unscientific, utopian, and subversive; by the same token the existing order of society is made to appear not only as the only possible one but as the only conceivable one.

The contradiction between the increasing rationality of society's methods of production and the organizations which embody them on the one hand and the undiminished elementality and irrationality in the functioning and perception of the whole creates that ideological wasteland which is the hallmark of monopoly capitalism. But we must insist that this is not, as some apologists of the status quo would have us believe, "the end of ideology"; it is the displacement of the ideology of rising capitalism by the ideology of the general crisis and decline of the world capitalist order. That its main pillar is anti-communism is neither accidental nor due to a transient conjunction of political forces, any more than is the fact that the main content of the political and economic policies of modern capitalism is armaments and Cold War. These policies can only be *anti*; there is nothing left for them to be *pro*.

Class Conflict and Class Collaboration

Clark Kerr

Former president of the University of California, Clark
Kerr is also a distinguished economist specializing in
labor and industrial relations problems.

As seen from a more modern viewpoint than that of Marx, the conflict
over class has largely dissolved. Instead of six classes or five or two, there
are said to be none at all in the communist world—all men are equal and
some are more equal than others; and, in the capitalist world, there are
such infinite variations and gradations that it is better to speak of interest
groups or status positions rather than class at all in the sense of a class set
apart by its common attachment to grievances or to privileges or to a
common ideology—all men are unequal and some are more unequal
than others.

Morality attaches more to individual men than to classes, although there
are now those who would urge a special moral position for the intellectuals. Evolution is leading towards an all-pervasive middle class—a middle
class that expands its coverage so widely that it is no longer a class at all.
There are few hard and fast lines in this middle group but, rather, many
minor grades that shade off into one another; except that an 'under-class'
may be clearly distinguished and is in some places more visible where it
has a special racial composition, as in the United States. The under-class
stands outside the embrace of the great productive 'middle' segment.

Conflict is not concentrated at one place and at one time—at the
barricades that separate the proletariat and the bourgeoisie. Friction is
spread around in the ball-bearing society that has evolved. Protest is

Excerpted from Clark Kerr, "Class Conflict and Class Collaboration" from *Marshall, Marx and Modern
Times: The Multi-Dimensional Society* (London: Cambridge University Press, 1969), pp. 37–41, 122,
129–30. Reprinted by permission of the publisher.

fractionalized. It is not over property but over countless prices and rules. It is not against the capitalist alone, but also against the merchant and bureaucrat and politician. The evolution of industrial society has helped this. There are fewer isolated masses in the lumber camp or textile town or mining village with common grievances against a single source of authority. The one-industry community is less frequent, and employer paternalism gradually passes away. Workers are concentrated into larger communities but these communities are so heterogeneous that the individual and the group are absorbed and contained and subdued. Conflict is everywhere and this saves it from being anywhere to a degree that causes revolution—it is too scattered over time and place.

Marx saw a process that went on stage by stage until its ultimate conclusion—but the process stopped at about the stage he saw and went little further. Workers coalesced into trade unions and in some capitalist countries into political parties, but the trade unions remained bread-and-butter trade unions and the political parties remained cooperating political parties, and neither became revolutionary instruments. In England, at the time of the General Strike, and in the United States, with the I.W.W.s, it looked for a time as though the process might go on as Marx saw it, but the process was arrested. The process of developing increasing group consciousness stopped at the stage of economic trade unions and participating political parties.

Relations of workers and employees became less violent, not more. Real wages rose. Trade unions developed power and influence in the work place—enough to get better rules and to settle grievances; and in individual industries—enough to be concerned with the profitability and growth of 'their' industry. As Bendix has noted, the willingness of entrepreneurial classes to compromise may increase along with the capitalist development[1]—not hold steady or decrease. Political parties with worker support came to rule governments. Marx never thought that the capitalists would yield so easily the authority he believed they had over the state—for this, to him, was 'suicide.' The state turned to welfare. The law was, to a degree, impartial and was not just a tool of the dominant class. Many buffers were created between contending parties. The 'new economics' of Cambridge replaced the old. Slichter once wrote of the crucial race between the engineer and the union leader, the one pushing greater productivity and the other higher money wages. A far more important race was between Cambridge economists and the Great Depres-

---

[1] Reinhard Bendix, *Work and Authority in Industry* (New York: John Wiley, 1956), p. 438.

sions, and Cambridge won.[2] The hard and intricate problem of counter-cyclical policy was solved.

Marx was wrong about the evolution of class in maturing capitalist nations. He expected revolution from the workers during an industrial crisis as the standard case. Communist revolutions have come instead more from the peasants and from war. Peasants to Marx represented 'barbarians' rather than civilized men. That they should have been impor-tant in Russia and particularly China and Cuba would have surprised him. Through foresight or by chance, however, he envisioned a war between Germany and Russia which 'will act as the midwife to the inevita-ble social revolution in Russia.' But Russia was not an advanced capitalist nation and thus fell outside his central theory.

Communism has appealed less to the stage of late capitalism and more to early development than Marx had thought it would. It has had a special appeal to people undergoing the transition from a traditional to a modern society. It speaks to their sense of revulsion against the old dynastic elite or against foreign domination. It speaks to their sense of exploitation. It speaks to their increasing sense of misery as they face the psychological impact of the 'revolution of rising expectations.' Com-munism, also, has some answers to the problems of the transition —control by the state, a social plan, fast capital accumulation. It is less well adapted to the complexities of an advanced industrial society where many small decisions must be made, and where individuals and groups achieve a degree of independence. Thus, in a world marked by many countries in the early transitional stages into industrialization, Marxism has come to have substantial influence even though it has little appeal in more ad-vanced societies.

THE NEW STRUGGLE

The old struggle was seen by Marx as being over the ownership of property since property determined power. The new struggle is directly over power, almost regardless of the ownership of property: power to set the rules, fix the rewards, influence the style of life. It takes place in modern industrial societies between the several forms of pluralism as against the monolithic society of Stalinism on the one extreme and anarchism without any central coercive authority at the other, and within and among the several forms of pluralism themselves. The old struggle

[2] [Kerr is referring here to the work of John Maynard Keynes, who was a Cambridge (England) University economist.]

pitted the workers under the banners of socialism against the capitalists with control of the state as the major prize. The new struggle pits the managed under the banners of freedom and participation against the managers with the control and the conduct of a myriad of organizations involved. Instead of trying to concentrate power in the state, the new effort is to fractionalize it everywhere—the old salvation is the new tyranny; and general revolution gives way to piecemeal evolution. Communism, not capitalism, now faces the greatest challenge; for power there is most centrally held—the old radicalism is the new conservatism.

The new problems of modern industrial society call for more flexibility, for more individuality. The new imperative is to 'humanize' the communities of work, adapt them to individual preferences. Rather than the unfolding of class relations or the perfecting of market mechanisms, the new force at work is further adaptation to individual preferences in many situations and for many reasons. The challenge once was to absorb and adjust to the factory, the worker and the capitalist; now it is to adjust to the more aggressive individual. Instead of socialism challenging the old capitalism, it is now anarchistic and individualistic and syndicalistic tendencies challenging the new communism and the new capitalistic pluralism. A new synthesis is in process.

Industrial pluralism has developed as the realistic alternative to both the monolithic and the atomistic society. Pluralism now struggles with some of the ultimate issues that go beyond class versus class and monopoly versus the market: (1) the role of the managed as against the managers, of the semi-managed as against the semi-managers, of the individual against the group; (2) the pressure of the ever-newer technology to change the lives of men as against the desire of men to rule technology, to exercise their options in relation to it; (3) the interests of those inside the productive process as against those standing outside; and (4) the contrast between the imperfectibility of man and the hope for a more perfect society. No revolution, no alchemy of morality and knowledge can rid man of all his chains, can make all men into gentlemen; or so it seems one century later.

GREAT DEBATE THREE

ECONOMIC DEVELOPMENT VERSUS DEMOCRACY?

ECONOMIC DEVELOPMENT VERSUS DEMOCRACY?

I N the preceding Great Debate, when discussing Marx's predictions of the revolutionary ending of advanced capitalistic societies, we noted that communism, in fact, has had its greatest appeal in the less-developed nations of the world: Russia in 1917, China, Vietnam, North Korea, Cuba, Albania. Some of these cases are mixed—Russia, for example, had shown substantial economic progress in the late nineteenth and early twentieth centuries, and, some commentators believe, was on her way to a modified Western-style development when World War I and the revolution intervened—but clearly none of these countries were examples of mature capitalism when Communist regimes gained power. Thus, the spread of communism has to a degree discredited Marxian theory, but, by the same token, created a new apprehension and a new great debate. Is a communist takeover of the underdeveloped Third World an historical inevitability? More generally, have the special problems of development in Asia, Africa and Latin America virtually ruled out the application of such Western concepts as individualism, personal liberty, voter participation and parliamentary democracy? Or do authoritarian, including communist, regimes suffer from their own serious disabilities in promoting economic improvement in conditions of extreme poverty? Is there one "wave of the future," or are there many paths, all difficult and all different?

ECONOMICS OF THE "BIG PUSH"

In the reading selections that follow, much of the emphasis is on the political and sociological aspects of the development process. For this reason, it is important to emphasize the significant economic issues that are also at stake. The key point in Heilbroner's argument may perhaps be conveyed by the single word, *haste* (p. 99). "Haste" is enjoined upon us by the very fact of the enormous misery of the countless millions who still live in poverty and despair. But it may also be a technical requirement of successful development. Much of the economic theorizing about the plight of the less-developed world has centered on the requirement for speed in the initial stages of growth, or, to use the phrase commonly employed, on the need for a "big push."

"Big push" theories are usually based on a recognition both of the general obstacles to launching a development process in a poor country, and also of the special difficulties that face Third World countries today, particularly those in overpopulated Asia. Take population growth for example. Both Malthus and Ricardo, as we earlier noted in passing (p. 12), felt that population growth was a threat to any permanent improvement in the economic lot of the mass of mankind. If wages rose, population would quickly increase and this would force wages back down to some bare subsistence level. Subsequent experience has suggested that the Malthusian approach failed to weigh fully the favorable effects of the development process on restraining population growth. A widely held view today[1] is that although in the initial phases of economic development, population growth may be stimulated by improved conditions, nevertheless in the longer run the process of urbanization, rising living standards, gradual emancipation of women, increasing education and so on will have the effect of lowering the birth rate. Crudely put: economic development first lowers the death rate and then, after a time, also lowers the birth rate. The suggestion is that the problem of a very rapid population growth is limited to the early stages of development, when death rates have been lowered and birth rates are still high. Later on, the fall in birth rates moderates the rate of population increase, and, consequently, population growth ceases to be a major obstacle to still further development.

Now one can see even in this very general sense why the population problem would require a certain amount of "haste" in the early stages of development. The problem is to get past the population bulge and raise living standards sufficiently so that falling birth rates begin to produce their favorable effects. A "big push"—rapid initial development—may be much more desirable than a gradual process because the latter may simply be soaked up by the concurrent population increase, with none of the improvements in living standards, education and so forth that might lead to a moderation of that population increase.

But this general argument is greatly intensified for most of the poor countries today because their population problems, on the average, are infinitely worse than those of countries like the United States, Britain, Germany and so on who developed earlier. Because of the modern medical and public health revolutions, these countries are facing extremely rapid rates of population increase even *before* general economic development begins. Furthermore, especially in Asia, where the great majority of the world's poor people live, these rapid population increases are taking place in heavily populated areas where the pressure of people on limited natural resources is already very intense. In the absence of massive development efforts, economic conditions in these countries may not only remain unchanged but

[1] Sometimes called the "theory of demographic transition."

seriously decline: to make actual *progress*, one must either have a very big "big push," or an effective population control campaign in advance of development (which, despite Wrong's tentative optimism, p. 115, has yet to be demonstrated in fact), or possibly rapid development *and* significant population control *simultaneously,* that is, an enormous all-out effort to promote modern growth.

Moreover, the population problem is only one of a group of problems that give weight to the "big push" strategy for the less-developed countries. Thus, one of the advantages that these countries have is supposed to be the storehouse of modern technology, largely developed in the West, that these countries can "borrow" to achieve great increases in productivity. However, this technology is often best suited to large-scale production, and frequently makes large demands in terms of capital (machinery, equipment, building facilities and so on) and skilled workers and management personnel, as opposed to unskilled, purely manual labor. To establish a few large-scale industries in a generally depressed economic environment may mean that they lack adequate markets, and hence fail not because they are unproductive but because they are too productive. One may need to do several things at once to ensure success. But moving on several fronts simultaneously may make extremely heavy demands on the society's ability to accumulate sufficient capital. A people already at or near the verge of starvation may have to be told to pull in their belts still further, to work harder, to wait longer. To make less than this massive demand on the populace may guarantee failure. Again, a "big push" in terms of the maximum speed and size of the development effort in the early stages seems to be called for.

Of course, not all economists accept this analysis, or certainly every feature of it. Some years ago, for example, Professor A. O. Hirschman published a provocative book[2] in which he argued for concentrating on certain specific sectors of the economy rather than trying to promote progress on all fronts at once. The very interdependence ("linkages" as he called them) between different industries and sectors that prompted the all-or-nothing school suggested to him that a selective strategy would be better. The reason: because progress in a few of several linked sectors would exert pressure on the lagging sectors to catch up; general development might be best fostered by *creating* tensions between different parts of the economy rather than *easing* them. However, even economists who favor this kind of "unbalanced" growth usually recognize that the strains of early development in today's poor countries are great and that a really major mobilization of resources will be required to solve them.

THE STATE AND PLANNING

The consequence of the "big push" doctrine in its various manifestations has been widespread agreement among economists that economic development today will require far more state planning than was the case, say, in England in the late

[2] Albert O. Hirschman, *The Strategy of Economic Development* (New Haven: Yale University Press, 1958).

eighteenth century Industrial Revolution or in the United States in the early nineteenth century when our growth began to accelerate. And this has clearly been the case so far. India is often cited in contrast to China as a case of relatively mild government intervention in the economy, but India has proceeded (or attempted to proceed) on the basis of various Five Year Plans ever since 1951. Development on a "big push" basis requires a greater degree of conscious, centralized direction as opposed to the more haphazard, fragmented efforts of the past.

Disagreement begins to arise, however, when one asks just how total, and how authoritarian, this greater state intervention need be. There are two main reasons for doubting the wisdom of those who would turn everything over to the state as a panacea for development problems. First, there is the fact that in many underdeveloped countries there exist important private sources of business enterprise and initiative. To introduce government too heavily into the picture is to introduce various taxes, subsidies, quotas, licensing systems and so on that, in total, may so discourage private enterprise that this important potential source of development is wasted.

Second, there is the fact that, in many instances, the governments of these countries are themselves "underdeveloped." It would be easy if one were turning the development and execution of economic planning over to a highly efficient, incorruptible, fair-minded and hard-working bureaucracy. But such governments are a rarity everywhere in the world, and certainly in the less-developed countries. It is not a choice between a highly efficient public sector and a bungling private sector, but between relatively inefficient (and sometimes corruptible) civil servants, and equally inefficient (and also corruptible) private entrepreneurs. In such circumstances, the choice may often come down to the specific analysis of a given country and of where, by history and tradition, its particular strengths and weaknesses lie.

RUSSIA VERSUS JAPAN

A frequent approach to the issue is to look at the experience of nations that have developed relatively recently: Russia and Japan, as opposed to, say, England and the United States. Heilbroner cites the "enormous economic strides" that Russia has made and, even more significantly, "the gradual emancipation of its people from the 'idiocy of rural life,' their gradual entrance upon the stage of contemporary existence" (p. 97). Wrong cites the success at modernization in the case of Japan under the direction of an "essentially conservative regime" (p. 116). The trouble is that neither example really carries much weight. Conditions in the less-developed world are basically different today. Heilbroner sums up these differences as follows (p. 120):

1. The population crisis enjoins a much greater degree of haste for the contemporary backward world.
2. There has been no period of preparation comparable to the three centuries of European commercialization.
3. The backward world is handicapped by the deformations of imperialism.

Curiously, these conditions would seem to rule out the Russian example far more than the Japanese, yet Heilbroner himself largely excludes the Japanese case, and often points to the achievements of the U.S.S.R. Russia has large resources and no population problem; Russia did participate to some degree in the "three centuries of European commercialization" and, in fact, was clearly making economic progress before the revolution; and Russia was not under the control of a Western imperialist power. Japan, by contrast, has few resources and a very large population; it was in nearly total isolation from the West for two centuries before Perry's visit in 1853; and, if never a Western colony, as was India or Indo-China, it at least came closer to sharing the general Asiatic experience with the West than did Russia.

However, even the Japanese case is of only mixed relevance. Although its population density is heavy, the rate of increase of Japanese population never reached the very high rates common in many poor countries today. Further, Japan was able to exploit certain export markets—textiles and other light industry—that have become progressively more crowded as development has spread more widely around the globe. Further, Japanese development was accomplished with a very unequal income distribution—a pattern that might be difficult to replicate in the twentieth century except under a much more interventionist state. Closer than the Russian experience certainly; but still a very doubtful guide to the less-developed countries of today.

THE ISSUE OF IDEOLOGY

Thus, the debate very quickly tends to move towards the clearly relevant, but difficult to assess, experience of the less-developed countries themselves—China, Cuba, India, Indonesia, Egypt, Algeria and the like. Heilbroner's position is that this experience suggests that authoritarian, left-leaning and very probably communist regimes are likely to be the agents to bring economic development to the Third World. Wrong's position is that there are many paths to development, including authoritarian right-wing regimes, and not really ruling out either communist or more democratic (in a Western sense) regimes.

How are these positions expressed in terms of the economic issues we have been discussing? In the case of population growth, Heilbroner stresses the urgency of the problem and suggests that noncommunist governments are essentially unable to mobilize the necessary response. The "vague, well-meaning leaders of India," despite all their talk, have been totally ineffective in their effort to "control the birth rate" (p. 98). Dennis Wrong expresses more of a hope than a conviction that the population problem may be improving already, but also notes that, as far as birth control is concerned, there "is not the slightest evidence that China has had any greater success" (p. 114). In fact, China has had (until fairly recently) serious doctrinal disagreements with the view that population growth *could* be a problem. Karl Marx rejected Malthusian theory as a "libel on the human race." The problem was not human nature but the nature of the capitalistic system. In the past several years, there is strong evidence that the Chinese have overcome this particular ideological hurdle and are now seeking to promote later marriages, birth control and family planning. Wrong argues that, at a minimum, the Chinese lagged behind the noncommunist underdeveloped countries in promoting population control; Heilbroner replies, in effect, that if the Chinese don't succeed in their new efforts, nobody will. The reason is essentially that they, with their communist ideology, have shown themselves capable of the "Herculean effort to reach and rally the great anonymous mass of the population." This, in fact, is *the* great accomplishment of communism" (p. 98).

The ideological argument is, indeed, central to Heilbroner's overall thesis. The strength of communist ideology will make it easier for poor peoples to make the necessary sacrifices that are involved in a massive effort of capital accumulation. This ideology will lead to the uprooting of traditions, the destruction of apathy, the promotion of education, the implanting of modern techniques and attitudes, the freeing of the underdeveloped country from all those features of the past that stand in the way of modernization and rapid development. And—perhaps most important of all—there is simply no alternative. "What other force," Heilbroner asks, "does anyone suggest" (p. 122)?

Wrong replies that the Communist ideology is, in fact, often extremely defective when it comes to promoting economic development. There is the confusion on the population problem, already mentioned. There is the waste of capital and other resources associated with the holy wars and massive defense expenditures that revolutionary, and especially communist, regimes tend to initiate and perpetuate. Nor is their attitude to economic development as single-minded as Heilbroner suggests. Chairman Mao's cultural revolution "appears to be directed *against* assigning high priority to economic development and the materialism it inevitably brings rather than the reverse" (p. 125). If a strong ideology can promote, it can also cripple the efforts of educators, scientists, technicians, and other experts to bring true modernization.

Further, Wrong continues, people are too ready to sell democratic institutions short when it comes to fostering development. After all, a sense of participation in the process of change is what is needed, and democracy excels in promoting communication and consultation between the masses and the government. History does not rule out the combination of democracy and a strong central state, and it certainly does not rule out democracy together with vigorous economic growth.

THE AMERICAN ROLE

These issues vitally affect one's conception of the United States' role in relation to the Third World. Heilbroner's original article is entitled "Counterrevolutionary America." Starkly put, his argument is this: Only communist regimes can effectively promote development in the poor countries of the world; American intervention in those poor countries has been heavily influenced by the attempt to prevent communist revolutions from occurring; therefore, the United States has effectively been in opposition to true economic development in these countries.

This argument conflicts sharply with the whole underlying rationale of the American foreign aid program ever since the Point Four assistance program under Truman. Apart from the genuine humanitarian element in this program (which every realist should acknowledge, though he may question how large an element it was), there was the view that communist revolutions and the installation of governments aggressively opposed to the interests of the United States could be largely prevented if successful economic development efforts could be sustained in the uncommitted underdeveloped countries. Putting it in equally crude terms, this logic was: Aid promotes economic development; economic development promotes political stability; political stability minimizes the chances of revolutionary communist takeovers. By this logic, America was not opposed to economic development, but highly favorable to it because, apart from its human appeal, it made the spread of communism unlikely.

Thus, in weighing the issues in this debate, one is not only assessing the prospects of relief from poverty of the world's poor and hungry; one is also making some kind of judgment as to what stance this country can and should assume in the international arena in the years ahead. Are we inevitably linked with the dead hand of the past? Or is there still more life and spirit and potency in democracy than its critics may have imagined?

Counterrevolutionary America

Robert L. Heilbroner

Robert L. Heilbroner is Norman Thomas Professor of
Economics at the New School for Social Research.

Is the United States fundamentally opposed to economic development?
The question is outrageous. Did we not coin the phrase, "the revolution
of rising expectations"? Have we not supported the cause of development
more generously than any nation on earth, spent our intellectual energy
on the problems of development, offered our expertise freely to the
backward nations of the world? How can it possibly be suggested that the
United States might be opposed to economic development?

The answer is that we are not at all opposed to what we conceive
economic development to be. The process depicted by the "revolution of
rising expectations" is a deeply attractive one. It conjures up the image of
a peasant in some primitive land, leaning on his crude plow and looking
to the horizon, where he sees dimly, but for the *first time* (and that is what
is so revolutionary about it), the vision of a better life. From this electrify-
ing vision comes the necessary catalysis to change an old and stagnant way
of life. The pace of work quickens. Innovations, formerly feared and
resisted, are now eagerly accepted. The obstacles are admittedly very
great—whence the need for foreign assistance—but under the impetus of
new hopes the economic mechanism begins to turn faster, to gain traction
against the environment. Slowly, but surely, the Great Ascent begins.

There is much that is admirable about this well-intentioned popular
view of "the revolution of rising expectations." Unfortunately, there is
more that is delusive about it. For the buoyant appeal of its rhetoric

conceals or passes in silence over by far the larger part of the spectrum of realities of the development process. One of these is the certainty that the revolutionary aspect of development will not be limited to the realm of ideas, but will vent its fury on institutions, social classes, and innocent men and women. Another is the great likelihood that the ideas needed to guide the revolution will not only be affirmative and reasonable, but also destructive and fanatic. A third is the realization that revolutionary efforts cannot be made, and certainly cannot be sustained, by voluntary effort alone, but require an iron hand, in the spheres both of economic direction and political control. And the fourth and most difficult of these realities to face is the probability that the political force most likely to succeed in carrying through the gigantic historical transformation of development is some form of extreme national collectivism or communism.

In a word, what our rhetoric fails to bring to our attention is the likelihood that development will require policies and programs repugnant to our "way of life," that it will bring to the fore governments hostile to our international objectives, and that its regnant ideology will bitterly oppose capitalism as a system of world economic power. If that is the case, we would have to think twice before denying that the United States was fundamentally opposed to economic development.

But is it the case? Must development lead in directions that go counter to the present American political philosophy? Let me try to indicate, albeit much too briefly and summarily, the reasons that lead me to answer that question as I do.

I begin with the cardinal point, often noted but still insufficiently appreciated, that the process called "economic development" is not primarily economic at all. We think of development as a campaign of production to be fought with budgets and monetary policies and measured with indices of output and income. But the development process is much wider and deeper than can be indicated by such statistics. To be sure, in the end what is hoped for is a tremendous rise in output. But this will not come to pass until a series of tasks, at once cruder and more delicate, simpler and infinitely more difficult, has been commenced and carried along a certain distance.

In most of the new nations of Africa, these tasks consist in establishing the very underpinnings of nationhood itself—in determining national borders, establishing national languages, arousing a basic national (as distinguished from tribal) self-consciousness. Before these steps have been taken, the African states will remain no more than names insecurely affixed to the map, not social entities capable of undertaking an enormous collective venture in economic change. In Asia, nationhood is generally much further advanced than in Africa, but here the main impediment to development is the miasma of apathy and fatalism, superstition and distrust that vitiates every attempt to improve hopelessly inefficient modes of work and patterns of resource use: while India starves, a quarter of the world's cow population devours Indian crops, exempt either from effective employment or slaughter because of sacred taboos. In still other areas, mainly Latin America, the principal handicap to development is not an absence of national identity or the presence of suffocating cultures (although the latter certainly plays its part), but the cramping and crippling inhibitions of obsolete social institutions and reactionary social classes. Where land-holding rather than industrial activity is still the basis for social and economic power, and where land is held essentially in fiefdoms rather than as productive real estate, it is not surprising that so much of society retains a medieval cast.

Thus, development is much more than a matter of encouraging economic growth within a given social structure. It is rather the *modernization* of that structure, a process of ideational, social, economic, and political change that requires the remaking of society in its most intimate as well as its most public attributes.[1] When we speak of the revolutionary nature of economic development, it is this kind of deeply penetrative change that we mean—change that reorganizes "normal" ways of thought, established patterns of family life, and structures of village authority as well as class and caste privilege.

What is so egregiously lacking in the great majority of the societies that are now attempting to make the Great Ascent is precisely this pervasive modernization. The trouble with India and Pakistan, with Brazil and Ecuador, with the Philippines and Ethiopia, is not merely that economic growth lags, or proceeds at some pitiable pace. This is only a symptom of deeper-lying ills. The trouble is that the social physiology of these nations remains so depressingly unchanged despite the flurry of economic planning on top. The all-encompassing ignorance and poverty of the rural regions, the unbridgeable gulf between the peasant and the urban elites, the resistive conservatism of the village elders, the unyielding traditionalism of family life—all these remain obdurately, maddeningly, disastrously unchanged. In the cities, a few modern buildings, sometimes brilliantly executed, give a deceptive patina of modernity, but once one journeys into the immense countryside, the terrible stasis overwhelms all.

---

[1] See C. E. Black, *The Dynamics of Modernization.*

To this vast landscape of apathy and ignorance one must now make an exception of the very greatest importance. It is the fact that a very few nations, all of them communist, have succeeded in reaching into the lives and stirring the minds of precisely that body of the peasantry which constitutes the insuperable problem elsewhere. In our concentration on the politics, the betrayals, the successes and failures of the Russian, Chinese, and Cuban revolutions, we forget that their central motivation has been just such a war *à l'outrance* against the archenemy of backwardness—not alone the backwardness of outmoded social super-structures but even more critically that of private inertia and traditionalism.

That the present is irreversibly and unqualifiedly freed from the dead hand of the past is, I think, beyond argument in the case of Russia. By this I do not only mean that Russia has made enormous economic strides. I refer rather to the gradual emancipation of its people from the "idiocy of rural life," their gradual entrance upon the stage of contemporary existence. This is not to hide in the smallest degree the continuing back-wardness of the Russian countryside where now almost 50—and formerly perhaps 80—percent of the population lives. But even at its worst I do not think that life could now be described in the despairing terms that run through the Russian literature of our grandfathers' time. Here is Chekhov:

During the summer and the winter there had been hours and days when it seemed as if these people [the peasants] lived worse than cattle, and it was terrible to be with them. They were coarse, dishonest, dirty, and drunken; they did not live at peace with one another but quarreled continually, because they feared, suspected, and despised one another. . . . Crushing labor that made the whole body ache at night, cruel winters, scanty crops, overcrowding, and no help, and nowhere to look for help.

It is less certain that the vise of the past has been loosened in China or Cuba. It may well be that Cuba has suffered a considerable economic decline, in part due to absurd planning, in part to our refusal to buy her main crop. The economic record of China is nearly as inscrutable as its political turmoil, and we may not know for many years whether the Chinese peasant is today better or worse off than before the revolution. Yet what strikes me as significant in both countries is something else. In Cuba it is the educational effort that, according to the New York *Times*, has constituted a major effort of the Castro regime. In China it is the unmistakable evidence—and here I lean not alone on the sympathetic account of Edgar Snow but on the most horrified descriptions of the rampages of the Red Guards—that the younger generation is no longer fettered by the traditional view of things. The very fact that the Red Guards now revile their elders, an unthinkable defiance of age-old Chinese custom, is testimony of how deeply change has penetrated into the texture of Chinese life.

It is this Herculean effort to reach and rally the great anonymous mass of the population that is the great accomplishment of communism—even though it is an accomplishment that is still only partially accomplished. For if the areas of the world afflicted with the self-perpetuating disease of backwardness are ever to rid themselves of its debilitating effects, I think it is likely to be not merely because antiquated social structures have been dismantled (although this is an essential precondition), but because some shock treatment like that of communism has been administered to them.

By way of contrast to this all-out effort, however short it may have fallen of its goal, we must place the timidity of the effort to bring modernization to the peoples of the noncommunist world. Here again I do not merely speak of lagging rates of growth. I refer to the fact that illiteracy in the noncommunist countries of Asia and Central America is increasing (by some 200 million in the last decade) because it has been "impossible" to mount an educational effort that will keep pace with population growth. I refer to the absence of substantial land reform in Latin America, despite how many years of promises. I refer to the indifference or incompetence or corruption of governing elites: the incredible sheiks with their oildoms; the vague, well-meaning leaders of India unable to break the caste system, kill the cows, control the birthrate, reach the villages, house or employ the labor rotting on the streets; the cynical governments of South America, not one of which, according to Lleras Camargo, former president of Colombia, has ever prosecuted a single politician or industrialist for evasion of taxes. And not least, I refer to the fact that every movement that arises to correct these conditions is instantly identified as "communist" and put down with every means at hand, while the United States clucks or nods approval.

To be sure, even in the most petrified societies, the modernization process is at work. If there were time, the solvent acids of the twentieth century would work their way on the ideas and institutions of the most inert or resistant countries. But what lacks in the twentieth century is time. The multitudes of the underdeveloped world have only in the past two decades been summoned to their reveille. The one thing that is certain about the revolution of rising expectations is that it is only in its inception, and that its pressures for justice and action will steadily mount as the voice of the twentieth century penetrates to villages and slums where it is still almost inaudible. It is not surprising that Princeton historian C. E. Black, surveying this labile world, estimates that we must anticipate "ten to fifteen revolutions a year for the foreseeable future in the less developed societies."

In itself, this prospect of mounting political restiveness enjoins the speediest possible time schedule for development. But this political urgency is many times compounded by that of the population problem. Like an immense river in flood, the number of human beings rises each year to wash away the levees of the preceding year's labors and to pose future requirements of monstrous proportions. To provide shelter for the 3 billion human beings who will arrive on earth in the next 40 years will require as many dwellings as have been constructed since recorded history began. To feed them will take double the world's present output of food. To cope with the mass exodus from the overcrowded countryside will necessitate cities of grotesque size—Calcutta, now a cesspool of 3 to 5 millions, threatens us by the year 2000 with a prospective population of from 30 to 60 millions.

These horrific figures spell one importunate message: haste. That is the *mene mene, tekel upharsin* written on the walls of government planning offices around the world. Even if the miracle of the loop is realized—the new contraceptive device that promises the first real breakthrough in population control—we must set ourselves for at least another generation of rampant increase.

But how to achieve haste? How to convince the silent and disbelieving men, how to break through the distrustful glances of women in black shawls, how to overcome the overt hostility of landlords, the opposition of the Church, the petty bickerings of military cliques, the black-marketeering of commercial dealers? I suspect there is only one way. The conditions of backwardness must be attacked with the passion, the ruthlessness, and the messianic fury of a jehad, a Holy War. Only a campaign of an intensity and single-mindedness that must approach the ludicrous and the unbearable offers the chance to ride roughshod over the resistance of the rich and the poor alike and to open the way for the forcible implantation of those modern attitudes and techniques without which there will be no escape from the misery of underdevelopment.

I need hardly add that the cost of this modernization process has been and will be horrendous. If communism is the great modernizer, it is certainly not a benign agent of change. Stalin may well have exceeded Hitler as a mass executioner. Free inquiry in China has been supplanted by dogma and catechism; even in Russia nothing like freedom of criticism or of personal expression is allowed. Furthermore, the economic cost of industrialization in both countries has been at least as severe as that imposed by primitive capitalism.

Yet one must count the gains as well as the losses. Hundreds of millions who would have been confined to the narrow cells of changeless lives have been liberated from prisons they did not even know existed. Class structures that elevated the flighty or irresponsible have been supplanted by others that have promoted the ambitious and the dedicated. Economic systems that gave rise to luxury and poverty have given way to systems that provide a rough distributional justice. Above all, the prospect of a new future has been opened. It is this that lifts the current ordeal in China may finally have been galvanized into social, political, and eco- that country who have perished over the past centuries from hunger or neglect, is beyond computation. The present revolution may add its dreadful increment to this number. But it also holds out the hope that China may finally have been galvanized into social political, and economic attitudes that for the first time make its modernization a possibility.

Two questions must be answered when we dare to risk so favorable a verdict on communism as a modernizing agency. The first is whether the result is worth the cost, whether the possible—by no means assured —escape from underdevelopment is worth the lives that will be squandered to achieve it.

I do not know how one measures the moral price of historical victories or how one can ever decide that a diffuse gain is worth a sharp and particular loss. I only know that the way in which we ordinarily keep the books of history is wrong. No one is now toting up the balance of the wretches who starve in India, or the peasants of Northeastern Brazil who live in the swamps on crabs, or the undernourished and permanently stunted children of Hong Kong or Honduras. Their sufferings go unrecorded and are not present to counterbalance the scales when the furies of revolution strike down their victims. Barrington Moore has made a nice calculation that bears on this problem. Taking as the weight in one pan the 35,000 to 40,000 persons who lost their lives—mainly for no fault of theirs—as a result of the Terror during the French Revolution, he asks what would have been the death rate from preventable starvation and injustice under the *ancien regime* to balance the scales. "Offhand," he writes, "it seems unlikely that this would be very much below the proportion of .0010 which [the] figure of 40,000 yields when set against an estimated population of 24 million."[2]

[2] *Social Origins of Dictatorship and Democracy,* p. 104.

Is it unjust to charge the *ancien regime* in Russia with 10 million preventable deaths? I think it not unreasonable. To charge the authorities in prerevolutionary China with equally vast and preventable degradations? Theodore White, writing in 1946, had this to say: . . . "some scholars think that China is perhaps the only country in the world where the people eat less, live more bitterly, and are clothed worse than they were five hundred years ago."[3]

I do not recommend such a calculus of corpses—indeed, I am aware of the license it gives to the unscrupulous—but I raise it to show the onesidedness of our protestations against the brutality and violence of revolutions. In this regard, it is chastening to recall the multitudes who have been killed or mutilated by the Church which is now the first to protest against the excesses of communism.

But there is an even more terrible second question to be asked. It is clear beyond doubt, however awkward it may be for our moralizing propensities, that historians excuse horror that succeeds; and that we write our comfortable books of moral philosophy, seated atop a mound of victims—slaves, serfs, laboring men and women, heretics, dissenters—who were crushed in the course of preparing the way for our triumphal entry into existence. But at least we are here to vindicate the carnage. What if we were not? What if the revolutions grind flesh and blood and produce nothing, if the end of the convulsion is not exhilaration but exhaustion, not triumph but defeat?

Before this possibility—which has been realized more than once in history—one stands mute. Mute, but not paralyzed. For there is the necessity of calculating what is likely to happen in the absence of the revolution whose prospective excesses hold us back. Here one must weigh what has been done to remedy underdevelopment—and what has not been done—in the past twenty years; how much time there remains before the population flood enforces its own ultimate solution; what is the likelihood of bringing modernization without the frenzied assault that communism seems most capable of mounting. As I make this mental calculation I arrive at an answer which is even more painful than that of revolution. I see the alternative as the continuation, without substantial relief—and indeed with a substantial chance of deterioration—of the misery and meanness of life as it is now lived in the sinkhole of the world's backward regions.

I have put the case for the necessity of revolution as strongly as possible, but I must now widen the options beyond the stark alternatives I have

[3]*Thunder Out of China*, p. 32.

posed. To begin with, there are areas of the world where the immediate tasks are so far-reaching that little more can be expected for some decades than the primary missions of national identification and unification. Most of the new African states fall into this category. These states may suffer capitalist, communist, fascist, or other kinds of regimes during the remainder of this century, but whatever the nominal ideology in the saddle, the job at hand will be that of military and political nation-making.

There is another group of nations, less easy to identify, but much more important in the scale of events, where my analysis also does not apply. These are countries where the pressures of population growth seem sufficiently mild, or the existing political and social framework sufficiently adaptable, to allow for the hope of considerable progress without resort to violence. Greece, Turkey, Chile, Argentina, Mexico may be representatives of nations in this precarious but enviable situation. Some of them, incidentally, have already had revolutions of modernizing intent —fortunately for them in a day when the United States was not so frightened or so powerful as to be able to repress them.

In other words, the great arena of desperation to which the revolutionizing impetus of communism seems most applicable is primarily the crowded land masses and archipelagoes of Southeast Asia and the impoverished areas of Central and South America. But even here, there is the possibility that the task of modernization may be undertaken by noncommunist elites. There is always the example of indigenous, independent leaders who rise up out of nowhere to overturn the established framework and to galvanize the masses—a Gandhi, a Marti, a pre-1958 Castro. Or there is that fertile ground for the breeding of national leaders—the army, as witness Ataturk or Nasser, among many.[4]

Thus there is certainly no inherent necessity that the revolutions of modernization be led by communists. But it is well to bear two thoughts in mind when we consider the likely course of noncommunist revolutionary sweeps. The first is the nature of the mobilizing appeal of any successful revolutionary elite. Is it the austere banner of saving and investment that waves over the heads of the shouting marchers in Jakarta and Bombay, Cairo and Havana? It most certainly is not. The banner of economic

---

[4] What are the chances for modernizing revolutions of the Right, such as those of the Meiji Restoration or of Germany under Bismarck? I think they are small. The changes to be wrought in the areas of greatest backwardness are much more socially subversive than those of the nineteenth century, and the timespan allotted to the revolutionists is much smaller. Bourgeois revolutions are not apt to go far enough, particularly in changing property ownership. Still, one could imagine such revolutions with armed support and no doubt Fascistic ideologies. I doubt that they would be any less of a threat than revolutions of the Left.

development is that of nationalism, with its promise of personal immortality and collective majesty. It seems beyond question that a feverish nationalism will charge the atmosphere of any nation, communist or not, that tries to make the Great Ascent—and as a result we must expect the symptoms of nationalism along with the disease: exaggerated xenophobia, a thin-skinned national sensitivity, a search for enemies as well as a glorification of the state.

These symptoms, which we have already seen in every quarter of the globe, make it impossible to expect easy and amicable relations between the developing states and the colossi of the developed world. No conceivable response on the part of America or Europe or, for that matter, Russia, will be able to play up to the vanities or salve the irritations of the emerging nations, much less satisfy their demands for help. Thus, we must anticipate an anti-American, or anti-Western, possibly even anti-white animus from any nation in the throes of modernization, even if it is not parroting communist dogma.

Then there is a second caution as to the prospects for noncommunist revolutions. This is the question of what ideas and policies will guide their revolutionary efforts. Revolutions, especially if their whole orientation is to the future, require philosophy equally as much as force. It is here, of course, that communism finds its special strength. The vocabulary in which it speaks—a vocabulary of class domination, of domestic and international exploitation—is rich in meaning to the backward nations. The view of history it espouses provides the support of historical inevitability to the fallible efforts of struggling leaders. Not least, the very dogmatic certitude and ritualistic repetition that stick in the craw of the Western observer offer the psychological assurances on which an unquestioning faith can be maintained.

If a noncommunist elite is to persevere in tasks that will prove Sisyphean in difficulty, it will also have to offer a philosophical interpretation of its role as convincing and elevating, and a diagnosis of social and economic requirements as sharp and simplistic, as that of communism. Further, its will to succeed at whatever cost must be as firm as that of the Marxists. It is not impossible that such a philosophy can be developed, more or less independent of formal Marxian conceptions. It is likely, however, to resemble the creed of communism far more than that of the West. Political liberty, economic freedom, and constitutional law may be the great achievements and the great issues of the most advanced nations, but to the least developed lands they are only dim abstractions, or worse, rationalizations behind which the great powers play their imperialist tricks or protect the privileges of their monied classes.

Thus, even if for many reasons we should prefer the advent of non-communist modernizing elites, we must realize that they too will present the United States with programs and policies antipathetic to much that America "believes in" and hostile to America as a world power. The leadership needed to mount a jehad against backwardness—and it is my main premise that only a Holy War will begin modernization in our time—will be forced to expound a philosophy that approves authoritarian and collectivist measures at home and that utilizes as the target for its national resentment abroad the towering villains of the world, of which the United States is now Number One.

All this confronts American policy makers and public opinion with a dilemma of a totally unforeseen kind. On the one hand we are eager to assist in the rescue of the great majority of mankind from conditions that we recognize as dreadful and ultimately dangerous. On the other hand, we seem to be committed, especially in the underdeveloped areas, to a policy of defeating communism wherever it is within our military capacity to do so, and of repressing movements that might become communist if they were allowed to follow their internal dynamics. Thus, we have on the one side the record of Point Four, the Peace Corps, and foreign aid generally; and on the other, Guatemala, Cuba, the Dominican Republic and now Vietnam.

That these two policies might be in any way mutually incompatible, that economic development might contain revolutionary implications infinitely more far-reaching than those we have so blandly endorsed in the name of rising expectations, that communism or a radical national collectivism might be the only vehicles for modernization in many key areas of the world—these are dilemmas we have never faced. Now I suggest that we do face them, and that we begin to examine in a serious way ideas that have hitherto been considered blasphemous, if not near-traitorous.

Suppose that most of Southeast Asia and much of Latin America were to go communist, or to become controlled by revolutionary governments that espoused collectivist ideologies and vented extreme anti-American sentiments. Would this constitute a mortal threat to the United States?

I think it fair to claim that the purely *military* danger posed by such an eventuality would be slight. Given the present and prospective capabilities of the backward world, the addition of hundreds of millions of citizens to the potential armies of communism would mean nothing when there was no way of deploying them against us. Even the total communization of the backward world would not effectively alter the present balance of military strength in the world.

However small the military threat, it is undeniably true that a communist or radical collectivist engulfment of these countries would cost us the loss of billions of dollars of capital invested there. Of our roughly $50 billions in overseas investment, some $10 billions are in mining, oil, utility, and manufacturing facilities in Latin America, some $4 billions in Asia including the Near East, and about $2 billions in Africa. To lose these assets would deal a heavy blow to a number of large corporations, particularly in oil, and would cost the nation as a whole the loss of some $3 to $4 billions a year in earnings from those areas.

A Marxist might conclude that the economic interests of a capitalist nation would find such a prospective loss insupportable, and that it would be "forced" to go to war. I do not think this is a warranted assumption, although it is undoubtedly a risk. Against a gross national product that is approaching three-fourths of a trillion dollars and with total corporate assets over $1.3 trillions, the loss of even the whole $16 billions in the vulnerable areas should be manageable economically.

By these remarks I do not wish airily to dismiss the dangers of a communist avalanche in the backward nations. There would be dangers, not least those of an American hysteria. Rather, I want only to assert that the threats of a military or economic kind would not be insuperable, as they might well be if Europe were to succumb to a hostile regime.

But is that not the very point?, it will be asked. Would not a communist success in a few backward nations lead to successes in others, and thus by degrees engulf the entire world, until the United States and perhaps Europe were fortresses besieged on a hostile planet?

I think the answer to this fear is twofold. First, as many besides myself have argued, it is now clear that communism, far from constituting a single unified movement with a common aim and dovetailing interests, is a movement in which similarities of economic and political structure and ideology are more than outweighed by divergencies of national interest and character. Two bloody wars have demonstrated that in the case of capitalism, structural similarities between nations do not prevent mortal combat. As with capitalism, so with communism. Russian communists have already been engaged in skirmishes with Polish and Hungarian communists, have nearly come to blows with Yugoslavia, and now stand poised at the threshold of open fighting with China.

Second, it seems essential to distinguish among the causes of dangerous national and international behavior those that can be traced to the tenets of communism and those that must be located elsewhere. "Do not talk to me about communism and capitalism," said a Hungarian economist with whom I had lunch this winter. "Talk to me about rich nations and poor ones."

I think it *is* wealth and poverty, and not communism or capitalism, that establishes much of the tone and tension of international relations. For that reason I would expect communism in the backward nations (or national collectivism, if that emerges in the place of communism) to be strident, belligerent, and insecure. If these regimes fail—as they may —their rhetoric may become hysterical and their behavior uncontrolled, although of small consequence. But if they succeed, which I believe they can, many of these traits should recede. Russia, Yugoslavia or Poland are simply not to be compared, either by way of internal pronouncement or external behavior, with China, or, on a smaller scale, Cuba. Modernization brings, among other things, a waning of the stereotypes, commandments, and flagellations so characteristic of (and so necessary to) a nation engaged in the effort to alter itself from top to bottom.

Nevertheless, there *is* a threat in the specter of a communist or near-communist supremacy in the underdeveloped world. It is that the rise of communism would signal the end of capitalism as the dominant world order, and would force the acknowledgement that America no longer constituted the model on which the future of world civilization would be mainly based. In this way, as I have written before, the existence of communism frightens American capitalism as the rise of Protestantism frightened the Catholic Church, or the French Revolution the English aristocracy.

It is, I think, the fear of losing our place in the sun, of finding ourselves at bay, that motivates a great deal of the anti-communism on which so much of American foreign policy seems to be founded. In this regard I note that the nations of Europe, most of them profoundly more conservative than America in their social and economic dispositions, have made their peace with communism far more intelligently and easily than we, and I conclude that this is in no small part due to their admission that they are no longer the leaders of the world.

The great question in our own nation is whether we can accept a similar scaling-down of our position in history. This would entail many profound changes in outlook and policy. It would mean the recognition that communism, which may indeed represent a retrogressive movement in the West, where it should continue to be resisted with full energies, may nonetheless represent a progressive movement in the backward areas, where its advent may be the only chance these areas have of escaping misery. Collaterally, it means the recognition that "our side" has neither the political will, nor the ideological wish, nor the stomach for directing those changes that the backward world must make if it is ever to cease being backward. It would undoubtedly entail a more isolationist policy for the United States *vis-à-vis* the developing continents and a greater willingness to permit revolutions there to work their way without our interference. It would mean in our daily political life the admission that the ideological battle of capitalism and communism had passed its point of usefulness or relevance, and that religious diatribe must give way to the pragmatic dialogue of the age of science and technology.

Economic Development and Democracy

Dennis H. Wrong

Dennis H. Wrong is Professor of Sociology at New York University.

I

Robert Heilbroner's essay, "Counterrevolutionary America," is the most intelligent and forceful statement of a point of view that is widely held by writers on economic development in the Third World. Although Heilbroner is an economist, his conclusions rest only to a minor degree on economic expertise. Both in the article and in his earlier book-length essay, *The Great Ascent,* he fully recognizes that economic development necessarily involves massive social and political changes in addition to the changes in the techniques and the organization of production that the term connotes in its narrow sense. Heilbroner's argument, anticipated in his earlier book but stated far more strongly and without qualification in the more recent article, is that the obstacles posed to rapid economic development by traditional values and old established ruling elites are so great that a revolution bringing to power a communist-type totalitarian dictatorship can alone be expected to overcome them and proceed with the urgent task of modernizing backward societies.

It is worth reviewing step by step the reasoning by which Heilbroner reaches this conclusion. The essentials of his position are shared by many other writers—indeed, some of them have become virtual commonplaces in discussions of economic development. By summarizing the argument as schematically as possible, shorn of Heilbroner's considerable eloquence and richness of allusion, it should be possible to see its main structure

From Dennis H. Wrong "Economic Development and Democracy: A Debate on Some Problems of the Third World" in *Dissent* (November–December 1967), pp. 723–33. Reprinted by permission of the publisher. Not all footnotes appear.

and to separate the truths from the assumptions and hypotheses contained in it.

Only the starting point of the argument involves an economic proposition: namely, that the task of initial capital accumulation in underdeveloped countries requires the holding down for a time of the living standards of the peasants, who constitute the mass of the population; not until the "infrastructure" of a modern economy has been built will it be possible for the resulting gains in productivity to be widely distributed.

But strictly economic considerations are transcended as soon as we ask what groups and agencies in contemporary underdeveloped countries are capable of organizing and directing the economic task of drawing a portion of the peasantry off the land to build capital, and of collecting part of the agricultural produce of the remaining peasants to feed this new nonagricultural labor force. The absence of rising commercial and entrepreneurial classes resembling the European *bourgeoisie,* or of any group inbued with an ethos favoring, like the Protestant ethic, hard work and the sacrifice of present material gains for the future, means that the state alone can play the necessary role in today's backward countries. Most experts on economic development concede (in the large at least) that the state must assume the entrepreneurial function in the majority of the nations of the Third World and that these nations are therefore likely to adopt some form of collectivism or "state socialism." Only a handful of neoclassical economists disagree. The state must be a strong state if it is to initiate successful programs of economic development. That is, it must, in the first instance, possess the power and the will to coerce or buy off traditional elites that resist modernizing measures. But, more important, it must command the allegiance of a significant portion of the population.

II

There is little in this analysis so far that is likely to arouse much disagreement. The next step in Heilbroner's argument, however, goes beyond the limits of general consensus. In order to win the support of the masses, the argument runs, the state must promote a new ideological creed that will penetrate their minds and hearts, win them away from traditional habits, beliefs and loyalties—"reach and rally them," as he puts it—and induce them to acquiesce in the sacrifices and rigors of the period of capital accumulation. Such a creed is bound to be intolerant of all dissent and is likely to contain a strong negative component, branding foreigners, in particular the West, as carriers of evil and as actual or potential supporters of oppositionists at home. Clearly, this description is matched most closely by a revolutionary regime which has seized power after mobilizing a sizable segment of the population against the old order or foreign imperialists, or, most probably, a combination of both. Only a militant revolutionary state can make the sharp break with the past and impose the strict totalitarian discipline on a sprawling agrarian society that are needed to begin "the Great Ascent" to the heights of modernization.

Heilbroner's rejection of the belief or hope that democratic, constitutional governments, preserving and fostering the political liberties of the individual citizen, are capable of achieving economic development is presented in less detail than his reasons for thinking that some form of totalitarian collectivism can do the job. But his case against democratic government is implicit in much of his argument and has been more fully stated by other writers who share his general outlook. I shall draw on some of them to flesh out his thesis.[1]

Most of the states in the Third World are far from being genuine nations. Democratic institutions and practices, it is held, can only delay the task of nation building by encouraging all the diverse ethnic, religious, tribal and linguistic groups that make up the populations of the new states to articulate their distinctive values and interests. The new states must create an overriding sense of national purpose and identity transcending parochial group loyalties if they are to carry out effective economic development programs. A democratic multiparty system will perpetuate and even accentuate the fragmentation of their populations. This argument has been applied most widely in defense of one-party dictatorships in Africa. It makes a specifically *political* case against democracy in the Third World, seeing nation building as the prime requisite for the strong state that is in turn a prime requisite for economic development.

Unlike Africa, most Asian and Latin American nations do not confront the immediate necessity of welding together collections of tribal peoples who have often been traditional enemies and have never acknowledged any central political authority. The case against democracy in Asia and Latin America rests less on the alleged requirements of nation building than on the contention that democratic governments cannot succeed in breaking the resistance to far-reaching social reform offered by old classes and elites—parasitic landlords, village moneylenders, *compradore* merchants, corrupt military and bureaucratic cliques, hoary priestly oligarchies. Democracy is likely to be no more than a facade behind which

[1] For a critique resembling in some respects the present one of prevalent assumptions about modernization in the Third World, see Charles C. Moskos, Jr., and Wendell Bell, "Emerging Nations and Ideologies of American Social Scientists," *American Sociologist*, 2 (May 1967), 67–72.

these groups retain full power, occasionally lulling the masses with token reforms.

A more general argument against democracy in the Third World, one that is more closely linked to the initial prerequisites for economic development, holds that the masses are likely to vote themselves welfare state benefits, opting for immediate improvements in their standard of living rather than for capital investment and thus defeating long-range development programs. Argentina under Peron, and particularly the persistence of Peronist sympathies among the industrial workers long after the dictator's fall from power, are frequently cited as the standard horrible example. There is an obvious contradiction between the assertion that democracy in the Third World is doomed to be a mere facade manipulated by the traditional ruling classes and the expressed fear that it will result in the mass electorate voting for immediate, "uneconomic" gains in income; but we shall let this pass for the moment.

Such in broad outline is Heilbroner's thesis, omitting only his observations on the probable attitude of the United States to revolutionary regimes in the Third World, which I shall discuss very briefly later. The thesis, both in Heilbroner's and other versions, has evoked vigorous objections from liberals and democrats unwilling to accept the necessity and inevitability of the totalitarian trend it postulates. Their reactions, however, have usually failed to go beyond ringing reaffirmations of democratic and humanitarian values, and expressions of moral outrage at the apparent readiness of so many Western writers to regard violence and repressive government as the unavoidable price of modernization. Heilbroner is entitled to reply to such protests—indeed, he has already so replied (see the correspondence columns of the July 1967 *Commentary*)—"don't blame me for being the bearer of bad news. To refute me you must first show that the news is not as bad as I've reported, that my analysis is mistaken, and this you have failed to do."

III

The Heilbroner thesis outlines certain social prerequisites for economic development and maintains that democratic institutions are bound to present obstacles to fulfilling them. Since democracy runs the risk of promoting anarchic factionalism, permitting privileged classes to retain covert control over the government, and encouraging all groups to seek to use the state to advance their material interests, the thesis possesses an immediate plausibility. This plausibility carries over to the next step in the argument, where it is asserted that a government lacking democratic features will be able to avoid the problems of democracy and meet the requirements of modernization. But what if we start by asking what are the difficulties that a totalitarian revolutionary regime is likely to face in carrying out development programs? These difficulties are conceded in passing by Heilbroner, but they fail to receive the attention they deserve because of the initial critical focus on the difficulties apt to be encountered by "mild," democratic governments.

To begin with, the inflammatory nationalism, the xenophobia, and the exaltation of the state—which are, according to Heilbroner, invariable ingredients of the "mobilizing appeal" of revolutionary elites—lead to the investment of considerable resources in armaments and the maintenance of large standing armies. Such expenditures are, of course, an utter waste from the standpoint of economic development. If demonstration steel mills and airlines are to be regarded as economically irrational national status symbols, how much more so are jet planes, tanks, and well-drilled armies? True, the desire for national strength and military glory may powerfully motivate a nation to modernize its capital equipment and thus lay the foundation for eventual increases in productivity that will wipe out mass poverty and improve every citizen's material lot. A nation that can send sputniks into outer space is presumably capable of mass-producing shoes and automobiles, although the Soviet Union has yet to confirm this. However, underdeveloped nations are more likely to purchase the sinews of war from the advanced nations by intensifying their production of staple raw materials—the very syndrome that is part of the whole syndrome of their economic backwardness. Moreover, the trouble with large defense expenditures is that they tend to become self-perpetuating, not merely because they create vested interests, but because they persuade insecure neighbors to arm themselves, thus justifying the claim that a large military establishment is necessary for national security. Surely, those nations that have followed most closely Heilbroner's prescription—Russia, China, Egypt, Sukarno's Indonesia—have diverted enormous human and material resources from peaceful economic development to military uses.

In addition, the enhanced importance of the army makes a military takeover more probable should the revolutionary regime falter. If any "wave of the future" is discernible in the Third World at the present moment, it is in the direction of military dictatorships rather than communist revolutions. Since 1960 revolutionary national socialist or left-nationalist reformist regimes have been overthrown in Argentina, Brazil, Bolivia, Algeria, Ghana and Indonesia, and have been discredited—to put it mildly—in Egypt and Syria. It is still altogether possible that in China,

Mao's "cultural revolution" will be terminated by an army takeover. Military dictatorships have also replaced shaky democratic civilian governments in Nigeria, the Congo, Greece, and a number of smaller African nations. A few of these new regimes are national socialist and even procommunist in ideological orientation (e.g. Algeria); a larger number are right-wing, strongly anticommunist or even proto-fascist (e.g. Argentina, Brazil, Greece, Indonesia).

Finally, aggressive nationalism and militarism may induce nations to seek territorial expansion, causing wars that risk spreading to engulf entire subcontinents, if not the world. Barrington Moore, Jr., observes that military defeat in World War II was part of the price paid by Japan for following a conservative-fascist path to modernization.[2] In other words, the dead of Hiroshima and Nagasaki, the Tokyo fire-bomb raids, and the Pacific islands campaigns must be cast into the balance against the "preventable deaths" from starvation and injustice under the old regime in toting up the costs of Japanese modernization. Should not the Soviet Union's enormous losses in World War II be assessed, along with the victims of Stalin's purges and enforced collectivizations, as part of the price of totalitarian communist modernization? Stalin's army purges, his opportunistic foreign policy toward Germany, and his unpopularity with the peasants who first hailed the Nazi invaders as liberators, stemmed from his totalitarian rule and contributed to Russian military defeats in the early stages of the war.

Some Western nations also went through a military-expansionist phase in the course of their modernization. But in the present century technology has made even "conventional" warfare far more destructive than in the past. If, as Heilbroner argues, greater population growth and density make economic development more urgent in the Third World today than in the West in the last century, then the changed scale of warfare and a more unstable international environment should also be taken into account if militaristic regimes are to be recommended as arch modernizers.

What countries have achieved economic development to date as a result of nationalist-communist revolutions? Let us concede the case of the Soviet Union, although the entire issue of whether the Bolshevik October revolution as distinct from the February revolution, let alone Stalin's totalitarian rule, was necessary for Russian economic development remains highly debatable among economists and historians. Heilbroner tells us that for himself he would rather be "an anonymous peasant" in China or Cuba than in India, Peru or Ecuador. But by his own admission "it may

[2] Barrington Moore, Jr., *The Social Origins of Dictatorship and Democracy* (Boston: Beacon Press, 1966), p. 271.

well be that Cuba has suffered a considerable economic decline" since Castro took power, and "we may not know for many years whether the Chinese peasant is better or worse off than before the revolution." He praises Cuba for its educational effort, and China for having freed its youth from the bondage of the traditional family system. However, these achievements—assuming their reality—at most facilitate economic development rather than constituting development itself. Heilbroner might also reflect that the peasants of India and Peru evidently do not share his view of their prospects, having rejected in large numbers the opportunity to vote for communist parties in free elections. In short, with the ambiguous exception of the Soviet Union, the communist promise of rapid industrialization remains no more than a promise.

IV

Heilbroner's case for the necessity of totalitarian ruthlessness to achieve modernization rests ultimately on his conviction of the enormous urgency of the problems of the backward countries. They cannot proceed according to the more leisurely timetable of past Western industrialization; they must take a giant step forward within the next three or four decades, or mass famine and internal chaos are sure to be their fate. Essentially, Heilbroner sees the continuing population explosion as imposing the need for an all-out attack on backwardness which must have priority over other values and objectives. Not the entire Third World, but "primarily the crowded land masses and archipelagos of Southeast Asia and the impoverished areas of Central and South America" must look to revolutions led by modernizing elites to rescue them from deepening poverty. The extent to which Heilbroner's argument rests on the population explosion is striking, considering that, though there are many exceptions, economists as a rule are more optimistic than demographers in their estimates of the prospects for economic development in backward countries. Economists perceive the economic job to be done and are impressed by the ample technical resources—including their own counsel—available to do it, while demographers, horrified by the floods of additional people indicated by extrapolated population growth rates, insist that without birth control any development program is doomed to founder.

But are communist countries likely to check population growth? Heilbroner refers patronizingly to India's failure to control the birth rate, but there is not the slightest evidence that China has had any greater success. Indeed, China's leaders lag behind India's in their awareness of the need for an antinatalist population policy. The relatively sparsely-settled Soviet

Union never faced a population explosion comparable to that of Southeast Asia—a further reason, incidentally, for questioning the necessity of totalitarianism for Russian economic development. The doctrinal anti-Malthusianism of communist ideology imposes a special handicap on communist countries with regard to birth control. Nor do noncommunist revolutionary elites imbued with aggressive nationalism and anti-Western fervor seem promising candidates to assign high priority to diffusing family planning over building steel mills and armies.

But what if birth rates should turn downwards *before* the "take-off" point in economic development has been reached? In a recent article in *Public Interest,*[3] Donald Bogue, the University of Chicago demographer, departed from the conventional pessimism of his colleagues, to predict the imminent end of the population explosion in the Third World. There is good reason to believe, he insists, that by the end of the present decade the efforts of government and private agencies promoting family planning will at last pay off and birth rates in India and several other Asian countries will begin unmistakably to decline. Bogue is unable to present decisive evidence supporting his forecast—he claims that the "catching on" of new birth control methods in peasant populations is still too recent to have been statistically recorded. His main tangible evidence is based on studies in several countries, the most impressive of which was conducted in South Korea, showing that peasant women have in surprising numbers adopted in an exceedingly short space of time such recently developed contraceptive methods as intra-uterine devices and even pills. Maybe Bogue wil turn out to be a false prophet, but it is worth recalling that sharp reversals of demographic trends have happened simultaneously before in a number of quite different countries, so there is no reason why sudden mass adoption of family planning resulting in lower birth rate might not occur in large areas of the Third World. Writing about Latin America, another demographer, J. Mayone Stycos of Cornell, also expresses cautious optimism in a recent book reporting his research in Peru and several Caribbean nations.[4]

V

I have argued that, though the difficulties faced by democratic governments in carrying out economic development are real ones, totalitarian revolutionary regimes also face difficulties peculiar to them that Heil-

[3] Donald Bogue, "The End of the Population Explosion," *Public Interest,* 2 (Spring 1967), pp. 11–20.

[4] J. Mayone Stycos, *Human Fertility in Latin America* (Ithaca, New York: Cornell University Press, 1967).

broner and others tend to slight. Military dictatorships, a third and at present the most common type of regime in the Third World, have not been notoriously successful modernizers either. One might conclude in an even more pessimistic vein than Heilbroner that neither democracy, revolutionary collectivism, nor military rule are capable of achieving modernization, and that it is therefore unlikely to take place at all. Yet such a conclusion would clearly be unjustified. In the past there have been a variety of paths to modernization: it has been achieved by essentially conservative regimes in Germany and Japan, by postrevolutionary bourgeois democracies in England and France, under a pure bourgeois democracy in the United States, and by communist dictatorship in Russia; even a few military regimes have made considerable progress as in Turkey and Mexico. There is apparently no intrinsic connection at all between economic progress and formal political institutions. The pace of economic development has also varied greatly, particularly among smaller nations free from the tensions of international rivalry.

Democratic institutions such as parliamentary government, elementary civil liberties and the rule of law, though not—except in the United States—universal suffrage, preceded economic development in the Western bourgeois democracies. Why should it be so widely assumed that democracy can only emerge in the Third World after modernization has been carried out by authoritarian governments? Those who argue this confuse the *strong* state that is indeed required for economic development with a monolithic, authoritarian state. The skeptics about democracy, with all their talk of avoiding ethnocentric evaluations of the institutions of non-Western people, often project the experience of Western democracies into the different social context of backward societies when they contend that Asian and African electorates will use the ballot to advance their short-term interests like voters in the West accustomed to government whose rationalized welfare and service functions have succeeded, as Michael Walzer has argued, in de-mystifying the very idea of the state itself. Actually, the demands of the masses in underdeveloped areas are likely to be too modest rather than excessive from the standpoint of stimulating development. Democracy, moreover, may take many different forms: ancient village communal bodies like the old Russian *mir* and the Indian *panchayats* can serve as two-way communication channels between modernizing elites and the base of the social structure, giving rise to a kind of "democratic centralism" that is a reality rather than a facade for unilateral dictation by the leadership. Also, even after universal suffrage was in effect in the Western democracies, the political organization and mobilization of the lower classes was a long, slow process. The masses in the Third World are not going to leap at once into the political arena to make short-sighted and selfish immediate group demands. There is no reason why they cannot be trusted to accept the guidance of enlightened modernizing elites that truly consult them and give them a sense of participation in the process. It is precisely such a sense of participation that Heilbroner sees as the *forte* of communist revolutionaries, but there is no inherent reason why they alone should be capable of instilling it.

What about American policy toward the Third World? Although a secondary issue, this was ostensibly the main subject of Heilbroner's essay. Heilbroner's denial notwithstanding, the United States has not been consistently antirevolutionary nor indeed consistently anything except opposed to states that have directly aligned themselves politically and militarily with the Soviet Union or China. The United States has given aid to communist Yugoslavia; to nationalist, procommunist and anti-American states such as Ghana under Nkrumah, Algeria and Egypt; as well as to noncommunist revolutionary regimes such as Bolivia in the 1950s. Admittedly, the bulk of American aid has gone to such "client states" ruled by conservative dictatorships as South Korea, Taiwan and South Vietnam. But American policy has on the whole been shortsightedly opportunistic rather than ideologically consistent, willing to support almost any government, Left or Right, that is not a direct dependency of Russia or China. When Heilbroner suggests that the United States is unlikely to allow any nations in the Third World to remain neutral in the Cold War, he seems to be taking seriously Dulles's rhetoric of a decade ago—even then the rhetoric did not correspond to American practice. More probably, he has in mind the war in Vietnam, but the flimsy American justification for the war rests on the assumption that China is the "real" enemy, not the Viet Cong or Hanoi. The United States accepted, after all, a neutral government in Laos.

Latin America, however, is obviously the area where Heilbroner's label "Counterrevolutionary America" is most applicable. Not only do the pocketbook interests of American businessmen have a greater influence on government policy there than elsewhere in the world, but the fall-out in domestic politics of victories by communist or proto-communist revolutionaries is bound to be far greater. The Dominican tragedy reveals the panic which may strike an American administration if it persuades itself that there is even the slightest possibility of a repetition of the Cuban experience. It is indeed hard to imagine the United States passively tolerating *any* anti-American revolutionary government in this hemisphere.

Finally, let us suppose that American policy-makers accept Heilbroner's analysis and become convinced that modernization of the Third World is possible only under communist or authoritarian left-nationalist auspices. The results may be curious indeed. *The New Republic* of July 8, 1967, reports that a privately distributed newsletter subscribed to by Wall Street insiders suggests that it may very well be in the American national interest to allow the Third World to go communist. The United States will save money in economic aid as the new communist regimes seek development by sweating their own peasantries whose labor will have to carry the whole burden of capital accumulation. If they fail, the United States cannot be blamed. If they succeed, they will in a decade or two become moderate and "bourgeois" in spirit like the Russians and not only can we live in peace with them but we can engage them in mutually profitable trade. Such a view may very well spread among those whom C. Wright Mills once called "sophisticated conservatives," and it may become more influential than the anger and frustration at the failure of American capitalism to convert the world that Heilbroner imputes to our leaders. And, as is so often the case in politics, the diagnosis may become self-confirming if America reduces instead of expands its aid to the Third World in expectation of a wave of totalitarian revolutions. The Heilbroner thesis might thus ironically help bring about the conditions it claims to deplore in counseling us to resign ourselves to their inevitability.

Reply to "Economic Development and Democracy"

Robert L. Heilbroner

I am grateful to Dennis Wrong for his thoughtful and carefully argued reply to my article in *Commentary* and to *The Great Ascent*. Here and there I disagree with him on small points, most of which will emerge in the paragraphs below. But in the main I feel that somehow even Wrong, who so scrupulously avoids the rhetoric of outrage, has failed to come squarely to grips with the contentions on which my own point of view is based. Let me therefore attempt to answer him by restating my position and emphasizing where I think the issue lies between us.

I

The essential starting point must be whether or not one believes that modernization will take place under the aegis of *present* governments in most of Latin America, Southeast Asia and the Near East. I have made it clear that I do not think it will. What is more, I rather doubt that Wrong would disagree with this pessimistic appraisal, although he would no doubt wish to see it qualified. If this is so, then economic development will have to wait until the regimes that now seem incapable of mounting a successful modernization program are replaced by other regimes. The question is, what kinds will they be?

From Robert L. Heilbroner, "Robert L. Heilbroner Replies," in "Economic Development and Democracy," *Dissent* (November-December 1967), pp. 734–41. Reprinted by permission of the publisher. Footnotes have been omitted.

II

Are the chances propitious for the emergence of democratic governments as the modernizing forces in these areas? I do not think so for the following reasons, some mentioned by Wrong and some not:

1. In many states only a revolutionary party will be able to oust the incumbent regimes.

2. In most nations the tradition of democratic opposition is unknown or thinly held, and the tradition of "strong man" government very widely accepted.

3. The changes needed to bring modernization are not only political, but economic, social, intellectual, and even religious. Such deep-seated changes are extraordinarily difficult to achieve under the best of circumstances. I suspect that only authoritarian regimes can impose them.

Against these doubts Wrong suggests some counterarguments. One of these is that "democracy" is capable of many guises. This is certainly true and some measure of "democracy" in a *consultative* sense (e.g., the Russian soviets, at least in theory) may exist even under dictatorships. What cannot, I think, be tolerated is a recognized and potentially powerful *opposition party.*

A second counterargument of Wrong's is that the Western nations have climbed to modernity under various sorts of governments, including a number of democratic (although not always very consultative) ones. This is of course so. The question then arises as to the relevance of Western (or Japanese post-Meiji) experience to the critical areas of the underdeveloped world. I think the relevance is slight for the following reasons:

1. The population crisis enjoins a much greater degree of haste for the contemporary backward world.

2. There has been no period of preparation comparable to the three centuries of European commercialization.

3. The backward world is handicapped by the deformations of imperialism.

Thus I hesitate to apply the lessons of the West to the East and South. However, if Wrong is merely arguing that the developing elites need not display the worst forms of totalitarianism; that a degree of tolerance is compatible with a strong modernization movement; and that a measure of freedom may be functional rather than otherwise, I would not disagree. Much depends on the personalities of the development leader and his opposition, on the tradition and circumstances of the country, etc. Nonetheless, I would argue (and again I doubt that Wrong would disagree) that strong tendencies must exist for extending and deepening the control of leadership, not only over political and economic life, but into social and intellectual life as well. Perhaps I should point out, although Wrong has been good enough to do so for me, that in making this prediction I am not saying what I wish to have happen, but only what I think will happen, whether I wish it or not.

III

Taking off from these premises, I go on to state that left-authoritarian regimes, very likely, although not necessarily communist, probably offer the best chance for a breakthrough in the backward areas. Here several points are to be examined:

1. Is such a breakthrough needed? Will not a slower process of change suffice? As Wrong points out, my prognosis rests heavily on the urgency of the population program. It is this above all that sets the timetable. If Bogue is right, the timetable may be much extended and the necessity for rapid and radical action accordingly reduced. But is Bogue right? I am certainly far from convinced, and evidently neither is Wrong. Moreover, even if population growth *slows down,* will the deceleration come in time to avert economic and social crisis? Do not forget that populations will double in the most impoverished areas by the year 2000.

2. Will a revolutionary regime succeed in "breaking through"? One cannot be sure. As Wrong points out, a communist government may be ideologically unable to institute birth control. Or its ideological fervor, etc., may fall on deaf ears. Or it may just make terrible mistakes. In that case, I should think the probable outcome would be that mentioned at the end of his piece—there will be *no* modernization, and the future will be one of gradual deterioration, starvation, etc. I consider this an entirely possible state of affairs for the next generation. Yet one must ask, what is the chance for modernization if there is not an all-out revolutionary effort? This brings us back to my initial two premises.

3. Is there any evidence that the communists can mount a successful development effort? Wrong states that the communists have so far delivered no more than promises. I would reply that promises are better than nothing. But are they only promises? Russia, to be sure, is a great mystery—is her development due to communism or to pre-1913 industrialization? I would suggest that without communism Russia would today be a kind of Brazil, with the extremes of Sao Paulo and the San Francisco Valley. But that is only a guess. The evidence as to Cuba buttresses my feeling that Castro has instituted a genuine and deeply-rooted change. Reston's New York *Times* articles (written after my *Commentary* piece) provide grist for my mill. As for China, who knows? What matters is the outcome after the present power struggle is resolved. I am impressed by Edgar Snow's observation in *The Other Side of the River* that whatever one may think of the communist effort, there is no doubt that China has been profoundly and irreversibly changed. It is this kind of change that I believe to be an absolutely necessary condition for development; and at the base of my argument is my belief that among the existing political forces in the world only communism is likely to be able to administer such a change. What other force does anyone suggest?

IV

Wrong emphasizes the destructive side of authoritarianism and its penchant for war. There is something to be said for this, although I fear that democracy provides no guarantee of peace. (Do I dare mention India and Goa; England and Suez; France and Algeria; and the U.S. and its military adventures?)

But once again I am forced back to choosing between ugly alternatives. Revolutionary regimes bring a ruthless will and a desire to change everything; nonrevolutionary regimes seem unable to change even the few things that cry out for it. *If* we could have the best of both worlds—the enthusiasm, the dedication, the clear-cut program of the revolutionary, and the tolerance, open-mindedness and decency of the gradualist—who would not welcome it? But I fear that in the existing condition of things we will have to make a far less palatable choice. If so, I opt for the party of "total" change. I repeat that if I had to take my chances here and now as an anonymous particle of humanity in China or India or in Cuba or Brazil, I would unhesitatingly choose the communist side. Furthermore, I suspect Wrong would too. (To be sure, if I could choose to be an intellectual in both nations I would opt for the other side. But only a tiny few of the particles of humanity are intellectuals.)

V

Last, I am not much alarmed over the possibility of my counsel becoming a self-fulfilling prophecy. Even if it were, I would prefer the difficulties of living in a world that was largely communist in the backward areas and isolationist here in the U.S., to one that threatens to go communist and that evokes from us the military response of a Vietnam. But in the end I am interested in making a historical forecast, not in preparing a blueprint for action. My forecast is that if modernization takes place in the backward world (and again I caution that it may not), it will be because of the efforts of revolutionary, and very likely Communist, regimes. I forecast as well that the successes of milder, democratic government in bringing modernization to the peoples of Latin America, Southeast Asia and the Middle East will be small, if any. Let us wait 10 or 20 years and see which of us is right.

"Economic Development and Democracy": A Rebuttal
Dennis H. Wrong

I am glad Robert Heilbroner finds that I have correctly understood and presented his views. He has done as well with mine. Hopefully, the absence of rhetoric and polemical flourishes in our exchange will clarify the issues between us.

Heilbroner reiterates his conviction that left-authoritarian or communist movements "offer the best chance for a breakthrough in the backward areas." Whether he is right or wrong in this belief, he fails fully to confront the prior question of how likely in the near future such movements are to come to power at all and win the chance to show what they can do. Far from foreseeing any upsurge of democratic modernizing forces in the Third World, I argued that the present trend was toward the overthrow of *both* democratic governments and left-authoritarian regimes by the armed forces. Heilbroner is more hopeful—given his assumptions—than I am that there will be successful communist revolutions; I am more hopeful than he that some modernization will take place under a variety of political regimes. He apparently regards such recent events as China's declining prestige in the Third World, the turmoil inside China, the overthrow of left-nationalist "strong men" in Indonesia, Algeria and Ghana, the misadventures of "Arab socialism," and the repeated failures and defeats of Cuban-sponsored guerrillas in Latin America as mere eddies in a broad historical current favoring revolutionary authoritarian regimes and movements. I, on the contrary, think that the Viet Cong may be the leaders of the last communist-directed "war

Excerpted from Dennis H. Wrong, "A Rebuttal by Dennis H. Wrong," in "Economic Development and Democracy," *Dissent* (November–December 1967). Reprinted by permission of the publisher.

of national liberation" rather than the forerunners of a new revolutionary wave.

But if Heilbroner is right and communist revolutions do take place in much of the Third World, can they achieve modernization? Communists have won power primarily by their own efforts in only five countries: Russia, Yugoslavia, China, North Vietnam, and Cuba. None of the three conditions Heilbroner adduces for doubting relevance of past Western experience to the contemporary underdeveloped world was fully present in Russia or Yugoslavia, so their record is scarcely more pertinent to the argument than the successful modernization achieved under democratic auspices by England and the United States. As to China, I agree with Heilbroner—who knows? China may indeed have been "profoundly and irreversibly changed," but such change may or may not in the end facilitate the particular kind of "profound and irreversible change" we call modernization. In its exaltation of an ascetic, chiliastic revolutionary brotherhood, Mao's "cultural revolution" appears to be directed *against* assigning high priority to economic development and the materialism it inevitably brings rather than the reverse. North Vietnam has been involved in wars for over a decade. Cuba, a partially modernized country before Castro, has at most established some of the prerequisites for balanced modernization (e.g., mass literacy) while undergoing actual economic decline. I agree that promises are better than nothing, but communists are not the only people in the Third World promising modernization.

The very polycentrism of the communist world that makes nonsense out of the anticommunist slogans invoked by Washington to justify the Vietnam war reduces the likelihood that future national communist regimes will be the ruthless modernizers Heilbroner expects them to be. Would Egyptian national communism differ in any important way from Nasser's regime? Would an Algerian revolution create a state markedly different from the Ben Bella and Boumedienne dictatorships? Revolutions led by hard-bitten, Moscow-trained Stalinist orgmen might have a chance of successfully using totalitarian methods to impose the drastic surgery of modernization on a recalcitrant peasantry. So might revolutions led by men like Mao's original cadres. So might revolutions led by orthodox Marxist-Leninists like most of the national communists of Eastern Europe. But post-Stalinist Moscow no longer tightly controls the communist parties in the Third World (or, indeed, anywhere), and Maoism today has little in common with traditional Marxist-Leninist doctrine. Revolutionary movements in the Third World are likely to be shaped to a greater extent by national character traits than was the case in past communist revolutions and such traits have usually been an obstacle—though by no means the only one—to modernization. The degree to which communist parties in the Third World base themselves on dissatisfied ethnic, religious and caste minority groups in their struggle against existing governments has been documented by Donald Zagoria. Can we really expect such parties, should they win power, to be as relentlessly future-minded as the puritanical, iron-willed Bolsheviks who are the prototypes for our model of totalitarian modernization?

If Heilbroner is right that communist revolutions offer the only hope for modernization and I am right in doubting that there will be many successful revolutions in the near future, then the obvious conclusion is that there may be little or no modernization and that economic deterioration and political fragmentation are likely results. I agree that this is an entirely possible outcome for the next generation. It seems to me much more probable that disciplined, authoritarian revolutionaries will be able to seize power under conditions of mass famine and chaos than that they will succeed in overthrowing present governments which are maintaining some degree of order and economic progress, painfully slow though the latter may be. After all, in four of the five countries where indigenous communist movements have triumphed (Cuba is the one exception), the communist seizure of power occurred during or immediately after devastating wars and foreign invasions that had disrupted agricultural life and destroyed the control of the previous governments over much of their territories. In such circumstances, determined revolutionary movements have their best chance of succeeding. But this possibility is not what Heilbroner has in mind: he sees communist revolutions as a way of *averting* political and economic collapse rather than as an eventual consequence of collapse.

The issue of the timetable for modernization is really the crucial one. I agree that none of the existing regimes in the Third World, neither the formal democracies, the collectivist one-party states nor the military dictatorships, have achieved full modernization. But "when we look at the positive side of our ledger sheet, we perceive an astonishing fact. Against all the obstacles to development that we have described, economic progress has in fact been taking place, and at a pace which by comparison with the past amazes us with its rapidity." So writes Robert Heilbroner on page 89 of his book *The Great Ascent*. He immediately observes that both the gains already achieved as well as future gains risk "being washed out by population growth."

Now I am indeed not fully convinced that Donald Bogue is right in predicting the imminent end of the population explosion. Who can have complete confidence in any forecast of something that has never happened before, like the mass adoption of birth control by peasant populations within a decade or two? But the probability of this happening seems to me somewhat greater than the probability of a wave of communist revolutions in the Third World followed by the rapid achievement of modernization by the revolutionary regimes. The populations of the advanced countries, including Japan, have altered their childbearing habits in very short periods of time and without having been exposed to large-scale, state-directed campaigns urging them to do so. Since I wrote my original article, another leading American demographer, Frank Notestein, president of the Population Council, has expressed in the October *Foreign Affairs* qualified optimism over the prospect of new birth control methods spreading in the underdeveloped world and reducing current rates of population growth before the end of the century. If this should happen it will not remove entirely the urgency of the need for rapid modernization in the larger, more densely-populated areas, for even a rate of growth that is half the present one (and this Notestein considers possible) will still be an economic burden. But slower population growth will certainly make it easier for any regime committed to modernization to make some progress and will allow a wider margin for retrievable error.

I am aware that Heilbroner is making a forecast rather than advocating a course of action. But forecasts can become self-fulfilling if those who possess power are persuaded by and act on them. I too would prefer a communist Third World and an isolationist United States to a succession of Vietnams; but is Heilbroner really prepared to give up all hope that the United States and the West in general can have any constructive influence on the economic development of the backward areas? Did the author of *The Future as History* mean by that phrase that it is as futile in the end to reflect on what still might be as it is to mourn over what might have been?

GREAT
DEBATE
FOUR
THE LIMITS TO
ECONOMIC GROWTH

THE LIMITS TO
ECONOMIC GROWTH

N THE early 1970s, a number of documents were published purporting to
show that economic growth in the industrialized world was not only of
questionable benefit but harmful and, in the not so very distant future,
would be potentially disastrous. These works included Jay Forrester's *World
Dynamics* (Cambridge, Mass.: Wright-Allen Press, 1971), the Club of Rome's *Limits
to Growth* (New York: Universe Books, 1972), and the British "A Blueprint for
Survival" (*The Ecologist,* 1972). The Doomsday views presented in these works
stimulated numerous rebuttals and attacks. Some said that these writers were
nothing but modern Malthusians, raising the specter of rapid population growth and
waning food supplies. Other said that they made rigid projections of the past into
the future without allowing for the capacity of the economic system to make
adjustments to problems as they developed.

. At a minimum, the antigrowth school clearly placed into question one of the great
assumptions of modern industrial society: that growth, with its accompanying
benefits of rising living standards, more goods, increased leisure, education and
welfare, would continue on into the indefinite future more or less as it had in the
recent past. And this, in turn, raised the possibility that the central economic
experience of the Western World since the Industrial Revolution was a once-for-all
phenomenon, unsustainable into the future, destined for modification, or—if, as
some believed, the time for modification was already past—for devastating
collapse.

THE VAST SCOPE OF MODERN GROWTH

To understand the depth of the issues at stake, one must appreciate how enormous
and all-pervasive a phenomenon modern economic growth has been for those

countries that have experienced it.[1] The United States' growth record, although in some respects unique, suggests the central characteristics of this transforming social and economic development.

First of all, growth has meant more people. Rapid population growth, by previous historical standards, has been characteristic of all nations that have experienced an industrial revolution. In the United States, rapid population growth was accentuated by substantial immigration from abroad through most of our history. We have grown from a nation of 5 or 6 million in 1800 to well over 200 million in the 1970s. But immigration was only part of this story. The more significant part was a persistent excess of births over deaths caused by improving economic and sanitary conditions and better health and medical care. Life expectancy, at birth, in the United States was around 40 years in 1850; it is over 70 years today. There is no one-to-one relationship between population growth and economic growth. The poor countries of the world—because of public health and medical advances—are experiencing rapid population growth in advance of general economic development. Furthermore, the rich nations of the world are now experiencing declines in their rate of population increase. Historically, however, the growth explosion and the population explosion went hand in hand, the former reinforcing and making possible the latter.

Economic growth has also been associated with vast transformations in the way in which people live and in the character of their work. Three-quarters of our people now live in urban areas; a century ago, the figure was one-quarter. In 1800, the characteristic American worker was a farmer; today, our agricultural output is produced by about 5 percent of the population. Figure 1 suggests the amazing transformation in the kinds of work Americans do that is occurring within the present century. The characteristic American today, furthermore, has vastly more leisure and a much higher degree of formal education than did his counterpart in the nineteenth century. In the 1870s the average standard work week was about 67 hours; in the 1970s it is 37 hours. In 1900 only about 7 percent of all children attended college; in the 1970s the figure is around 40 percent. Changes of these orders of magnitude are very uncommon historically. It is appropriate to say that the industrial revolution has proved to be not one but a continuing revolution, and this not only in industry but in every feature of our social and economic life.

Finally, of course, economic growth has meant—and this is really the definition of the term—an enormous expansion in the quantity and variety of goods and services our economy produces. The remarkable thing is that this expansion has been so enormous that it has far more than equaled the very rapid rates of population growth with which it has been associated. Figure 2 suggests the path of American economic growth on a *per capita* basis. In less than three-quarters of a century—a century, moreover, that included perhaps the greatest depression of all

---

[1] And, of course, half the world has not yet experienced this phenomenon. This is the "development" problem discussed in the Great Debate Three (pp. 87–129). The fact that many nations are still poor and are trying to duplicate the growth "successes" of the industrialized West only intensifies the issues at stake in the present limits-to-growth debate.

Figure 1   Changing Composition of the Labor Force, 1900–1970.

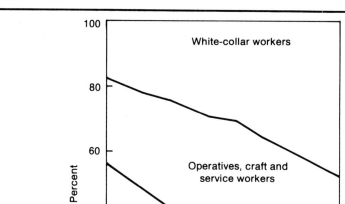

Source: U.S. Department of Labor and U.S. Department of Commerce.

time (notice what happened to per capita GNP in the 1930s)—output per capita in the United States increased nearly three times. This is an enormous increase. At such rates, per capita output would grow ninefold every century and a half. Consider what this suggests about living standards in 1825. Consider what, if such growth continued, it would suggest about living standards in 2125.

It is this vast process, affecting all industrial nations in a similar though not identical way, that we call modern industrial growth. And it is about whether this process can and/or should continue that the growth-versus-antigrowth debate is concerned.

IS GROWTH DESIRABLE?

In view of what we have just said about increased leisure, education, living standards, and the like, it might seem curious to ask, as our very first question, whether this process is desirable. If modern economic growth could be continued into the indefinite future, is it conceivable that anyone would actually oppose it? The answer is definitely yes. Many people would argue that in the future the costs of

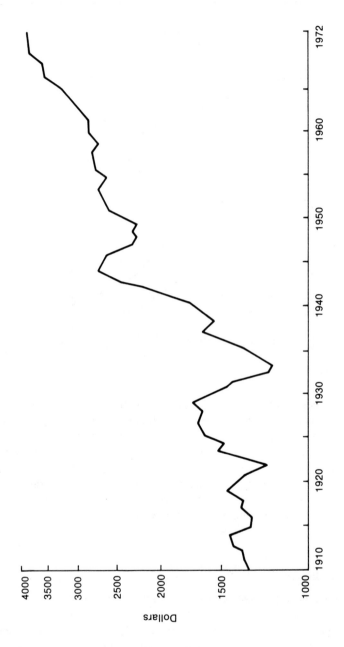

Figure 2 Growth in U.S. per capita GNP (in "constant" 1958 prices)

Over this 62 year stretch, per capita output in the United States has increased by over 190 percent.

Source: Department of Commerce.

modern growth are likely to exceed its benefits. Indeed, many believe that this has already been the case for some time.

Such an idea was being voiced well back into the nineteenth century. As Lewis notes (p. 168), the philosopher John Stuart Mill yearned for the day when mankind would look for "better things" than a continuation of the constant "struggle for riches." Mill wrote:

I confess I am not charmed with an ideal of life held out by those who think that the normal state of human beings is that of struggling to get on; that the trampling, crushing, elbowing, and treading on each other's heels, which form the existing type of social life, are the most desirable lot of human kind, or anything but the disagreeable symptoms of one of the phases of industrial progress.

Mill actually looked forward to the coming of a "stationary state," provided, of course, that the population problem that had worried his predecessor, Malthus, could be handled, and a decent standard of life could be guaranteed the working classes.

The present-day opponents of economic growth would argue that the working classes have indeed been taken care of, and that, in point of fact, the growth of material production has long since passed any reasonable limit of economic need or desirability. In this context, there are few, if any, benefits to continued growth. Why do we seem to want still more goods? they ask. Essentially, they answer, because a growing society creates the very wants that it, in turn, supplies. These wants may be created by other consumers in the manner of "keeping up with the Joneses": My neighbor has a new and fancy automobile, and thus I, too, must have a new and fancy automobile. Or they may be created by the industrial producers through advertising and other means of public persuasion—if you do not buy such-and-such a product, your personal and social life will be jeopardized if not ruined. In either case, a kind of self-canceling process of want-creation and want-satisfaction is established. If I buy more because my neighbor buys more, and if he buys more because I buy more, then we can both keep on accumulating purchases indefinitely without either being any better off than if we had remained content with less in the beginning. Similarly, in the case of producer-induced demand: business firms advertise to convince the consumer that he needs the goods that he would not have missed had the advertising and the additional production never occurred.

Such criticisms of the benefits of increased production are then combined with the belief that this increased production has decidedly serious economic costs. Some critics would go so far as to say that, on any proper calculus, economic growth in terms of providing for increased human satisfactions is not even occurring any more. To the curve showing an increased output of "goods," as depicted in Figure 2, they would say, along with this, comes an increased production of "bads." These "bads" are befouled air, polluted water, scarred land, billboard-defaced fields and meadows, the nightmare of subways, commuter traffic, urban sprawl, congestion, anxiety, crime in the streets—indeed, the whole catalog of ills of modern industrial society. A great part of our production now is not a net addition to our output, they say, but simply an attempt to counterbalance these overwhelming costs. Suppose we lay tracks and set up a commuter service between the city and the suburbs. We call this additional output, but in fact it is simply an attempt to make possible an awkward, irrational, and ultimately dehumanizing pattern of life. Better to change the pattern to produce fewer "goods" *and* "bads"; better, in fact, to aim towards Mill's stationary state—a stable, less dynamic, but more contented society.

IS GROWTH POSSIBLE?

A consideration of these economic costs of growth soon leads to an even deeper problem. In particular, it has led many observers to the conclusion that continued economic growth, whether desirable or not, is not really possible. The writers of the "Blueprint for Survival" announce this difficulty in their very first sentences: "The principal defect of the industrial way of life with its ethos of expansion is that it is not sustainable. Its termination within the lifetime of someone born today is inevitable—unless it continues to be sustained for a while longer by an entrenched minority at the cost of imposing great suffering on the rest of mankind" (p. 141). According to the "Blueprint," we shall either stop the growth process in a conscious, rational, humane way or it will end in "a succession of famines, epidemics, social crises and wars" (p. 141). A similar conclusion is suggested by the computer models developed under the auspices of the Club of Rome. Professor Jay W. Forrester of MIT is quoted as saying that "a society with a high level of industrialization may be nonsustainable" (p. 177); "we may now be living in a 'golden age' when . . . the quality of life is, on the average, higher than ever before in history and higher now than the future offers" (p. 176). We face not future growth—but stability, and perhaps inevitable decline.

The general danger that causes growth to be self-limiting and unsustainable in the view of the critics is that it is inconsistent with the ecological balance of planet earth. More specifically, the forces that break the bounds of environmental possibility are scarcity of natural resources, excessive population growth, and pollution and other damaging "external effects" of growth.

In one sense, there is no argument between the growth and the antigrowth schools: if the exploitation of resources, population growth, and pollution were to increase along the same pattern as they have in the past century or more, then eventually—and not so eventually at that—they would produce an untenable situation. The case of population growth is an obvious one. At the rates of world population increase prevalent in the past 40 years, the world's population would soon pass the standing-room-only phase and create an obviously impossible economic and environmental situation. Similarly, it is evident that, if we continue our heavy dependence on certain particular natural resources, in due course we shall exhaust them: a simple reflection of the fact that they are finite and not infinite. Also, continuing increases in pollution over time would lead not only to discomforts and disamenities but to such disruption of the world's ecological system that human life would no longer be sustainable on the planet.

Such basic propositions are not really in dispute. What is in question is the degree to which corrective forces are already, or can be with relatively minor cost, built into the economic system so that (1) continued growth can occur for a very considerable length of time; and (2) when growth halts or slows down, it is not via a general collapse of the economies of the world, but in a fairly gradual way and at a reasonably high standard of living.

POSSIBLE CORRECTIVE FORCES

Consider again the case of population growth. We have admitted that recent historical experience projected into the future would lead to disaster. But then we have to ask: how strong are the corrective forces that may come into play to moderate these historically high rates of population increase? For the industrialized world, at least, such corrective forces seem clearly to exist.[2] Birth rates have been falling in the United States and other developed societies. Awareness of the population problem has itself undoubtedly influenced attitudes towards having children in a corrective direction. Nor, as Solow points out, is there any evidence that, if growth should drop off and our standard of living decline, we would go back to the high birth rates associated with lower incomes in the past. "Common sense suggests that a society in such a position would fight to preserve its standard of living by reducing the desired family size" (p. 182). In other words, apart from any radical change in the society's economic and political system, population growth may be modified by corrective forces that grow naturally out of human responses to new problems and conditions.

Another important corrective force is new technology. The attitudes of the progrowth and antigrowth groups towards new technology are often sharply opposed. If particular resources are in short supply, Wallich is fairly confident that the shortage "will stimulate research and development to produce substitutes" (p. 170). The "Blueprint" writers, by contrast, are highly suspicious of most modern technology already. They note how the new intensive agriculture with its high-yield seeds and heavy use of fertilizers and pesticides can "disrupt local ecosystems" (p. 146). They tend to rely on technological substitutes only in the short run. In the long run these substitutes should be replaced "by 'natural' or self-regulating ones (p. 149). For those who favor continued growth, new inventions, scientific advances, innovations and breakthroughs are part of the solution; for the ecology-minded advocates of stability, they are part of the problem.

Still a further corrective force is the capacity of the economic system to adjust to such scarcities as develop. If a resource is in short supply, its price will rise and this will not only encourage the development of those new technologies referred to above but will lead producers and consumers to substitute more plentiful resources for those that are now more expensive. As Solow explains: "To the extent that it is impossible to design around or find substitutes for expensive natural resources, the

[2] For the special population problem of the less developed "Third World," see the previous Great Debate, pp. 88–89.

prices of commodities that contain a lot of them will rise relative to the prices of other goods and services that don't use up a lot of resources. Consumers will be driven to buy fewer resource-intensive goods and more of other things. All these effects work automatically to increase the productivity of natural resources, i.e. to reduce resource requirements per unit of GNP" (p. 178).

The opponents of growth are highly doubtful that the price system will adequately perform these adjustments automatically, unless there is "controlled and well-orchestrated change on numerous fronts" (p. 149). Moreover, even those who believe continued growth is possible admit that the price system is defective in one very significant way. Pollution of the air, land and water of the industrial societies usually involves social costs for which the polluter, whether individual consumer or private business corporation, is not charged. Economists call these costs "external diseconomies." The price system has no way of mitigating these effects precisely because they are "external" to that system. The motorist who pollutes the air is not charged for the cost to society of his pollution. Therefore, the price system itself gives him no motive to reduce such pollution. The situation of the business firm that discharges its chemicals and other effluents into the river or the sea is similar.

Here, then, the debaters agree that some conscious public policy will have to be developed if pollution is to be abated. The issue really is the extent of the modifications of the present system that will be required to lessen the pollution problem. The antigrowth writers tend to feel that a massive change in social outlook and the economic and political system will be required. The progrowth writers tend to feel that reform through particular pieces of useful legislation will be sufficient. Do we alter the whole society? Or, because many natural corrective forces are at work in any event, can we get by with a few supplementary regulations here and a few extra dollars of public monies there?

SHAPE OF THE FUTURE SOCIETY

The willingness to contemplate massive social change depends, to a degree, on one's image of what a world without growth would really look like. Would it, as our earlier quotation from Mill suggests, be rather nice to go to a "stationary state"? Or would it involve extremely painful, perhaps insoluble, social and economic problems?

The authors of the "Blueprint" clearly find a world without growth quite tenable and, in many ways, very attractive. They urge a future economy that is based on the concept of "the earth as a space ship" (p. 148). This notion of *spaceship earth* has been advanced by Kenneth Boulding and other economists who contrast it with our present-day *throughput economy*.[3] In a throughput economy, we take natural resources, create goods with them, and these goods, along with the

[3] See Kenneth E. Boulding, "Fun and Games with the Gross National Product," *The Environmental Crisis,* Harold W. Helfrich, Jr., ed. (New Haven: Yale University Press, 1970), pp. 162–3. For further discussion of the concepts of a throughput or spaceship economy, see Edwin G. Dolan, *TANSTAAFL* (*There ain't no such thing as a free lunch)* (New York: Holt, Rinehart and Winston, 1971), Chapter 1.

useless byproducts created in the course of their production, ultimately become wastes that we dispose of in various sinks, sewers, dumps and the like. Natural resources are put through the system and become garbage. By contrast, in spaceship earth, the economy is based on the recycling of resources, much as it would be on an actual space vehicle. A permanent equilibrium is maintained as natural resources are converted into goods, which are converted into wastes, which, in turn, are converted back into resources for further production. There is no net drain, or at most a miniscule drain, on the society's exhaustible natural resources and, at the same time, the wastes of the society, rather than causing pollution, become the sources of new recycled resources.

This is a very pretty picture, but we have to ask what kind of society is it that would be able to effect such a change in its basic economic structure? The authors of the "Blueprint" envision a really major change in social-political-economic organization. They urge, in particular, a massive decentralization of society into "neighborhoods of 500, represented in communities of 5,000, in regions of 500,000, represented nationally, which in turn as today should be represented globally" (p. 156). These small communities would be largely self-sufficient; they would contain a balance of agriculture and industry; many modern appliances would have to be given up, but handicraft skills would make a comeback, and the arts, generally, would flourish. "It is probable that only in the small community can a man or woman be an individual. In today's large agglomerations he is merely an isolate" (p. 155). Thus, the stable economy emerges not merely as the only hope of humankind to avoid collapse, but actually as a preferred environment in which, by reducing his impact on Nature, man achieves a new personal and social harmony that has been lost in the urban complexes of a growth-oriented society.

The critique of this hopeful portrait of the new society involves many elements. For many people, the proposed alterations in the structure of society are not beguiling but pernicious. The editors of Nature wonder if people will really "be better off if they are organized in small communities in which social mobility is deliberately restricted and in which agriculture is central to everybody's life. Are these not potentially illiberal arrangements? Is there not a serious danger that to strive for them will weaken the will of civilized communities, developed and developing, to work towards humane goals—the removal of poverty and the liberty of the subject" (p. 165).

There is disagreement about the degree to which economic productivity would have to be sacrificed if spaceship earth, especially if organized around small agro-industrial, handicraft-oriented communities, were to become a reality. Indeed, one of the strong arguments for growth is that it may provide the tools for combating some of the deficiencies of growth. How do we pay to correct for pollution? In a growing society, the reduction of pollution may not have to come out of our current standard of living, but may be paid for out of the proceeds of growth itself. In a relatively low-productivity, stable society, it may be very difficult to bear the added cost of purifying the air and land and water, and properly treating our chemical and other wastes.

And then there is the large question of income distribution. There are substantial inequalities of income within the industrialized nations and, of course, really massive inequalities between the developed and underdeveloped world. Growth, at least in principle, provides the resources for raising low-income groups in a rich society without lowering the incomes of the upper classes. It also provides the means for the poor societies to catch up to, or approximate, the standard of living of the richer societies. Even so strong a critic of growth as Lewis recognizes that limiting growth would transform "the whole question of equality as a social goal" (p. 168). Wallich fears that "the ecologists do not seem to be aware of what it would mean to freeze total income anywhere near today's level. Do they mean that the present income distribution is to be preserved with the poor frozen into their inadequacies? Would that go for the underdeveloped countries too?" (p. 171). The reduction of the average American standard of living to that of the average citizen of the world today would cause a social seismic wave that would make the Great Depression look like a gentle roller. Are the antigrowth people living in a fool's paradise? Or are they simply trying to shock people into an awareness of a problem, hoping that at least some beneficial changes will be stimulated thereby?

A MATTER OF TIMING

So the debate goes on. In many respects, it reduces to a matter of style and timing. In the 1960s, economists often talked about self-sustaining growth forever. No one does that anymore. Whether because of, or in spite of, the Doomsday prophets, everyone now recognizes that the experience of the developed world since the industrial revolution cannot simply be extrapolated across national boundaries in space and future centuries in time. We have been living through a relatively unique historical period, and we are doubtless due for some slowing down of the feverish tempo that has characterized the "progressive" societies of our era. How abrupt should the change be? And how self-consciously planned and directed?

It is to these questions of tempo and design that the limits to growth debate is likely to address itself increasingly in the years ahead.

A Blueprint for Survival
The Ecologist

This document has been drawn up by a small team of
people involved in the study of global environmental
problems.

I. INTRODUCTION: THE NEED FOR CHANGE

The principal defect of the industrial way of life with its ethos of expansion is that it is not sustainable. Its termination within the lifetime of someone born today is inevitable—unless it continues to be sustained for a while longer by an entrenched minority at the cost of imposing great suffering on the rest of mankind. We can be certain, however, that sooner or later it will end (only the precise time and circumstances are in doubt), and that it will do so in one of two ways: either against our will, in a succession of famines, epidemics, social crises and wars; or because we want it to—because we wish to create a society which will not impose hardship and cruelty upon our children—in a succession of thoughtful, humane and measured changes.

Radical change is both necessary and inevitable because the present increases in human numbers and per capita consumption, by disrupting ecosystems and depleting resources, are undermining the very foundations of survival. At present the world population of 3,600 million is increasing by 2 percent per year (72 million), but this overall figure conceals crucially important differences between countries. The industrialized countries with one-third of the world population have annual growth rates of between 0.5 and 1.0 percent; the undeveloped countries on the other hand, with two-thirds of the world population, have annual growth rates of between 2 and 3 percent, and from 40 to 45 percent of their population is under fifteen. It is commonly overlooked that in countries with an unbalanced age structure of this kind the population will continue to increase for many years even after fertility has fallen to the replacement level. As the Population Council has pointed out: "If replacement is achieved in the developed world by 2000 and in the developing world by 2040, then the world's population will stabilize at nearly 15.5 billion (15,500 million) about a century hence, or well over four times the present size."

The per capita use of energy and raw materials also shows a sharp division between the developed and the undeveloped parts of the world. Both are increasing their use of these commodities, but consumption in the developed countries is so much higher that, even with their smaller share of the population, their consumption may well represent over 80 percent of the world total. For the same reason, similar percentage increases are far more significant in the developed countries; to take one example, between 1957 and 1967 per capita steel consumption rose by 12 percent in the U.S. and by 41 percent in India, but the actual increases (in kg per year) were from 568 to 634 and from 9.2 to 13 respectively. Nor is there any sign that an eventual end to economic growth is envisaged, and indeed industrial economies appear to break down if growth ceases or even slows, however high the absolute level of consumption. Even the U.S. still aims at an annual growth of GNP of 4 percent or more. Within this overall figure much higher growth rates occur for the use of particular resources, such as oil.

The combination of human numbers and per capita consumption has a considerable impact on the environment, in terms of both the resources we take from it and the pollutants we impose on it. A distinguished group of scientists, who came together for a "Study of Critical Environmental Problems" (SCEP) under the auspices of the Massachusetts Institute of Technology, state in their report the clear need for a means of measuring this impact, and have coined the term *ecological demand*, which they define as "a summation of all man's demands on the environment, such as the extraction of resources and the return of wastes." Gross domestic product (GDP), which is population multiplied by material standard of living, appears to provide the most convenient measure of ecological demand, and according to the UN *Statistical Yearbook* this is increasing annually by 5 to 6 percent, or doubling every 13.5 years. If this trend should continue, then in the time taken for world population to double (which is estimated to be by just after the year 2000), total ecological demand will have increased by a factor of six. SCEP estimate that "such demand-producing activities as agriculture, mining and industry have global annual rates of increase of 3.5 percent and 7 percent respectively. An integrated rate of increase is estimated to be between 5 and 6 percent per year, in comparison with an annual rate of population increase of only 2 percent."

It should go without saying that the world cannot accommodate this continued increase in ecological demand. *Indefinite* growth of whatever type cannot be sustained by *finite* resources. This is the nub of the environmental predicament. It is still less possible to maintain indefinite *exponential* growth—and unfortunately the growth of ecological demand is proceeding exponentially (i.e., it is increasing geometrically, by compound interest).

The implications of exponential growth are not generally appreciated and are well worth considering. As Professor Forrester explains it, ". . . pure exponential growth possesses the characteristic of behaving according to a 'doubling time.' Each fixed time interval shows a doubling of the relevant system variable. Exponential growth is treacherous and misleading. A system variable can continue through many doubling intervals without seeming to reach significant size. But then in one or two more doubling periods, still following the same law of exponential growth, it suddenly seems to become overwhelming."

Thus, supposing world petroleum reserves stood at 2,100 billion barrels, and supposing our rate of consumption was increasing by 6.9 percent per year, then as can be seen from Figure 1, demand will exceed supply by the end of the century. What is significant, however, is not the

Figure 1 World Reserves of Crude Petroleum at Exponential Rate of Consumption

Note that in 1975, with no more than fifteen years left before demand exceeds supply, the total global reserve has been depleted by only 12½ percent.

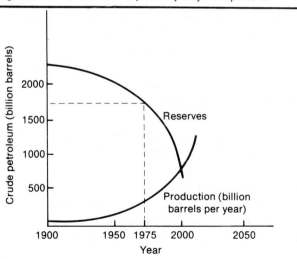

speed at which such vast reserves can be depleted, but that as late as 1975 there will appear to be reserves fully ample enough to last for considerably longer. Such a situation can easily lull one into a false sense of security and the belief that a given growth rate can be sustained, if not indefinitely, at least for a good deal longer than is actually the case. The same basic logic applies to the availability of any resource including land, and it is largely because of this particular dynamic of exponential growth that the environmental predicament has come upon us so suddenly, and why its solution requires urgent and radical measures, many of which run counter to values which, in our industrial society, we have been taught to regard as fundamental.

If we allow the present growth rate to persist, total ecological demand will increase by a factor of 32 over the next 66 years—and there can be no serious person today willing to concede the possibility, or indeed the desirability, of our accommodating the pressures arising from such growth. For this can be done only at the cost of disrupting ecosystems and exhausting resources, which must lead to the failure of food supplies and the collapse of society. It is worth briefly considering each in turn.

DISRUPTION OF ECOSYSTEMS

We depend for our survival on the predictability of ecological processes. If they were at all arbitrary, we would not know when to reap or sow, and we would be at the mercy of environmental whim. We could learn nothing about the rest of nature, advance no hypotheses, suggest no "laws." Fortunately, ecological processes *are* predictable, and although theirs is a relatively young discipline, ecologists have been able to formulate a number of important "laws," one of which in particular relates to environmental predictability: namely, that all ecosystems tend towards stability, and further that the more diverse and complex the ecosystem the more stable it is; that is, the more species there are, and the more they interrelate, the more stable is their environment. By stability is meant the ability to return to the original position after any change, instead of being forced into a totally different pattern—and hence predictability.

Unfortunately, we behave as if we knew nothing of the environment and had no conception of its predictability, treating it instead with scant and brutal regard as if it were an idiosyncratic and extremely stupid slave. We seem never to have reflected on the fact that a tropical rain forest supports innumerable insect species and yet is never devastated by them; that its rampant luxuriance is not contingent on our overflying it once a month and bombarding it with insecticides, herbicides, fungicides, and what-have-you. And yet we tremble over our wheatfields and cabbage patches with a desperate battery of synthetic chemicals, in an absurd attempt to impede the operation of the immutable "law" we have just mentioned—that all ecosystems tend towards stability, therefore diversity and complexity, therefore a growing number of different plant and animal species until a climax or optimal condition is achieved. If we were clever, we would recognize that successful long-term agriculture demands the achievement of an artificial climax, an imitation of the preexisting ecosystem, so that the level of unwanted species could be controlled by those that did no harm to the crop-plants.

Instead we have put our money on pesticides, which although they have been effective, have been so only to a limited and now diminishing extent: according to SCEP, the 34 percent increase in world food production from 1951 to 1966 required increased investments in nitrogenous fertilizers of 146 percent and in pesticides of 300 percent. At the same time they have created a number of serious problems, notably resistance—some 250 pest species are resistant to one group of pesticides or another, while many others require increased applications to keep their populations within manageable proportions—and the promotion of formerly innocuous species to pest proportions, because the predators that formerly kept them down have been destroyed. The spread of DDT and other organochlorines in the environment has resulted in alarming population declines among woodcock, grebes, various birds of prey and seabirds, and in a number of fish species, principally the sea trout. SCEP comments: "the oceans are an ultimate accumulation site of DDT and its residues. As much as 25 percent of the DDT compounds produced to date may have been transferred to the sea. The amount in the marine biota is estimated to be in the order of less than 0.1 percent of total production and has already produced a demonstrable impact upon the marine environment. . . . The decline in productivity of marine food fish and the accumulation of levels of DDT in their tissues which are unacceptable to man can only be accelerated by DDT's continued release to the environment. . . ."

There are half a million manmade chemicals in use today, yet we cannot predict the behaviour or properties of the greater part of them (either singly or in combination) once they are released into the environment. We know, however, that the combined effects of pollution and habitat destruction menace the survival of no less than 280 mammal, 350 bird, and 20,000 plant species. To those who regret these losses but greet them with the comment that the survival of *Homo sapiens* is surely more important than that of an eagle or a primrose, we repeat that *Homo sapiens* himself depends on the continued resilience of those ecological networks of which eagles and primroses are integral parts. We do not need to utterly destroy the ecosphere to bring catastrophe upon ourselves: all we have to do is to carry on as we are, clearing forests, "reclaiming" wetlands, and imposing sufficient quantities of pesticides, radioactive materials, plastics, sewage, and industrial wastes upon our air, water and land systems to make them inhospitable to the species on which their continued stability and integrity depend. Industrial man in the world today is like a bull in a china shop, with the single difference that a bull with half the information about the properties of china as we have about those of ecosystems would probably try to adapt its behaviour to its environment rather than the reverse. By contrast, *Homo sapiens industrialis* is determined that the china shop should adapt to him, and has therefore set himself the goal of reducing it to rubble in the shortest possible time.

FAILURE OF FOOD SUPPLIES

Increases in food production in the undeveloped world have barely kept abreast of population growth. Such increases as there have been are due not to higher productivity but to the opening up of new land for cultivation. Unfortunately this will not be possible for much longer: all the good land in the world is now being farmed, and according to the FAO, at present rates of expansion none of the marginal land that is left will be unfarmed by 1985—indeed some of the land now under cultivation has been so exhausted that it will have to be returned to permanent pasture.

For this reason, FAO's program to feed the world depends on a program of intensification, at the heart of which are the new high-yield varieties of wheat and rice. These are highly responsive to inorganic fertilizers and quick-maturing, so that up to ten times present yields can be obtained from them. Unfortunately, they are highly vulnerable to disease, and therefore require increased protection by pesticides, and of course they demand massive inputs of fertilizers (up to 27 times present ones). Not only will these disrupt local ecosystems, thereby jeopardizing long-term productivity, but they force hard-pressed undeveloped nations to rely on the agrochemical industries of the developed world.

Whatever their virtues and faults, the new genetic hybrids are not intended to solve the world food problem, but only to give us time to devise more permanent and realistic solutions. It is our view, however, that these hybrids are not the best means of doing this, since their use is likely to bring about a reduction in overall diversity, when the clear need is to develop an agriculture diverse enough to have long-term potential. We must beware of those "experts" who appear to advocate the transformation of the ecosphere into nothing more than a food-factory for man.

The concept of a world consisting solely of man and a few favoured food plants is so ludicrously impracticable as to be seriously contemplated only by those who find solace in their own wilful ignorance of the real world of biological diversity.

We in Britain must bear in mind that we depend on imports for half our food, and that we are unlikely to improve on this situation. The 150,000 acres which are lost from agriculture each year are about 70 percent more productive than the average for all enclosed land, while we are already beginning to experience diminishing returns from the use of inorganic fertilizers. In the period 1964–9, applications of phosphates have gone up by 2 percent, potash by 7 percent, and nitrogen by 40 percent, yet yields per acre of wheat, barley, lucerne and temporary grass have leveled off and are beginning to decline, while that of permanent grass has risen only slightly and may be leveling off. As per capita food availability declines throughout the rest of the world, and it appears inevitable it will, we will find it progressively more difficult and expensive to meet our food requirements from abroad. The prospect of severe food shortages within the next 30 years is not so much a fantasy as that of the continued abundance promised us by so many of our politicians.

EXHAUSTION OF RESOURCES

As we have seen, continued exponential growth of consumption of materials and energy is impossible. Present reserves of all but a few metals will be exhausted within 50 years if consumption rates continue to grow as they are. Obviously there will be new discoveries and advances in mining technology, but these are likely to provide us with only a limited stay of execution. Synthetics and substitutes are likely to be of little help, since they must be made from materials which themselves are in short supply: while the hoped-for availability of unlimited energy would not be the answer, since the problem is the ratio of useful metal to waste matter (which would have to be disposed of without disrupting ecosystems), not the need for cheap power. Indeed, the availability of unlimited power holds more of a threat than a promise, since energy use is inevitably polluting, and in addition we would ultimately have to face the problem of disposing of an intractable amount of waste heat.

COLLAPSE OF SOCIETY

The developed nations consume such disproportionate amounts of protein, raw materials and fuels that unless they considerably reduce their consumption there is no hope of the undeveloped nations markedly improving their standards of living. This vast differential is a cause of much and growing discontent, made worse by our attempts at cultural uniformity on behalf of an expanding market economy. In the end, we are altering people's aspirations without providing the means for them to be satisfied. In the rush to industrialize we break up communities, so that the controls which formerly regulated behavior are destroyed before alternatives can be provided. Urban drift is one result of this process, with a consequent rise in antisocial practices, crime, delinquency and so on, which are so costly for society in terms both of money and of well-being.

At the same time, we are sowing the seeds of massive unemployment by increasing the ratio of capital to labor so that the provision of each job becomes ever more expensive. In a world of fast diminishing resources, we shall quickly come to the point when very great numbers of people will be thrown out of work, when the material compensations of urban life are either no longer available or prohibitively expensive, and consequently when whole sections of society will find good cause to express their considerable discontent in ways likely to be anything but pleasant for their fellows.

It is worth bearing in mind that the barriers between us and epidemics are not so strong as is commonly supposed. Not only is it increasingly difficult to control the vectors of disease, but it is more than probable that urban populations are being insidiously weakened by overall pollution levels, even when they are not high enough to be incriminated in any one illness. At the same time international mobility speeds the spread of disease. With this background, and at a time of widespread public demoralization, the collapse of vital social services, such as power and sanitation, could easily provoke a series of epidemics—and we cannot say with confidence that we would be able to cope with them.

At times of great distress and social chaos, it is more than probable that governments will fall into the hands of reckless and unscrupulous elements, who will not hesitate to threaten neighboring governments with attack, if they feel that they can wrest from them a larger share of the world's vanishing resources. Since a growing number of countries (an estimated 36 by 1980) will have nuclear power stations, and therefore sources of plutonium for nuclear warheads, the likelihood of a whole series of local (if not global) nuclear engagements is greatly increased.

By now it should be clear that the main problems of the environment do not arise from temporary and accidental malfunctions of existing economic and social systems. On the contrary, they are the warning signs of a profound incompatibility between deeply rooted beliefs in continuous growth and the dawning recognition of the earth as a space ship,[1] limited

[1] See discussion of this concept, pp. 138–139.

in its resources and vulnerable to thoughtless mishandling. The nature of our response to these symptoms is crucial. If we refuse to recognize the cause of our trouble the result can only be increasing disillusion and growing strain upon the fragile institutions that maintain external peace and internal social cohesion. If, on the other hand, we can respond to this unprecedented challenge with informed and constructive action, the rewards will be as great as the penalties for failure.

Our task is to create a society which is sustainable and which will give the fullest possible satisfaction to its members. Such a society by definition would depend not on expansion but on stability. This does not mean to say that it would be stagnant—indeed it could well afford more variety than does the state of uniformity at present being imposed by the pursuit of technological efficiency. We believe that the stable society, as well as removing the sword of Damocles which hangs over the heads of future generations, is much more likely than the present one to bring the peace and fulfilment which hitherto have been regarded, sadly, as Utopian.

II. TOWARDS THE STABLE SOCIETY

INTRODUCTION

The principal conditions of a stable society—one that to all intents and purposes can be sustained indefinitely while giving optimum satisfaction to its members—are: (1) minimum disruption of ecological processes; (2) maximum conservation of materials and energy—or an economy of stock rather than flow; (3) a population in which recruitment equals loss; and (4) a social system in which the individual can enjoy, rather than feel restricted by, the first three conditions.

The achievement of these four conditions will require controlled and well-orchestrated change on numerous fronts, and this change will probably occur through seven operations: (1) a control operation whereby environmental disruption is reduced as much as possible by technical means; (2) a freeze operation, in which present trends are halted; (3) asystemic substitution, by which the most dangerous components of these trends are replaced by technological substitutes, whose effect is less deleterious in the short-term, but over the long-term will be increasingly ineffective; (4) systemic substitution, by which these technological substitutes are replaced by "natural" or selfregulating ones, i.e., those which either replicate or employ without undue disturbance the normal processes of the ecosphere, and are therefore likely to be sustainable over very long periods of time; (5) the invention, promotion and application of alternative technologies which are energy and materials conservative, and which because they are designed for relatively "closed" economic communities are likely to disrupt ecological processes only minimally (e.g. intermediate technology); (6) decentralization of polity and economy at all levels, and the formation of communities small enough to be reasonably self-regulating and self-supporting; and (7) education for such communities.

In putting forward these proposals we are aware that hasty or disordered change is highly disruptive and ultimately self-defeating; but we are also mindful of how the time-scale imposed on any proposal for a remedial course of action has been much abbreviated by the dynamic of exponential growth (of population, resource depletion and pollution) and by the scarcely perceived scale and intensity of our disruption of the ecological processes on which we and all other life-forms depend. Within these limitations, therefore, we have taken care to devise and synchronize our program so as to minimize both unemployment and capital outlay. We believe it possible to change from an expansionist society to a stable society without loss of jobs or an increase in real expenditure. Inevitably, however, there will be considerable changes, both of geography and function, in job availability and the requirements for capital inputs—and these may set up immense counter-productive social pressures. Yet given the careful and sensitive conception and implementation of a totally integrated program these should be minimized, and an open style of government should inspire the trust and cooperation of the general public so essential for the success of this enterprise.

MINIMIZING THE DISRUPTION OF ECOLOGICAL PROCESSES

Ecological processes can be disrupted by introducing into them either substances that are foreign to them or the correct ones in the wrong quantities. It follows therefore that the most common method of pollution "control," namely dispersal, is not control at all, but a more or less useful way of playing for time. Refuse disposal by dumping solves the immediate problem of the householder, but as dumping sites are used up it creates progressively less soluble problems for society at large; smokeless fuels are invaluable signs of progress for the citizens of London or Sheffield, but the air pollution from their manufacture brings misery and ill-health to the people near the plants where they are produced; in many cases the dispersal of pollutants through tall chimneys merely alters the proportion of pollution, so that instead of a few receiving much, many receive some; and lastly, in estuarine and coastal waters—crucial areas for fisheries —nutrients from sewage and agriculture run-off in modest quantities probably increase productivity, but in excess are as harmful as organochlorines and heavy metals.

Thus dispersal can be only a temporary expedient. Pollution control proper must consist of the recycling of materials, or the introduction of practices which are so akin to natural processes as not to be harmful. The long-term object of these pollution control procedures is to minimize our dependence on technology as a regulator of the ecological cycles on which we depend, and to return as much as possible to the natural mechanisms of the ecosphere, since in all but the short-term they are much more efficient and reliable.

CONVERSION TO AN ECONOMY OF STOCK

The transfer from flow to stock economics can be considered under two headings: resource management and social accounting.

Resource management. It is essential that the throughput of raw materials be minimized both to conserve nonrenewable resources and to cut down pollution. Since industry must have an economic incentive to be conservative of materials and energy and to recycle as much as possible, we propose a number of fiscal measures to these ends:

(*a*) A raw materials tax. This would be proportionate to the availability of the raw material in question, and would be designed to enable our reserves to last over an arbitrary period of time, the longer the better, on the principle that during this time our dependence on this raw material would be reduced. This tax would penalize resource-intensive industries and favor employment-intensive ones. Like (*b*) below it would also penalize short-lived products.

(*b*) An amortization tax. This would be proportionate to the estimated life of the product, e.g., it would be 100 percent for products designed to last no more than a year, and would then be progressively reduced to 0 percent for those designed to last 100+ years. Obviously this would penalize short-lived products, especially disposable ones, thereby reducing resource utilization and pollution, particularly the solid-waste problem. Plastics, for example, which are so remarkable for their durability, would be used only in products where this quality is valued, and not for single trip purposes. This tax would also encourage craftsmanship and employment-intensive industry.

Social accounting. By the introduction of monetary incentives and disincentives it is possible to put a premium on durability and a penalty on disposability, thereby reducing the throughput of materials and energy so that resources are conserved and pollution reduced. But another important way of reducing pollution and enhancing amenity is by the provision of a more equitable social accounting system, reinforced by antidisamenity legislation. Social accounting procedures must be used not just to weigh up the merits of alternative development proposals, but also to determine whether or not society actually wants such development. Naturally, present procedures require improvement: for example, in calculating "revealed preference" (the values of individuals and communities as "revealed" to economists by the amount people are willing and/or can afford to pay for or against a given development), imagination, sensitivity and common sense are required in order to avoid the imposition on poor neighborhoods or sparsely inhabited countryside of nuclear power stations, reservoirs, motorways, airports and the like; and in calculating the "social time preference rate" (an indication of society's regard for the future) for a given project, a very low discount should be given, since it is easier to do than undo, and we must assume that unless we botch things completely many more generations will follow us who will not thank us for exhausting resources or blighting the landscape.

The social costs of any given development should be paid by those who propose or perpetrate it—"the polluter must pay" is a principle that must guide our costing procedures. Furthermore, accounting decisions should be made in the light of stock economics: in other words, we must judge the health of our economy not by flow or throughput, since this inevitably leads to waste, resource depletion and environmental disruption, but by the distribution, quality and variety of the stock. At the moment, as Kenneth Boulding has pointed out, "the success of the economy is measured by the amount of throughput derived in part from reservoirs of raw materials, processed by 'factors of production,' and passed on in part as output to the sink of pollution reservoirs. The gross national product (GNP) roughly measures this throughput." Yet, both the reservoirs of raw materials and the reservoirs for pollution are limited and finite, so that ultimately the throughput from the one to the other must be detrimental to our well-being and must therefore not only be minimized but be regarded as a cost rather than a benefit. For this reason Boulding has suggested that GNP be considered a measure of gross national cost, and that we devote ourselves to its minimization, maximizing instead the quality of our stock. "When we have developed the economy of the spaceship earth," he writes, "in which man will persist in equilibrium with his environment, the notion of the GNP will simply disintegrate. We will be less concerned with income-flow concepts and more with capital-stock concepts. Then technological changes that result in the maintenance of the total stock with *less* throughput (less production and consumption) will be a clear gain." We must come to assess our standard of living not by calculating the value of all the air-conditioners we have made and sold, but by the freshness of the air; not by the value of the antibiotics, hormones, feedstuff and broiler-houses, and the cost of disposing of their wastes, all of which put so heavy a price on poultry production today, but by the flavor and nutritional quality of the chickens themselves; and so on. In other words, accepted value must reflect real value, just as accepted cost must reflect real cost.

STABILIZING THE POPULATION

We have seen already that however slight the growth rate, a population cannot grow indefinitely. It follows, therefore, that at some point it must stabilize of its own volition, or else be cut down by some "natural" mechanism—famine, epidemic, war or whatever. Since no sane society would choose the latter course, it must choose to stabilize.

Our task is to end population growth by lowering the rate of recruitment so that it equals the rate of loss. A few countries will then be able to stabilize, to maintain that ratio; most others, however, will have to slowly *reduce* their populations to a level at which it is sensible to stabilize. Stated baldly, the task seems impossible; but if we start now, and the exercise is spread over a sufficiently long period of time, then we believe that it is within our capabilities. The difficulties are enormous, but they are surmountable.

First, governments must acknowledge the problem and declare their commitment to ending population growth; this commitment should also include an end to immigration. Secondly, they must set up national population services with a fourfold brief:

1. to publicize as widely and vigorously as possible the relationship between population, food supply, quality of life, resource depletion, etc., and the great need for couples to have no more than two children. The finest talents in advertising should be recruited for this, and the broad aim should be to inculcate a socially more responsible attitude to child-rearing. For example, the notion (derived largely from the popular women's magazines) that childless couples should be objects of pity rather than esteem should be sharply challenged; and of course there are many similar notions to be disputed.

2. to provide at local and national levels free contraception advice and information on other services such as abortion and sterilization;

3. to provide a comprehensive domiciliary service, and to provide contraceptives free of charge, free sterilization, and abortion on demand;

4. to commission, finance and coordinate research not only on demographic techniques and contraceptive technology but also on the subtle cultural controls necessary for the harmonious maintenance of stability.

We know so little about the dynamics of human populations that we cannot say whether the first three measures would be sufficient. It is self-evident that if couples still wanted families larger than the replacement-size no amount of free contraception would make any difference. However, because we know so little about population control, it would be difficult for us to devise any of the socioeconomic restraints which on the face of it are likely to be more effective, but which many people fear might be unduly repressive. For this reason, we would be wise to rely on the first three measures for the next 20 years or so. We then may find they are enough—but if they aren't, we must hope that intensive research during this period will be rewarded with a set of socioeconomic restraints that are both *effective* and *humane*. These will then constitute the third stage, and should also provide the tools for the fourth stage—that of persuading the public to have average family sizes of slightly *less* than replacement size, so that total population can be greatly reduced. If we achieve a decline rate of 0.5 percent per year, the same as Britain's rate of growth today, there should be no imbalance of population structure, as the dependency ratio would be exactly the same as that of contemporary Britain. Only the makeup of dependency would be different: instead of there being more children than old people, it would be the other way round. The time-scale for such an operation is long of course.

CREATING A NEW SOCIAL SYSTEM

Possibly the most radical change we propose in the creation of a new social system is decentralization. We do so not because we are sunk in nostalgia for a mythical little England of fetes, olde worlde pubs, and perpetual conversations over garden fences, but for four much more fundamental reasons:

1. While there is good evidence that human societies can happily remain stable for long periods, there is no doubt that the long transitional stage that we and our children must go through will impose a heavy burden on our moral courage and will require great restraint. Legislation and the operations of police forces and the courts will be necessary to reinforce this restraint, but we believe that such external controls can never be so subtle nor so effective as internal controls. It would therefore be sensible to promote the social conditions in which public opinion and full public participation in decision making become as far as possible the means whereby communities are ordered. The larger a community the less likely this can be: in a heterogeneous, centralized society such as ours, the restraints of the stable society if they were to be effective would appear as so much outside coercion; but in communities small enough for

the general will to be worked out and expressed by individuals confident of themselves and their fellows as individuals, "us and them" situations are less likely to occur—people having learned the limits of a stable society would be free to order their own lives within them as they wished, and would therefore accept the restraints of the stable society as necessary and desirable and not as some arbitrary restriction imposed by a remote and unsympathetic government.

2. As agriculture depends more and more on integrated control and becomes more diversified, there will no longer be any scope for prairie-type crop-growing or factory-type livestock-rearing. Small farms run by teams with specialized knowledge of ecology, entomology, botany, etc., will then be the rule, and indeed individual smallholdings could become extremely productive suppliers of eggs, fruit and vegetables to neighborhoods. Thus a much more diversified urban-rural mix will be not only possible, but because of the need to reduce the transportation costs of returning domestic sewage to the land, desirable. In industry, as with agriculture, it will be important to maintain a vigorous feedback between supply and demand in order to avoid waste, overproduction or production of goods which the community does not really want, thereby eliminating the needless expense of time, energy and money in attempts to persuade it that it does. If an industry is an integral part of a community, it is much more likely to encourage product innovation because people clearly want qualitative improvements in a given field, rather than because expansion is necessary for that industry's survival or because there is otherwise insufficient work for its research and development section. Today, men, women and children are merely consumer markets, and industries as they centralize become national rather than local and supranational rather than national, so that while entire communities may come to depend on them for the jobs they supply, they are in no sense integral parts of those communities. To a considerable extent the "jobs or beauty" dichotomy has been made possible because of this deficiency. Yet plainly people want jobs *and* beauty; they should not in a just and humane society be forced to choose between the two, and in a decentralized society of small communities where industries are small enough to be responsive to each community's needs, there will be no reason for them to do so.

3. The small community is not only the organizational structure in which internal or systemic controls are most likely to operate effectively, but its dynamic is an essential source of stimulation and pleasure for the individual. Indeed it is probable that only in the small community can a man or woman be an individual. In today's large agglomerations he is merely an isolate—and it is significant that the decreasing autonomy of

communities and local regions and the increasing centralization of decision making and authority in the cumbersome bureaucracies of the state have been accompanied by the rise of self-conscious individualism, an individualism which feels threatened unless it is harped upon.

4. The fourth reason for decentralization is that to deploy a population in small towns and villages is to reduce to the minimum its impact on the environment. This is because the actual urban superstructure required per inhabitant goes up radically as the size of the town increases beyond a certain point. For example, the per capita cost of high-rise flats is much greater than that of ordinary houses; and the cost of roads and other transportation routes increases with the number of commuters carried. Similarly, the per capita expenditure on other facilities such as those for distributing food and removing wastes is much higher in cities than in small towns and villages. Thus, if everybody lived in villages the need for sewage treatment plants would be somewhat reduced, while in an entirely urban society they are essential, and the cost of treatment is high. Broadly speaking, it is only by decentralization that we can increase self-sufficiency—and self-sufficiency is vital if we are to minimize the burden of social systems on the ecosystems that support them.

Although we believe that the small community should be the basic unit of society and that each community should be as self-sufficient and self-regulating as possible, we would like to stress that we are not proposing that they be inward-looking, self-obsessed or in any way closed to the rest of the world. Basic precepts of ecology, such as the interrelatedness of all things and the far-reaching effects of ecological processes and their disruption, should influence community decision making, and therefore there must be an efficient and sensitive communications network between all communities. There must be procedures whereby community actions that affect regions can be discussed at regional level and regional actions with extraregional effects can be discussed at global level. We have no hard-and-fast views on the size of the proposed communities, but for the moment we suggest neighborhoods of 500, represented in communities of 5,000, in regions of 500,000, represented nationally, which in turn as today should be represented globally. We emphasize that our goal should be to create *community feeling* and *global awareness*, rather than that dangerous and sterile compromise which is nationalism.

III. THE GOAL

There is every reason to suppose that the stable society would provide us with satisfactions that would more than compensate for those which, with the passing of the industrial state, it will become increasingly necessary to forgo.

We have seen that man in our present society has been deprived of a satisfactory social environment. A society made up of decentralized, self-sufficient communities, in which people work near their homes, have the responsibility of governing themselves, of running their schools, hospitals, and welfare services, in fact of constituting real communities, should, we feel, be a much happier place.

Its members, in these conditions, would be likely to develop an identity of their own, which many of us have lost in the mass society we live in. They would tend, once more, to find an aim in life, develop a set of values, and take pride in their achievements as well as in those of their community.

It is the absence of just these things that is rendering our mass society ever less tolerable to us and in particular to our youth, and to which can be attributed the present rise in drug addiction, alcoholism and delinquency, all of which are symptomatic of a social disease in which a society fails to furnish its members with their basic psychological requirements.

REAL COSTS

We might regard with apprehension a situation in which we shall have to make do without many of the devices such as motor-cars and various domestic appliances which, to an ever greater extent, are shaping our everyday lives.

These devices may indeed provide us with much leisure and satisfaction, but few have considered at what cost. For instance, how many of us take into account the dull and tedious work that has to be done to manufacture them, or for that matter to earn the money required for their acquisition? It has been calculated that the energy used by the machines that provide the average American housewife with her high standard of living is the equivalent of that provided by five hundred slaves.

In this respect, it is difficult to avoid drawing a comparison between ourselves and the Spartans, who in order to avoid the toil involved in tilling the fields and building and maintaining their homes employed a veritable army of helots. The Spartan's life, as everybody knows, was a misery. From early childhood, boys were made to live in barracks, were fed the most frugal and austere diet and spent most of their adult life in military training so as to be able to keep down a vast subject population, always ready to seize an opportunity to rise up against its masters. It never occurred to them that they would have been far better off without their slaves, fulfilling themselves the far less exacting task of tilling their own fields and building and maintaining their own homes.

In fact "economic cost," as we have seen, simply does not correspond to "real cost." Within a stable society this gap must be bridged as much as possible.

This means that we should be encouraged to buy things whose production involves the minimum environmental disruption and which will not give rise to all sorts of unexpected costs that would outweigh the benefits that their possession might provide.

REAL VALUE

It is also true, as we have seen, that "economic value" as at present calculated does not correspond to real value any more than "economic cost" corresponds to real cost.

In a stable society, everything would be done to reduce the discrepancy between economic value and real value, and if we could repair some of the damage we have done to our physical and social environment, and live a more natural life, there would be less need for the consumer products that we spend so much money on. Instead we could spend it on things that truly enrich and embellish our lives.

In manufacturing processes, the accent would be on quality rather than quantity, which means that skill and craftsmanship, which we have for so long systematically discouraged, would once more play a part in our lives. For example, the art of cooking would come back into its own, no longer regarded as a form of drudgery, but correctly valued as an art worthy of occupying our time, energy and imagination. Food would become more varied and interesting and its consumption would become more of a ritual and less a utilitarian function.

The arts would flourish: literature, music, painting, sculpture and architecture would play an ever greater part in our lives, while achievements in these fields would earn both money and prestige.

A society devoted to achievements of this sort would be an infinitely more agreeable place than is our present one, geared as it is to the mass production of shoddy utilitarian consumer goods in ever greater quantities. Surprising as it may seem to one reared on today's economic doctrines, it would also be the one most likely to satisfy our basic biological requirements for food, air and water, and even more surprisingly, provide us with the jobs that in our unstable industrial society are constantly being menaced.

There must be a fusion between our religion and the rest of our culture, since there is no valid distinction between the laws of God and

Nature, and Man must live by them no less than any other creature. Such a belief must be central to the philosophy of the stable society, and must permeate all our thinking. Indeed it is the only one which is properly scientific, and science must address itself much more vigorously to the problems of cooperating with the rest of Nature, rather than seeking to control it.

This does not mean that science must in any way be discouraged. On the contrary, within a stable society, there would be considerable scope for the energies and talents of scientist and technologist.

Basic scientific research, plus a good deal of multidisciplinary synthesis, would be required to understand the complex mechanisms of our ecosphere with which we must learn to cooperate.

There would be a great demand for scientists and technologists capable of devising the technological infrastructure of a decentralized society. Indeed, with the application of a new set of criteria for judging the economic viability of technological devices, there must open a whole new field of research and development.

The recycling industry which must expand very considerably would offer innumerable opportunities, while in agriculture there would be an even greater demand for ecologists, botanists, entomologists, mycologists, etc., who would be called upon to devise ever subtler methods for ensuring the fertility of the soil and for controlling "pest" populations.

Thus in many ways, the stable society, with its diversity of physical and social environments, would provide considerable scope for human skill and ingenuity.

Indeed, if we are capable of ensuring a relatively smooth transition to it, we can be optimistic about providing our children with a way of life psychologically, intellectually and aesthetically more satisfying than the present one. And we can be confident that it will be sustainable as ours cannot be, so that the legacy of despair we are about to leave them may at the last minute be changed to one of hope.

A Response to the Blueprint
Nature

Nature is one of Britain's leading scientific publications.

I. THE CASE AGAINST HYSTERIA

Britain is being assaulted by the environmentalists. This weekend, Dr. Paul Ehrlich, president of Zero Population Growth Inc., and a professor of biology at Stanford University, is to recite for the Conservation Society his now familiar dirge that the world is about to breed itself to death. Last week, a distinguished group of doctors, many of whom should have known better, published in *The Lancet* and the *British Medical Journal* a declaration that Britain is so overcrowded that there is "a direct threat to the mental and physical well-being of our patients" and a plea that doctors should unite "to combat the British disease of overpopulation." At the same time, the new magazine *The Ecologist* published what it called "A Blueprint for Survival" which reflects and sometimes amplifies a good many of the half-baked anxieties about what is called the environmental crisis. On this occasion, the doctrine that dog should not eat dog notwithstanding, the magazine deserves to be taken to task if only for having recruited a "statement of support" from 33 distinguished people, many of them scientists, at least half of whom should have known better. Nobody pretends that there are no serious problems to be worried about but the time seems fast approaching when the cry of disaster round the corner will have to be promoted to the top of the list of causes for public concern.

That professional people should lend their names to attempts like these to fan public anxiety about problems which have either been exaggerated

"A Response to the Blueprint," excerpted from editorials in *Nature* (January 14, 1972 and January 28, 1972). Reprinted by permission of the publisher.

or which are nonexistent is reprehensible. It is especially regrettable that declarations like these should myopically draw attention to the supposed difficulties of moderating population growth in Britain when there is no evidence worth speaking of to suggest that Britain is overpopulated (which is not, of course, the same thing as to say that the country is properly managed). The doctors who signed the round robin to the medical weeklies say that the problems of the developing countries "are formidable and may defy any rational solution," but that they are also "gravely concerned" at the pace of growth of the British population, which exceeds 55 million, and which is expected to increase to 66.5 million by the end of the century.

In reality, the doctors seem to have added an extra 500,000 to the latest estimates of the population of the United Kingdom in the year 2000, for the Government Actuary's latest calculation, published three months ago, gives an even 66 million for that date. It is, however, much more relevant that the forward projections of the British population have been declining steadily over the past decade, as the statisticians have been persuaded by experience that the trend of fertility in Britain, like that in much of the rest of Western Europe, is downward. The doctors also choose, by design or ignorance, to overlook the plain truth that only a quarter of such increase of the British population as there may be between now and the end of the century can be attributed to what they call "the present reproductive bonanza." The rest is simply a consequence of their own craft, which has now made it possible for people to live longer and to survive a good many of the previously fatal hazards of middle life. So is it to be expected that the same people will band together in public to wring their hands about the once and for all increase of the British population which is likely to come about when, at some time in the next two decades, ways are found of treating or even preventing some forms of cancer?

The same unreflectiveness appears to have marred *The Ecologist's* "Blueprint for Survival." Those who have compiled it say that "the relevant information available has impressed upon us the extreme gravity of the global situation today." They foresee "the collapse of society" and consider that if present trends persist, "life support systems on this planet" will be irreversibly disrupted if not by the end of the century then "within the lifetime of our children." Governments, they say, are either refusing to face facts or are "briefing their scientists in such a way that their seriousness is played down." So, the argument goes, there must be a redefinition of the philosophy of civilized life and a restructuring of society as a whole.

The errors in this simplistic view of the present stage in the history of the human race are by now familiar. Much turns on the way in which industrialized societies are at present consuming raw materials at a substantial rate, and it is true that it seems increasingly unlikely that petroleum companies will be able indefinitely to discover new reserves at such a pace that future supplies are always ensured. Oil, indeed, may be the most vulnerable of the resources at present used, just as in Europe 2000 years ago native stands of timber proved not to be inexhaustible. But does it follow from this simple-minded calculation that there will come a time when, to everybody's surprise, petroleum deposits are worked out and industry is forced to grind to a halt? Is it not much more likely, about a century from now, that prices for petroleum will be found to be so high that even the least successful nuclear power companies will find themselves able to sell reactors more easily?

In the same way, is it not likely that the apparently impending scarcity of copper (belied for the time being by the obstinately low price at which the metal is at present marketed) will encourage the use of aluminum as a conductor of electricity? To be sure, as the developing countries gather economic momentum, they will begin to make larger demands on raw materials such as these, yet it does not follow that they will have to repeat in every detail the industrial history of the countries now industrialized, and it remains a comforting truth that the raw materials on which the products of modern industry are based loom less large in economic terms than the products of the Industrial Revolution. Computers, after all, need very little copper for their manufacture. In general, the problem of raw materials is not a problem of the exploitation of a finite resource, however much it might be made to seem as such, but is a problem in economics —how best to regulate the prices of raw materials so as to balance the present demand against the probable demand in the future, how best to encourage what kinds of substitutions, how best to bring into production new reserves (not the least of which are the oceans of the world). Nobody should think that there is nothing to worry about. Good planetary housekeeping, as *The Ecologist* would no doubt describe it, should be an important objective of public policy. But it is a public disservice to describe such intricate and interesting problems in such simple and scarifying terms.

Similar fallacies attend *The Ecologist's* analysis of the supply of food. The document says that food production in the developing world has "barely kept abreast of population growth" and that such increases as there have been are a consequence of the "opening up of new land for cultivation." It goes on to say that this will not be possible for much longer, for "all the good land in the world is now being farmed." Factually, these statements are incorrect. In many parts of Southeast Asia, the past few years have seen dramatic improvements in agricultural productivity, acre for acre. In any case, it remains a fact and even something about which agronomists should hang their heads that tropical regions are still comparatively unproductive of food. But the chief complaint of this declaration is that the "FAO program to feed the world" depends on an intensification of agriculture and that the strains of wheat and rice likely to be the work horses of Asian agriculture are more vulnerable to disease and more demanding of fertilizer.

So what? must surely be the moderate reply. In North America and Western Europe, after all, agriculture is much more intensive than most agricultural practices likely to be common in Asia in the next few years. And the benefits of intensive agriculture are not merely that a given acre of land can produce more food each year but that it can be made to do so at a lower labor cost. Indeed, it might well be calculated that until the populations of the developing world are able to feed themselves without employing more than half of their labor force on the land, they will not be free to develop either along the lines of Western industrialization or along some other route that they might prefer. The fact that intensive agriculture entails crops which are highly specialized and therefore vulnerable to epidemic diseases of one kind or another is no more relevant in Asia than in, for example, North America.

The abiding fault in these discussions is their naivete, and nowhere is this more true than in speculations about the social consequences of the phenomena over which *The Ecologist* wrings its hands. Starting with the assertion that the developed nations have already collared the raw materials with which developing nations might seek to improve their standards of living, the journal goes on to say that "we are altering people's aspirations without providing the means for them to be satisfied. In the rush to industrialize, we break up communities, so that the controls which formerly regulated behavior are destroyed. Urban drift is one result of this process, with a consequent rise in antisocial practices, crime, delinquency and so on. . . ." This is an echo of the distinguished doctors' declaration about the consequences of crowding, but is it fair to describe this, as *The Ecologist* does, as a portent of the collapse of society? Is it reasonable to say that in such circumstances, "it is more than probable that governments will fall into the hands of reckless and unscrupulous elements, who will not hesitate to threaten neighboring governments with attack if they feel they can wrest from them a larger share of the world's vanishing resources?" The truth is, of course, that this is mere speculation. All the attempts which there have been in the past few years to discover correlations between such factors as population density and prosperity per head of population with the tendency to violence, either civil or international, have been fruitless. Who will say that the crowded Netherlands are more violent than the uncrowded United States? And who will say that the forces which have in the past 2000 years helped to make civilized communities more humane can now be dismissed from the calculation simply because a new generation of seers sees catastrophe in the tea leaves?

II. CATASTROPHE OR CHANGE?

Predictably, anxiety about environmental catastrophe has spread to Britain, and it is hard not to remember Professor D. J. Bogue's description of the same phenomenon in the United States as the "nonsense explosion." Many readers of *Nature* appear to have been surprised that a journal which counts Sir Julian Huxley's grandfather as one of its sponsors should have taken such a fierce line on the warnings of environmental catastrophe now commonly to be heard. The truth is that public confusion which has been created in the past few years by warnings of catastrophe is a serious impediment to the rational conduct of society. A part of the difficulty is technical, for whether the prophets are complaining of the hazards of DDT, carbon dioxide in the environment, the threatened exhaustion of natural resources or the growth of population, a proper understanding of what happens and is likely to happen is fraught with uncertainty, complexity and error. Understandably, people at large are puzzled to know what weight to give to warnings of catastrophe around the corner and to assurances that the problems are not nearly as alarming as they are said to be.

The question whether the years immediately ahead will bring catastrophe is not so much technical as philosophical. The document published two weeks ago by *The Ecologist* says that "the principal defect of the industrial way of life . . . is that it is not sustainable. Its termination within the lifetime of somebody born today is inevitable—unless it continues to be sustained for a while longer by an entrenched minority at the cost of imposing great suffering on the rest of mankind." The calculations supposedly implicit in statements like this are that particular resources, petroleum for example, may be seriously depleted on time scales of the order of a century, or that, after a century of unrestricted growth, the population of the world may have grown to such a point that life is intolerable or even insupportable. As yardsticks which show what kinds of problems may in future be important, pieces of arithmetic like this are no doubt of some value. The error in supposing that they constitute a proof of imminent calamity is the assumption that administrative and social mechanisms which exist already or which are in the course of being developed will do nothing to fend them off, but this is to ignore the beneficent tendencies already apparent—the rapid decline of fertility in the past decade in Southeast Asia and the Caribbean and the working of the Classical economic laws of scarcity, originally described by the great Victorians, to strike a balance between exploitation and conservation and the way in which governments in North America and Western Europe have succeeded in improving the quality of urban air and water by laying out money on pollution control. In short, those who prophesy disaster a century or more from now and ask for apocalyptic remedies overlook the way in which important social changes have historically been effected by the accumulation of more modest humane innovations.

In the circumstances, it is not surprising that the remedies suggested for the avoidance of catastrophe are often unpleasantly unrealistic. *The Ecologist's* manifesto may be controversial because of its over-sharp definition of the supposed threat, but it shares with other declarations of this kind the advocacy of thoroughly pernicious changes in the structure of society. It is tempting to ask how many of those who gave their names to the document solemnly consider that industrialized societies such as Britain will be better off if they are organized in small communities in which social mobility is deliberately restricted and in which agriculture is central to everybody's life. Are these not potentially illiberal arrangements? Is there not a serious danger that to strive for them will weaken the will of civilized communities, developed and developing, to work towards humane goals—the removal of poverty and the liberty of the subject?

To Grow and to Die

Anthony Lewis

Anthony Lewis is a Pulitzer-prize-winning journalist with
the *New York Times*.

I

Our diverse worlds—developed, underdeveloped, East, West—have at
least one article of faith in common: economic growth. For individuals,
for economic enterprises and for nations, growth is happiness, the
specific for ills and the foundation of hope. Next year our family will be
richer, our company bigger, our country more productive.

Now the ecologists have begun to tell us that growth is self-defeating,
that the planet cannot long sustain it, that it will lead inevitably to social
and biological collapse. That was the central thesis of the recent "Blueprint for Survival" published in Britain, and it is a theme increasingly
found in analytical studies of the earthly future.

The proposition is so shocking that the natural reaction is to wish it
away. Some economists, the apostles of growth, do just that. There was an
especially acute example of wishfulness in a *Newsweek* column by Henry C.
Wallich, Yale professor and former U.S. economic adviser, condemning
the opposition to growth as dangerous heresy.

"It is an alarming commentary on the intellectual instability of our
times," Professor Wallich said, "that today mileage can be made with the
proposal to stop America dead in her tracks. Don't we know which way
is forward?"

As long as there is growth, he said, "everybody will be happier." By
"allowing everybody to have more" and refusing to "limit resources avail-

able for consumption," we shall also have "more resources" to clean up the environment.

If Professor Wallich's opinion is representative of the American intellectual community, it is an alarming comment on our awareness of the most important facts of life today. For he is evidently in a state of ecological illiteracy.

There are no such things as endless growth and unlimited resources for everyone and everything. We live in a finite world, and we are approaching the limits. Discussion of growth as an environmental factor has to begin with some understanding of such considerations.

The crucial fact is that growth tends to be exponential. That is, it multiplies. Instead of adding a given amount every so often, say 1,000 tons or dollars a year, the factors double at fixed intervals. That tends to be true of population, of industrial production, of pollution and of demand on natural resources—some of the main strains of planetary life.

The rate of increase determines the doubling time. If something grows 7 percent a year, it will double in 10 years. Right now world population is growing 2.1 percent a year; at that rate it doubles in 33 years. And with each doubling, the base is of course larger for the next increase. The world had about 3.5 billion people in it in 1970. At the present rate of increase, it will have 7 billion in 2003.

Exponential growth is a tricky affair. It gives us the illusion for a long time that things are going slowly; then suddenly it speeds up. Suppose the demand for some raw material is two tons this year and doubles every year. Over the next 15 years it will rise to only 32,768 tons, but just 5 years later it will be 1,048,576 tons.

That phenomenon is what makes it so hard for people to understand how rapidly we may be approaching the limits of growth. For as population and per capita consumption both grow, the curves of demand suddenly zoom upward.

Consider the case of aluminum as a sample of resource demand and supply. The known reserves of aluminum are enough to supply the current demand for 100 years. But the use is increasing exponentially, and at the rate of increase the supply will be enough for only 31 years. Moreover, the multiplying demand is a much larger factor, mathematically, than any likely discovery of new sources of supply. If reserves were multiplied by five, the same growth of demand would still exhaust them in 55 years.

The example of aluminum is not especially chosen to disturb, for there are others that even more dramatically indicate the way exponential growth can run up to projected limits. One is simply arable land. At the present rate of world population growth, the supply of land necessary for food production will run out by the year 2000. If agricultural productivity were doubled, the limit would be pushed back 30 years.

II

A hundred years ago John Stuart Mill urged human society to limit its population and wealth and seek "the stationary state." He had a vision of a cramped and depleted earth. He sincerely hoped, he said, that men "will be content to be stationary long before necessity compels them to it."

Mill's was a premature vision, and for a long time hardly anyone shared it. Now, suddenly, impressive scientific evidence is being put to us that necessity compels an early end to the dominant earthly ambition of economic growth. For the exponential growth of population and production is putting strains on our environment that cannot be sustained.

To talk about limiting growth as a philosophical matter is easy enough. But when one begins to consider the specific changes of course that would be required of mankind, the difficulties are soon seen to be enormous. The economic habits of a millennium, the motivations, the very conception of a good society would be affected.

The whole question of equality as a social goal, for example, would be transformed. In most societies, East and West, there are gross inequalities of wealth today. They are made politically tolerable in good part by the notion of the whole economic pie growing constantly larger so that everyone can have a bigger slice. That is why politicians from Brezhnev to Edward Heath promise their constituents faster economic growth.

But what happens if everyone in a society knows that there can be no increase in the total volume of material goods? Is it still bearable that one man has three cars in his garage and another not enough to eat?

Similar considerations affect our traditional view of competition as a motivating economic force. Leading ecologists say we must adopt a policy of no net increase in capital investment from now on—only enough to match depreciation of capital.

But if the United States had such a policy, how could manufacturers compete in the traditional way of more productive machinery? Would it not follow that new forms of social control would have to be imposed on production, on marketing, on advertising? And how would they be squared with our ideas of freedom?

Equality is an issue not only within but between societies. If the ecologists are right, then it is foolish and dangerous for developing countries to dream of having industrial economies and a standard of material wealth like the developed world's.

But how can the rich few advise the poor many that they will be better off forsaking the old material goals? And does not that again imply a change in one's whole view of social organization, toward a less material society on the Chinese model, with enough for everyone to eat but little competition for goods or ease? Does it not follow in international as in national life that an end to growth must not be an imposition by the rich on the poor and hence requires a fresh commitment to a decent level of equality?

Merely to state such problems is to make one thing evident: the complete irrelevance of most of today's political concerns to the most important problem facing the world in the long run. And not very long at that.

A World Without Growth?

Henry C. Wallich

Henry C. Wallich, formerly a member of the President's
Council of Economic Advisers, is a member of the Board
of Governors of the Federal Reserve System.

Anthony Lewis, in two recent issues of The New York *Times*, warns us of the deadly consequences of growth. Running out of resources, running into total pollution, running to the point of total exhaustion and collapse—those are the ultimate rewards of growth. We must stop growth, not just of population, but of production and income.

The group of ecologists who generated this well-meaning scare are members of an old club. Its founder, the Rev. Thomas Malthus, issued dire warnings of inevitable starvation in 1798. This having proved a poor bet, the emphasis today shifts to a dearth of all natural resources and mounting pollution.

It does not take an ecologist to explain that if the world's population doubles every so many years, after a while there will be Standing Room Only, at least on the surface of this planet. Likewise, it is fairly obvious that if we deplete existing resources without discovering new sources, developing methods of recycling, and inventing substitutes, we shall some day run out. But perhaps an economist can be helpful in clarifying why these problems are not top priority today.

In the first place, the economy will simply substitute things that are plentiful for things that become scarce. If we run out of aluminum, the price of aluminum will go up. That will encourage manufacturers to use something else, and will stimulate research and development to produce substitutes.

Some scientists believe that matter and energy are fundamentally interchangeable in many forms, but as a layman, I would not bet on any near-term miracles. The simple processes of economics will keep us going. If they don't, the ecologists' advice to slow down will not be worth much—it would only postpone the day of disaster without avoiding it.

In the course of centuries, more basic adjustments will probably be needed. Population may stop growing, production may stop growing. The chances are that the world will adapt to the changing environment gradually. Lack of space will cause families to shrink, if families then still exist. Great per capita income will reduce interest in producing and consuming more. We do not need to rely on "misery," as the Rev. Malthus thought, to bring about the adjustment.

The real question is at what time this transition will have to be faced. New York restaurants carry signs to the effect that occupancy by more than some maximum number is unlawful. If half a dozen persons were to gather in an otherwise empty restaurant with such a sign and discuss heatedly the urgency of keeping newcomers out, they would be in something like the position of Americans debating the zero growth notion. To stop growing now, generations before the real problems of growth arise if ever, would be to commit suicide for fear of remote death.

The ecologists do not seem to be aware of what it would mean to freeze total income anywhere near today's level. Do they mean that the present income distribution is to be preserved, with the poor frozen into their inadequacies? Would that go for the underdeveloped countries too? Or do they have in mind an equalization of incomes? It will take pretty drastic cuts in upper income bracket standards to bring them down to the average American family income of about $10,000, to say nothing of a cut to average world income. We can and perhaps should approach this condition over generations. Trying to do it quickly would create completely needless problems.

The ecologists also do not seem to be aware of what their prescriptions, contrary to their wishes, might do to the environment. If growth came to a halt, it is obvious that every last penny of public and private income would be drawn upon to provide minimal consumer satisfactions. There would be very little left for the cleaning-up job that needs to be done. Growth is the main source from which that job must be financed.

I would like to end with a quote from my *Newsweek* column on which Mr. Lewis commented. "A world without growth, that is, without change, is as hard for us to imagine as a world of everlasting growth and change. Somewhere in the dim future, if humanity does not blow itself up, there may lie a world in which physical change will be minimal . . . hopefully a much more humane and less materialistic world. We shall not live to see it."

The Club of Rome Model

W. E. Schiesser

W. E. Schiesser is a professor at the Computer Center
and Department of Chemical Engineering, Lehigh
University.

The mathematical modeling and computer analysis of economic and
social systems, epitomized by the Club of Rome world model, has developed rapidly in the last decade. This activity, which has arisen because
of the need to better understand the evolution of our complex, highly
structured society, has become possible with the availability of powerful
computers which provide solutions to large, complex mathematical models. However, until recently the quantitative analysis of economic and
social systems has been essentially limited to studies of segments of society, such as the operations of a corporation, the growth and decay of an
urban area or the development of a particular industry. The Club of
Rome model is the first attempt to analyze the evolution of the entire
world system. The model provides long-term projections of such major
factors as world population, pollution, per capita food supply, natural
resource utilization and capital investment. The model and its computer
output have received widespread comment, both favorable and unfavorable. Much of the reaction has been based on an incomplete understanding
of the model and how it generates numerical results.[1]

The availability of computers was a prerequisite for the development of
the Club of Rome model because the model equations are sufficiently

---

[1] The author has available a FORTRAN IV computer program for the global model which
can be executed on essentially any computer if one wishes to obtain an in-depth understanding of the model.

Excerpted from W. E. Schiesser, "The Club of Rome Model," in Andrew Weintraub, Eli Schwartz, J. Richard
Aronson, eds., The Economic Growth Controversy (White Plains, N.Y. International Arts and Sciences
Press, 1973), pp. 219–21; 224–29. Copyright © 1973 by International Arts and Sciences Press, Inc. Re-
printed by permission.

complex and nonlinear so that they cannot be solved by analytical methods that one might use, for example, to solve a set of linear algebraic equations. Rather, a numerical step-by-step procedure is used to compute the time-evolution of variables such as the world's population and per capita food supply. Furthermore, since all of the major variables of the model are interrelated in a complex structure, the complete set of equations must be solved simultaneously. Consequently, the number of numerical operations required to move the model through time is very large and can only be done practically through the use of a computer.

With this in mind, perhaps it would be helpful here to provide a brief historical perspective of the Club of Rome model and to discuss some of the output of the global model.

The Club of Rome is a group of internationally prominent individuals who have met informally since 1968 to discuss what they consider to be certain alarming developments in the world today. Specifically, the Club of Rome is interested in the analysis of the evolving world system and especially such trends as the growing world population and level of pollution, the depletion of natural resources, and the need for an ever-increasing food supply. In order to obtain a better overall perspective of these trends, the Club of Rome commissioned Professor Jay W. Forrester of MIT to undertake a quantitative analysis of the world system. In particular, the Club sought a comprehensive analysis which would include the interaction of all major factors which affect the evolving world system. This approach was new at the time and stood in contradistinction to the piecemeal approach which had characterized quantitative economic model-building up to that time.

Professor Forrester was eminently qualified to undertake such a study since he had pioneered the field of "systems dynamics" in which mathematical modeling and computer simulation are applied to the quantitative analysis of complex systems. Forrester's analysis resulted in a preliminary model, generally termed World 2, which is thoroughly described and documented in his book *World Dynamics*[2]. World 2 contains as the major worldwide outputs: (1) population, (2) pollution level, (3) level of natural resources, (4) total capital investment, (5) capital investment in agriculture, and (6) "quality of life." The latter is an arbitrarily defined quantity which essentially reflects human well-being in terms of a composite of material standards, food supply, crowding and pollution.

[2] The World 2 model and the summary of Forrester's conclusions which follow are reprinted with permission of Wright-Allen Press, Inc., Cambridge, Mass.

The World 2 model is highly simplified, is based essentially on assumed relationships (rather than relationships based on data), and is highly aggregated (i.e., no attempt is made, for example, to distinguish between segments of the world's population on the basis of the relative availability of capital, wealth, etc.). These features of the model have all been the basis for criticism. However, the model is the first of its kind and therefore can be viewed as a pioneering effort that should be refined and extended to increase its realism and reliability with respect to the accuracy of the long-term projections.

There has been much criticism of the model. But critics should realize that the initial effort to model the world system should logically be limited in detail so that it can be implemented with reasonable effort and the results can be obtained within a reasonable period of time. If the initial results are judged to be interesting and worthwhile, there is justification for additional work. Clearly, it would be difficult to attempt to model in detail every aspect of the world system, since much of the required information is unavailable; moreover, such a rigorous requirement would make even the initial results impossible to achieve. To reason by analogy, one could argue that Henry Ford's first car should have looked like the Ford cars which now roll off the assembly line. Obviously it required many years of research and development before the industry learned how to build today's cars. Similarly, continuing development of the global model will be required to give it essential detail and realism.

Another point of criticism (and also a source of confusion) is the fact that two global models have been discussed in the open literature. Professor Meadows and a group of coworkers, also at MIT, extended the Forrester model. The output of this model, called World 3, forms the basis of the much publicized book *The Limits to Growth*. Unfortunately, the technical details of World 3 are described quite superficially in *The Limits to Growth*. The situation is analogous to one in which a scientist reports a series of experimental results without indicating how the results were obtained. Other scientists who are interested in the work cannot verify the reported results by repeating the experiments or extend the results through additional research. The technical details (i.e., the equations) of the World 3 model were published several years after the original publication of *The Limits to Growth* (see Meadows, Dennis L., et al., *Dynamics of Growth in a Finite World*, Cambridge, Mass.: Wright–Allen Press, 1974).

The structure of a relatively detailed global model consists of a complex interconnection of "feedback loops." . . . A detailed discussion of (these "feedback loops") is not possible here. One can say, however, that the information and predictions generated by the model yield little hope for continuing increases in our present standard of living beyond the year

2100. Indeed, many disamenities begin to show themselves much sooner. Figure 1, for example, is a graphic depiction which shows the "quality of life" steadily declining in the future, the decline resulting from the depletion of natural resources. Figure 2, however, depicts a model which assumes that the rate at which natural resources are used up can be reduced, and that the decline in the "quality of life" is not as precipitous.

The two examples of the model output in Figures 1 and 2 are not isolated cases, but rather are typical of the serious degradation or total collapse of the world system as projected by the model. Generally, whenever one source of pressure which causes worldwide catastrophe is relieved, another source develops, usually a relatively short time later, to also cause eventual collapse. This general mode of response of the World 2 model has been summarized by Forrester in *World Dynamics* (pp. 11–13):

1. Industrialization may be a more fundamental disturbing force in world ecology than is population. In fact, the population explosion is perhaps best viewed as a result of technology and industrialization. (Medicine and public health are included here as a part of industrialization.)

2. Within the next century, man may face choices from a four-pronged dilemma—suppression of modern industrial society by a natural-resource

Figure 1   Response of the World 2 Model with the depletion of natural resources.

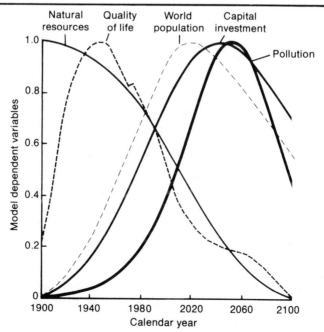

Figure 2 Response of the World 2 Model for the pollution crisis case: depletion of natural resources rate reduced by 75 percent relative to Figure 1.

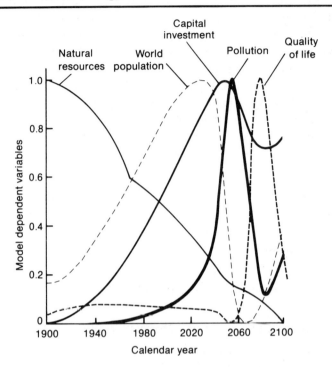

shortage; decline of world population from changes wrought by pollution; population limitation by food shortage; or population collapse from war, disease, and social stresses caused by physical and psychological crowding.

3. We may now be living in a "golden age" when, in spite of a widely acknowledged feeling of malaise, the quality of life is, on the average, higher than ever before in history and higher now than the future offers.

4. Exhortations and programs directed at population control may be inherently self-defeating. If population control begins to result, as hoped, in higher per capita food supply and material standard of living, these very improvements may relax the pressures and generate forces to trigger a resurgence of population growth.

5. The high standard of living of modern industrial societies seems to result from a production of food and material goods that has been able to outrun the rising population. But, as agriculture reaches a space limit, as industrialization reaches a natural-resource limit, and as both reach a pollution limit, population tends to catch up. Population then grows until the "quality of life" falls far enough to stabilize population.

6. There may be no realistic hope of the present underdeveloped countries reaching the standard of living demonstrated by the present industrialized nations. The pollution and natural-resource load placed on the world environmental system by each person in an advanced country is probably 20 to 50 times greater than the load now generated by a person in an underdeveloped country. With 4 times as many people in underdeveloped countries as in the present developed countries, their rising to the economic level that has been set as a standard by the industrialized nations could mean an increase of 10 times in the natural-resource and pollution load on the world environment. Noting the destruction that has already occurred on land, in the air, and especially in the oceans, capability appears not to exist for handling such a rise in standard of living. In fact, the present disparity between the developed and underdeveloped nations may be equalized as much by a decline in the developed countries as by an improvement in the underdeveloped countries.

7. A society with a high level of industrialization may be nonsustainable. It may be self-extinguishing if it exhausts the natural resources on which it depends. Or, if unending substitution for declining natural resources were possible, a new international strife over pollution and environmental rights might pull the average world-wide standard of living back to the level of a century ago.

8. From the long view of a hundred years hence, the present efforts of underdeveloped countries to industrialize may be unwise. They may now be closer to an ultimate equilibrium with the environment than are the industrialized nations. The present underdeveloped countries may be in a better condition for surviving forthcoming world-wide environmental and economic pressures than are the advanced countries. If one of the several forces strong enough to cause a collapse in world population does arise, the underdeveloped countries might suffer far less than their share of the decline because economies with less organization, integration, and specialization are probably less vulnerable to disruption.

These pessimistic conclusions are clearly tied to the potential problems of unrestricted growth. The Club of Rome report, embodied in the quantitative studies of Forrester and Meadows, has dramatically called these problems to the attention of the world society. Much additional research now remains to be done. The models must be developed and refined to improve their reliability. Nevertheless, if the principal results remain essentially unaltered, we must face their critical economic, sociological and ecological implications for the future world society.

Is the End of the World at Hand?

Robert M. Solow

Robert M. Solow, an economist of wide-ranging accomplishments, is Professor of Economics at the Massachusetts Institute of Technology.

There is, as you know, a school of thought that claims that continued economic growth is in fact not possible any more, or at least not for very long. This judgment has been expressed more or less casually by several observers in recent years. What distinguishes the Doomsday Models from their predecessors is that they claim to much more than a casual judgment: they deduce their beliefs about future prospects from mathematical models or systems analysis. They don't merely say that the end of the world is at hand—they can show you computer output that says the same thing.

Characteristically, the Doomsday Models do more than just say that continued economic growth is impossible. They tell us why: in brief, because (a) the earth's natural resources will soon be used up; (b) increased industrial production will soon strangle us in pollution; and (c) increasing population will eventually outrun the world's capacity to grow food, so that famine must eventually result. And, finally, the models tell us one more thing: the world will end with a bang, not a whimper. The natural evolution of the world economy is not at all toward some kind of smooth approach to its natural limits, wherever they are. Instead, it is inevitable—unless we make drastic changes in the way we live and organize ourselves—that the world will overshoot any level of population and production it can possibly sustain and will then collapse, probably by the middle of the next century.

Excerpted from Robert M. Solow, "Is the End of the World at Hand?" in Andrew Weintraub, Eli Schwartz, J. Richard Aronson, eds., *The Economic Growth Controversy* (White Plains, N.Y.: International Arts and Sciences Press, Inc., 1973), pp. 46–49; 52–61. Copyright © 1973 by International Arts and Sciences Press, Inc. Reprinted by permission.

I would like to say why I think that the Doomsday Models are bad science and therefore bad guides to public policy. I hope nobody will conclude that I believe the problems of population control, environmental degradation and resource exhaustion to be unimportant, or that I am one of those people who believe that an adequate response to such problems is a vague confidence that some technological solution will turn up. On the contrary, it is precisely because these are important problems that public policy had better be based on sound and careful analysis. I want to explain some of my reasons for believing that the global models don't provide even the beginnings of a foundation of that kind.

The first thing to realize is that the characteristic conclusion of the Doomsday Models is very near the surface. It is, in fact, more nearly an assumption than a conclusion, in the sense that the chain of logic from the assumptions to the conclusion is very short and rather obvious.

The basic assumption is that stocks of things like the world's natural resources and the waste-disposal capacity of the environment are finite, that the world economy tends to consume the stock at an increasing rate (through the mining of minerals and the production of goods), and that there are no built-in mechanisms by which approaching exhaustion tends to turn off consumption gradually and in advance. You hardly need a giant computer to tell you that a system with those behavior rules is going to bounce off its ceiling and collapse to a low level. Then, in case anyone is inclined to relax into the optimistic belief that maybe things aren't that bad, we are told: Imagine that the stock of natural resources were actually twice as big as the best current evidence suggests, or imagine that the annual amount of pollution could be halved all at once and then set to growing again. All that would happen is that the date of collapse would be postponed by T years, where T is not a large number. But once you grasp the quite simple essence of the models, this should come as no surprise. It is important to realize where these powerful conclusions come from, because, if you ask yourself "Why didn't I realize earlier that the end of the world was at hand?" the answer is not that you weren't clever enough to figure it out for yourself. The answer is that the imminent end of the world is an immediate deduction from certain assumptions, and one must really ask if the assumptions are any good.

It is a commonplace that if you calculate the annual output of any production process, large or small, and divide it by the annual employment of labor, you get a ratio that is called the productivity of labor. At the most aggregative level, for example, we can say that the GNP in 1971 was $1,050 billion and that about 82 million people were employed in producing it, so that GNP per worker or the productivity of a year of labor was about $12,800. Symmetrically, though the usage is less common, one could just as well calculate the GNP per unit of some particular natural resource and call that the productivity of coal, or GNP per pound of vanadium. We usually think of the productivity of labor as rising more or less exponentially, say at 2 or 3 percent a year, because that is the way it has in fact behaved over the past century or so since the statistics began to be collected. The rate of increase in the productivity of labor is not a constant of nature. Sometimes it is faster, sometimes slower. For example, we know that labor productivity must have increased more slowly a long time ago, because if we extrapolate backward at 2 percent a year, we come to a much lower labor productivity in 1492 than can possibly have been the case. And the productivity of labor has risen faster in the past twenty-five years than in the fifty years before that. It also varies from place to place, being faster in Japan and Germany and slower in Great Britain, for reasons that are not at all certain. But it rises, and we expect it to keep rising.

Now, how about the productivity of natural resources? All the Doomsday Models will allow is a one-time hypothetical increase in the world supply of natural resources, which is the equivalent of a one-time increase in the productivity of natural resources. Why shouldn't the productivity of most natural resources rise more or less steadily through time, like the productivity of labor? . . .

SCARCITY AND THE PRICE SYSTEM

There is at least one reason for believing that the Doomsday story is almost certainly wrong. The most glaring defect of the Forrester-Meadows models is the absence of any sort of functioning price system. I am no believer that the market is always right, and I am certainly no advocate of *laissez-faire* where the environment is concerned. But the price system is, after all, the main social institution evolved by capitalist economies (and, to an increasing extent, socialist economies too) for registering and reacting to relative scarcity. There are several ways in which the working of the price system will push our society into faster and more systematic increases in the productivity of natural resources.

First of all, [consider] the analogy between natural resources and labor. We are not surprised to learn that industry quite consciously tries to make inventions that save labor, i.e., permit the same product to be made with fewer man-hours of work. After all, on the average, labor costs amount to almost three-fourths of all costs in our economy. An invention that reduces labor requirements per unit of GNP by 1 percent reduces all costs by about 0.75 percent. Natural resource costs are a much smaller proportion of total GNP, something nearer 5 percent. So industry and engineering have a much stronger motive to reduce labor requirements by 1 percent than to reduce resource requirements by 1 percent, assuming —which may or may not be true—that it is about as hard to do one as to do the other. But then, as the earth's supply of particular natural resources nears exhaustion, and as natural resources become more and more valuable, the motive to economize those natural resources should become as strong as the motive to economize labor. The productivity of resources should rise faster than now—it is hard to imagine otherwise.

There are other ways in which the market mechanism can be expected to push us all to economize on natural resources as they become scarcer. Higher and rising prices of exhaustible resources lead competing producers to substitute other materials that are more plentiful and therefore cheaper. To the extent that it is impossible to design around or find substitutes for expensive natural resources, the price of commodities that contain a lot of them will rise relative to the prices of other goods and services that don't use up a lot of resources. Consumers will be driven to buy fewer resource-intensive goods and more of other things. All these effects work automatically to increase the productivity of natural resources, i.e., to reduce resource requirements per unit of GNP.

As I mentioned a moment ago, this is not an argument for *laissez-faire*. We may feel that the private decisions of buyers and sellers give inadequate representation to future generations. Or we may feel that private interests are in conflict with a distinct public interest—strip-mining of coal is an obvious case in point, and there are many others as soon as we begin to think about environmental effects. Private market responses may be too uncoordinated, too slow, based on insufficient and faulty information. In every case there will be actions that public agencies can take and should take; and it will be a major political struggle to see that they are taken. But I don't see how one can have the slightest confidence in the predictions of models that seem to make no room for the operation of everyday market forces. If the forecasts are wrong, then so are the policy implications, to the extent that there are any realistic policy implications.

Every analysis of resource scarcity has to come to terms with the fact that the prices of natural resources and resource products have not shown any tendency to rise over the past half century, relative to the prices of other things. This must mean that there have so far been adequate offsets to any progressive impoverishment of deposits—like improvements in the technology of extraction, savings in end uses, or the availability of cheaper substitutes. The situation could, of course, change; and very likely some day it will. If the experienced and expert participants in the market now believed that resource prices would be sharply higher at some foreseeable time, prices would *already* be rising, as I will try to explain in a moment. The historical steadiness of resource prices suggests that buyers and sellers in the market have not been acting as if they foresaw exhaustion in the absence of substitutes, and therefore sharply higher future prices. They may turn out to be wrong; but the Doomsday Models give us absolutely no reason to expect that—in fact, they claim to get whatever meager empirical basis they have from such experts.

Why is it true that if the market saw higher prices in the future, prices would already be rising? It is a rather technical point, but I want to explain it because, in a way, it summarizes the important thing about natural resources: conserving a mineral deposit is just as much of an investment as building a factory, and it has to be analyzed that way. Any owner of a mineral deposit owns a valuable asset, whether the owner is a private capitalist or the government of an underdeveloped country. The asset is worth keeping only if at the margin it earns a return equal to that earned on other kinds of assets. A factory produces things each year of its life, but a mineral deposit just lies there: its owner can realize a return only if he either mines the deposit or if it *increases in value*. So if you are sitting on your little pile of X and confidently expect to be able to sell it for a very high price in the year 2000 because it will be very scarce by then, you must be earning your 5 percent a year, or 10 percent a year, or whatever the going rate of return is, each year between now and 2000. The only way this can happen is for the value of X to go up by 5 percent a year or 10 percent a year. And that means that anyone who wants to use any X any time between now and 2000 will have to pay a price for it that is rising at that same 5 percent or 10 percent a year. Well, it's not happening. Of course we are exploiting our hoard of exhaustible resources; we have no choice about that. We are certainly exploiting it wastefully, in the sense that we allow each other to dump waste products into the environment without full accounting for costs. But there is very little evidence that we are exploiting it too fast.

POPULATION GROWTH

I have less to say about the question of population growth because it does not seem to involve any difficult conceptual problems. At any time, in any place, there is presumably an optimal size of population—with the property that the average person would be somewhat worse off if the population were a bit larger, and also worse off if the population were a bit smaller. In any real case it must be very difficult to know what the optimum population is, especially because it will change over time as technology changes, and also because it is probably more like a band or zone than a sharply defined number. I mean that if you could somehow plot a graph of economic welfare per person against population size, there would be a very gentle dome or plateau at the top, rather than a sharp peak.

I don't intend to guess what the optimal population for the United States may be. But I am prepared to hazard the guess that there is no point in opting for a perceptibly larger population than we now have, and we might well be content with a slightly smaller one. (I want to emphasize the likelihood that a 15 percent larger or 15 percent smaller population would make very little difference in our standard of well-being. I also want to emphasize that I am talking only about our own country. The underdeveloped world offers very special problems.) My general reason for believing that we should not want a substantially larger population is this. We all know the bad consequences of too large a population: crowding, congestion, excessive pollution, the disappearance of open space —that is why the curve of average well-being eventually turns down at large population sizes. Why does the curve ever climb to a peak in the first place? The generic reason is what economists call economies of scale, because it takes a population of a certain size and density to support an efficient chemical industry, or publishing industry, or symphony orchestra, or engineering university, or airline, or computer hardware and software industry, especially if you would like several firms in each, so that they can be partially regulated by their own competition. But after all, it only takes a population of a *certain* size or density to get the benefit of these economies of scale. And I'm prepared to guess that the U.S. economy is already big enough to do so; I find it hard to believe that sheer efficiency would be much served in the United States by having a larger market.

As it happens, recent figures seem to show that the United States is heading for a stationary population: that is to say, the current generation of parents seems to be establishing fertility patterns that will, if continued, cause the population to stabilize some time during the next century. Even so, the absolute size of the population will increase for a while, and level off higher than it is now, because decades of population growth have left us with a bulge of population in the childbearing ages. But I have already argued that a few million more or less hardly make a difference; and a population that has once stabilized might actually decrease, if that came to seem desirable.

At the present moment, at least for the United States, the danger of rapid population growth seems to be the wrong thing to worry about. The main object of public policy in this field ought to be to ensure that the choice of family size is truly a voluntary choice, that access to the best birth-control methods be made universal. That seems to be all that is needed. Of course, we know very little about what governs fertility, about why the typical notion of a good family size changes from generation to generation. So it is certainly possible that these recent developments will reverse themselves and that population control will again appear on the agenda of public policy. This remains to be seen.

In all this I have said nothing about the Doomsday Models because there is practically nothing that needs to be said. So far as we can tell, they make one very bad mistake: in the face of reason, common sense and systematic evidence they seem to assume that at high standards of living, people want more children as they become more affluent (though over most of the observed range, a higher standard of living goes along with smaller families). That is certainly a bad error in terms of the recent American data—but perhaps it explains why some friends of mine were able to report that they had run a version of the Forrester World Dynamic Model starting with a population of two people and discovered that it blew up in 500 years. Apart from placing the date of the Garden of Eden in the fifteenth century, what else is new?

There is another analytical error in the models. . . . Suppose resource exhaustion and increased pollution conspire to bring about a reduction in industrial production. The model then says that birth rates will rise because, in the past, low industrial output has been associated with high birth rates. But there is nothing in historical evidence to suggest that a once-rich country will go *back* to high birth rates if (as I doubt will happen) its standard of living falls from an accustomed high level. Common sense suggests that a society in such a position would fight to preserve its standard of living by reducing the desired family size. In any case, this is another example of a poorly founded—or unfounded—assumption introduced to support the likelihood of overshoot-and-collapse.

PAYING FOR POLLUTION

Resource exhaustion and overpopulation: that leaves pollution as the last of the Doomsday Devils. The subject is worth a whole lecture in itself, because it is one of those problems about which economists actually have something important to say to the world, not just to each other. But I must be brief. Fine print aside, I think that what one gets from the Doomsday literature is the notion that air and water and noise pollution are an inescapable accompaniment of economic growth, especially industrial growth. If that is true, then to be against pollution is to be against growth. I realize that in putting the matter so crudely I have been unjust; nevertheless, that is the message that comes across. I think that way of looking at the pollution problem is wrong.

A correct analysis goes something like this. Excessive pollution and degradation of the environment certainly accompany industrial growth and the increasing population density that goes with it. But they are by no means an inescapable byproduct. Excessive pollution occurs because of an important flaw in the price system. Factories, power plants, municipal sewers, drivers of cars, strip-miners of coal and deep-miners of coal, and all sorts of generators of waste are allowed to dump that waste into the environment, into the atmosphere and into running water and the oceans, without paying the full cost of what they do. No wonder they do too much. So would you, and so would I. In fact, we actually do—directly as drivers of cars, indirectly as we buy some products at a price which is lower than it ought to be because the producer is not required to pay for using the environment to carry away his wastes, and even more indirectly as we buy things that are made with things that pollute the environment.

This flaw in the price system exists because a scarce resource (the waste-disposal capacity of the environment) goes unpriced; and that happens because it is owned by all of us, as it should be. The flaw can be corrected, either by the simple expedient of regulating the discharge of wastes to the environment by direct control or by the slightly more complicated device of charging special prices—user taxes—to those who dispose of wastes in air or water. These effluent charges do three things: they make pollution-intensive goods expensive, and so reduce the consumption of them; they make pollution-intensive methods of production costly, and so promote abatement of pollution by producers; they generate revenue that can, if desired, be used for the further purification of air or water or for other environmental improvements. Most economists prefer this device of effluent charges to regulation by direct order. This is more than an occupational peculiarity. Use of the price system has certain advantages in efficiency and decentralization. Imposing a physical limit on, say, sulfur dioxide emission is, after all, a little peculiar. It says that you may do so much of a bad thing and pay nothing for the privilege, but after that the price is infinite. Not surprisingly, one can find a more efficient schedule of pollution abatement through a more sensitive tax schedule.

But this difference of opinion is minor compared with the larger point that needs to be made. The annual cost that would be necessary to meet decent pollution-abatement standards by the end of the century is large, but not staggering. One estimate says that in 1970 we spent about $8.5

billion (in 1967 prices), or 1 percent of GNP, for pollution abatement. An active pollution-abatement policy would cost perhaps $50 billion a year by 2000, which would be about 2 percent of GNP by then. That is a small investment of resources: you can see how small it is when you consider that GNP grows by 4 percent or so every year, on the average. Cleaning up air and water would entail a cost that would be a bit like losing one-half of one year's growth between now and the year 2000. What stands between us and a decent environment is not the curse of industrialization, not an unbearable burden of cost, but just the need to organize ourselves consciously to do some simple and knowable things. Compared with the possibility of an active abatement policy, the policy of stopping economic growth in order to stop pollution would be incredibly inefficient. It would not actually accomplish much, because one really wants to reduce the amount of, say, hydrocarbon emission to a third or a half of *what it is now*. And what no-growth would accomplish, it would do by cutting off your face to spite your nose.

In the end, that is really my complaint about the Doomsday school. It diverts attention from the really important things that can actually be done, step by step, to make things better. The end of the world *is* at hand—the earth, if you take the long view, will fall into the sun in a few billion years anyway, unless some other disaster happens first. In the meantime, I think we'd be better off trying to pass a strong sulfur-emissions tax, or getting some Highway Trust Fund money allocated to mass transit, or building a humane and decent floor under family incomes, or overriding President Nixon's veto of a strong Water Quality Act, or reforming the tax system, or fending off starvation in Bengal —instead of worrying about the generalized "predicament of mankind."

GREAT DEBATE FIVE

ENERGY AND GROWTH

ENERGY AND
GROWTH

IN THE course of the previous debate on the limits to growth, comments
were frequently made about the exhaustibility of certain natural resources,
including particularly petroleum and other energy resources. This debate,
therefore, is to a degree simply a specific aspect of the growth-antigrowth debate.
However, the issues are not the same in every respect. For example, the authors of
the "Blueprint for Survival" argue that unlimited sources of energy, if discovered,
would only worsen the global growth problem because of the enormous pollution
and waste consequences that boundless energy would bring (p. 147).

Furthermore, the "energy crisis" of 1973–1974 brought energy problems to the fore
as a national concern of considerable dimensions in their own right. At that same
time, the Ford Foundation was bringing out (at a well-publicized cost of $4 million)
an elaborate report on America's energy future. The authors of this report, *A Time
to Choose,* hoped that their work would spark a nationwide discussion of energy
policies, and it did almost immediately. A number of economists had within a few
months published a rebuttal to the Ford report, calling it *No Time to Confuse.* Some
commentators found the Ford report an "important document . . . worth the serious
concern of the country" (p. 215); another commentator found it "so fatally dosed
with economic error, fallacy, and confusion . . . as to border on dishonesty" (p.
217). So the sides were drawn, and a new great debate was underway.

ROLE OF PROJECTIONS IN THE FORD REPORT

Although the Ford report deals to some degree with the specifics of the energy
crisis of 1973–74—the joining together of the (mainly Arab) oil-producing nations in
the Organization of Petroleum Exporting Countries (OPEC), the temporary embargo
on oil exports to the United States in 1973, the quadrupling of oil prices in 1973–74

and the associated industrial, employment and balance-of-payments problems then arising—its main concern is with the long-term growth of energy consumption in this country, and with the options open to us over the next two or three decades.

In this connection, they employ three projections or "scenarios," as they call them, reflecting different patterns of energy consumption over the years 1970 to 2000. The first of these is called the *historical growth scenario*. It is based essentially on the "continuation of recent trends" in the American economy.[1] This does not mean that the economy in year 2000 is assumed to have exactly the same structure as at present. Various developments, evident at the present time, affect the trends within this scenario. Present low fertility rates imply a gradual slowdown of the rate of population increase and therefore of the increase in the labor force and GNP; inflation is expected to take place at about 3.75 percent per year (slower than the present rate, but faster than the rate over the last 10 to 15 years); electricity output is expected to grow much more rapidly than GNP, manufacturing at about the same rate as GNP, services and government faster and agriculture and construction slower than GNP; and other similar projections. In other words, the historical growth scenario does not assume that the economy in year 2000 is simply the 1970 economy writ larger, but that it is modified by certain changes already in prospect. It also assumes that the energy for this path—through domestic production and/or imports—is, in fact, available in sufficient quantity to permit these historical growth rates to occur.

The second scenario is called the *technical fix scenario*. This scenario is designed to bring out the impact of large price increases for petroleum products and electricity on projected patterns of economic growth. Say that the energy resources assumed in the historical growth scenario are not available because of unfavorable domestic and international supply conditions. This would result in substantial increases in the prices of oil and electricity, which, in turn, would lead to a different pattern of growth in the economy as a whole. Energy savings in response to higher prices would occur in the consumer sectors (smaller cars, better home insulation, and so on) and in the producing sectors (for example, substitution of labor for energy-using capital goods). The curtailment of energy supplies could be expected to slow down the growth of GNP to some degree and also, because of higher fuel and electricity prices, to increase the rate of inflation.

The third and final projection is called the *zero energy growth* scenario, athough, as is evident from Figure 1 (p. 197), energy consumption continues to increase on this scenario until near the end of the century when zero growth finally takes over. This scenario is produced by adding to the technical fix scenario an energy sales tax (3.3 percent in 1985 and 15 percent in 2000), and this has two major effects. First, the further increase in the cost of energy discourages the use of energy by

[1] Energy Policy Project of the Ford Foundation, *A Time to Choose: America's Energy Future* (Cambridge, Mass.: Ballinger Publishing Co., 1974), Appendix F, p. 497. The comments in the above section on the assumptions behind the three energy growth scenarios are based on Appendix F, prepared by Edward A. Hudson and Dale W. Jorgenson for Data Resources, Inc.

Table 1. Summary of differences between growth paths (percentage difference in the level of each variable between growth paths)

	Historical Growth vs. Technical Fix		Historical Growth vs. Zero Energy Growth		Technical Fix vs. Zero Energy Growth	
	1985	2000	1985	2000	1985	2000
Real GNP	−1.64	−3.78	−1.61	−3.54	0.03	0.25
Price of GNP	2.00	4.81	2.26	6.03	0.25	1.17
Employment	0.90	1.52	1.25	3.32	0.35	1.77
Capital input	−1.02	−1.83	−0.88	−1.17	0.15	0.67
Energy input	−16.60	−37.70	−19.30	−46.10	−3.20	−13.40

both consumers and industry. Second, the government is assumed to spend the revenues from this tax ($131 billion in year 2000—$50 billion at today's prices) on such things as health and education, thus encouraging the demand for labor and services, and further reducing the demand for energy.

A convenient way of looking at these three scenarios is through Table 1, taken from p. 494, Appendix F of the Ford Report. The way to read this table is as follows: Take, for example, the second column of figures. What it says is that if the economy follows the path of the technical fix scenario as opposed to the historical growth scenario, then, in the year 2000, our real GNP (total physical output) will be 3.78 percent lower than it would have been under the historical growth pattern, our price level will be 4.81 percent higher, our employed labor force will be 1.52 percent higher, our use of capital goods will be 1.83 percent lower, and our consumption of energy will be a substantial 37.70 percent lower.

One interesting comparison is that between technical fix and zero energy growth. According to this table, GNP actually grows faster under zero energy growth than under technical fix. The reason for this is essentially that the government is using its tax revenues to purchase nonenergy intensive goods and services; this change in final demand slightly more than counterbalances the constraints on growth caused by the reduced consumption of energy.

CRITIQUE OF THE SCENARIOS

The Ford report concludes with a favorable assessment of the technical fix and especially the zero energy growth scenarios as opposed to the historical growth scenario. They are also in favor of substantial governmental action to produce a redirection of our energy consumption patterns.

But, first, we have to ask about the significance of the scenarios themselves. How valid are these tools? Alchian regards them as *"at best,* worthless for identifying or understanding energy issues" (p. 217).[2] Kahn feels that they are labeled in a highly misleading way. The technical fix is closer to a scenario reflecting historical forces; Ford's historical growth scenario is more properly labeled "naive" (p. 232).

The basic problem is that although the historical growth scenario reflects certain ongoing historical trends, it does not reflect certain other developments, including especially the fact that oil is much more expensive now that it was a few years ago and that a rise in the price of energy resources is a predictable response of a market economy to energy shortages if, in fact, such shortages occur. Kahn feels that the way the report projects its historical growth scenario is like taking the rate of growth of a 6-year-old boy as a given trend and then asking how tall he would be at age 16, 20 and 50. A *proper* historical growth scenario in this case would take into account the natural factors that would limit the boy's growth rate in future years. Since Kahn feels that the present higher prices of energy and the ability of the economy to make upward price adjustments to energy shortages are part of the natural historical pattern of our society, he argues that they should be included (like the forces limiting a boy's growth rate) in any properly historical projection. For this reason, he believes that the technical fix scenario is actually closer to a "business-as-usual or historical forces scenario" than is the Ford-labeled historical growth scenario (p. 232).

Further, Kahn feels that the zero growth scenario is also misleading. It incorporates within it important government actions—taxing energy at high rates and spending this revenue in a certain pattern—that are controversial at best. Indeed, he considers this particular outcome highly improbable because "it assumes that the government will be willing to interfere in American life for a period long after the crisis ends, for the sake of attitudes and ideologies that are not widely shared" (p. 233). In short, none of the three scenarios seems very enlightening in the eyes of these particular commentators.

ROLE OF PRICES AND MARKETS

A crucial issue, as is apparent from the above, is just how effective prices and markets can be in regulating the production and consumption of energy over the years ahead. Both Alchian and Kahn argue that the report has vastly underestimated the role of natural price adjustments in solving the energy problem. Alchian, indeed, argues that the whole report is based on a false sense of energy shortages, needs, unfulfilled demands and the like. In his three diagrams (pp. 218–220), he shows the difference between supply and demand interpreted as fixed quantities at any particular moment of time, and supply and demand interpreted as schedules in which the quantity supplied and the quantity demanded vary

[2] Though Alchian is somewhat more favorable to the discussion of the scenarios in Appendix F than in the body of the Ford report.

according to the price of the product in question. In his Figure 3, there would be a "shortage" of petroleum in 1975 at a price of $4 per barrel; but natural market forces would tend to raise the price to $10, and then the "shortage" would miraculously disappear.

Now no economist would argue that a completely unregulated market system would handle our energy problems in a thoroughly satisfactory way. For one thing there is the pollution problem. As we discussed in Great Debate Four (pp. 138–139) there are certain "external diseconomies" involved in the production and consumption of many different goods, and energy is, of course, a prime example in this area. Whether we are talking about automobile pollution, space-heating, the environmental hazards of nuclear energy, the problems of strip mining coal or what have you, these external effects are clearly part of the picture. And they create a *prima facie* case for public intervention and modification of the free-market outcome.

Furthermore, because oil and coal and many other energy sources are essentially exhaustible natural resources, they raise another rather difficult theoretical problem. How can we be sure that the market will lead us to "use up" these resources at a socially desirable rate? A moment's reflection will convince anyone that what we are dealing with here is a balancing of the claims of the present generation against those of future generations. But the decisions we make today are made by the present generation only. There is no way to count the "votes" of the as yet nonexistent future generations. This may lead to a preference for the claims of the present above the claims of the future or, at least, above the claims of the distant future. If, after careful thought, we consider that it is ethically indefensible to weigh our claims more heavily than the future's, then we may decide that an unregulated market will lead to too rapid an exploitation of our energy and other nonrenewable natural resources.[3]

In other words, the issue is not pure market versus total government regulation. It is whether the Ford report has fairly represented or underestimated the contribution that prices and markets *can* make in the energy area. And also it is a disagreement about what the probable effects of government intervention would be. Certain government actions could, after all, make things even worse.

DEBATE OVER EFFECTS OF GOVERNMENT INTERVENTION

And, in fact it is evident that a fundamental difference in point of view about the efficacy of government action runs through this entire debate.

The basic position of the authors of the Ford report is fairly clear. The very title of the report—*A Time to Choose*—suggests that a self-conscious decision, probably involving major federal legislative action, is called for. "Drift" is to be avoided.

What kind of policy action does the Ford report call for? Essentially, it suggests

[3] For a discussion of some further reasons why the present generation might undervalue future needs, see Robert Solow, "The Economics of Resources or the Resources of Economics," *American Economic Review*, Vol. LXIV, 2 (May 1974).

that Congress should establish conservation of energy as a matter of "highest national priority" and that it should set as a goal "significant reductions in the average national rate of growth in energy consumption as compared to historical trends" (p. 209). In the long run, the authors clearly prefer to move towards zero energy growth, and they urge that a new Energy Policy Council be established to consider, among other things, how such a policy could be implemented.

The tools the report proposes include a variety of measures: taxes (for example, to reflect the pollution costs of energy extraction and consumption); subsidies (for example, to make available easy credit for householders who want to make energy-saving investments in their houses); regulations (for example, setting certain fuel economy standards for automobiles); and research (to promote the development of energy-saving technologies). The report suggests that not much more government intervention is required on the technical fix scenario than takes place at the present time. If, however, the move were made towards zero energy growth, presumably there would have to be the higher energy excise taxes and increased government expenditures (directed to non-energy-intensive goods and services) that are built into the construction of that scenario.

What do the critics say to this general approach? Kahn feels that the report is biased in favor of government control and regulation and overlooks both the strength of natural forces and the possible inadequacy of government action. It was, after all, government action which, in recent years, has kept the price of natural gas artificially low, thus leading to inefficient consumption and insufficient storage (p. 234). Ideal regulation might be beneficial; in practice, regulation may do more harm than good.

Alchian argues that the whole regulatory approach of the report is paternalistic and economically inefficient. Should, for example, the government set standards for car-size and speed, fuel economy, and the like? Alchian argues that higher prices for energy will be quite sufficient to get us to "drive smaller cars with greater (not maximum!) mileage per gallon, drive less often, drive slower, all *without* rationing or reduced speed limits or weekend closing of service stations" (p. 224). To add government regulations to this natural response to higher prices is to indulge in "*overconservation.*" Essentially what such regulations do is to divert energy from higher to lower valued uses. The state requires us to use energy not in the way we would like, but in the way our legislators would like. This means that there is a deadweight loss to society in consequence.

As far as taxes are concerned, Alchian recognizes the need for supplementing the market in the particular case of pollution and other external effects. However, to add taxes to rising prices (as for example in moving towards zero energy growth) to suppress the use of energy is to engage in "overkill." It is "to arrogantly assume that people *over*value energy uses (as we are prone to assume they do for smoking, drinking, pornography and gambling) and should be restrained even more than justified by the *true* costs of energy" (p. 222). Because these regulatory distortions lead to losses in consumer welfare, Alchian notes that the zero energy growth scenario—where heavy excise taxes on energy use are employed—actually has a greater cost in terms of economic growth foregone than suggested by our Table 1 above.

A deeper criticism of both the report and the critics is that neither relates the issue of government intervention to the overall question of present versus future generations. We have noted that there may be reasons for believing that the market will not adequately reflect our considered judgments about the resource needs of future generations. This might seem to lead to a call for government action. But then we have to ask, can we expect that the state will be more future-oriented than will be private individuals or business firms? The government is, after all, subject to all kinds of pressures, some of which, like the desire to keep the prices of "necessities" such as fuel as low as possible, may be counter-productive.

Thus the energy debate must be said to be still in its early stages. This is not surprising. As recently as 1970, economists, with the exception of a few specialists, were hardly aware of an energy problem. It is probably premature to speak of "a time to choose"; it is more accurately a time to study and consider. This study and consideration must include a realistic and practical weighing of the options before us, but it cannot really escape the philosophic problem—embedded also in the limits to growth debate—of what true economic "progress" in terms of our own and future generations is all about.

A Time to Choose

Energy Policy Project of The Ford Foundation

The authors of the Ford Report are: S. David Freeman,
Director, Pamela Baldwin, Monte Canfield, Jr., Steven
Carhart, John Davidson, Joy Dunkerley, Charles Eddy,
Katherine Gillman, Arjun Makhijani, Kenneth Saulter,
David Sheridan, and Robert Williams.

It is this Project's conclusion that the size and shape of most energy problems are determined in large part by how fast energy consumption grows. Some problems, of course, such as high prices and their impact on the poor, must be faced whatever the policy adopted on conservation. But slower growth makes many energy-related problems less formidable.

It is, of course, a mistake to regard energy conservation as an end in itself; that puts the cart before the horse. Conservation is worthwhile as a means to alleviate shortages, preserve the environment, stretch out the supply of finite resources and protect the independence of U.S. foreign policy.

By the same token, energy growth is valuable only because it brings us more useful goods and services, warms our houses, and makes possible our vacation trips. More mundanely, energy gets us to work and keeps the office machinery and industrial plant going. If we could continue to enjoy these things in much the same way with slower energy growth through greater efficiency, that achievement is worth considerable effort and perhaps some small sacrifice.

ENERGY FUTURES

To assist our analysis of energy choices, the Energy Policy Project has constructed three different versions of possible energy futures for the United States through the year 2000. Figure 1 offers a comparative sketch

Excerpted from Final Report by the Energy Policy Project of the Ford Foundation, *A Time to Choose* (Cambridge, Mass.: Ballinger Publishing Co., 1974), pp. 11–17; 131–137; 325–334.

of these three possible paths to the future. The three alternate futures, or scenarios, are based upon differing assumptions about growth in energy use. In many ways they are quite dissimilar, but each scenario is consistent with what we know about physical resources and economic effects.

The scenarios are not offered as predictions. Instead, they are illustrative, to help test and compare the consequences of different policy choices. In reality, there are infinite energy futures open to the nation, and it is not likely that the real energy future will closely resemble any of our scenarios. Our purpose is to spotlight three possibilities among the many, in order to think more clearly about the implications of different rates of energy growth. What are their effects on the economy, the environment, foreign policy, social equity, life styles? What policies would

Figure 1   Scenarios: energy use in 1985 and 2000

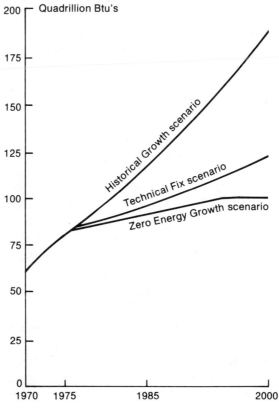

Source: Energy Policy Project

be likely to bring about each one? What resources are needed to make each of them work?

Certain common characteristics have been built into all three scenarios. They all include enough energy to provide the population with warmth in winter and air conditioning in summer; several "basic" appliances that would seem the height of luxury to most people in the world; and cars for most families, as well as other means of transportation.

We recognize that fundamental reforms are needed in America to bring "the good life" to all citizens. But we have included enough energy in our three versions of the future to allow it to happen. Where people live, how they get to work, how much they drive the family car, and the kind of car they own differ from one scenario to the next. But none of them skimps on amenities. All the scenarios provide for energy growth over today's levels, and household comforts take a major share of such growth in each. All three scenarios include enough energy for more material prosperity than the country now enjoys.

A most important similarity among the scenarios is that all are based on full employment and steady growth in gross national product and personal incomes. The lower energy growth scenarios provide major savings in energy with small differences in the GNP from historical growth trends. Employment opportunities are, if anything, better. In all three scenarios, the real GNP for the year 2000 (discounting the effect of inflation) is more than twice what it is today. Of course, we recognize that the chief economic ills of the early 1970s are inflation and high unemployment, and we offer no cures for them here. But in the energy futures we are exploring, a lack of energy will not be a cause for these problems. . . .

Our first scenario, *Historical Growth,* assumes that energy use in the United States would continue to grow till the end of the century at about 3.4 percent annually, the average rate of the years from 1950 to 1970. It assumes that no deliberate effort would be made to alter our habitual patterns of energy use. Instead, we assume that a vigorous national effort would be directed toward enlarging energy supply to keep up with rising demand. By 2000 we assume energy use would amount to about 187 quadrillion Btu's annually.

Present price and productivity trends cast some doubt on the likelihood that historical growth trends will persist. Even so, there are two persuasive reasons for exploring a *Historical Growth* scenario. First, it is the one assumed by many government and industry leaders, and it has been the basis for important government and industry planning. Second, any analysis of future energy policy must examine the consequences of a continuation of historical growth. No one can be sure it will not take place; if the future is like the past, new uses of energy may appear that cannot be foreseen.

The second scenario, *Technical Fix*, differs little from *Historical Growth* in its mix of goods and services. The rate of economic growth is very slightly slower so that by 2000 the real GNP is nearly 4 percent less than in *Historical Growth* (but still more than twice as high as in 1973). This scenario reflects a conscious national effort to use energy more efficiently through engineering know-how—that is, by putting to use the practical, economical, energy-saving technology that is either available now or soon will be.

The Project's work indicates that if we were to apply these techniques consistently, an energy growth rate of 1.9 percent annually would be adequate to satisfy our national needs. This is little more than half the rate of *Historical Growth*. *Technical Fix* would use about 124 quadrillion Btu's a year in 2000—one-third less than *Historical Growth*, a saving four-fifths as large as our current total consumption. Yet the effect on the way people live and work—on material possessions, jobs, comfort, travel convenience—would be, our research tells us, quite moderate. *Technical Fix* is leaner and trimmer, but basically on the same track as *Historical Growth*.

Our *Zero Energy Growth (ZEG)* scenario represents a modest departure from that track. It would not require austerity, nor would it preclude economic growth. The real GNP in this scenario is approximately the same as in *Technical Fix,* and it actually provides more jobs. It includes all the energy-saving devices of *Technical Fix,* plus extra emphasis on efficiency. Its main difference lies in a small but distinct redirection of economic growth, away from energy-intensive industries toward economic activities that require less energy. An energy excise tax, by making energy more expensive, would encourage the shift.

Compared with the other energy futures, a *ZEG* future would have less emphasis on making things and more on offering services—better bus systems, more parks, better health care. About 2 percent of GNP would be diverted through the higher energy taxes to these public purposes —purposes designed to enhance the quality of life, as defined in the scenario.

The *ZEG* scenario assumes a modest rise in total energy use by 2000 but a declining rate of growth, which slows to zero before 1990. Total energy use would reach a level of 100 quadrillion Btu's a year, and remain on that lofty plateau.

Where would the energy come from to supply these various growth patterns? We must keep in mind the long lead time required for enlarging energy supply. The next few years are likely to be tight under any option, and brand new sources of energy are a decade or more away. Looking to the late 1970s and beyond, however, the supply problem can be solved if we decide on a policy now—and implement it.

The Project's research, as well as the results of independent studies we have commissioned, lead us to conclude that it is physically possible, even from domestic sources alone, to fuel the *Historical Growth* rate, during the later years of the century. It would not be easy, and we have serious doubts that it is desirable. But it could be done. It would mean very aggressive development of all available energy sources—oil and gas onshore and offshore, coal, shale, nuclear power. Increased reliance on imported oil could somewhat relieve the pressure on domestic energy sources.

Under the *Historical Growth* scenario there would be little scope to pick and choose among sources of supply, no matter what economic, foreign policy, or environmental problems they might raise. For example, no matter how we juggle the mix of sources, coal and nuclear power would have to be the mainstays of energy supply by the year 2000. Together they would furnish more energy than all sources combined provided in 1973.

Supply options are more flexible in the *Technical Fix* scenario. The slower growth in energy consumption permits more flexibility and a more relaxed pace of development. The nation could halt growth in at least one of the major domestic sources of energy—nuclear power, offshore oil and gas, or coal and shale from the Rocky Mountain region—and still demand less from the other supply sources than *Historical Growth* requires.

Zero Energy Growth would allow still more choice in supply from conventional sources. After 1985 this scenario could also permit use of cleaner, renewable, but smaller scale energy sources such as windpower, rooftop solar power, and recycled waste to meet a larger share of the total energy demand. Still, it should be remembered that even in this scenario the national energy appetite would be very large. Even if there were no further annual growth in energy use after the 1980s, the nation would still need to find enough supplies every year to meet an energy demand one-third larger than that of 1973. . . .

ENERGY, EMPLOYMENT AND ECONOMIC GROWTH

The *Technical Fix* and *Zero Energy Growth* scenarios describe how reduced growth in energy use in the United States can yield many economic, social and environmental benefits. Nonetheless, a crucial question must be answered. Can energy growth be reduced while economic activity grows at historical rates? Our research indicates that energy growth could be reduced while growth continues in the output of goods and services —without sacrificing national economic goals. This appears possible, particularly in the industrial sector of the U.S. economy, where most of our energy is consumed. Current studies indicate that the same is likely to be true for the household, commercial and transportation sectors.

What about the impact of slower energy growth on employment? Would it prevent the growth of new job opportunities? We think not. The energy and manufacturing industries that are the most energy-intensive activities in the economy employ relatively few people. Slower growth in these sectors could be more than offset by more jobs in the service sector, which does not depend heavily on energy, and in industries that make and install energy-saving equipment.

We believe that the fear of the ripple effect of economic disruption and lost jobs, if we do not continue high rates of energy growth, is unfounded. This fear confuses the impact of sudden supply disruptions with the quite different longer-term effects of a slowdown in the growth of energy demand by way of economically efficient energy conservation.

Regardless of our energy future, major changes will occur in the U.S. economy before the year 2000. Some trends now discernible, especially population trends, may have the effect of slowing down growth in energy demand. If we anticipate such changes and their energy implications, public decisions on transportation, housing, and similar social programs can help to shape future patterns of personal consumption to be less energy demanding.

Our conclusions are based upon two quite different analytical approaches. We looked broadly at the energy-economy connection, dividing the economy into nine separate sectors. We also looked at individual energy consuming activities, projected their normal growth, and then worked out the effects of applying available technologies to improve the energy efficiency in each activity. The results of both analytical techniques are remarkably similar. The general conclusion of the analyses, stated simply, is that neither the economy nor employment necessarily suffers from lower growth in overall energy use.

Periods of rapid economic expansion in this country have generally coincided with rapid growth in energy consumption. In order to decide whether this relationship is necessary to the nation's economic well-being, we must examine the underlying question: what are the principal determinants of economic growth, and how do they relate to growth in energy consumption?

ECONOMIC GROWTH

Economic growth in the consumption of goods and services occurs in four broad areas: personal consumption expenditures by consumers, gross private domestic investment by business, government purchases of goods and services, and the trade balance—the difference between exports of U.S. goods and services and imports from abroad.

Because personal consumption expenditures are larger than the other three combined, changes in their pattern have a major influence on the pattern of economic growth. Advancing production technology is a key element in changing consumer buying patterns over time by the introduction of new products. For any given year, consumer spending patterns determine to a large extent the mix of goods and services that make up the gross national product. But over a period of years, technical advances in production can and do change consumer spending patterns. The advent of the automobile is an example.

Many other factors interact to determine the growth of the economy. Productive capacity grows as a result of new investments in capital stock, and technical change makes that capacity steadily more efficient; better education and training improves the quality of the labor force. These kinds of changes combine to increase the productivity of both capital and labor, permitting Americans to enjoy a rising standard of living.

Other elements are growth in population and the labor force, which create potential for greater output and provide the demand to absorb it. Economic growth is also influenced by countless government actions and changing policies and by the availability of raw materials from domestic and foreign sources.

ENERGY DEMAND

The five factors that chiefly affect energy demand are: population growth, price, personal income, technical efficiency and the growth and mix of the stock of capital goods. In general, as income and population increase, the demand for energy also increases. Energy demand tends to decline as price or efficiency increases. The impact of changing growth and mix of the capital stock upon energy use is variable. In the past, energy demand grew as capital stock increased, but more efficient equipment, or energy-saving substitutes for capital equipment, can both change the pattern of the past.

Consumer, or final demand for energy (such as electricity for air conditioning or gasoline for cars) is influenced by price, consumer preferences and income. Relative price—the price of energy in relation to prices for other goods—is especially important. But energy demand may increase while prices are rising, if strong preferences for such services as air conditioning or auto trips offset the dampening effect of higher prices. (This is referred to as "inelastic," or nonresponsive, consumer demand.) Rising personal income can also counteract the effect of rising prices. Falling real prices for energy-using goods, such as freezers and air conditioners, also tend to increase the demand for energy. This is true for most goods whose demand is "derived," and is based on the demand for intermediate goods (electricity demand by the aluminum industry), or is complementary to the demand for different goods (gasoline demand and auto demand).

Industrial and commercial demand for energy is indirect. Energy is an input needed to produce goods and services. If the demand for the products grows, then demand for the energy it contains also grows. For example, the aluminum industry's demand for electricity is based on the economy's demand for aluminum. If aluminum demand is up, then, all other things being equal, electricity demand also will be up.

In the United States, most energy is used in or by machines, equipment, buildings and appliances, which in general constitute the capital stock of the economy. Energy cannot be eaten or worn. It is used through the medium of capital goods, from complicated industrial machinery to the lowly household iron. The rate of growth in this capital stock, its changing mix and changes in the efficiency with which it transforms energy into goods and services are fundamental determinants of the growth in U.S. energy demand. Higher prices and uncertainty about availability have compelled closer attention to the ways in which energy is used. Industry's efforts to reduce energy requirements by conservation measures and by developing and applying engineering devices are increasing the efficiency of energy use.

A decline in future U.S. energy growth could occur if we increase the energy efficiency of capital goods, that is, add to or replace existing capital stock with energy efficient substitutes, or change consumption patterns to conserve energy.

Capital investment is crucial to economic growth because it leads to productivity increases and greater efficiency in resource use. It plays an equally important role in determining energy demand. Public policies such as investment tax credits that accelerate the rate of capital spending have in the past contributed to growth in energy demand, especially when, as in the past two decades, energy prices were low relative to the prices of other resources. When it becomes economically attractive to conserve energy, then the same new capital investment that spurs economic growth may slow down energy growth rates because it uses energy more efficiently.

ECONOMICS OF ENERGY CONSERVATION

Our scenarios concentrate on technically efficient changes in specific activities to reduce energy demand. For these changes to become probable, they must also be economically attractive or "cost effective": the money value of the energy savings must exceed the cost required to achieve it. (Both benefits and costs properly discounted over the life of the activity.)

To determine what is economically efficient is not easy. Calculations may be based on incomplete information concerning future prices for energy and uncertainty concerning the availability of certain fuels. Our expectations about future prices of energy are now dramatically different from those of the past two decades. When energy prices were constant, or falling, relative to the general price level, machinery was purchased and plants built in order to use "money saving" processes, even if these were technically inefficient and wasteful of "cheap" energy. Given current energy price levels, the installation of an energy-wasting manufacturing process is apt to be economically inefficient as well.

SOME FINDINGS

Given these rather straightforward relationships, what can we say about the future? An economic model developed for the Project by Data Resources, Inc. provides a broad based measure of the impact of reduced energy growth, and concludes that a transition to slower growth—even zero energy growth—can indeed be accomplished without major economic cost or upheaval. The study indicates that it is economically efficient, as well as technically possible, over the next 25 years, to cut rates of energy growth at least in half. Energy consumption levels could be 40 to 50 percent lower than continued historical growth rates would produce, at a very moderate cost in GNP—scarcely 4 percent below the cumulative total under historical growth in the year 2000, but still more than twice the level of 1975.

The following are the chief conclusions of the Data Resources report.

1. Substantial economies are possible in U.S. energy input with the present structure of the economy, without sacrificing the continued growth of real incomes.

2. Such energy conservation does have a "nontrivial" economic cost in real income; in 2000, both under *Technical Fix* and *Zero Energy Growth,* real income would be about 4 percent below the *Historical Growth* figure.

3. Our adaptation to a less energy-intensive economy would not reduce employment; in fact, it would result in a slight increase in demand for labor.

Other Project-sponsored studies also support the conclusion that we can safely uncouple energy and economic growth rates.

For example, the Conference Board and the Thermo Electron Corporation have completed Project studies showing that energy/output ratios for U.S. manufacturing are expected to fall rapidly in the future. Some energy intensive industries such as steel could maintain current levels of output with one-third less energy than now used. The Conference Board study included actual field surveys, and a detailed mail questionnaire completed prior to the 1973–74 oil embargo, and was thus based on normal trends in prices and costs. It found that

Significant savings in energy use have been realized by the manufacturing sector in the past. Energy use per unit of product declined at a 1.6 percent rate from 1954 to 1967. As a result, while total manufacturing output rose 87 percent, total energy use rose only 53 percent. This was achieved in a period of stable or declining relative prices of energy.

Recent sharp increases in energy prices, together with present and expected interruptions in supplies of energy, will result in an acceleration in energy savings in manufacturing. The projections presented in this report indicate that energy use per unit of output will decline at an average rate of 2.0 percent from 1967 to 1980.

. . . The existing stock of productive equipment and likely rate of replacement in the industries studied were taken into account, together with known technology. Because of this, the projections represent economically probable developments, [at pre-embargo prices] rather than technically possible optimums. . . .

CONCLUSIONS AND RECOMMENDATIONS

As a result of a two-year study, the Energy Policy Project has reached a number of conclusions on major issues that go to the heart of the debate over national energy policy. We hope these conclusions will be useful to citizens as they make the choices that will add up to an energy policy for the nation.

The major finding from our work is that it is desirable, technically feasible and economical to reduce the rate of energy growth in the years ahead, at least to the levels of a long-term average of about 2 percent annually, as set forth in our *Technical Fix* scenario. Such a conservation-oriented energy policy provides benefits in every major area of concern—avoiding shortages, protecting the environment, avoiding problems with other nations and keeping real social costs as low as possible.

The future rate of growth in the GNP is not tied to energy growth rates. Our research shows that with the implementation of the actions to conserve energy in the years ahead, GNP could grow at essentially historical rates, while energy consumption grows at just under 2 percent. And employment opportunities would also be essentially the same as under a continuation of the historical pattern of increased energy consumption. Investments would shift from more power plants to energy-saving technologies. In fact, the *Technical Fix* scenario would result in a net saving in capital investment requirements of some $300 billion over the next 25 years. The capital requirements for the energy industry, which would otherwise absorb 30 percent of total capital, would be reduced to about 20 percent, or near the current percentage.

The Project also finds that it appears feasible, after 1985, to sustain growth in the economy without further increases in the annual consumption of energy. Such a *Zero Energy Growth* scenario can be implemented if needed for reasons of resource scarcity or environmental degradation, or it may occur as a result of policies that reflect changing attitudes and goals.

The great bulk of the savings over historical growth in energy consumption can be achieved by "technical fixes" in three key areas:

1. Construction and operation of buildings to reduce energy needed for heating and cooling.

2. Better mileage for automobiles.

3. Greater energy efficiency in industrial plants through investments in new technology and self-generation of electricity to use waste heat instead of more fuel to make process steam.

We have given a great deal of thought to the key question of how to make these opportunities for saving energy, which are technically feasible and economical, become a reality. We believe that market forces can and should be encouraged to help balance energy supply and demand, but there are a number of specific areas where market forces are ineffective.

Environmental degradation and foreign policy concerns are not automatically reflected in the market price of energy. Electric power and natural gas utilities are natural monopolies and, therefore, governmental price controls are necessary to protect the consumer. And the market is also weak in areas such as investments in new, energy-efficient buildings, where the investor has a stake in reducing initial costs and often passes up economical investments that would save energy. Nor is it clear that major savings from improved gas mileage for automobiles can be achieved on the most rapid timetable without supplementing market forces with specific performance requirements or tax incentives.

Furthermore, we do not write on a clean slate. There is a whole host of ongoing governmental controls and interventions in the marketplace that need to be removed or reformed, if the nation is to balance its energy budget in a satisfactory manner. Tax subsidies to the petroleum industry, promotional rate making policies by the utility commissions, leasing policies of the federal government, one-sided investments in R&D and counterproductive restrictions on the railroads by the Interstate Commerce Commission are all examples of where reform is needed. Government policies and regulatory actions already play a major role in both the availability of energy supplies and the quantities that are consumed. Legislative and executive actions are needed no matter what energy policy the nation adopts.

We have examined three widely different patterns of future growth in demand. Each scenario will require government actions; the degree of governmental interaction with the marketplace is no greater in the *Technical Fix* scenario than in *Historical Growth.* The governmental actions differ for the different scenarios, but they each require certain specific items of legislation, administrative action, industry initiative and citizen action to "make them happen" in a manner that serves the public interest.

The package of problems that is called the energy crisis constitutes one of the most formidable challenges facing this nation. Meeting future energy requirements without shortages, unnecessary environmental degradation, or adverse impacts on foreign policy will not be easy. Producing the energy required for even the lower energy growth options will be a tremendous task for industry. We recommend a specific set of actions because if we simply drift, the nation will inevitably suffer a series of energy-related crises in the years ahead.

ENERGY CONSERVATION ACTIONS

To achieve all the energy conservation goals of the *Technical Fix* scenario requires a broad spectrum of policy actions. However, the most substantial energy savings could be achieved through the pursuit of four goals:

1. Setting prices to eliminate promotional discounts and reflect the full costs of producing energy—especially important in achieving industrial energy conservation goals.

2. Adopting national policies to assure the manufacture and purchase of more efficient automobiles.

3. Developing incentives for increased energy efficiency in space conditioning of buildings.

4. Initiating government programs to spur technological innovation in energy conservation.

To achieve these goals we recommend the following specific policies.

1. Changes in energy pricing.

Redesign the rates for electricity to eliminate promotional discounts and to reflect peak load costs.

Eliminate subsidies to energy producers such as the depletion allowance and expensing of intangibles, unwarranted use of the foreign tax credit and cut-rate government accident insurance for nuclear power.

Enact pollution taxes supplementary to regulatory actions to reflect environmental costs of fuels extraction and energy operations.

Reflect in the price of oil the costs of stockpiling oil to guard against emergencies.

2. Incentives for more efficient space conditioning.

Establish a federal loan program so that easy credit is available to householders and small businessmen to make economical energy saving investments in existing buildings.

Revise FHA standards for mortgages to specify minimum levels of heat loss and gain for buildings and minimum efficiency of space conditioning systems based on life-cycle economics.

Initiate federal, state and local government programs to provide credit to builders and owners to finance energy-saving technology, to upgrade state and local building codes, and to provide technical assistance to builders.

3. Government action on automobile performance.

Enact minimum fuel economy performance standards for automobiles, supplemented by taxes and tax credits, to encourage the manufacture and purchase of more efficient cars (so as to achieve an average fuel economy of at least 20 miles per gallon by 1985).

4. Government programs to spur technological innovation.

Shift a sizeable share of federal R&D funds to development of energy conservation technology and research on problems of implementing it.

Direct government purchasing toward energy-conserving equipment—efficient cars, tighter buildings, efficient space conditioning systems such as heat pumps, recycled materials—to provide a market for the most advanced energy-saving technologies that are feasible on the basis of life-cycle economies.

It is important that Congress debate and enact legislation which declares that energy conservation is a matter of highest national priority and which establishes energy-conservation goals for the nation.

The goals should provide generally that:

1. There should be significant reductions in the average national rate of growth in energy consumption as compared to historical trends. A target for the long-term growth rate should be set at 2 percent per year and reviewed annually by the Congress;

2. All possible measures should be taken to encourage the most efficient production and use of energy;

3. Each sector of the economy should achieve the lowest possible energy requirements subject to economic efficiency and the state of technology.

All federal government energy-related programs should be coordinated, so that in their cumulative effect they fall within the national goal.

Congress should establish a new Energy Policy Council within the Executive Office of the President, with responsibility for developing and coordinating national energy policy. It would be responsible for translating the national conservation goals into guidelines that would be useful as a reference point to both government and private planners.

The guidelines should be broken down by major sectors and by geographic regions and should be developed with input from governments in the regions, industry and public hearings. An essential element of such a program is to institute a uniform system of accounting for energy in our economy so that we know better where and how energy is used, and in what sectors of the economy it will be needed in the future. We also need hard facts on the energy required to produce all the various energy sources so that we know how much net energy the economy gains from various supply options.

The conservation guidelines would provide government planners and decision makers a yardstick against which to measure their programs and regulatory actions. At the federal government level, they should be mandatory for program planning. Thus, for example, a federal coal-leasing program would be based on the guidelines for coal consumption for the geographic regions to be served. State and local governments could also make use of these criteria in exercising their energy-related responsibilities. Thus state utility rate-making commissions (or, preferably, a regional agency) could assess projected capital expansion plans of utilities, on the basis of projected needs for regional electric growth under a policy of energy conservation. They would have a basis for deciding how many power plants are really needed.

The Energy Policy Council would also perform a comprehensive energy monitoring function. It would continually evaluate growth trends by sector and region, and would modify the conservation guidelines as necessary. It would report annually to Congress and the public on the nation's energy situation; and would recommend any needed legislative reform. It would be assisted by a Citizens' Advisory Board.

SUPPLY ACTIONS

Our work indicates that with the achievement of the energy conservation opportunities in the *Technical Fix* scenario, energy supply will need to be approximately 28 percent larger in 1985 than in 1973. Achieving this increase in supply over the next decade will require a strong effort by the energy producing industry. But unlike *Historical Growth,* the energy savings in this scenario will make unnecessary additional developments which threaten serious environmental damage, or increased oil imports which pose foreign policy concerns.

The lower rate of growth in the supply requirements from now through 1985 could be filled without massive new commitments to energy supply systems that are the source of major controversy: large-scale development of western coal and shale where land cannot be reclaimed, imported oil, nuclear power and presently undeveloped offshore provinces such as the Atlantic and Pacific coasts and the Gulf of Alaska. During the next decade, new supplies would come from the following sources:

1. New discoveries of oil and natural gas in the lower 48 states and Alaska onshore, and offshore in the Gulf of Mexico;

2. Coal from deep mines and areas where surface mining reclamation is feasible;

3. Electric power plants that are already in some stage of construction;

4. Secondary and tertiary recovery of oil and gas from existing wells.

The development of these supplies will not prevent shortages in the very short term because of the lead times involved in any new developments. But if no effort is made to improve efficiency in energy consumption, any near-term shortages would be worse.

In the period after 1985 significant development of substantial additional supplies from controversial sources will be required even to support 2 percent growth. But the lower growth rate compared with the *Historical Growth* scenario permits much greater selectivity. The nation will be able to pick and choose, avoiding the most undesirable sources that would still be needed under historical growth.

In this same post-1985 period some supplies can be expected from unconventional sources, including solar energy, geothermal energy, and solid and organic wastes. However, total energy requirements even at the lower rate of growth will be so large as to require continued expansion of conventional supplies. We must either make major commitments to at least two of the four troublesome energy sources noted earlier—oil imports, nuclear power, the Rocky Mountain coal and shale, and drilling in the Gulf of Alaska and off the East and West Coasts—or we must go ahead with all four on a more moderate scale. In addition coal production will be required approximately to double from current levels by 2000. If pollution technology to control small particles, especially sulfates, can be available by then, increased coal production in the latter part of the century could come from midwestern areas, where reclamation can be readily accomplished.

Our judgment is that the oil and gas resource base in this country is far from exhausted and can supply over half the U.S. energy supply in the *Technical Fix* scenario for the remainder of the century. Limitations on oil and gas availability are likely to stem from a combination of environmental, social and political constraints on rates of development rather than from a physical limit on the quantities in the ground that could in theory be available. In the long run, when oil and gas prices rise relative to more abundant energy sources, oil and gas may have even greater value as chemical feedstocks and protein sources—uses that may be expected to take an increasing fraction of available supplies.

The nation is gradually moving toward a predominantly electric energy economy. This places a premium on reforms in the pricing, regulation and institutional arrangements of the electric power industry to assure maximum efficiency and environmental protection in its production, and maximum efficiency in its use. Electric power has steadily become a larger and larger share of our energy supply, and now over 25 percent of all fuel is converted to electricity. This trend has been due to the unique flexibility of electricity for use in industry and in the home, as well as to a long period of falling prices relative to other fuels. The trend to electric power is apt to continue even under the lower growth rates of the *Technical Fix* or *Zero Energy Growth* scenarios.

One important conclusion from our work is that the expansion program of the electric power industry now underway is substantially greater than needed to supply the electricity that the *Technical Fix* scenario requires. Demand for electric power in this scenario would grow faster than 2 percent per year overall growth rate; but it would still amount to only about half the 7 percent which is the electric power industry's historical growth rate. Power plants now on order for completion by 1980 could satisfy the demand for electricity until 1985 under such an energy conservation policy. This would mean that a pause of several years in new power plant starts is possible for the nation as a whole. During this period, technical progress could diminish concerns about the safety of nuclear power and about air pollution from burning coal or oil in power plants.

In our view, at the present time there are ample incentives in the existing price of crude oil and coal for industry to produce the required quantities of fuel. Indeed the incentives are excessive, in view of the existing tax subsidies, and taking into account that prices of new production do not reflect free and open competition but are the same high prices that were fixed by a cartel of oil-producing nations. However, a few specific governmental actions are required to stimulate the necessary growth in environmentally preferred energy sources without underwriting excessive profits to industry:

1. Adoption of a combined policy covering oil and natural gas pricing and federal income tax payments, with the purpose of eliminating special tax advantages, yet providing high-enough prices to attract sufficient capital for the development of these resources;

2. Establishment of oil stockpiles to provide at least a 90-day backup to imports as a safeguard. The federal government should adjust the size of the stockpile in the future as an integral part of its energy policy. A tariff on imported oil should be levied to finance the stockpile program;

3. Redirecting research and development of new sources of energy to enlarge the effort on near- and medium-term opportunities, such as organic wastes and geothermal energy, and toward solving environmental protection and safety problems with existing sources.

ZERO ENERGY GROWTH

The policies for the *Technical Fix* scenario and *Zero Energy Growth* are virtually identical for the next five years. However, in the years that follow, additional energy conservation measures and small, but important, shifts in the pattern of economic growth would be required to move toward a stable level of energy consumption with a healthy economy. Our work suggests that such a policy direction would be desirable to meet certain social goals that would improve the quality of life, at least in the view of a growing number of citizens. We also believe that, with a transition over a 10- to 15-year-period, it could well be technically and economically feasible to achieve stability in energy consumption while continuing healthy economic growth. Furthermore, it is altogether possible that one or more environmental concerns or resource constraints will force us to such a policy, whether we like it or not.

It is therefore our recommendation that the new Energy Policy Council, as an undertaking of the highest priority, make an intensive, continuing study of the desirability, feasibility and necessity of moving to zero energy growth. The Council should publish annual reports on their studies to the Congress and the American people; these could serve as the basis of widespread public discussion and congressional hearings, so that timely decisions could be made if the nation decides that zero energy growth should, or must, be our national policy.

We stress that the quantity of energy required by the United States when it reaches a stable level as presented in the *Zero Energy Growth* scenario is by no means sacrosanct. The quantity we use, based on near-term technology, is meant to illustrate the point that we can level off energy consumption and continue with an economy in which consumer well-being continues to improve. We have not examined in detail what might be accomplished in the way of additional efficiencies (what might be called a "super technical fix"), but our research suggests that a satisfactory economy after the turn of the century might be possible with appreciably less energy than shown in our *Zero Energy Growth* scenario.

Comment on the Ford Report
Harvey Brooks and Carl Kaysen

Harvey Brooks is Dean of the Division of Engineering and Applied Physics, Harvard University. Carl Kaysen, an economist, is Director of the Institute for Advanced Study in Princeton.

The major propositions which the report presents deserve wide attention. We believe that some of the deficiencies in the report—rhetorical excesses and disproportionate attention to certain matters of detail—unfortunately detract from its persuasiveness and may divert the attention of readers away from the central questions which it fairly poses. The most important of these is the simple proposition that as a nation we are faced with a long-run energy problem with which we are unlikely to deal in a desirable way by relying chiefly on the workings of the market. This is what we have done until now, with sporadic, diffuse and uncoordinated interventions by government—sometimes to assist producers, sometimes to protect consumers, sometimes to preserve the environment, sometimes in the name of national security. Further, the Report argues—in our view, properly—that a wise policy will be one which includes a substantial decrease in the rate of growth of energy use in the United States as an essential element. It is a virtue of the report to make clear the potential gains in both security and in our capacity to control the environmental costs of energy use from such a decrease, and to show that it is both feasible and not so costly in terms of other values, including the values of prosperity and consumer satisfaction, as to be impossible of achievement. . . .

Further, the report's discussion of the possibility that after 1985 we should seek to order our affairs so that there is no further growth in the demand for energy is interesting and provocative in an important way.

Excerpted from Advisory Board Comments, in *A Time to Choose, op. cit.*, pp. 361–62.

We think the discussion of this issue removes it from the realm of faddishness into that of serious discussion. While we ourselves are unpersuaded that this is a necessary goal, we certainly think it wise to give its possibility every detailed examination.

Unfortunately, the good features of the report are marred by many superficial defects. The level of sophistication with which political issues are presented is unfortunately low. This is especially true of those involving conflicts between consumers and producers, or between producers desirous of expanding output at minimum costs and citizens concerned about the impact of their activities on the environment, and other similar issues which form the substance of political conflict. The populist speech writer seems at times to have taken over from the analyst in these discussions. . . .

Despite these reservations, we consider the report an important document and its major propositions worth the serious concern of the country.

An Introduction to Confusion
Armen A. Alchian

Armen A. Alchian is Professor of Economics at the
University of California, Los Angeles.

A Time to Choose—better titled *A Time to Confuse*—regrettably confuses energy and environmental issues, enters the Guinness book of records for most errors of economic analysis and fact in one book, is arrogant in assertions of waste and inefficiency, is paternalist in its conception of energy consumption management, is politically naive, and uses demagoguery. That is a shocking indictment of a final Report of a $4 million project financed by the Ford Foundation. Let us see why it is deserved.

SCENARIOS: CRYSTAL BALL VISIONS

The Report proposes three "scenarios" of 1975–2000; one, the first (*Historical Growth*) assumes continued growth of energy use at the historical rate; the second (*Technical Fix*) assumes energy use at about half the past rate, with adjustments in use responsive to higher price and value of energy with presently known technologies for substitution of other materials and less energy-using activity; the third (*Zero Energy Growth*) projects a zero increase in energy use after 1985. All scenarios terminate at the century's end—a remarkably short horizon. The thesis is that once "we" understand the implications of these scenarios, "we" can better choose upon which to embark.

The Report commends the technical fix future, but recommends a zero energy growth because it is "desirable, technically feasible and economical

Excerpted from Armen A. Alchian, "An Introduction to Confusion," in Morris A. Adelman, *et al.*, *No Time to Confuse* (San Francisco, Calif.: Institute for Contemporary Studies, 1975), pp. 1–25. Reprinted by permission.

to reduce the rate of energy growth [to] 2 percent annually," and "provides benefits in every major area of concern, avoiding shortages, protecting the environment, avoiding problems with other nations and keeping the real social costs as low as possible" [p. 205]. In fact, it does none of those, as should have been evident to the authors. . . .

The scenarios are, *at best,* worthless for identifying or understanding energy issues. Instead, they present some facts about energy uses and possibilities for adjusting to higher-cost energy supplies—issues better understood outside the context of *any* presumed future path. The scenarios are neither predictions of the future nor accurate guidelines for achieving future goals. They are *imagined* future itineraries. In fact, of course, whether we experience faster, lower or possibly negative energy growth depends upon yet-to-be-revealed costs and values of energy uses.

ECONOMIC ANALYTIC ERRORS

Unfortunately, the Report is inexcusably ignorant of economics—indeed, it is so fatally dosed with economic error, fallacy and confusion at critical stages as to border on dishonesty.

NEEDS: SINGULAR OR PLURAL?

A serious, fatal analytic error is the Report's too-frequent refusal to use the fact that the amount of energy demanded can, has been, and will be reduced by a higher price to match the supplies that are available at that price. A famous economic principle of demand is ignored in the Report: the principle that the amount of petroleum demanded depends on the *price* of petroleum. The lower that price, the more we "need," require, or demand. That the Report of a $4 million project would ignore such a well-established, powerful fact of life would be incredible were it not that so many politicians, bureaucrats and even oil industry people also ignore or ignorantly deny it. A similarly powerful, general proposition is that the amount supplied will be larger, the higher the price offered to sellers or producers.

These fundamental, inescapable propositions are shown graphically in the elementary demand diagram in Figure 1. As curve *DD* (for *demand*) plainly shows, the amount of a good that is consumed, needed, required, or demanded depends on the price of the good. That "demand" curve slopes from the upper left to the lower right, suggesting a whole *series of alternative* amounts we "need," "require," or "demand," depending on the price. We have needs, requirements, demands—depending on the price. Anyone who ignores these facts of life is irresponsibly playing a dangerous and expensive game. He is increasing society's problems. The way he

Figure 1 Needs are variable depending on price

Needs are really a range of petroleum uses not all equally valuable. The lower the price, the more petroleum we will put to our lower valued uses. At a higher price, we will deem those lower valued uses not worth achieving. They will no longer be in our "needs." Failure to understand that the variety of petroleum uses have different values leads some people to argue fallaciously that existing supplies will not cover our needs. They are saying all our current uses are of equal importance or value, that we do not regard some uses as more valuable than others; this is a totally incorrect conception, as illustrated by the simplistic fantasy theory graphed in Figure 2.

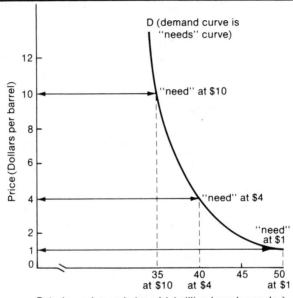

Petroleum demands (needs) (million barrels per day)

conceals those facts of life is to talk of a need or requirement as if it was a natural, unique, given quantity—independent of the cost or price of getting more. Such an intellectually bankrupt—though commonly held —conception is shown in Figure 2; "need-requirement-demand" is expressed as a vertical line, with price having no effect. The counterpart to this error is the notion of supply as a fixed amount, regardless of price. Then the difference between the two is naturally called a shortage or gap. And anyone who swallows that propaganda probably deserves the consequence: the espousal of political control over the consumer's use of the available supply by allocations, rationing or political pressures, in order to divert that supply to politically approved "needs."

In fact, the diagnosis is simply wrong, no matter how often it is repeated in the media by political aspirants, bureaucrats and even some energy industry officials—who of all people should know better. The actual reason, as shown in Figure 3, surprisingly, that supply does not

Figure 2   Naive, but common, view of demand and supply

The vertical line of Demand, or Need, portrays the false conception that there is no ranking of alternative uses with some having lower values than others and that regardless of how costly it is to get petroleum we are incapable of deciding that some uses are less valuable than that cost and hence we will not curtail our demand or "need" for so much petroleum. This is the absurd model of human behavior and valuation of petroleum uses employed by people who talk about our "needs," "requirements," and basic necessities and wish us to believe that an increased market price will not bring about a voluntary revision in our uses to match the available supply at the higher equilibrating price, as portrayed in Figure 3.

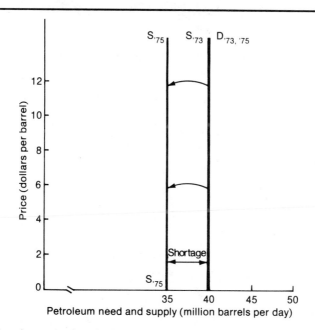

approach what people want to consume at the "market price" is that the price is kept too *low*. This is shown in Figure 3. If you think the price is too high at $10 a barrel, why did you not think it was too high at $3 a barrel? After all, $1 a barrel or even $.20 a barrel would be better and feasible—*if* there were so much oil that we could put it to such low-valued uses as would be worth only $.20 a barrel.

Today, like it or not, and whatever the reason—embargo, less resources, increased population, you name it—the amount of petroleum available to us is such that, as we progress down to its lower-valued uses, we *still* have unsatisfied uses worth on the margin as much as $10 a barrel. That is why the price of available petroleum is now $10 on the world markets. The issue of why we have *only as much* petroleum available as we do is another thing entirely. To fail to separate the two issues—how much oil is available and how much each extra barrel of petroleum is worth to us—is to lead the nation into confusion, not toward rational choice. And it

Figure 3 Price rations out lower-valued uses

At an open-market price, the amount "needed" or demanded is restrained along the demand curve to match available supply. Suppose marketed supplies were reduced—shown by the leftward shifted supply line. If price *within* the U.S. is held below the $10 equilibrating price, shortages occur as people seek to satisfy lower-valued uses requiring more petroleum than is available. With a curtailed price, competition by queueing, political and arbitrary allocations, favoritism and side payments will determine which claims will be denied. If price is allowed to rise to $10, individuals themselves decide which lower-valued uses are to be eliminated, so only higher-valued uses are satisfied by supplies. (The leftward shift in the supply line only crudely depicts the effect of an oil cartel's output restriction from existing sources by existing producers from existing fields. Also, the effects of higher price on discovery of new fields by other producers should be considered. Therefore, this diagram shows *no* more than the effect of an open-market price in changing our "needs" to match whatever supplies are available.)

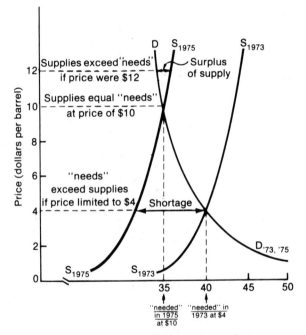

Petroleum (million barrels per day)

is the demand curve that reflects the use value of extra barrels of petroleum. The less we have, the greater the value of a barrel of petroleum, the more that is supplied, the lower the value of the uses to which the extra oil is put.

Irresponsible talk about an oil or energy shortage leads the nation to confuse (1) the fact of a reduced supply of oil with (2) the fact of people using oil in some low-valued uses while other higher-valued uses are unfulfilled. Thus, the unfulfilled higher-valued uses provoke talk of shortages with regard to *those* uses. Why *do* we use some petroleum in the less-valuable ways? The answer is clear and simple. We are told the "price" should be low; therefore, at that price we try to use the petroleum in ways that have use values as low as that artificially low price. In exactly the same way, too-low privately perceived energy costs (that do not include environmental effects) mislead us to abuse the environment—a factor rightly to be deplored.

Those low prices restrained (by domestic price controls) literally mislead us into trying to achieve such low-valued uses of oil, rather than restricting it to our higher-valued uses. Each of us is led to think, as if by a malicious devil, that oil is plentiful enough to satisfy those lower-valued uses. None of us is effectively impressed with the fact that the oil we use in those low-valued ways is of greater value to other people in other uses. Prices, as measures and signals that restrain and control the way we use petroleum or energy, are destroyed by such politically imposed price controls.

Seeing the damage wreaked by our attempts to use available petroleum wastefully, politicians complain that the market system of prices and free enterprise won't work—that it must be replaced by political controls. Indeed it must; break the horse's leg and then say it can't gallop. It is no accident that the strongest appeals for political action in the present situation are made by the strongest opponents of free-enterprise activity: those who would prefer to cripple the process of voluntary exchange through market prices, which might otherwise help us reserve petroleum for its highest-value uses.

The failure to perceive the fundamental distinction between (1) *schedules* of associated alternative possible amounts demanded or supplied at *alternative* prices, and (2) *a* particular amount demanded and *a* particular amount supplied at some one price leads the Report to other confusions. The word *shortage* is used to mean situations where prices rise because of increased demand *schedules* relative to a supply *schedule*. But it is also used to refer to a very different situation created by political controls on permissible price: where the amount *demanded* at that price exceeds the amount *supplied* at that price, because price is politically fixed below the open-market price. This *undervalued* price *is* the energy adjustment obstacle. That is a crucial part of our energy problem.

The battle lines are now drawn between politically ambitious people and those who would rely on a liberal society in which individuals can express, compare, and be guided by their individual use values relative to those of other people—the condition fulfilled by market exchange prices! The energy situation is one of the critical battlefields. The issues of the appropriate degree of environmental protection, Arab wealth and foreign dependence have been transformed—wittingly or unwittingly, into smokescreens to hide the real field of battle.

CONTRIVED VS. NATURAL SUPPLY CHANGE

A reduction in petroleum availability can result from either a naturally decreasing supply relative to demands or a government cartel, or both. Each situation commands a different response. Unfortunately, though the Report discusses both, its recommended responses do not account for the differences involved. To recommend higher use taxes to *suppress energy uses,* where prices are rising in response to natural forces that reduce available supply, is to overkill. The higher market price *alone* is sufficient to restrict use and channel available energy to the highest valued uses. To impose, in addition, taxes or mandatory controls over uses is to arrogantly assume that people *over*value energy uses (as we are prone to assume they do for smoking, drinking, pornography and gambling) and should be restrained even more than justified by the *true* costs of energy. This is the implication of conservation proposals directed to situations in which energy costs are rising because of decreasing relative supplies.

But if the price rise is caused by a *cartel* of producers who have banded together to restrict available petroleum, then sale by us to foreign governments of rights to sell oil in the U.S. market (not imposition of tariffs) would make more sense in liberal free society—as a means of taxing the monopoly rents of the cartel without raising domestic prices. This is a subtle issue, apparently too subtle for the Report. Indeed, it may be too subtle for political application, because it is too easily diverted to other objectives. Nevertheless, the Report should have considered the import quota sale tactic.

EFFICIENCY: TECHNICAL OR SOCIAL COST?

The Report, incorrectly, focuses on technical instead of economic or social cost efficiency. Technical efficiency simply means minimizing the amount of *one* input per unit of output—number of towels used in the washroom per unit of gasoline produced in a refinery, or pounds of steel per automobile produced, or "this" input per unit of "that" output. But total *costs* of *all* inputs are pertinent, not just one component. No engineer or economist worth his salt seeks to minimize gasoline used per mile driven, or electricity or fuel oil per cubic foot of house kept warm—criteria which the Report repeatedly *does* employ in bewailing alleged inefficiency and waste of energy in the past. On the contrary, to use *less* energy in the past would have been wasteful; it would have meant sacrificing more of other useful and desirable things than the energy was worth. This broad, inclusive view of costs and values escaped the attention of the authors of the Report, despite correct statements in Appendix F, "Economic Analysis of Alternative Energy Growth Patterns, 1975–2000."

Ironically, this disastrous failure to acknowledge the totality of inputs and their costs rather than the physical amounts of one input (whose costs can always be reduced by increasing other costs) is cited in the Report as a criticism of *other* peoples' behavior. The Report *accurately* expresses the well-known fact that not all consequences are contained or reflected in market prices—in particular some (not all!) sacrificed values of the environment. The environment is a resource (air, water, land) and the costs of using it should be known by or imposed on users. Why are they not? Because *no one owns* those resources; no one can control their use, as one can control the use of one's own labor or one's own goods. Otherwise, the abuse would be avoided, as with my labor for which I am paid more by its "abusers" than I would be for any other alternative use. In the same fashion, water or air would be used in some particular way only if that use or abuse were of greater value than the best alternative use. That selectivity is what ownership and marketability of a resource at open market prices induces.

And so it might be with water and air, if only we knew how to enforce property rights in those fleeting, unappropriable assets. But those goods are not yet appropriable as marketable property; everyone uses them as if they were costless. No one has to compensate others for their use and thereby heed the costs that do, in fact, exist. Prices do not reflect *those* costs—abuses of nonowned resources. That is why the environment is abused—exactly as my labor would be abused if I did not have rights to myself, or as my car would be abused if I had no marketable, defined property rights to the car. *That* is the problem of environmental control. Yet, we repeat, it is precisely this *same error of excluding* some components of cost that the Report commits in persistently advocating *technical* efficiency. No useful analysis can be derived by using "technical efficiency" as the criterion. . . .

WASTE OR PATERNALISM?

The Report flies in the face of analysis and evidence in alleging energy waste in automobiles or inefficiently insulated buildings. True, many airconditioned buildings have big windows that lose heat and use heating and cooling equipment that use up lots of energy. Indeed they do, but that was *not* wasteful when the costs of energy use *were* lower than the value of window views and comfortable temperatures. Big cars, with powerful motors, air conditioning and power steering were *not* inefficient or wasteful. The energy used provided more valuable services than any other use to which that energy could have been put. If that were not true, *no* one would have obtained gasoline for those end services. After all, no one was compelled to buy those cars; those were all options. As prices of energy are bid up, reflecting the higher values of available energy, people use less energy for those particular end results. Those options are still worth as much as before, but are now too costly to indulge in to the same extent. Higher prices induce us to curtail our amounts demanded (needs?) to the amounts available and to use what little is available in ways that give us the highest personal values. With *higher prices* to inform and impress us about the higher value of a gallon of the reduced supply of gasoline, we will forsake the least-valuable marginal uses. We will drive smaller cars with greater (not maximum!) mileage per gallon, drive less often, drive slower, all *without* rationing or reduced speed limits or weekend closing of service stations.

Such paternalist, political controls *are wasteful*, because they divert some energy from higher- to lower-valued uses. If 60 cents a gallon for gasoline permits each user to buy as much as he demands (needs?) *at that price*, he will use it in the ways that are of most value to him. If quick starts and faster trips at 70 mph are worth more to him than more miles slowly, he will get more value from the gasoline through 70 mph speeds than if he, *or anyone else,* used that gasoline or petroleum in some other way. Shouldn't he? Are we to become paternalist life arrangers under the guise of "conserving" energy?

To say that no one could or should value driving 70 mph more than any other use he or anyone else might have for the gasoline, or any other good he could have had if he did not use that gasoline is to say paternalistically that "we" know what is best for everyone else. To advocate a reduced speed limit to conserve energy is to commit an arrogant intellectual error. It does *not* conserve energy. Instead, it *diverts* some of the available supply to less-valuable uses. Whatever is made available will be used in one way or another. Petroleum prohibited from use for high-speed driving is diverted in part to fuel oil. The reduced speed limit can hardly be viewed as anything but a political power play to divert petroleum to people with political influence who want fuel oil for their own lower-valued uses.

Political controls on our use of energy—whether for outdoor lighting, household heating or swimming pool heating—means simply that an elite group is undertaking to limit the options of other people. Has the lesson of Nixon's administration been ignored? The Report recommends a higher gasoline tax and mandatory gasoline mileage standards to conserve gasoline—even beyond the amount available at costs that match the price people are willing to pay to get the gasoline (the value they place on it). Such *over*conservation, making the costs of energy use appear higher than they really are, is a kind of masochism. . . .

LEISURE IS UNEMPLOYMENT

The Report repeatedly calms fears of unemployment with remarkable assurances that reduced use of energy, whether by deliberate policy or natural reduction of available supply, will not create long-term unemployment. Indeed, it would increase employment—it could even bring back the man-drawn plough. If cheaper and more plentiful supplies of energy tend, happily, to reduce voluntary employment by increasing the supply of other goods relative to leisure, then surely less nonhuman energy will induce us to work harder. One cent would be too high a price to pay for the revelation that long-term employment could be increased by reducing the supply of *non*human power—let alone $4 million. Yet the Report treats reduced nonhuman power and the consequent inducement to work more (i.e., more employment) as an *advantage* of zero energy growth. Less is more! . . .

ENERGY-RELATED ISSUES

Throughout the Report, the authors refer to "policy" without defining it, or as though none existed. But the absence of a national political energy policy does not mean the absence of extensive, continuous, private economy-wide planning of energy uses and production for both present and future. The lack of political management on a national level is not "drift." The Report fails to comprehend economic markets and property rights as controlling and coordinating devices that enable us to anticipate future possibilities and respond promptly to information on current issues.

FOREIGN SUPPLY

The Report provides no careful discussion or exposition of problems possibly caused by reliance on foreign supplies. If foreign *governments* (not private concerns!) can interrupt energy supplies, what do we do? The Report presents a knee-jerk response. Go independent by using less energy, at least to the extent of what would have been imported, and find new domestic sources of energy. To treat the events of Fall 1973 (the so-called Arab boycott) as identical to the cartel policy of restricting output is to generate more confusion. The interruption effects of the

Arab actions were not serious enough to change any country's foreign policy toward Arab interests. And *cartel pricing* is not an *interruption* threat. It is a device to increase Arab wealth. To confuse cartel pricing with interruptions is a disservice to economic understanding and efficient response. But the Report is not alone in this error; it is by no means uncommon.

The use of foreign supplies over the long pull (by importing, say, 20 percent of our petroleum) will affect our foreign policy. But *how,* and what will these effects be? And if we are energy independent, but Europe and other western nations depend on imports, are we asked to be so naive as not to revise our foreign actions? The Report would have been of some value had it more carefully analyzed the potential gains from *our* energy independence, instead of naively referring to "independence," "cooperation," "shared interests." The Report suggests "no artificial barriers to . . . trade" while proposing to limit our oil imports.

RISING ENERGY COSTS

Energy prices rise because the demand *schedule* expands more than the supply *schedule* does. That implies that higher prices will be needed to equalize the amount demanded and the amount supplied. As we observed earlier, the Report confuses *an* amount demanded at *a* price with "needs," as if the current demand did not depend on price or costs. This failure to distinguish between (a) "shortages" (resulting from price controls), (b) reduced supply resulting in higher prices and (c) costs of environmental use not reflected in existing market prices, is pervasive. We adapt to reduced supply (relative to demand) by private actions in response to higher market prices; this process is the economic market in action, doing its job as it always has except when disrupted by government controls on use and price. Unless one understands this operation, one tends to assume that any economic upheaval demands a purposive political response—while in actuality, such intervention works to destroy the effective national energy policy *already* in existence.

After World War II, the government—wisely—refrained from adopting a political policy in response to falling energy costs (due to more plentiful supplies). Market prices and the economic system induced adaptation, exactly as they will today if current higher energy costs continue. No one has to use political power to enforce a pattern of decreed behavior intended to shape the future; the authors of the Report should heed the principles of substitution and pricing described in Appendix F. The market's pricing system *works,* as long as we do not disable it with political controls and allocations (ordered by officials who, unlike private energy providers, are relatively immune to the consequences of such actions).

The Report contends that energy adjustments can be achieved without resorting to government compulsion or force, and then blithely recommends mandatory controls and taxes not to mention such deceptively authoritative recommendations as "It is important that Congress debate *and enact* legislation which declares that energy conservation is a matter of *highest* national priority and which establishes energy conservation goals for the nation" [p. 209, italics added]. . . .

ENVIRONMENT

The Report also clouds the problem of environmental use values that are not captured or reflected in market prices. We need an accurate technique for evaluating environmental use, and we must be able to use that measurement to ensure that users will balance environmental considerations against other priorities. Preventing *all* deterioration of environment is not the object, as even the Report (at one point) concedes: ". . . there is a limit to what clean air is worth." Close, but not close enough. It is not a question of *clean* air, but clean*er* or *less* clean; the problem is how to ascertain the values of changes in the environment relative to consequent value changes in other goals and goods. What is the cost (value sacrificed) of more pollution, relative to the value of other benefits thereby attainable? Most of us work—we pollute our leisure and our lives with sweat, tedium, and occupational hazards because we think the gains outweigh the value of our unpolluted leisure. Should any man who is not now working be forbidden to work, to avoid polluting his leisure? Should *any* deterioration in the environment be intolerable, regardless of values thereby achieved?

Reduced energy use does not necessarily improve the environment. On the contrary, greater use of a greater supply of energy could be an effective means of *improving* (not just preserving) our surroundings. While energy production may injure the quality of some natural resources in some areas, cheaper, more plentiful energy permits improvements in other areas (possibly even the energy production locale). Air conditioning improves our environment (in a sense); more gasoline for engines with lower mileage but greater effectiveness in curtailing pollutants would also help; pumping water to arid areas (by means of energy) makes the desert bloom. The correct issue is the optimal degree and type of pollution, the optimal mix of environmental effects, the optimal degree of personal abuse via work or loss of leisure. Despite the Report's seeming bias in favor of energy reduction, nowhere does it actually demonstrate that decreased energy growth or a return to our original environment is the ideal objective.

The Report is not alone in the belief that an all-out rescue plan for the environment is indicated. Some of our laws and judicial decisions prohibit *any* air pollution, regardless of subsequent benefits. But this approach imposes waste on society and requires belated correction after the damages are incurred and revealed. . . .

There is a role for government action: to help ensure that the cost of resources used in producing and consuming energy are accurately and effectively revealed in market prices or user fees. Given that some of those resources are unowned, they cannot be accurately priced, nor can users be effective charged for them. Yet it appears sensible and desirable that people who use those resources should be made to heed those costs by compensating the owners. Three tasks are involved: (1) assessing the value of the abuse, (2) making that cost impinge on the user and (3) identifying the resource owners. Those *may* be roles for governmental personnel, *if* we believe that gains from government participation would outweigh gains from continued abuse of the resource—which is not a foregone conclusion. Politicians and bureaucrats (as recent legislation controlling any new use of the California coastline suggests) tend to be overly protective. Why assume that *new* uses are less valuable than old ones? What do political controllers gain or lose by seeking to under- or over-value alternative uses of a resource? These problems are germane to a discussion of *any* scarce resource—natural or not.

An acknowledgement that the market system has not and will not work in these areas is no more earthshaking than the fact that past political actions have opposed clear, secure and transferrable property rights that enable us to possess and exchange goods. The question is, what is the best way to help both open market *and* government fulfill their proper roles —and why have they sometimes performed unsatisfactorily in the past?

CONTROL OF ENERGY INDUSTRY AND ENERGY USERS

Since no government agency overtly controls the energy industry, some political action is needed—in the Report's view—to make private producers responsive and answerable to the public. But the absence of political control by a public *group* does not mean the absence of public control. Consumer decisions on the value of various kinds of energy control the actions of major corporations. General Motors could not make us all buy Cadillacs, or even 1975 models; nor could Ford make us all buy Pintos. Private producers offer, at their risk, the kind of cars they *predict* we will prefer, as evidenced by our willingness to pay the costs. Control is exercised by the people through market-revealed willingness to work at various wages in light of their range of work opportunities, and by their willingness to buy the offered cars in the open market. Producers propose, consumers dispose.

But the authors of the Report, seeing that a few auto company managers are sensitive and responsive to this public control by consumers and workers, confuse response with control and proposers with disposers. Even U.S. senators must consider the wishes of their constituents; in formulating policies, they are trying to forecast what the public will accept. The same holds true for the private sector. But very important differences lie in the speed and accuracy with which true desires are revealed, compared and enforced and the performers rewarded, punished, or displaced.

A Review of a Time to Choose

Herman Kahn

Herman Kahn is the head of a research center, the Hudson Institute, in Croton-on-Hudson, New York.

At first sight Americans in general and analysts like myself should be very pleased by this Ford Report. First of all the timing was almost perfect —the study was started in December 1971 and largely finished in late 1974, at a time when its results could still be extremely relevant. In fact that is one of the problems of the Report: people may take it too seriously. Yet it does illustrate one of the important advantages the United States has over many countries. It has many organizations willing to support timely and "impartial" studies that are or could be of great value to the nation, and these studies are often quite adequately funded. This particular study cost $4 million and had an excellent advisory board.

Unfortunately this study also illustrates an important weakness of such projects. They are often staffed by groups who not only have a very narrow ideological focus but, to some extent, don't realize that this is the case. As a result, they don't even protect themselves adequately from criticisms by those who do not share their views. I often explain to potential employees of the Hudson Institute that, although it's very difficult to get truly objective people, at least we try to find people who are careful; very often care and prudence make up for a good deal in a lack of objectivity. All too often, today, studies like this one express a view that is largely characteristic of upper-middle-class progressive intellectuals. This group is highly influential in Japan and the Atlantic Protestant culture area; indeed, a good many readers of this review are no doubt among its

Excerpted from Herman Kahn, "A Review of *A Time to Choose*," in Morris A. Adelman *et al.*, *No Time to Confuse* (San Francisco, Calif.: Institute for Contemporary Studies, 1975), pp. 131–36; 143–44. Reprinted by permission.

charter members. But we must remember that intellectuals don't have a monopoly on wisdom and knowledge. I would argue, indeed, that something approaching the opposite is often the case.

The Ford Report makes heavy use of the scenario technique, superficially in much the same fashion as the Hudson Institute. In many cases they use terminology very similar to ours. However, I'd like to comment on some important differences between the Report's use of this technique and ours. At Hudson we distinguish quite carefully between at least four different kinds of scenarios, labeled respectively as follows: (1) the naive projection; (2) projections associated with business-as-usual, historical forces and/or the programmed system; (3) the surprise-free scenario and projection; and, finally, (4) special scenarios such as excursions, examples, prototypes, archetypes, hedging recommendations and so on. Although this is not necessarily the case, the four categories usually involve dichotomies. The distinctions between these scenarios are important in trying to understand and evaluate studies. The naive scenario arbitrarily freezes certain aspects of the present, and then extrapolates as if this arbitrary freezing were valid. For example, one might take a six-year-old boy, freeze his growth rate, and then ask how tall he would be at age 16, 20, and 50. Or one could freeze some economic or population growth rate. Such experiments may be quite interesting, but it is almost always misleading to take the extrapolation literally, as if it reflects some kind of reality. The label "naive" clearly warns the reader of this pitfall. In scenarios of the business-as-usual, historical forces or programmed system variety, one assumes that the forces and policies that have operated in the past will either continue to operate in the future or that certain recent or probable changes will be operating in the future. To go back to the analogy of the six-year-old boy, we would assume that certain forces would tend to slow down his growth rate, even if he were placed in a brand new environment.[1]

Thus, if there is a change in the price of oil, we normally expect more "conservation" (i.e., moves to greater efficiency and to substitution), as a reflection of these changes. In the surprise-free scenario, we are willing to consider new policies, or events that are not necessarily already programmed or even terribly likely but would not surprise us very much if they occurred. Generally speaking, when the Ford study recommends new policies, these should be included in the surprise-free scenario, since

[1] Thus, if we are studying the future economic growth of Japan, we would assume that the programmed system would phase out low-productivity industries rather quickly and efficiently in favor of high-productivity industries. In the case of most European countries we would expect the programmed system to try to "save" these low-productivity industries or defer their phasing out in order to reduce the hardships associated with adjustment.

analysts normally don't recommend doing something which they do not believe has any serious chance of being adopted. However, recommendations are sometimes made in the hope of preventing something from happening; if that occurred anyway, it would be quite a surprise for the analyst who wrote the scenario. In other cases, recommendations are made simply for educational purposes or to make certain kinds of points that in no sense reflect likely events. Also, very often changes are made or adopted only as a result of crisis or other unexpected events. One may think that a certain kind of crisis or event was quite unlikely to occur, but still be interested in hedging against such an occurrence. In that case, the scenario illustrating these possibilities may not be a surprise-free scenario.

The fourth category is self-explanatory.

The Ford study revolves around three scenarios, designated respectively Historical, Technical Fix, and Zero Energy growth. Their "historical" scenario we would have called "naive"; the difference in terminology is important because it explicitly emphasizes that the scenario takes no account of the almost automatic adjustments in the system. The study's authors would probably argue that they are entitled to use any name they wish; this is true to some extent. However, in the Ford treatment the scenario is taken with such excessive seriousness that there is a tendency to assume that we have a real historical scenario or "programmed system." As a result the reader is likely to enormously exaggerate the kinds of changes introduced by the study's Technical Fix and Zero Growth scenarios. The approach is like trying to illustrate the value of a certain medicine on the growth of a young boy by claiming that it will slow down his growth rate, when in fact the rate will decrease eventually for natural reasons. To go back to our earlier example, the concerns expressed in the Ford historical scenario are no less artificial than would be anxiety about how to clothe or feed the six-year-old boy who grew to be a giant because his growth rate was frozen. The historical growth scenario depends upon the fact that in the past oil was available in the Persian Gulf for about $1 to $2 a barrel, and natural gas in this country cost only about $0.15 or $0.20 per thousand cubic feet. In reality, such prices are not likely to be seen again in this century. As the Report points out, the government could keep prices down by very large subsidies, but this would encourage some highly irrational growth patterns. Again, the Report itself suggests that what it calls wasteful use of energy by Americans would not be nearly as prevalent in a context of much higher prices (which now exists).

What the study calls the "Technical Fix" is relatively close to what we call the business-as-usual or historical forces scenario, since there is a great tendency for a society such as ours to act sensibly as a result of the operation of the price mechanism. That is, the basic assumption of high prices for oil may turn out to be wrong; but given this assumption, much of the Ford Technical Fix scenario follows almost automatically (plus a small number of recommendations and new programs—but mostly more or less straightforward actions which facilitate the adjustment to the new condition). The similarity is not really great enough, however, to suggest that the differences between the Ford historical scenario and Technical Fix scenario are due to the recommended program. One trouble with this scenario is that it confuses the almost automatic effects of the new high prices with a number of other effects. The government does, of course, make some significant decisions, such as the direction to be taken by official research and development programs. But, given the new level of prices, even these decisions are not as effective as might be assumed.

Finally, Hudson would put in category 4 what is, in effect, the recommended zero growth program (the authors' preference is not explicitly stated, but it is clear from many of the biases and implications in the study). This is a very improbable outcome, for a number of reasons. First, it assumes that the government will be willing to interfere in American life for a period long after the crisis ends, for the sake of attitudes and ideologies that are not widely shared (only by the upper-middle progressive elites). While the Report is not maniacally antigrowth, and indeed shows a surprising awareness of arguments against such a mania, it nevertheless accepts much of the ideology and assumptions of the antigrowth group.

One interesting and by no means minor aspect of this ideology is its enormous hostility to the automobile—and to the concept that Americans have had a blind and irrational desire for quantity at the expense of quality. It is the "in" thing today to blame most of the problems of society on this assumed desire for growth for growth's sake in general and/or the pervasiveness of the automobile in particular. However, if one looks at the bulk of the American population, one finds, for example, that a family with median income often can't make ends meet if living in suburbia. And yet, overwhelmingly, Americans choose this form of life as the preferred compromise over everything else that's available. Of course, many anti-suburbia planners and ideologists say that better things can be made available, but this remains very much a statement to be proved.

It should be noted that the American passion for the single house on its own land goes back very far in our history. In most countries in the world, farmers lived in villages and went out to the farm to work. In the United States, they lived on their separate farms. Indeed they often preferred to risk casualties from Indians than live too close to their neighbors. Almost every survey of Americans today indicates a firm, well-informed, almost passionate attachment to the single-family house, in either a suburban small town or rural setting. This implies that the U.S. economy and society will be based on the private automobile, which does indeed supply a flexible, convenient, and generally desirable means of transportation. Of course the car has a large number of defects; but the average American who, despite the critics, is really well-informed about his own needs and desires is willing to accept these shortcomings and try to overcome them over time.[2]

. . . The study refers frequently to the need for all sorts of government control and regulation; indeed, it is clearly biased in favor of such action. People who take this stance, unfortunately, tend to underestimate the enormous role high prices can play in a free market and to ignore the harm governments can do. In many cases regulation would be useful if carried out with great skill, but disastrous if such skill is not forthcoming. For example, I would argue that the Arab oil embargo of 1973 could not have had serious effects in this country, had our government not made at least two serious mistakes. The first was to allow our energy stocks to reach dangerously low levels. In fact, if there had been a very cold winter or very warm summer in 1973 or 1974, our home heating and air conditioning needs would have been so great that a large part of our industry might have been forced to shut down. Behavior like this is similar to the disastrous gamble of the British Labour Party on a warm winter in 1948. The second major mistake by our government was to keep the domestic price of natural gas at an artificially low level, at a time when we were negotiating to buy it abroad for a dollar or more per thousand cubic feet (at this writing the domestic price is still about 50 cents). I really don't know of any sensible person who will still defend this policy. As a result of this mistake, perhaps 40 percent of our natural gas has been

[2] An interesting sidelight on this issue shows up in an informal poll I have conducted with literally hundreds of American audiences, particularly upper-middle-class audiences. I ask them to choose between a $12,000 Cadillac and $4,000 cash. The Cadillac is designed to be economical in fuel use and maintains its value over time. These gifts are to be given tax-free; the only catch is that the receiver has to drive the Cadillac for about five years. He can, however, turn in his current car. Overwhelmingly, academic audiences choose the $4,000 by ratios of 10 or 20 to 1. Upper-middle-class audiences generally take the $4,000 by ratios of 2 or 2 to 1. This includes intellectually enlightened boards of directors and trustees of many corporations. If you change the choice to $4,000 or a Mercedes Benz, one finds a large shift in favor to the Mercedes Benz over the $4,000. If you ask people why they chose as they did, they admit after a few minutes' conversation that in their minds a Cadillac is associated less with the wealthy plutocrat than with the Mafia, the successful black, and the affluent Jewish contractor; who wants to be associated with such people? In other words, the Cadillac is, of course, the car of the wealthy in America; but it is even more a car of the upward mobile middle-class square, and there's a kind of contempt for this kind of person in academe today.

consumed inefficiently. If the price had been more rational, much of our gas would have been kept in storage, and, quite probably, more would have been discovered.

It is often argued that our concern for the environment has caused some very serious mistakes in recent years. It is of course clear that air and water are no longer free commodities in this country; we certainly must take serious steps to protect and preserve the quality of our environment. Significant policy changes in this direction were and are necessary. Nevertheless, we must learn from our mistakes and not permit excesses in our pursuit of a clean environment. Let me use the Alaska pipeline as an example. If we are to cope with our energy problems, some damage must be done to the environment; the question is, how much and where? I have asked many people where they would put an 800 mile pipeline if one must be built somewhere. Siberia usually comes in first, followed by Alaska. I can only agree. Since there are about 600,000 square miles in Alaska, I would argue that plenty of unmoved landscape will be left over, even after a pipeline is built. We really have so much low quality real estate in Alaska that we can afford to regard it as expendable, if the goal is urgent and important enough. . . .

PART II

ANALYSIS AND POLICY

GREAT DEBATE SIX

SIX

GALBRAITH AND THE NEW INDUSTRIAL STATE

GALBRAITH AND THE NEW INDUSTRIAL STATE

I N a series of three books—*The Affluent Society* (1958), *The New Industrial State* (1967), and *Economics and the Public Purpose* (1973)—Professor John Kenneth Galbraith has launched a major attack on received economic doctrine concerning the structure and performance of a modern industrial society. Commentators will disagree about the originality of Galbraith's ideas and about their overall coherence. But none will doubt their impact. These three books, together with his other writings, have made him perhaps the most well-known of all contemporary economists. He has taken his critique of the profession not simply to his colleagues but also to the public at large.

In this introduction, we shall try to indicate the broad scope of Galbraith's differences with what he would call the "conventional wisdom" of his fellow economists. In the debate proper, we shall concentrate on some exchanges that took place just after the publication of *The New Industrial State* in 1967 and early 1968. These exchanges are sharp and, at times, quite personal. Behind them, however, is a deep general issue: what is the best overall framework for analyzing the complexities of modern industrial organization? For if Galbraith is right, a great part of what is usually taught in courses on the principles of economics, and especially in the sections on microeconomics, should be consigned to the trash heap. It is not only irrelevant, but also misleading, and, very probably, a cover for the hidden purpose of defending the status quo.

THE OBJECT OF GALBRAITH'S ATTACK

Galbraith's main object of attack is the standard body of neoclassical economic theory that deals with business firms, consumers, factors of production and markets and how these individuals and institutions are related in a private economy. Historically, this theory focused almost exclusively on one particular

241

market structure, pure competition, and, even to this day, the full analysis of competitive markets occupies a central place in most economics instruction. A major condition for this particular market structure is that all units in the economy be small. In the case of business firms, it is assumed that each one is so small that it has no effect on the price of the product which it is selling. The firm's primary economic task is to adjust its quantity of the product produced in light of the given market conditions. It has no need to advertise because it can already sell all that it can produce at the going price and because, its product being identical (homogeneous product) with that of thousands of similar firms, it could not sell at a price higher than that of any of its rivals. Examples of such economic impotence are hard to find; usually, economists refer to agriculture, say, a small-scale wheat farmer.

Similar conditions are applied to factors of production and consumers. The laborers hired by our small business firm are not collectively organized, but come as separate individuals each of whom takes the market wage as given and independent of any bargaining that he might attempt. The same would be true of the owners of capital and land. Furthermore, if the business firm wished to invest in more machines and equipment, it would go to an external capital market to borrow the funds for this expansion of its plant. The small competitive business firm would not have large sums of profits for engaging in internal financing of investment.

Similarly, the consumer is small, isolated, and powerless to affect the prices he must pay for goods and services in the purely competitive world. In one sense, he is "sovereign": his preferences and tastes are assumed to be original and independent with himself. An important test for the economy is how well it responds to his preferences. If it gives him what he wants (subject, of course, to the limitations of resources and technology), then we say that "consumer sovereignty" holds sway. This, of course, does not imply that all consumers do equally well because the degree of each person's "sovereignty" depends on his initial endowment of funds and/or earning power.

The capstone of this neoclassical analysis of the competitive economy is general equilibrium theory. We imagine all these small economic units meeting together in various markets, each governed by its desire to do the best it can for itself. The business firms, all being private, owner-operated enterprises, focus on the goal of maximizing profits. The individual consumer or laborer will try to maximize his "utility," or, in modern terms, to reach his highest possible indifference curve.

When all these "maximizing" individuals and firms are brought together, the result could be chaos. The great achievement of neoclassical economics, however, was to show that under certain circumstances, the result could be overall equilibrium—that is, each firm and individual would find a resting place such that he could not improve his position by any indicated alteration of his behavior. Furthermore, barring external effects and various other important limitations, this equilibrium could be shown to be *efficient*. If we tried to improve one person's position, it would have to be at the expense of someone else. For example, if we could reallocate our labor and capital so as to produce more of some commodities and no less of other commodities, this would suggest that the *pre*-reallocation position was *in*efficient; in principle, these extra commodities would allow us to make everybody better off. Such inefficiencies (again, subject to the required conditions) would not occur under a purely competitive regime.

Thus, the world of the small wheat farmer. But surely no one would identify this world with that of the modern industrial economy! Galbraith is not so sure that this identification has not, rather subtly, taken place. However, he, like every other economist in the world, recognizes that neoclassical theory does not leave the matter there, without making some further comments.

Beginning in the 1930s, especially with the work of Chamberlin and Robinson,[1] economists have regularly considered various forms of imperfectly competitive market structures: monopoly, monopolistic competition, duopoly and especially oligopoly. In these market structures, the various restrictive assumptions of pure competition are modified and the resulting changes in business conduct and performance analyzed. Perhaps the most important assumptions have to do with the number and size of firms in an industry. In oligopoly theory, economists attempt to analyze the case where a few large firms dominate a particular industry. But they also analyze some of the effects of product differentiation (dropping the assumption of a homogeneous product), advertising, internal financing of investment and so on. In the case of labor markets, they also consider the effects of unions and collective bargaining.

The main impact of the amended neoclassical theory is to suggest that where monopoly "elements" are present, firms will tend to produce outputs that are too low, which they will tend to sell at prices that are too high, and which, in turn, will lead to abnormal profits. In the case of labor unions, a similar analysis suggests too high a wage and too low a level of employment in organized as opposed to unorganized industries. These departures from pure competition can, under certain conditions, be shown to be inefficient in our sense. The analysis of imperfect competition has not had so long a history, and it tends to be a lot more messy, than that of pure competition, but it does exist and is a standard component of traditional economic thought.

ECONOMIC STRUCTURE OF THE REAL WORLD

In this context, it can be said that part, but only part, of Galbraith's criticism of the economics profession is that it has given too little emphasis to this component of economic thought dealing with imperfect competition. He considers that the imperfectly competitive sector of our economy is far more important in actuality than current theory has admitted. In *The New Industrial State,* his sole concern is with this sector of the economy. In his later *Economics and the Public Purpose,* he

[1] Edward H. Chamberlin, *The Theory of Monopolistic Competition* (Cambridge: Harvard University Press, 1933); and Joan Robinson, *The Economics of Imperfect Competition* (London: Macmillan, 1933).

explicitly divides the present-day American economy into two sectors: a "market system" and a "planning system." The traditional purely competitive analysis applies, at best, to the market system. But the planning system is terribly important and must be coped with. In this latter system, the large firm is a dominating factor. He cites various statistics on the degree of concentration in the manufacturing sector.[2] He stresses that in these large firms the divorce of ownership and control makes the old owner-operated firm concept outmoded. He argues that all really major technological innovation takes place in the planning system, and not in the market system. He even suggests that much of the market system derives its character from its relation *to* the planning system: "Numerous service enterprises are the byproduct of the rise of the large firm. They are, in effect, a subsidiary and supporting development of the planning system. This is especially the case with that part of the service sector which, from outward evidence, is expanding most rapidly."[3]

This planning system, Galbraith suggests, comprises about half of the U.S. economy. And one element in his critique of traditional theory is that it has given this system far less than half its attention. Economists have paid lip-service to the large firm, to the divorce of ownership and control, and so on, but they have not given such developments the massive study their importance requires.

PLANNING VERSUS MARKET RESPONSE

But this is not the whole of his argument, by any means. Even more important is his contention that economists have tended to *mis*analyze this sector of the economy, even when they have noticed it.

A major part of his argument is suggested by the very term *planning system.* Galbraith insists that the large modern corporation will not simply sit back and respond to the dictates of the market. On the contrary, it will attempt to control its economic environment. It will engage in elaborate *planning* in an attempt to free itself from the vagaries of the marketplace.

He writes: "So the firm controls the prices at which it buys materials, components and talent and takes steps to insure the necessary supply at these prices. And it

[2] Thus, he writes: "The two largest industrial corporations, General Motors and Exxon, have combined revenues far exceeding those of California and New York. With Ford and General Electric they have revenues exceeding those of all farm, forest and fishing enterprises. In the first quarter of 1971, the 111 industrial corporations with assets of a billion dollars or more had more than half of all the assets employed in manufacturing and received substantially more than half of the earnings on more than half of the sales. The 333 industrial corporations with assets of more than $500 million had a full 70 percent of all assets employed in manufacturing. In transportation, communications, power utilities, banking and finance, although the concentration is somewhat less, the tendency is similar; in merchandising the concentration is also high. An assembly of the heads of the firms doing half of all the business in the United States would, except in appearance, be unimpressive in a university auditorium and nearly invisible in the stadium." *(Economics and the Public Purpose,* p. 43).

[3] *Op. cit.,* p. 55.

controls the prices at which it sells and takes steps to insure that the public, other producers or the state take the planned quantities at these prices . . . Prices, costs, production and resulting revenues are established not by the market but, within broad limits . . . by the planning decisions of the firm" (p. 251).[4]

The firm achieves these goals by, for example, integrating its suppliers into the firm to achieve dependability of supply and by financing its expansion out of retained funds rather than going to external capital markets. As far as consumers are concerned, they are subject to "partial management" by means of advertising. Also, firms produce large quantities of goods for the government, and there is a substantial "influence of producers on public procurement including, in particular, weaponry" (p. 252). This relative freedom from the market, through planning, is what distinguishes this half of the economy from its weaker neighbor, the market system.

It is part of Galbraith's contention that traditional analysis, even when it is specifically focused on oligopoly and imperfect competition, has largely overlooked this planning apparatus. The large firm, in neoclassical analysis, has some freedom to set the price of its product, but this setting of prices still takes place in response to the overall instruction of the market. Not the price of the product, but the basic economic environment is given. Galbraith argues that this overlooks the fundamental purpose and power of these large firms to control and alter, not completely but in significant ways, the environment in which they operate. Conscious control through planning is closer to the truth than automatic response to the market.

GOALS OF THE FIRM

To the degree that it is successful in modifying its economic environment, the large corporation in the planning system can pursue its own chosen goals. Here again, Galbraith stresses the difference of his analysis from the textbook treatment of imperfect competition. In that treatment, the large firm (in this respect, like the small purely competitive firm) is a simple maximizer of profits. The test of any decision is clear: will it add more to revenues than to costs? If it does, adopt it. The equilibrium condition familiar to all students of economics, that marginal revenue must equal marginal cost ($MR = MC$) is, of course, nothing but a simple profit maximization condition. This is a bit of a caricature of the textbook treatment of this important subject, but there is certainly an element of truth in it.

In any event, Galbraith feels that such an approach is in fundamental error. Profit maximization is strictly appropriate only in the case of owner-operated firms. In this connection, Galbraith once again stresses the divorce of ownership and control. Management is in charge of the large corporations, but the management is not the

---

[4] When no source is given, page references will refer to pages within this book. This will be our practice in each of the debates.

owner. "Stock holdings by management are small and often nonexistent" (p. 252) Top management, furthermore, is only part of the controlling apparatus of the modern firm, there being an elaborate bureaucracy of scientists, engineers, contract negotiators, sales executives, and so on—the *technostructure*—who are involved in a serious way with the corporation and who help determine its goals.

Now the members of the technostructure do not get, and should not in principle get, the profits that they are allegedly trying to maximize. The doctrine of maximization thus rests on their supposed willingness to maximize profits for others (stockholders)—that is, the urge to make profits operates "not in the first person but the third" (p. 253). Because planning has given management some freedom of action, may they then not choose some other goals?

Yes, replies Galbraith. The picture he draws is essentially this: The large corporation must in the first instance pay some attention to profits, in particular trying to secure a certain minimum level of earnings so as to be able to pay dividends and ward off stockholder dissatisfaction, and, at the same time, to have funds available for reinvestment in the capital expansion of the firm. From this point on, however, its major objective is likely to be not maximum profits but maximum growth of sales and output. The growth of the firm does two major things: (1) it reinforces the planning efforts of the firm in its attempts to control prices, costs, consumer attitudes and the like; and (2) it serves the direct personal interests of members of the technostructure by maximizing "opportunity for, among other things, advancement, promotion and pecuniary return for itself" (p. 274). The difference in point of view can be significant. Traditional analysis of monopoly elements in the economy usually emphasizes their tendency to restrict output, as we mentioned earlier. Galbraith sees the large firm as largely dominated by the desire for growth, and hence, from a social point of view, producing, if anything, "too much" output.

PERSUASION OF THE CONSUMER

To secure its goals, especially the continuing growth of sales, the large corporation must win the compliance of the consumer. In American society, this compliance is secured not by threat, force or deprivation, but largely by persuasion. Persuasion by advertising or by other marketing techniques is the means by which the large corporation convinces the private consumer that he needs and desires that which the large corporations feel he needs and desires. In the case of the public consumer—the state—the technostructure works its influence (as in the so-called military-industrial complex) in ways both direct and indirect, overt and subtle. The very fact that the members of the technostructure are prestigious and respected individuals gives them undue influence on public policy.

Insofar as these efforts at persuasion work, then the basic system is not—as in the textbook picture—one in which the productive apparatus responds to the original and independent dictates of the consumer ("consumer sovereignty"), but rather one in which producer interests regularly and systematically bend the consumer to their own purposes. It is almost a case of society as a whole existing to serve the technostructure, rather than the technostructure existing to serve society.

SOCIAL CONSEQUENCES OF THE PLANNING SYSTEM

The main social consequence of the planning system, according to Galbraith, is to produce an economy which gives far too much weight to economic growth. "The technostructure is principally concerned with the manufacture of goods and with the companion management of the demand for these goods. It is obviously important that this be accorded high social purpose, and that the greater the production of goods, the greater the purpose served" (pp. 255–256). Thus, the influence of corporate structure and conduct on society as a whole is to produce an emphasis on more and more output when, in Galbraith's view, more output is of very dubious value. A higher standard of living only allows "avoiding muscular energy, increasing sensual pleasure and . . . enhancing caloric intake above any conceivable nutritional requirement" (p. 256).

It also has great costs to society. These are direct costs in terms of increased pollution, despoilation of nature and our natural resources, traffic accidents, urban congestion and so on. There are also indirect costs in terms of opportunities foregone. Galbraith favors a more leisured, cultured, artistically oriented society in which genuine public needs are served as opposed to the clamorous voices of private interest. The technostructure produces an economic performance which is quite good in terms of the goals set by the technostructure, and thereby influencing the rest of society, but which is quite bad in terms of the *real* needs of our present-day economy.

Thus the Galbraithian analysis.

CRITIQUE OF GALBRAITH

Virtually all economists would credit Galbraith with bringing a greater air of realism to the analysis of industrial organization than is found in much neoclassical reasoning. However, most economists (but only the older ones, Galbraith would say) would also fault him for his failure to appreciate the real achievements of traditional economic theory. Even the purely competitive model has important uses in showing the interdependence of an economic system and in providing a model for the concept of economic efficiency. Theorists of government spending and of socialist economics find it necessary to use important elements of this model. The work of John Maynard Keynes in the 1930s might never have occurred if there had not been a purely competitive model of the economy to work with.

The very simplicity and rigidity of the competitive model makes it easier to analyze the impact of departures from its assumptions. Galbraith's theory, the critics might argue, is much too loose. On some important issues, you hardly know where he stands. Does the large corporation of the planning system tend to charge prices that are too high or too low? Because there is this great emphasis on growth of output, one might assume that the large corporation in the Galbraithian world would opt for lower-than-usual prices. But Galbraith also stresses the readiness of the corporation to pass along wage increases to the consumer in terms of higher prices. Galbraith admits that "higher prices are inimical to growth,"[5] but recognition of the problem does not represent its solution. He seems to picture large corporations as responsible for both too much output and inflation at the same time. Indeed, having given up the neoclassical model of efficiency, Galbraith's theory offers no explicit standard of what "too high" or "too low" prices are. His greater realism is purchased, at times, at the expense of intellectual order.

There are also specific rebuttals to all the points we have presented in our summary of his theory. Very briefly:

STRUCTURE OF THE ECONOMY

If traditional theory overemphasizes the small-scale sector of the economy, Galbraith overemphasizes the large corporation, speaking, at times, as if it were the dominating and characteristic form of modern enterprise. But this is very probably already an historical anachronism. The most rapidly growing sector of the economy now is the service sector, characteristically small-scale in organization. As Professor Robert Solow says, it is by no means "clear which way the wind is blowing" (p. 263).

PLANNING VERSUS THE MARKET

The term "planning" as used by Galbraith implies far more control over its environment than most large firms have. Ford "planned" to have a success with the Edsel and totally failed (Solow, p. 264). General Motors undoubtedly "planned" to have a banner year in 1974, but the energy crisis and the recession reduced their sales and employment substantially. In short, Galbraith considerably overstates the actual power that businessmen have to alter their environment.

GOALS OF THE FIRM

Dr. Robin Marris offers Galbraith some partial support in his analysis of the goals of the large corporation (p. 283). Marris thinks it likely that the large firm will seek growth first, and then try to adjust other variables—the rate of profit, the amount of earnings that it pays out in dividends as opposed to what it retains for expansion, the price of its stocks on the market—to this prior goal. Maximum growth subject to a minimum stock price, he believes, describes the goals of many of these large firms. However, critics can point out that it is not clear empirically that the Galbraith-Marris view is correct nor is it clear that their view is really so different from the traditional view. Solow notes that favorable capital gains treatment in federal taxation may bring the goals of growth of the firm and maximum profits much closer together than they would be if only before-tax profits were considered

[5]*Economics and the Public Purpose*, p. 187.

(pp. 289–290). In seeking growth, the firm may simply be maximizing *after* tax profits.

PERSUASION OF THE CONSUMER

Galbraith offers no scientific evidence of the effect of advertising on the consumer and therefore there is no way of judging how much (or how little) success large corporations have in creating consumer tastes and altering consumer behavior. It is particularly unfortunate that he has no reply to Solow's important question about television (p. 266). Here was a new, apparently very powerful medium of communication and persuasion: Has it, in fact, made a massive difference to consumer buying habits and patterns? If so, where is the evidence to that effect?

SOCIAL CONSEQUENCES

As in the case of Galbraith's analysis of the structure of the economy, it can be argued that his analysis of the social consequences of modern industrial organization is already out of date. Recall that this succession of books began with *The Affluent Society* which described a world in which scarcity had largely disappeared (except in isolated areas, "case poverty," etc.), shortages did not exist, and the need for economic toil was becoming progressively less. In such a world, the criticism that the large corporation put far too much emphasis on growth of output had a weight that it does not carry today. Are we really in the affluent society at all, or will we have to work increasingly hard if we are even to preserve our standard of living, clean up our environment, avoid specific shortages of resources and the like? As economists who were writing in the Depression were perhaps overly fearful of imminent economic collapse, has Galbraith—writing mostly during the great American prosperity of the 1950s and 1960s—been too impressed by the ease with which economic growth occurs?

There is no certain answer to any of these questions. If there were, we would not have a debate but a conclusion. The following pages should make it clear that that conclusion is not yet with us. It should also make clear the depth of feeling that differences on matters of economic analysis can arouse. This is not dry science, but dramatic personal encounter as well.

The New Industrial State
John Kenneth Galbraith

John Kenneth Galbraith is the former United States
Ambassador to India and Paul M. Warburg Professor of
Economics Emeritus at Harvard University.

The market has only one message for the business firm. That is the
promise of more money. If the firm has no influence on its prices, as the
Wisconsin dairy farm has no influence on the price of milk, it has no
options as to the goals that it pursues. It must try to make money and, as a
practical matter, it must try to make as much as possible. Others do. To
fail to conform is to invite loss, failure and extrusion. Certainly a decision
to subordinate interest in earnings to an interest in a more contented life
for workers, cows or consumers would, in the absence of exceptional
supplementary income, mean financial disaster. Given this need to maximize revenue, the firm is thus fully subject to the authority of the market.

When the firm has influence on market prices—when it has the power
commonly associated with monopoly—it has also long been assumed that
it will seek as large a profit as possible. It could settle for less than the
maximum but it is assumed that it seeks monopoly power in order to be
free of the limitations set by competition on its return. Why should it seek
monopoly power and then settle for less than its full advantages? When
demand is strong, the monopolistic firm can extract more revenue from
the market; when demand slackens, it can get less. But so long as it tries
to get as much as possible it will still be subject to control by the market
and ultimately, as sustained by the compulsions of avarice, by the preferences of consumers, as expressed by their purchases. Were the mon-
opolist regularly to settle for something less than a maximum return,

Excerpted from John Kenneth Galbraith, *The New Industrial State* (Boston: Houghton Mifflin, 1967; London:
Andre Deutsch, 1967), pp. 109–11, 115–17, 160–65, 210–15. Copyright © 1967, 1971 by John Kenneth
Galbraith. Reprinted by permission of the publishers, Houghton Mifflin and Andre Deutsch.

the causes of this restraint would have to be explained by forces apart from the market. Along with the state of demand these forces would be a factor determining prices, production and profit. Belief in the market as the transcendent regulator of economic behavior requires, therefore, a parallel belief that participating firms will always seek to maximize their earnings. If this is assumed, there is, by exclusion, no need to search for other motives.

When planning replaces the market this admirably simple explanation of economic behavior collapses. Technology and the companion commitments of capital and time have forced the firm to emancipate itself from the uncertainties of the market. And specialized technology has rendered the market increasingly unreliable. So the firm controls the prices at which it buys materials, components and talent and takes steps to insure the necessary supply at these prices. And it controls the prices at which it sells and takes steps to insure that the public, other producers or the state take the planned quantities at these prices. So far from being controlled by the market, the firm, to the best of its ability, has made the market subordinate to the goals of its planning. Prices, costs, production and resulting revenues are established not by the market but, within broad limits later to be examined, by the planning decisions of the firm.

The goal of these planning decisions could still be the greatest possible profit. We have already seen that a high and reliable flow of earnings is important for the success of the technostructure. But the market is no longer specifying and enforcing that goal. Accordingly profit maximization—the only goal that is consistent with the rule of the market—is no longer necessary. The competitive firm had no choice of goals. The monopoly could take less than the maximum; but this would be inconsistent with its purpose in being a monopoly. But planning is the result not of the desire to exploit market opportunity but the result, among other factors, of the unreliability of markets. Subordination to the market, and to the instruction that it conveys, has disappeared. So there is no longer, *a priori*, reason to believe that profit maximization will be the goal of the technostructure. It could be, but this must be shown. And it will be difficult to show if other things are more important than profit for the success of the technostructure. It will also be difficult to show if the technostructure does not get the profit.

THE APPROVED CONTRADICTION

It is agreed that the modern large corporation is, quite typically, controlled by its management. The managerial revolution as distinct from that of the technostructure is accepted. So long as earnings are above a certain minimum it would also be widely agreed that the management has little to fear from the stockholders. Yet it is for these stockholders, remote, powerless and unknown, that management seeks to maximize profits. Management does not go out ruthlessly to reward itself—a sound management is expected to exercise restraint. Already at this stage, in the accepted view of the corporation, profit maximization involves a substantial contradiction. Those in charge forgo personal reward to enhance it for others.

The contradiction becomes much sharper as one recognizes the role of the technostructure. If power is regarded as resting with a few senior officers, then their pecuniary interest could be imagined at least to be parallel to that of the owners. The higher the earnings the higher the salaries they can justify, the greater the return on any stock they may themselves hold, and the better the prospect for any stock options they may have issued to themselves. Even these contentions stand only limited examination. There are few corporations in which it would be suggested that executive salaries are at a maximum. As a not uncritical observer has recently observed, ". . . [the] average level of salaries of managers even in leading corporations is not exceptionally high."[1] Astronomical figures, though not exceptional, are usually confined to the very top. Stock holdings by management are small and often non-existent. Stock options, the right to buy stock at predetermined prices if it goes up in value, though common, are by no means universal and are more widely valued as a tax dodge than as an incentive. So even the case for maximization of personal return by a top management is not strong.

But with the rise of the technostructure, the notion, however tenuous, that a few managers might maximize their own return by maximizing that of the stockholders, dissolves entirely. Power passes down into the organization. Even the small stock interest of the top officers is no longer the rule. Salaries, whether modest or generous, are according to scale; they do not vary with profits. And with the power of decision goes opportunity for making money which all good employees are expected to eschew. Members of the technostructure have advance knowledge of products and processes, price changes, impending government contracts and, in the fashionable jargon of our time, technical breakthroughs. Advantage could be taken of this information. Were everyone to seek to do so—by operations in the stock of the company, or in that of suppliers, in commodity markets, by taking themselves and their knowledge into the em-

---

[1] Wilbert E. Moore, *The Conduct of the Corporation* (New York: Random House, Inc. 1962), p. 13.

ploy of another firm for a price—the corporation would be a chaos of competitive avarice. But these are not the sort of thing that a good company man does; a remarkably effective code bans such behavior. Group decision making insures, moreover, that almost everyone's actions and even thoughts are known to others. This acts to enforce the code and, more than incidentally, a high standard of personal honesty as well. The technostructure does not permit of the privacy that misfeasance and malfeasance require.

So the technostructure, as a matter of necessity, bans personal profit making. And, as a practical matter, what is banned for the ordinary scientist, engineer, contract negotiator or sales executive must also be banned for senior officers. Resistance to pecuniary temptation cannot be enforced at the lower levels if it is known that the opportunity to turn a personal penny remains the prerogative of the high brass.

The members of the technostructure do not get the profits that they maximize. They must eschew personal profit making. Accordingly, if the traditional commitment to profit maximization is to be upheld, they must be willing to do for others, specifically the stockholders, what they are forbidden to do for themselves. It is on such grounds that the doctrine of maximization in the mature corporation now rests. It holds that the will to make profits is, like the will to sexual expression, a fundamental urge. But it holds that this urge operates not in the first person but the third. It is detached from self and manifested on behalf of unknown, anonymous and powerless persons who do not have the slightest notion of whether their profits are, in fact, being maximized. In further analogy to sex, one must imagine that a man of vigorous, lusty and reassuringly heterosexual inclination eschews the lovely, available and even naked women by whom he is intimately surrounded in order to maximize the opportunities of other men whose existence he knows of only by hearsay. Such are the foundations of the maximization doctrine when there is full separation of power from reward.

THE PRINCIPLE OF CONSISTENCY

The mature corporation, as we have seen, is not compelled to maximize its profits and does not do so. This allows it to pursue other goals and this accords similar alternatives to the members of the technostructure. The need for consistency, nonetheless, still holds. The goals of the corporation, though so freed, must be consistent with those of the society and consistent, in turn, with those of the individuals who comprise it. So also must be the motivations.

More specifically, the goals of the mature corporation will be a reflection of the goals of the members of the technostructure. And the goals of the society will tend to be those of the corporation. If, as we have seen to be the case, the members of the technostructure set high store by autonomy, and the assured minimum level of earnings by which this is secured, this will be a prime objective of the corporation. The need for such autonomy and the income that sustains it will be conceded or stressed by the society.

So with other goals, and so matters work also in reverse. If the society sets high store by technological virtuosity and measures its success by its capacity for rapid technical advance, this will become a goal of the corporation and therewith of those who comprise it. It may, of course, be subordinate, as a goal, to the need to maintain a minimum level of income—the fact that the goals of the mature corporation are plural rather than singular does not mean that all have the same priority. Rather, a hierarchy of goals is quite plausible. And given the requisite consistency between social, corporate and individual goals there is no *a priori* reason for assuming that the priorities will be exactly the same for any two corporations.

The same consistency characterizes motivation—the stimuli that set individuals and organizations in pursuit of goals. Pecuniary compensation is an extremely important stimulus to individual members of the technostructure up to a point. If they are not paid this acceptable and expected salary, they will not work. But once this requirement is met, the offer of more money to an engineer, scientist or executive brings little or no more effort. Other motivation takes over. Similarly, until the minimum requirements of the corporation for earnings are reached, pecuniary motivation will be strong. For it too, above a certain level, additional income brings little or no additional effort. Other goals become more important.

Consistency is equally necessary in the case of identification. The individual will identify himself with the goals of the corporation only if the corporation is identified with, as the individual sees it, some significant social goal. The corporation that is engaged in developing a line of life-preserving drugs wins loyalty and effort from the social purpose its products serve or are presumed to serve. Those engaged in the design or manufacture of a space vehicle identify themselves with the goals of their organization because it, in turn, is identified with the scientific task of exploring space or the high political purpose of outdistancing the Russians. The manufacturer of an exotic missile fuel, or a better trigger for a nuclear warhead, attracts the loyalty of its members because their organization is seen to be serving importantly the cause of freedom. It is felt no doubt that human beings, whose elimination these weapons promise, have an inherent tendency to abuse freedom.

There is no similar identification if the firm is simply engaged in making money for an entrepreneur and has no other claimed social purpose. It is noteworthy that when a corporation is having its assets looted by those in control it simultaneously suffers a very sharp reduction in executive and employee morale. All concerned recognize that the corporation is no longer serving any social purpose of any kind.

Consistency in the identification of individuals and organizations with social goals is possible because, running as a parallel thread from individual through organization to social attitudes, is the presence of adaptation as a motivating force. The individual serves organization, we have seen, because of the possibility of accommodating its goals more closely to his own. If his goals reflect a particular social attitude or vision, he will seek to have the corporation serve that attitude or vision. More important, he will normally think that the goals he seeks have social purpose. (Individuals have a well-remarked capacity to attach high social purpose to whatever—more scientific research, better zoning laws, manufacture of the lethal weapons just mentioned—serves their personal interest.) If he succeeds, the corporation in turn will advance or defend these goals as socially important. The corporation becomes, thus, an instrument for attributing social purpose to the goals of those who comprise it. Social purpose becomes by this process of adaptation what serves the goals of members of the technostructure.

This process is highly successful in our time. Much of what is believed to be socially important is, in fact, the adaptation of social attitudes to the goal system of the technostructure. What counts here is what is believed. These social goals, though in fact derived from the goals of the technostructure, are believed to have original social purpose. Accordingly, members of the corporation in general, and of the technostructure in particular, are able to identify themselves with the corporation on the assumption that it is serving social goals when, in fact, it is serving their own. Even the most acute social conscience is no inconvenience if it originates in one's own.

The process by which social goals become adapted to the goals of the corporation and ultimately the technostructure is not analytical or cerebral. Rather it reflects a triumph of unexamined but constantly reiterated assumption over exact thought. The technostructure is principally concerned with the manufacture of goods and with the companion management and development of the demand for these goods. It is obviously important that this be accorded high social purpose and that the greater the production of goods, the greater be the purpose served. This allows the largest possible number of people to identify themselves with social function.

From a detached point of view, expansion in the output of many goods is not easily accorded a social purpose. More cigarettes cause more cancer. More alcohol causes more cirrhosis. More automobiles cause more accidents, maiming and death; also more preemption of space for highways and parking; also more pollution of the air and the countryside. What is called a high standard of living consists, in considerable measure, in arrangements for avoiding muscular energy, increasing sensual pleasure and for enhancing caloric intake above any conceivable nutritional requirement. Nonetheless, the belief that increased production is a worthy social goal is very nearly absolute. It is imposed by assumption, and this assumption the ordinary individual encounters, in the ordinary course of business, a thousand times a year. Things are better because production is up. There is exceptional improvement because it is up more than ever before. That social progress is identical with a rising standard of living has the aspect of a faith. No society has ever before provided such a high standard of living as ours, hence none is as good. The occasional query, however logically grounded, is unheard.

There are other examples. Successful planning in areas of expensive and sophisticated technology requires that the state underwrite costs, including the costs of research and development, and that it insure a market for the resulting products. It is important to the technostructure, therefore, that technological change of whatever kind be accorded a high social value. This too is agreed. In consequence, the underwriting of sophisticated technology by the state has become an approved social function. Few question the merit of state intervention for such social purpose as supersonic travel or improved applications of nuclear power. Even fewer protest when these are for military purposes. Social purpose is again the result of adaptation. This is a matter of obvious importance and one to which I will return.

None of this is to suggest that all social attitudes originate with the technostructure and its needs. Society also has goals, stemming from the needs which are unassociated with its major productive mechanism, and which it imposes on the mature corporation. As elsewhere I argue only for a two-way process. The mature corporation imposes social attitudes as it also responds to social attitudes. Truth is never strengthened by exaggeration. Nor is it less the truth by being more complex than the established propositions that assert the simple eminence of pecuniary goals and pecuniary motivation.

THE REVISED SEQUENCE

In virtually all economic analysis and instruction, the initiative is assumed to lie with the consumer. In response to wants that originate within himself, or which are given to him by his environment, he buys goods and services in the market. The opportunities that result for making more or less money are the message of the market to producing firms. They respond to this message of the market and thus, ultimately, to the instruction of the consumer. The flow of instruction is in one direction—from the individual to the market to the producer. All this is affirmed, not inappropriately, by terminology that implies that all power lies with the consumer. There "is always a presumption of consumer sovereignty in the market economy." The uni-directional flow of instruction from consumer to market to producer may be denoted the Accepted Sequence.

We have seen that this sequence does not hold. And we have now isolated a formidable apparatus of method and motivation causing its reversal. The mature corporation has readily at hand the means for controlling the prices at which it sells as well as those at which it buys. Similarly, it has means for managing what the consumer buys at the prices which it controls. This control and management is required by its planning. The planning proceeds from use of technology and capital, the commitment of time that these require and the diminished effectiveness of the market for specialized technical products and skills.

Supporting this changed sequence is the motivation of the technostructure. Members seek to adapt the goals of the corporation more closely to their own; by extension the corporation seeks to adapt social attitudes and goals to those of the members of its technostructure. So social belief originates at least in part with the producer. Thus the accommodation of the market behavior of the individual, as well as of social attitudes in general, to the needs of producers and the goals of the technostructure is an inherent feature of the system. It becomes increasingly important with the growth of the industrial system.

It follows that the accepted sequence is no longer a description of the reality and is becoming ever less so. Instead the producing firm reaches forward to control its markets and on beyond to manage the market behavior and shape the social attitudes of those, ostensibly, that it serves. For this we also need a name, and it may appropriately be called the Revised Sequence.

The revised sequence sends to the museum of irrelevant ideas the notion of an equilibrium in consumer outlays which reflects the maximum of consumer satisfaction. According to this doctrine, beloved in economic instruction and still honored in economics textbooks, the individual or household arranges his or its purchases so there is approximately equal satisfaction from the last dollar spent for each of the several opportunities for consumption or use of goods. Were it otherwise—were it so that a dollar spent on cosmetics returned more satisfaction than a dollar spent on gasoline—then spending on cosmetics would have been increased and that on gasoline diminished. And the reverse being true of comparative satisfaction from cosmetics and gasoline, the reverse would have occurred. In other words, when the return to a small added outlay for different purposes is unequal, satisfaction can always be increased by diminishing the expenditure where the satisfaction is less, and enlarging it where the satisfaction is greater. So it follows that satisfaction is at a maximum when the return to a small increment of expenditure is the same for all objects of expenditure.

But it is also true that, since an individual's satisfaction from his various opportunities for expenditure is his own, there must be no interfering with this equalizing process. Dictation from any second person on how to distribute income, however meritorious, will not reflect the peculiar enjoyment pattern of the person in question. Presumably it will reflect the preferences of the instructor.

Such is the established doctrine. And if the individual's wants are subject to management this is interference. The distribution of his income between objects of expenditure will reflect this management. There will be a different distribution of income—a different equilibrium—in accordance with the changing effectiveness of management by different producers.[2] It is to the nature and purposes of this management, not simply to the effort of the individual to maximize his satisfactions, that the scholar must look if he is to have any adequate view of consumer behavior.

It is true that the consumer may still imagine that his actions respond to his own view of his satisfactions. But this is superficial and proximate, the result of illusions created in connection with the management of his wants. Only those wishing to evade the reality will be satisfied with such a simplistic explanation. All others notice that if an individual's satisfaction is less from an additional expenditure on automobiles than from one on housing, this can as well be corrected by a change in the selling strategy of General Motors as by an increased expenditure on his house. Similarly, a perfect state of equilibrium with marginal utilities everywhere equal can be upset not by a change in the individual's income or by a change in the goods available but by a change in the persuasion to which he is subject.

[2] What the lay reader will recognize, for example, to be the ordinary and expected result of the changing effectiveness of advertising campaigns.

The problem of economics here, once again, is not one of original error but of obsolescence. The notion of the consumer so ˏdistributing his income as to maximize satisfactions that originate with himself and his environment was not inappropriate to an earlier stage of economic development. When goods were less abundant, when they served urgent physical need and their acquisition received close thought and attention, purchases were much less subject to management. And, on the other side, producers in that simpler and less technical world were not under compulsion to plan. Accordingly they did not need to persuade—to manage demand. The model of consumer behavior, devised for these conditions, was not wrong. The error was in taking it over without change into the age of the industrial system. There, not surprisingly, it did not fit.

The New Industrial State or Son of Affluence

Robert M. Solow

Robert M. Solow is Professor of Economics at the
Massachusetts Institute of Technology.

More than once in the course of his new book Professor Galbraith takes
the trouble to explain to the reader why its message will not be enthusias-
tically received by other economists. Sloth, stupidity, and vested interest in
ancient ideas all play a part, perhaps also a wish—natural even in tourist-
class passengers—not to rock the boat. Professor Galbraith is too modest
to mention yet another reason, a sort of jealousy, but I think it is a real
factor. Galbraith is, after all, something special. His books are not only
widely read, but actually enjoyed. He is a public figure of some significance; he shares with William McChesney Martin the power to shake
stock prices by simply uttering nonsense. He is known and attended to all
over the world. He mingles with the Beautiful People; for all I know,
he may actually be a Beautiful Person himself. It is no wonder that
the pedestrian economist feels for him an uneasy mixture of envy and
disdain.

There is also an outside possibility that the profession will ignore *The
New Industrial State* (Houghton Mifflin) because it finds the ideas more or
less unhelpful. The world can be divided into big-thinkers and little-
thinkers. The difference is illustrated by the old story of the couple who
had achieved an agreeable division of labor. She made the unimportant
decisions: what job he should take, where they should live, how to bring
up the children. He made the important decisions: what to do about
Jerusalem, whether China should be admitted to the United Nations, how

From Robert M. Solow, "The New Industrial State or Son of Affluence," *The Public Interest,* No. 9 (Fall
1967), pp. 100–108. Copyright © National Affairs, Inc., 1967. Reprinted by permission of the publisher and
the author.

to deal with crime in the streets. Economists are determined little-thinkers. They want to know what will happen to the production of houses and automobiles in 1968 if Congress votes a 10 percent surcharge on personal and corporate tax bills, and what will happen if Congress does not. They would like to be able to predict the course of the Wholesale Price Index and its components, and the total of corporate profits by industry. They are not likely to be much helped or hindered in these activities by Professor Galbraith's view of Whither We Are Trending.

Professor Galbraith makes an eloquent case for big-thinking, and he has a point. Little-thinking can easily degenerate into mini-thinking or even into hardly thinking at all. Even if it does not, too single-minded a focus on how the parts of the machine work may lead to a careful failure ever to ask whether the machine itself is pointed in the right direction. On the other side, Professor Galbraith gingerly pays tribute to the little-thinkers whose work he has used, but it is evident that he has been exposed only very selectively to the relevant literature. There is no point squabbling over this: big-think and little-think are different styles, and the difference between them explains why this book will have more currency outside the economics profession than in it. It is a book for the dinner table, not for the desk.

I shall try to summarize the main steps in Galbraith's argument and shall then return to discuss them, one by one.

(1) The characteristic form of organization in any modern industrial society is not the petty firm but the giant corporation, usually producing many different things, and dominating the market for most of them. Nor is this mere accident. The complicated nature of modern technology and the accompanying need for the commitment of huge sums of capital practically demand that industry be organized in large firms.

(2) With few exceptions, the giant corporation is in no sense run by its owners, the common stockholders. The important decisions are made —have to be made—by a bureaucracy, organized in a series of overlapping and interlocking committees. The board of directors is only the tip of an iceberg that extends down as far as technicians and department managers. The members of the bureaucracy are all experts in something, possibly in management itself. Galbraith calls them the "technostructure," but that awkward word is probably a loser.

(3) It is the nature of the highly-capitalized bureaucratically controlled corporation to avoid risk. The modern business firm is simply not willing to throw itself on the mercy of the market. Instead, it achieves certainty and continuity in the supply of materials by integrating backward to produce its own, in the supply of capital by financing itself out of retained

earnings, in the supply of labor by bringing the unions into the act. It eliminates uncertainty on the selling side by managing the consumer, by inducing him, through advertising and more subtle methods of salesmanship, to buy what the corporation wants to sell at the price it wants to charge. The major risk of general economic fluctuations is averted by encouraging the government in programs of economic stabilization.

(4) It would be asking much too much of human nature to expect that the bureaucracy should manage the firm simply in the interests of the stockholders. There is, therefore, no presumption that the modern firm seeks the largest possible profit. Nor does it. The firm's overriding goal is its own survival and autonomy; for security it requires a certain minimum of profit and this it will try to achieve. Security thus assured, the firm's next most urgent goal is the fastest possible growth of sales. (Since firms grow by reinvesting their earnings, this goal is not independent of profits; nevertheless, once the minimum target in profits is achieved, the modern firm will expand its sales even at the expense of its profits.) There are two lesser goals: a rising dividend rate, presumably to keep the animals from getting restless, and the exercise of technological virtuosity.

(5) Modern industry produces mainly things, and it wishes to grow. Everyone will be happier if everyone believes that a growing production of things is the main object of the national life. People will be happier because that is what they in fact get, and the bureaucracy will be happier because they can feel that they serve the national purpose. This belief has been widely inculcated, but it takes effort really to believe it, because American society already has more things than it knows what to do with.

(6) The key resource in the modern industrial state is organized intelligence, especially scientific and managerial intelligence. One of the important things the government does to support the system is the extension of education to provide a supply of recruits for the bureaucracy, and the subsidization of scientific and technological research to provide something interesting for them to do. What Galbraith calls the "scientific and educational estate" therefore acquires a certain moral authority and even mundane power in the society. This is an important circumstance, because the scientific and educational estate—at least its youngest members—can see through the cult of the GNP and observe that it slights the claims of leisure, art, culture, architectural design, and even the innocent enjoyment of nature. Here is the most promising source of social change and of a rather more attractive national style of life.

There is a lot more in the book, much of it full of insight and merriment, but the main logic of the argument seems to be roughly as I have stated it.

It may be unjust and pointless to consider the degree of literal truth of each of the assertions that make up this argument. One would hardly discuss *Gulliver's Travels* by debating whether there really are any little people, or criticize the *Grande Jatte* because objects aren't made up of tiny dots. Nevertheless, it may help to judge the truth of Galbraith's big picture if one has some idea about the accuracy of the details. So, at the risk of judging big-think by the standards of little-think, I proceed.

(1) Professor Galbraith is right that modern economics has not really come to terms with the large corporation. Specialists in industrial organization do measure and describe and ponder the operations of the very large firm. Occasionally some of these specialists propound theories of their financial or investment or pricing behavior. It cannot be said that any of these theories has yet been so successful as to command widespread assent. Perhaps for that reason, much economic analysis, when it is not directly concerned with the behavior of the individual firm, proceeds as if the old model of the centralized profit-maximizing firm were a good enough approximation to the truth to serve as a description of behavior in the large. But this is not always done naively or cynically. Professor Galbraith is not the first person to have discovered General Motors. Most close students of industrial investment or pricing do make room in their statistical behavior equations for behavior that is neither perfectly competitive nor simply monopolistic. (The long debate over the incidence of the corporate profits tax hardly suggests universal reliance on any simple model.)

There is, after all, a moderate amount of economic activity that is not carried on by General Motors, or by the 100 largest or 500 largest corporations. In fact, only about 55 percent of the gross national product originates in nonfinancial corporations at all. Not nearly all of that is generated by the giant corporations (of course, some financial corporations are among the giants). Nor is it entirely clear which way the wind is blowing. The giant corporation is preeminently a phenomenon of manufacturing industry and public utilities; it plays a much less important role in trade and services. If, as seems to be in the cards, the trade and service sectors grow relative to the total, the scope of the large corporation may be limited. Alternatively, big firms may come to play a larger role in industries that have so far been carried on at small scale.

Enough has been said to suggest that it is unlikely that the economic system can usefully be described either as General Motors writ larger or as the family farm writ everywhere. This offers at least a hint that it will behave like neither extreme. In any case, counting noses or assets and recounting anecdotes are not to the point. What is to the point is a "model"—a simplified description—of the economy that will yield valid predictions about behavior.

(2) The "separation of ownership from control" of the modern corporation is not a brand new idea. It is to be found in Veblen's writings and again, of course, in Berle and Means' *The Modern Corporation and Private Property*. Recent investigation shows that the process has continued; only a handful of the largest American corporations can be said to be managed by a coherent group with a major ownership interest. (The nonnegligible rest of the economy is a different story.) I do not think the simple facts have ever been a matter for dispute. What is in dispute is their implications. It is possible to argue—and many economists probably would argue—that many management-controlled firms are constrained by market forces to behave in much the same way that an owner-controlled firm would behave, and many others acquire owners who like the policy followed by the management. I think it may be a fair complaint that this proposition has not received all the research attention it deserves. It is an error to suppose it has received none at all. Such evidence as there is does not give a very clear-cut answer, but it does not suggest that the orthodox presupposition is terribly wrong. Galbraith does not present any convincing evidence the other way, as I think he is aware. The game of shifting the burden of proof that he plays at the very end of this book is a child's game. Economics is supposed to be a search for verifiable truths, not a high-school debate.

(3) The modern corporation—and not only the modern corporation—is averse to risk. Many economic institutions and practices are understandable only as devices for shifting or spreading risk. But Galbraith's story that the industrial firm has "planned" itself into complete insulation from the vagaries of the market is an exaggeration, so much an exaggeration that it smacks of the put-on.

Galbraith makes the point that the planning of industrial firms need not always be perfect, that a new product or branch plant may occasionally go sour. By itself, therefore, the Edsel is not a sufficient argument against his position. His is a valid defense—but it is not one he can afford to make very often. No doubt the Mets "plan" to win every ballgame.

Consider the supply of capital. There is a lot of internal financing of corporations; it might perhaps be better if companies were forced more often into the capital markets. But external finance is hardly trivial. In 1966 the total flow of funds to nonfarm nonfinancial corporate business was about $96 billion. Internal sources accounted for $59 billion and external sources for the remaining $37 billion. Besides, depreciation allowances amounted to $38 billion of the internal funds generated by business, and much of this sum is not a source of net finance for growth. External sources provided about one-half of net new funds. In 1966, bond issues and bank loans alone added up to about two-thirds of undistributed profits. Trade credit is another important source of external funds, but it is complicated because industrial corporations are both lenders and borrowers in this market. I don't know how the proportions of external and internal finance differ between larger and smaller corporations, but the usual complaint is that the large firm has easier access to the capital market. I do not want to make too much of this, because self-finance is, after all, an important aspect of modern industrial life. But there is, I trust, some point in getting the orders of magnitude right. There might also be some point in wondering if the favored tax treatment of capital gains has something to do with the propensity to retain earnings.

Consider the consumer. In the folklore, he (she?) is sovereign; the economic machinery holds its breath while the consumer decides, in view of market prices, how much bread to buy, and how many apples. In Galbraith's counterfable, no top-heavy modern corporation can afford to let success or failure depend on the uninstructed whim of a woman with incipient migraine. So the consumer is managed by Madison Avenue into buying what the system requires him to buy. Now I, too, don't like billboards or toothpaste advertising or lottery tickets of unknown—but probably negligible—actuarial value with my gasoline. (Though I put it to Professor Galbraith that, in his town and mine, the Narragansett beer commercial may be the best thing going on TV.) But that is not the issue; the issue is whether the art of salesmanship has succeeded in freeing the large corporation from the need to meet a market test, giving it "decisive influence over the revenue it receives."

That is not an easy question to answer, at least not if you insist on evidence. Professor Galbraith offers none; perhaps that is why he states his conclusion so confidently and so often. I have no great confidence in my own casual observations either. But I should think a case could be made that much advertising serves only to cancel other advertising, and is therefore merely wasteful.

If Hertz and Avis were each to reduce their advertising expenditures by half, I suppose they would continue to divide the total car rental business in roughly the same proportion that they do now. (Why do they not do so? Presumably because each would then have a motive to get the jump on the other with a surprise advertising campaign.) What would happen to the total car rental business? Galbraith presumably believes it would shrink. People would walk more, sweat more, and spend their money instead on the still-advertised deodorants. But suppose those advertising expenditures were reduced too, suppose that all advertising were reduced near the minimum necessary to inform consumers of the commodities available and their elementary objective properties? Galbraith believes that in absence of persuasion, reduced to their already satiated biological needs for guidance, consumers would be at a loss; total consumer spending would fall and savings would simply pile up by default.

Is there anything to this? I know it is not true of me, and I do not fancy myself any cleverer than the next man in this regard. No research that I know of has detected a wrinkle in aggregate consumer spending behavior that can be traced to the beginning of television. Perhaps no one has tried. Pending some evidence, I am not inclined to take this popular doctrine very seriously. (It is perhaps worth adding that a substantial proportion of all the sales that are made in the economy are made not to consumers but to industrial buyers. These are often experts and presumably not long to be diverted from considerations of price and quality by the provision of animated cartoons or even real girls.)

Consider the attitude of the large corporation to the economic stabilization activities of the federal government. It is surely true that big business has an important stake in the maintenance of general prosperity. How, then, to account for the hostility of big business to discretionary fiscal policy, a hostility only lately ended, if indeed traces do not still persist? Here I think Professor Galbraith is carried away by his own virtuosity; he proposes to convince the reader that the hostility has not come from the big business bureaucracy but from the old-style entrepreneurial remnants of small and medium-sized firms. Their fortunes are not so dependent on general prosperity, so they can afford the old-time religion. Professor Galbraith is probably wrong about that last point; large firms are better able than small ones to withstand a recession. He is right that the more Paleolithic among the opponents of stabilization policy have come from smaller and middle-sized business.

But up until very recently, the big corporation has also been in opposition. Even in 1961 there was considerable hostility to the investment tax credit, mainly because it involved the government too directly and obviously in the management of the flow of expenditures in the economy at large. It was only after further acquaintance with the proposal excited their cupidity that representatives of the large corporation came around. More recently still, they have generally opposed the temporary suspension of the credit as a counterinflationary stabilization device, and welcomed its resumption. (This warm attachment to after-tax profits does not accord well with the Galbraith thesis.) There is a much simpler explanation for the earlier, now dwindling, hostility that would do no harm to the argument of the book: mere obtuseness.

(4) Does the modern industrial corporation maximize profits? Probably not rigorously and singlemindedly, and for much the same reason that Dr. Johnson did not become a philosopher—because cheerfulness keeps breaking in. Most large corporations are free enough from competitive pressure to afford a donation to the Community Chest or a fancy office building without a close calculation of its incremental contribution to profit. But that is not a fundamental objection to the received doctrine, which can survive if businesses merely *almost* maximize profits. The real question is whether there is some other goal that businesses pursue systematically at the expense of profits.

The notion of some minimum required yield on capital is an attractive one. It can be built into nearly any model of the behavior of the corporation. I suppose the most commonly held view among economists goes something like this (I am oversimplifying): for any given amount of invested capital, a corporation will seek the largest possible profits in some appropriately longrun sense, and with due allowance for cheerfulness. If the return on capital thus achieved exceeds the minimum required yield or target rate of return, the corporation will expand by adding to its capital, whether from internal or external sources. If the return on equity actually achieved (after corporation tax) is any guide, the target rate of return is not trivial. The main influence on profits in manufacturing is obviously the business cycle; for fairly good years one would have to name a figure like 12 percent, slightly higher in the durable-goods industries, slightly lower in nondurables. In recession years like 1954, 1958, 1961, the figure is more like 9 percent.

Alternatives to this view have been proposed. Professor Galbraith mentions William Baumol and Robin Marris as predecessors. Baumol has argued that the corporation seeks to maximize its sales revenue, provided that it earns at least a certain required rate of return on capital. This is rather different from Galbraith's proposal that corporations seek growth rather than size. These are intrinsically difficult theories to test against observation. Some attempts have been made to test the Baumol model; the results are not terribly decisive, but for what they are worth they tend to conclude against it. Marris's theory is very much like Galbraith's, only much more closely reasoned. He does propose that corporate management seeks growth, subject to a minimum requirement for profit. But Marris is more careful, and comes closer to the conventional view, because he is fully aware, as Galbraith apparently is not, of an important discipline in the capital market. The management that too freely sacrifices profit for growth will find that the stock market puts a relatively low valuation on its assets. This may offer an aggressive management elsewhere a tempting opportunity to acquire assets cheap, and the result may be a merger offer or a takeover bid, a definite threat to the autonomy of the management taken over. Naturally, the very largest corporations are not subject to this threat, but quite good-sized ones are.

Professor Galbraith offers the following argument against the conventional hypothesis. A profit-maximizing firm will have no incentive to pass along a wage increase in the form of higher prices, because it has already, so to speak, selected the profit-maximizing price. Since the modern industrial corporation transparently does pass on wage increases, it cannot have been maximizing profits in the first place. But this argument is a sophomore error; the ideal textbook firm will indeed pass along a wage increase, to a calculable extent.

There is, on the other hand, a certain amount of positive evidence that supports the hypothesis of rough profit-maximization. It has been found, for instance, that industries which are difficult for outsiders to enter are more profitable than those which are easily entered and therefore, presumably, more competitive. It has been found also, that there is a detectable tendency for capital to flow where profits are highest. Serious attempts to account for industrial investment and prices find that the profit-supply-demand mechanism provides a substantial part of the explanation, though there is room for less classical factors, and for quite a lot of "noise" besides.

(5) Professor Galbraith does not have a high opinion of the private consumption of goods and services. "What is called a high standard of living consists, in considerable measure, in arrangements for avoiding muscular energy, increasing sensual pleasure and for enhancing caloric intake above any conceivable nutritional requirement. . . . No society has ever before provided such a high standard of living as ours, hence none is as good. The occasional query, however logically grounded, is unheard." One wonders if that paragraph were written in Gstaad where, we are told, Professor Galbraith occasionally entertains his muse.

It is hard to disagree without appearing boorish. Nevertheless, it is worth remembering that in 1965 the median family income in the United States was just under $7000. One of the more persistent statistical properties of the median income is that half the families must have less. It does not seem like an excessive sum to spend. No doubt one could name an excessive sum, but in any case the reduction of inequality and the alleviation of poverty play negligible roles in Galbraith's system of thought. His attitude toward ordinary consumption reminds one of the Duchess who, upon acquiring a full appreciation of sex, asked the Duke if it were not perhaps too good for the common people.

(6) I have no particular comment on Professor Galbraith's view of the role of the scientific and educational estate as an agent of social and cultural improvement. But this is perhaps a convenient place for me to state what I take to be the role of this book. Professor Galbraith is fundamentally a moralist. His aim is to criticize seriously what he believes to be flaws in American social and economic arrangements, and to make fun of the ideological myths that are erected to veil the flaws. More often than not, in such expeditions, his targets are well chosen and he is on the side of the angels—that is to say, I am on his side. I trust that readers of his work will acquire some resistance to the notion that any interference by the government in a corporation's use of its capital is morally equivalent to interference in the citizen's use of his toothbrush. I share his belief that American society is under-provided with public services and over-provided with hair oil. I agree with him that men ought to be more free to choose their hours of work, and that this freedom is worth some loss of productivity.

But Professor Galbraith is not content to persuade people that his values ought to be their values. I don't blame him; it's slow work. He would like an elaborate theory to show that his values are, so to speak, objective, and opposition to them merely ideological. He would like to do, in a way, for the scientific and educational estate what Marx and "scientific socialism" tried to do for the proletariat. The ultimate point of the basic argument is that the economy does not efficiently serve consumer preferences—first because industrial corporations evade the discipline of the market by not seeking profit anyway, and second because the preferences are not really the consumer's own.

As theory this simply does not stand up, a few grains of truth and the occasional well-placed needle notwithstanding. There are, however, other powerful arguments against *laissez-faire:* the existence of monopoly power, inadequate information and other imperfections of the market, the presence of wide divergences between private and social benefits and costs, and a morally unattractive distribution of income. These need to be argued and documented from case to case. It is a kind of joke, but if Professor Galbraith would like to see more and better public services, he may just have to get out and sell them.

A Review of a Review
John Kenneth Galbraith

Professor Robert Solow is one of the most distinguished and prestigious economists of our time. He is a calm and confident scholar with rare mastery of the technical tools of economic and quantitative analysis. To the extent that economics qualifies as a science, it is men like Professor Solow who have earned it the reputation. The rather subjective standards of the social sciences in general and of economic theory in particular allow men a certain liberty in defining their own competence. A scholar is often what he claims to be. But Professor Solow's superior mastery of his discipline is acknowledged and admired, I think, by all.

It is because Professor Solow is so intimately associated with the scientific claims of our profession that I find myself writing this comment. It is not to dispute his view of *The New Industrial State;* this naturally differs from mine, and did I agree with it I would hardly have been justified in publishing the book. But the book is in the public domain and to a degree surpassing my far from modest expectations. Reviews of books that are technical or otherwise obscure are of no slight importance. Others depend on them as do theatre goers to whom first night admission is denied. But human vanity what it is, the person who has seen for himself will reach his own conclusions. So it is here, and this is the principal reason, as I have often said, why I years ago determined to seek a substantial audience. One is not at the risk of those who react adversely to that with which they disagree or find otherwise distasteful.

From John Kenneth Galbraith, "A Review of a Review," *The Public Interest*, No. 9 (Fall 1967), pp. 109–18. Reprinted by permission of the author.

However, Professor Solow's review seems to merit a word on its own account. It exemplifies a tendency of social scientists, unconscious but not above reproach, to divest themselves of the rules of scientific discourse when they encounter something they do not like. Carelessness also no doubt plays a part. This tendency acquires its special poignancy when, as in the case of Professor Solow, the writer is, and with reason, conscious of his scientific prestige. He is held to even higher standards than the rest of us. The phenomenon is worth explicit examination, and I trust that Professor Solow will not be perturbed by my using him, in effect, as a case study. Thus this review of his review.

2

Although the rules of scientific discourse have never been fully codified, a number enjoy wide acceptance in the common law. They can all best be stated in negative form. One should avoid comment *ad hominem*—that is to say, one should not attack a position by slighting or adverse comment on the personality or behavior of the person who defends it. One should be accurate. One should avoid *obiter dicta;* that is to say, nothing should be allowed to rest on the unsupported word of the speaker, however great his prestige. Both over- and understatement should be avoided—matters where I long ago learned to confess guilt. It is possible that another rule might be added although this may be a counsel of perfection. The scientist should be aware of, and disclose, personal interest. It is this, more than incidentally, that may cause him to violate the other rules. In the review in question Professor Solow is in more or less serious violation of the first three canons. There is at least a possibility that he violates the last. Even for a scholar with no special scientific pretensions this is a poor score. Let me specify.

He begins his review with a number of *ad hominem* observations—the alleged social life of the author and his association with what he calls the Beautiful People, the power that "he shares with William McChesney Martin . . . to shake stock prices by simply uttering nonsense," and this form of comment recurs when he takes exception to my suggestion that higher living standards are not a primary measure of social excellence. "One wonders if that paragraph were written in Gstaad where, we are told, Professor Galbraith occasionally entertains his muse."

Were this all and true, one would doubtless dismiss it as harmless needling, not damaging to careful discourse. I wouldn't, in reply, comment on Professor Solow's social preoccupations or choice of recreation or residence, but these are matters on which there is room for many levels of taste. But the reader will observe, I think, that these observations are in keeping with, and in some small measure serve, the larger design of his article. They suggest a certain frivolity of purpose. (One notices the use of the word nonsense.) Clearly, the deeply serious scholar should not be detained. It would surely be better scientific method though rather more demanding work simply to argue the case. More significant, perhaps, none of it is true. I regard most social activities, fashionable or otherwise, as a bore, and since I have been an ambassador there is even documentary evidence in the archives. In March of 1955 I gave testimony before the Senate Banking and Currency Committee, carefully prepared and not before described as nonsense, on the nature of the speculative fever in 1929 and the measures that might prevent a recurrence. I had just finished a book on the subject. While I testified the market dropped very sharply. On *no other* occasion have I ever seen it suggested that a remark of mine has affected the market. As opportunity allows, I certainly do go to Switzerland (as did Alfred Marshall), but in recent years it has been because I can work there free of both interruption and a disagreeable respiratory ailment. So even Professor Solow's personal comments, it will be evident, establish a rather disconcerting pattern of unreliability. Presumably, even *ad hominem* argument should be accurate. And his reliability does not become greater when he comes to substantial matters, and we measure his essay against the scientific canon that requires accurate meaning accurately conveyed. Let me offer what can only be a partial list.

3

The New Industrial State draws rather extensively from the empirical work of other economists. That, presumably, is one thing such empirical work is for. Professor Solow states that the author "gingerly pays tribute to the little-thinkers [his term and assuredly not mine] whose work he has used. . . ." That most readers will take to mean that I was miserly in my credit to others. Here, that the reader may judge, is what I said:

This book has not, it will be agreed, been confined to narrow points. But I have singularly little quarrel with those who so restrict themselves. I have drawn on their work, quantitative and qualitative at every stage; I could not have written without their prior efforts. So I have nothing but admiration and gratitude for the patient and skeptical men who get deeply into questions, and I am available to support their application to the Ford Foundation however minute the matter to be explored. I expect them to judge sternly the way their material has been used in this book.[1]

[1] John Kenneth Galbraith, *The New Industrial State* (Boston: Houghton Mifflin Co., 1967), p. 402.

In commenting on my contention that the large corporation is a highly important, strongly characteristic feature of the American economy Professor Solow says that "Professor Galbraith is not the first person to have discovered General Motors" and that "There is, after all, a moderate amount of activity that is not carried on by General Motors, or by the 100 largest or 500 largest corporations." Most readers would conclude from Professor Solow that I somehow claim originality as the discoverer of the great corporation and that I equate all economic activity with the large firms. There are no such suggestions in the book. I do say that the great firm has not made its way in modern economic theory. This Professor Solow concedes. I am careful to point out that the world of the large corporations, what I call the Industrial System, is not the whole of the economy. The remaining "part of the economic system is not insignificant. It is not, however, the part of the economy with which this book . . . [is] concerned."

I might add that Professor Solow then concludes this part of his discussion by saying that "enough has been said to suggest that it is unlikely that the economic system can usefully be described either as General Motors writ larger or the family farm writ everywhere." His logic here will surely seem casual. He is saying, in effect, that one cannot (as I do) describe a part of the economy, even a highly important part. One must do nothing unless he has a model that will cover all. This, I am sure, he does not intend.

Professor Solow says that "The 'separation of ownership from control' in the modern corporation is not a brand new idea," adding that it is to be found in Veblen's writings as well as in Adolf A. Berle, Jr. and G. C. Means.[2] Again the reader will suppose that Professor Solow is correcting, perhaps mildly rebuking, a spurious claim to novelty. None was made. Veblen's great point was, in fact, a different one. The engineers and the technicians he believed to be held in check by the greater power of the controlling pecuniary interest. The owners were unduly in control. Relying on his admitted competence on these matters, rather than more meticulous scholarship, Professor Solow uses error to rebuke precision. And my acknowledgement of the work of Adolf Berle, R. A. Gordon as well as of such later writers as Edward Mason, Carl Kaysen and Robin Marris on the separation of ownership from control could hardly be more

---

[2] *The Modern Corporation and Private Property* (New York: Macmillan, 1934). When this book first appeared economists and statisticians of high technical reputation, the men of the professional establishment, led in this instance by Professor W. L. Crum of Harvard, attacked it vigorously. They pointed to shortcomings in its measures of concentration and in its concept of control. These being present, it was held, in effect, that the book should be ignored.

complete or heartfelt.[3] But there is no need to argue a point that can otherwise be decided. Let Professor Berle, the scholar mentioned by Professor Solow as somehow slighted, say whether or not, both here and over the years, I have done less than justice to his work.

The reader will see what Professor Solow, however innocently, has sought to suggest. Here speaks the superior scholar. I must warn you against something that is not quite careful. I do not protest Professor Solow's superior view of his competence; it has much to commend it, and we are all allowed the enjoyment of our vanity. He has, however, gravely underestimated his task. An author will usually be more knowledgeable about his work than any critic. Accordingly, the latter has only slight leeway for error. And it will be evident that Professor Solow, so far from being careful, has been very careless. One final small example will show what he has let himself in for. In noting the importance that I attach to growth as a goal of the corporation he observes that Mr. Robin Marris, the distinguished British economist, has reached the same general conclusion, only his effort is "much more closely reasoned." Again the warning flag. But I do not disagree. Marris' reasoning occupies an entire book as compared with a chapter in my case. And as I told in the book, and most explicitly in the Reith lectures which have also been published, I made great use of Mr. Marris' argument. I did not duplicate it. In large measure I followed it. Professor Solow is in the odd position of finding something less well done that wasn't attempted.

In arguing against growth and in favor of profit maximization as a primary goal of the corporation, Professor Solow comes out on the side of the latter. That, of course, is his privilege; it is the received view and one that is vital if the omnipotence of the market is to be assumed. But it is hardly proper that Professor Solow should ignore what, from his viewpoint, is the most difficult point. If the technostructure—the autonomous and collegial guiding authority of the corporation—maximizes profits, it maximizes them, in the first instance at least for others, for the owners. If it maximizes growth, it maximizes opportunity for, among other things, advancement, promotion and pecuniary return for itself. That people should so pursue their own interest is not implausible. Professor Solow, as he elsewhere makes clear, does not think it so.

In attacking the importance that I attach to the control by the large corporation of its own capital supply—an importance that Professor

[3] One name, to my embarrassment, is missing, that of James Burnham. Scholars, perhaps put off by his subsequent extreme views on foreign policy, have not given sufficient credit to the ideas he offered in *The Managerial Revolution*. Their importance is at least suggested by the phrase he added to the language and which I do, of course, acknowledge.

Solow also concedes—he compares for 1966 the total flow of funds from within nonfarm, nonfinancial corporation to that coming from outside. More came from outside. Professor Solow then observes: "I don't know how the proportion of external and internal finance differs between large and smaller corporations although the usual complaint is that the larger firm has easier access to the capital market." It is hard to explain this by carelessness. For Professor Solow knows that construction and trade (the latter with its need to finance inventories and sales) rely heavily on borrowed funds. Firms here tend also to be relatively small—as he agrees elsewhere in the case of trade. It is from such firms as he also knows that complaints come when money is tight. And his reference to the easier access to the capital market of the larger firm is surely disingenuous. He knows that the security that is associated with an ample flow of funds from internal sources will favor the firm so blessed when it goes into the capital markets for additional supplies. Such "ease of access" proves nothing as regards reliance on outside funds.

When there is an industrywide wage increase a normal expectation is of a compensatory price increase with, perhaps, something more. I note that if an industry is able to so increase revenues the day after a wage increase, it could have done so the day before, always assuming that it could find some substitute for the wage increase as a signal for action. It follows that before the wage increase it was not maximizing its revenues; it had some unliquidated margin of monopoly gain. The conclusion is based, Professor Solow states, in language that many will think a trifle lofty if not otherwise unsuited to scholarly discourse, on "sophomore error." The textbook firm, already maximizing its profits, would also raise its prices "to a calculable extent." Alas, the error is again Professor Solow's—though I naturally forego any pejorative adjectives. He omitted to notice that the two responses—my full and immediate compensation for the wage increase and an unspecified response to a cost change—are not the same. The first would not generally be possible were profit already at a maximum. And he did not notice that I carefully allowed for the second.[4]

One will sense that Professor Solow's desire to attribute error has undermined his instinct to precision. This is most disturbingly evident in the last example I will cite. He suggests that I ignore the danger of a

---

[4] I fear that I, in some sense, tricked Professor Solow into this error. In an article in *The Review of Economics and Statistics* in 1957 I explored this problem in detail. I did not refer to it in *The New Industrial State*—I sought to ration footnotes beginning with those to my own work. Had Professor Solow been reminded of this earlier work he would not have fallen into the error of assuming a more simplistic rather than a more comprehensive view than his own. But it could be also argued that scholars should check the literature before reacting so strongly.

"takeover bid" for the firm that sacrifices earnings for growth and thus abnormally depresses the value of its securities thereby making them open to acquisition. Thus I am indifferent to the disciplines of the capital market. But then he concedes that the takeover is not a threat to the very large firms with which I am concerned. (It arises only farther down the size scale.) And he has elsewhere himself suggested that I write of an economy in which General Motors is writ large. The reader at this point will surely have begun to wonder. I am accused of being indifferent to dangers that by his admission do not exist for the large firms with which I am excessively concerned. In point of fact I considered this problem at length. The danger of involuntary takeover is negligible in the management calculations of the large firm and diminishes with growth and dispersal of stock ownership.

The list of the points on which Professor Solow has left himself vulnerable could be extended. I have not said, as he states, that the "industrial firm has 'planned' itself into complete insulation from the vagaries of the market." To have to make a point vulnerable by exaggeration is again to suggest a determination to find error so compulsive as to allow it to be invented. On the defense of consumer sovereignty, a vital matter as I will suggest presently, there is already something approaching an agreed line. To this Professor Solow adheres. I have not shown that demand can be managed fully and for all. So the effort can be safely dismissed. (Much or most advertising Professor Solow ventures "serves only to cancel other advertising and is therefore merely wasteful." He suspects that I am influenced by a dislike for billboards and singing commercials.) I argue only for a partial management of consumer choice. But it will hardly be suggested that what is imperfect or incomplete can, as a matter of sound scientific method, be ignored. Professor Solow to the contrary, I do deal with the stabilization of markets for nonconsumer's goods, and I treat at length of the influence of producers on public procurement including, in particular, weaponry. Enough has been said, I think, to indicate a fairly serious default in the canon of scientific discourse that requires careful attention to subject and statement. Let me now advert more briefly to the use of *obiter dicta*—to reliance not on evidence but on the undoubted scientific reputation of the speaker.

4

There are two of these which troubled me and which may well have troubled readers who have approached these matters with more care than Professor Solow. One is his concluding statement, which I confess I came upon with surprise, that "the reduction of inequality and the alleviation of poverty play negligible roles in Galbraith's system of thought." Rightly or wrongly the treatment of poverty in *The Affluent Society* has been widely cited as helping pave the way for the modern belief that, in the forms therein described, it would survive a steady increase in aggregate income. (The observations of Michael Harrington are perhaps relevant in this regard.) The same book had at least something to do with drawing attention to deficiencies in the public sector—shortcomings in education, the squalor of the cities—as sources of residual poverty and the anger we now experience in the ghettos.[5] A paper I presented before a special group working on the problem of "pockets of poverty" in the autumn of 1963 was at least well-timed in relation to the legislation establishing the Office of Economic Opportunity the following year.[6] I participated actively in drafting that legislation and served on the statutory advisory board to the Office until new legislation, plus possibly my views on Vietnam, brought my involuntary severance. I also served, though not with any great usefulness, on Mayor Lindsay's task force on this problem. None of this is final proof of a preoccupation with poverty and inequality, and in the nature of the case my own assessment is hardly to be trusted. But most fairminded readers will agree, I believe, that it is sufficient to place a certain burden of proof on Professor Solow. He could conceivably be suggesting, though the words do not imply it, that *The New Industrial State* is not directly concerned with poverty and inequality. But one does not cover all subjects in one book, and I was additionally careful to say:

There are many poor people left in the industrial countries, and notably in the United States. The fact that they are not the central theme of this treatise should not be taken as proof either of ignorance of their existence or indifference to their fate. But the poor, by any applicable tests, are outside the industrial system. They are those who have not been drawn into its service or who cannot qualify. And not only has the industrial system—its boundaries as here defined are to be kept in mind—eliminated poverty for those who have been drawn into its embrace but it has also greatly reduced the burden of manual toil. Only those who have never experienced hard and tedious labor, one imagines, can be wholly indifferent to its elimination.[7]

[5] The very first title of this book was *Why People are Poor*, and it was under this cachet that I negotiated a small grant for research from the Carnegie Corporation of New York in the early fifties. Later titles, *The Opulent Society* and then *The Affluent Society*, reflected my more mature view of the problem. That was less why people are poor than why residual poverty persists and other problems remain unsolved under conditions of generally high and rising income. I think it possible that Professor Solow might wish to plead that he has not read *The Affluent Society*. This is a wholly legitimate defense, one that would be offered by many other intelligent people, but it does, I would judge, deny him the right to pass on my preoccupations.

[6] "Let Us Begin" published in *Harper's Magazine* in the Spring of 1964.

[7] *The New Industrial State, op. cit.*, p. 318.

With equal absence of proof Professor Solow suggests that I have exposed myself only "very selectively" to the vast empirical literature relevant to the facets of the system I establish. Here again one is a poor witness for himself. I am naturally impressed by the time I have spent in the last ten years in tracking down and assimilating the distressingly vast material within the ambit of this volume—the case material on the management of the corporation, monographs on organization theory and practice, on the nature of scientific and technical development, trade union development and attitudes, socialist and Soviet planning including one substantial and one lesser journey for work on the ground, literature on political change and business ideology and the newer materials on the much more limited range of matters on which I consider myself a specialist and much, much more. (I need scarcely add that to my distress I keep on encountering materials that I should have seen.) Professor Solow as a teacher and scholar and distinguished public servant has, most plausibly, covered even more completely this same range of literature. Only as a result of having done so could he claim to pass on the adequacy or inadequacy of anyone else's coverage. But again the reader can rightly ask for at least some argument on behalf of his own greater and more systematic diligence. To let it stand on his own unsupported assertion is surely to trade unduly on scholarly reputation.

5

I come now to the point of it all. And here I am on less certain ground. Professor Solow's error and his use of *obiter dicta* are objective. They are visible to all. To ascribe reasons other than the obvious one of carelessness in the case of so distinguished a scholar involves elements of subjectivity. One could easily find himself in scientific default. Moreover, I am not wholly critical of Professor Solow for failing to disclose the interest which forces him into so unappealing a posture and performance. He may not be fully aware of it.

The issue concerns the future of economics in general and of the highly prestigious work with which Professor Solow is associated in particular. That work is within a highly specific frame. Within that frame it is the best of its kind. But it is only good if the frame is reasonably intact. When the frame goes so do the scholars it sustains.

What is the frame? It is that the best society is the one that best serves the economic needs of the individual. Wants are original with the individual; the more of these that are supplied the greater the general good. Generally speaking the wants to be supplied are effectively translated by the market to firms maximizing profits therein. If firms maximize profits they respond to the market and ultimately to the sovereign choices of the consumer. Such is the frame and given its acceptance a myriad of scholarly activities can go on within. Any number of blocks can be designed and fitted together in the knowledge that they are appropriate to—that they fit somewhere in—the larger structure. There can be differences of opinion as to what best serves the purposes of the larger structure. Mathematical theorists and model builders can squabble with those who insist on empirical measurement. But this is a quarrel between friends.

Should it happen, however, that the individual ceases to be sovereign—should he become, however subtly, the instrument or vessel of those who supply him, the frame no longer serves. Even to accommodate the possibility that humans are better served by collective than by individual consumption requires the framework to be badly warped. Should the society no longer accord priority to economic goals—should it accord priority to aesthetic accomplishment or mere idleness—it would not serve. And no one quite knows the effect of such change. One can only be certain that, for a long time, economics, like the lesser social sciences, will be struggling with new scaffolding. And the work of economists will be far less precise, far less elegant, seemingly far less scientific than those who are fitting pieces into a structure the nature of which is known and approved and accepted. And if social priority lies elsewhere, it will be less prestigious.

The threat to economics is a serious one; it could become like sociology and partly a branch of political theory. And there are even more pointed aspects. Students are attracted to economics partly by the fascination of working with men of precise and well articulated mind like Professor Solow. But they must be assured, also, that their work is within a framework of sound social purpose. (There remains considerable attraction, though not sufficient attraction, in being a member of a small band of technical initiates. It is somewhat like being a member of a fraternity, a lodge or a chess club.) To enhance the well-being of the individual has, in the past, seemed a sound social purpose. To assist the individual in his subordination to General Motors will not be so regarded. The sanctity of economic purpose will also be questioned if well-being as conventionally measured continues to improve and leaves unsolved the problems associated with collective need—those of the cities and their ghettos and the by-passed rural areas—or if this progress involves an unacceptable commitment to the technology of war. And the doubts so engendered will be especially acute if concentration on narrow economic priority appears to be a cause of other social shortcomings. The fate of the business schools is a warning of what happens when scholars lose their reputation for association with social purpose. The better students desert in droves and what is a scholar without a school?

I have been looking, however inadequately, at the frame. This, it is plain from the response, does not seem an unreasonable exercise to those outside the profession. Nor to those within who do not feel endangered—whose temperament allows them to watch and philosophically adjust. But it is a threat to those whose prestige and academic position is profoundly associated with the existing structure. It is perhaps not too surprising that it should inspire a counter-offensive. It is less agreeable that it should be compulsively negligent of the scientific mood which, given the old frame, could be so proudly avowed.

A Rejoinder

Robert M. Solow

I have always laughed at Professor Galbraith's jokes, even when they have been directed at me or my friends. So it is naturally a little disappointing that he should come on so solemn when I tease him a little.

There are one or two places where Professor Galbraith, and therefore possibly other readers, may have misunderstood me. I mentioned that the existence of very large corporations, and the separation of ownership from control within them, had been observed before now. My intention was not at all to hint that Professor Galbraith has tried to palm these off as brand new observations of his own. He has not. My purpose was to suggest to the reader that ideas so long in circulation must have evoked some response, one way or the other, from economists. I agreed that the response had not been wholly satisfactory from an analytical point of view, but I did not think Professor Galbraith had done it justice. The facts about the size and organization of industrial firms matter to the workaday economist mainly as they affect the substance of pricing, production and investment decisions. There is, in fact, a large body of empirical work on pricing, production and investment behavior in manufacturing industry. Much of it explains the data moderately well while staying loosely within the framework of supply-demand theory. The facts of large size and diffused stock-ownership do not seem to change that very much.

By the way, it was this range of material that I had in mind when I observed that Professor Galbraith seemed to have missed some of the relevant literature.

From Robert M. Solow, "A Rejoinder," *The Public Interest* No. 9 (Fall 1967), pp. 118–19. Copyright © National Affairs, Inc., 1967. Reprinted by permission of the publisher and the author.

I wrote that the reduction of inequality and the alleviation of poverty play negligible roles in Galbraith's system of thought. Professor Galbraith interprets me to be accusing him of indifference to the plight of the poor. But the context of my remarks was a discussion of the low valuation Professor Galbraith puts on the growth of private consumption and real output generally. My point was not that Professor Galbraith is hard-hearted, but that it is difficult to accommodate drastic reduction of the extent of poverty in a system of thought based on the unimportance of increased real output, except perhaps by sharply redistributive taxation. But the mean income is not so high as all that, and anyway Professor Galbraith does not talk much about redistribution.

Professor Galbraith is wrong to ascribe to me a belief in wants that are "original with the individual" and in "the omnipotence of the market." As to the first, it is hardly a deep thought that nearly all consumer wants beyond the most elementary physiological ones are socially or culturally determined. Indeed, that is precisely why I fear the whole issue is rather tricky. It is a very fine line between analytical statements about the creation of wants by advertising and elaborate indications that one believes one's own tastes to be superior to those of the middle classes.

As to the second, it is only to Professor Galbraith that I seem to believe in the omnipotence of the market. To people who really believe in it, I suppose I seem like Professor Galbraith. I do believe that market forces operate over a large part of the modern economy, sometimes loosely, sometimes tightly. That does not mean that whatever the market turns up is good, or immune from tinkering on the part of the political authority. It does suggest that it will often be efficient to accomplish the social good by *using* the market.

Finally, Professor Galbraith suggests that I disbelieve his argument not because it is unconvincing or unhelpful, but because I have a personal interest to protect. His doctrine is so subversive of conventional economics that if it were to be widely accepted my sort of work would fall in the academic pecking order, my students would diminish in number and quality, and economics would take a tack uncongenial to my sort of mind. About my motives, he may of course be right. Who knows what evil lurks in the hearts of men, as Lamont Cranston used to say. As for the rest, he may equally be right. I shall try to roll gracefully with the punch, and if I cannot, well, then *Après moi, la sociologie.*

Galbraith, Solow, and the Truth About Corporations

Robin Marris

Robin Marris, of Cambridge University, England, is an expert on the modern corporation.

I have volunteered to intervene in the Solow-Galbraith controversy, which began in the Fall issue of this journal, because I have some doubts whether, at the end of the day, the lay reader was left clear about the basic issues.

THE REAL WORLD OF THE FIRM

When we reach the core of the debate—i.e., the economic theory of corporate behavior—the truth is that Solow was disingenuous, but that Galbraith had left out vital elements and laid himself open to legitimate attack. What Solow omitted to tell was that my theory implies that *in spite* of the existence of "an important discipline in the capital market," the real-world system almost certainly behaves very differently from the way implied in the conventional theory: the conventional theory would imply that corporations would choose to grow considerably more slowly and reward stockholders significantly better. Galbraith, however, in failing to meet the argument that profits are needed for growth, failed to explain how this divergence can occur. In offering to put the record straight, I am motivated not only by vanity, but also by the conviction that an accurate theory about corporate growth is essential for a correct understanding of a wide range of contemporary problems of economic and social policy. The theory cannot be made simple, but can be summarized as follows.

A growing corporation faces two problems: the problem of creating a growing demand for its products, and the problem of financing the necessary growth of capacity. The corporation may strive to be as efficient as possible, in the sense of squeezing the maximum profit from its existing markets; but the search for (or creation of) *new* markets inevitably costs money (in research, marketing, and losses from failures), and so, as the growth process is accelerated, the average return realized on the *total* assets of the corporation must be adversely affected (even if the development expenditure is deployed as efficiently as possible). In theoretical language, we say there is consequently a "functional relationship" between the rate of return and the rate of growth of saleable output, which varies from corporation to corporation (in the sense that some can get a better return with a given growth rate than others) and from time to time, but that at a given phase in a particular corporation's history, when all the facts are known, the relationship is unique. At the same time, any given growth rate of sales must be supported by a corresponding growth rate of production capacity and hence requires an adequate supply of financial capital. If the main source of finance is internal, the existing level of profits is obviously a major factor governing the sums available, so we get a "feed-back" loop in which the rate of growth both influences and is influenced by the rate of profit. In fact, it is not difficult to see that if retained earnings were the only source of finance, and if the *proportion* retained were arbitrarily fixed by law or convention, we would already have what is called a "closed model"; given the relationships described, for each individual corporation there would be only one rate of growth which could satisfy both conditions simultaneously (the unique value would, however, vary *between* corporations). This would be an "equilibrium" relationship between growth rate and profit rate, in the sense that the profit rate was at the same time just *low* enough to be consistent with the growth rate of sales and just *high* enough to provide adequate finance. This is about the simplest and neatest "theory of the growth of the corporation" one can conceive. To the best of my knowledge it was invented by Carl Kaysen, now Director of the Institute for Advanced Studies at Princeton, New Jersey, in an unpublished seminar paper given in England about ten years ago. It is not difficult to make the theory more realistic by allowing for flexibility in the retention/pay-out decisions and by bringing in outside finance. In my earlier work I put considerable emphasis on the role of internal finance, and more particularly on the balance between internal and external finance in "closing" a more realistic model. More recently, I have become increasingly impressed by the theoretical work of other economists which suggests that the basic implications are much the same whether one assumes finance to be all internal, all external, or a mixture of the two. In other words, I now think it may not matter too much whether Galbraith or Solow was most right in their confrontation on this point. But to explain the next step in the argument most easily (and for that reason only), it is convenient to write as if all finance were internal.

If we accept that, within very wide limits, the retention ratio is effectively decided by the management, the basic structure of the theory remains unchanged—but it is turned around. If the management chooses to go for a certain growth rate, this will determine the profit rate, so there is now only one value of the retention ratio which will provide the continuous finance required. Once the management has decided its target growth rate, it *must* adopt a corresponding retention ratio; if not, the corporation will either (1) run out of money or (2) fail to achieve its target. Of course, Boards of Directors do not see their problems in these precise terms; but there is considerable evidence that they feel and understand the essential structure of the problem in this way.

PROFITS AND/OR GROWTH

If the process of growth were steady and continuous, and if the numerical values of the relations involved remained unchanged (neither conditions, of course, being satisfied in real life), a decision by the management to grow at a certain rate, and to choose the consistent retention ratio, must also evidently imply a unique level and expected rate of growth of the dividend; and so, in a rational stock market, the decision must imply a unique current price and prospective capital gain in the corporation's stock. Up to a point, actual or potential stockholders may be content to see increased growth creating prospects of future gain at the expense of current dividends; beyond this point, any further increase in the growth rate chosen by the management must have a depressing effect on the stock price. There is no reason to suppose that a growth-oriented management will always refrain from accelerating beyond this point; and if they go too far they will undoubtedly lay themselves open to a variety of dangers (e.g., a take-over raid). I suggested in my theory that we might describe a typical "managerial" objective as maximum growth subject to a *minimum* on the stock price.

Solow said that my theory, in recognizing the minimum stock-price constraint, "came closer to the conventional view." On the contrary, in the conventional view management exists only to serve stockholders, and the essential technical problem is to find decision rules that would establish the policy which will, in fact, *maximize* the price of the stock. The two theories become "similar" only in the special conditions where the minimum and maximum position lie close together. These conditions are most improbable; in other words, the traditional theory is literally a "special case."

Because large-scale, professional management, not personally owning large supplies of finance, has such predominant technical advantages in the modern economy; because, although it may *use* stockmarket investors and bankers, it no longer *depends* on them; because the (not insubstantial) true capitalists who remain in our system avoid speculating in large manufacturing businesses unless these are going very cheap (they prefer real estate); because the other potential take-over raiders are typically themselves management-controlled—because of all this and much more, it is inevitable that the safe minimum level of the price of a corporation's stock will be significantly lower, and the safe maximum growth rate correspondingly higher, than the values which would be chosen by a management that really did care only for the welfare of the stockholders. Numerical calculations based on statistical observation suggest that a rather growth-conscious management could typically grow almost twice as fast, setting the stock market value at all times about one-third lower, as compared to the values which would be obtained in an otherwise comparable corporation dominated by stockholders who knew all the facts. Furthermore, the growth-oriented management could safely continue the policy indefinitely, even if there were quite a number of others who chose to behave otherwise. Since the growth-oriented managements will by definition be located in the faster growing corporations, this type of behavior must in time drive out other types—a process which, I suggest, has been going on for some time. The further the process goes, the weaker is the power of the stock market to resist. Since the growth-oriented firms are technically efficient, they display not unattractive levels and growth rates of dividends, the incentive to resistance is dampened, and the latent preference for slower growth and higher current dividends remains unrecognized.

Furthermore, because managements, in fostering growth, also create technical progress, new wants, new goods and a generally different dynamic environment, the implications of the two types of theory cannot easily be compared. We cannot possibly assert that it would necessarily be in the public interest to compel managements to conform to the traditional norm; we might very likely make many people worse off and few better off. Galbraith, however, imposed the value judgment (the "affluent-society" thesis) that the higher rate of consumer innovation resulting from "managerial" behavior by the corporations is undesirable, because it is biased against the expression of leisure preferences and against the development of "public" goods. He does not, however (as maybe does Solow in saying "it might perhaps be better if companies were forced more often into the capital market"), suggest that the remedies lie in the direction of the traditional model.

The conclusion I draw (and it is an implication which I suspect to be one of the causes of the considerable ideological drive of "neoclassical" economics in the United States) would probably be disliked by both parties: namely, that once the classical idealization of capitalism is thus destroyed, there is no *economic* case for its superiority over socialism. Consequently, the attempt to impose capitalism all around the world, in some cases virtually by force, can only be justified on political grounds. The latter, however, seem to get thinner every day. In the miserable developing countries of the "free" world, where we cheerfully give aid to almost any form of dictatorship provided no industries are nationalized (the case of Tito being a historical freak, much disliked by the Congress, I understand), there is no dearth of greedy *profit* maximizers, many living in considerable luxury. What the nonaffluent majority of the world's population so badly needs is a much greater number of *growth* maximizers.

The Truth Further Refined: A Comment on Marris

Robert M. Solow

I want to welcome Robin Marris to this performance of Our Gang . . .

ON CORPORATE BEHAVIOR

Marris has summarized, with quite wonderful economy, his own theory of corporate behavior. It is a self-contained determinate theory, with implications that are testable at least in principle. Like any theory, this one raises two questions. Does it tell a true story? And, if it does, what are its larger implications about economic life?

As I mentioned in my review of Galbraith, it is not easy to invent a clearcut statistical test of the Marris theory of corporate growth against the more standard model of long-run profit maximization anchored by a target rate of return. I suggested that this is because the two theories do not have drastically different implications. Marris objects; like any student of advertising, he would like to stress the differences between his own product and Brand X. I should have been more precise. The two theories need not have very different implications, but they may. Whether they do depends on the height of the minimum acceptable-rate-of-return (or stock price) in Marris' model. The higher it is, or the closer to the target rate of return, the more similar a Marris economy will be to mine. I am uncertain about the source of Marris' conviction that the differences are in fact large, since so far as I know his theory has not yet been given a

Excerpted from Robert M. Solow, "The Truth Further Refined: A Comment on Marris," *The Public Interest* No. 11 (Spring 1968), pp. 47, 49–52. Copyright © National Affairs, Inc., 1968. Reprinted by permission of the publisher and the author.

large-scale run against the facts. One would like to know, for example, how well it does as a predictor of plant and equipment spending.

In the meanwhile, we are reduced to casual empiricism about the assumptions and implications of the Marris theory. This is hardly the place to discuss the matter in detail. I will simply say that the theory, interesting and attractive as it is, seems to me to rest on two fairly weak assumptions. The first is that for a given corporation in a given environment there must be a well-defined relation between its rate of growth (of output) and its rate of return on capital, independent of the absolute size of the corporation. It is not enough for the theory that, with everything else momentarily given, a corporation's profitability should depend on how rapidly it is trying to expand its sales and its capacity. What is required is that this relation hold for long intervals of time during which the corporation is actually growing. Both at the beginning of the period, when the company is small, and at the end, when it is large, it has to be true that to a particular, more or less steady rate of growth of x percent a year corresponds the same more or less steady rate of profit of y percent a year. This is not outlandish, but I think the assumption rests on too simple a view of the business of sales promotion, and on insufficient attention to the production-cost side of the problem.

The second dubious assumption is the one that names growth of sales as the prime object of the corporation. Marris does not simply assert this; he argues it with care and sociological circumstance in his book. He gives two versions: a management may "choose to go for a certain growth rate," or else it may seek "maximum growth subject to a minimum on the stock price." In a more technical statement of the theory he can allow profits and growth to be two separate objectives which have to be weighed against each other. The more weight a corporation attaches to profits and the less to growth, the more nearly it will behave according to the conventional theory.

There is certainly a lot of talk in the business press about growth and expansion. But this, by itself, is hardly support for the Marris-Galbraith doctrine. In the first place, the alternative theory—that corporations maximize long-run profits more or less, and expand whenever they earn more than a target rate of return—also entails that successful companies will be growing most of the time, and will no doubt be talking about it. In the second place, one must keep in mind that the federal government taxes long-term capital gains only half as heavily as dividends, and under some circumstances considerably less than that. Retention and reinvestment of earnings—i.e., internally financed growth—is the obvious way for a corporation to convert dividends into capital gains for its shareholders, including its officers. So devotion to growth is quite consistent with profit-maximization if profit is interpreted as the after-tax return to the stockholder.

Theories that emphasize the separation of ownership and control tend to ignore the fact that, if the common stockholder cannot control the policy of the corporation he owns, he can arrange to own a different corporation by merely telephoning his broker. He can even buy shares in a mutual fund that will tailor a portfolio to his expressed preferences between current dividends and capital gains. Indeed, such theories generally tend to ignore the large-scale institutional investors, whose presence on the other side of the market makes the balance of power between management and owner look a little different.

This would seem to be important, even within the framework of Marris' theory. He admits that some corporations can be more growth-oriented and less profit-oriented than others. If any substantial number of stockholders strongly favors immediate profits over growth, their demands can be mobilized by institutional investors. Corporate managements are sure to be found or created who will be prepared to get their kicks by catering to these demands.

I realize that these casual remarks about the plausibility of assumptions can never be decisive. For that we will have to wait for serious empirical testing. And if I am right that the two theories could turn out to have similar implications, we may have to wait even longer—but of course it will matter less.

ON IDEOLOGY

Marris considers his theory to be subversive of the existing order. Since the consumer is presumably manipulated and the stockholder presumably ignored, no intellectual case remains for capitalism as an efficient economic system. Even leaving aside the question whether this argument applies to the regulated mixed economy of today, it is the damnedest argument for socialism I ever heard. Who would storm the Winter Palace so that units of production could be "endowed with the social norm of growth maximization (subject to financial constraints)" even if "manipulation of the financial rules to offset various kinds of built-in bias . . . would be much easier"?

Marris also suspects that only an ideological drive can explain the persistence with which economists in the United States cling to some (incomplete) confidence in market mechanisms. I would not deny that some academic disputes have a genuine ideological content. But I would also assert that there is far less ideology wrapped up in academic economics in the United States than a man from Cambridge, England, can possibly realize. In fact, I don't think that my argument with Galbraith and Marris is really ideological in character. My own view is that any economic system can be made to work, if you go at it cleverly. But to do that, you have to get the analysis right. If Marris' theory of the firm turns out to work better, which is conceivable, I will buy it cheerfully.

GREAT DEBATE SEVEN

ECONOMIC JUSTICE AND THE DEBATE OVER INEQUALITY

ECONOMIC JUSTICE AND THE DEBATE OVER INEQUALITY

UNTIL the late 1960s, contemporary economists had largely sidestepped the question of what was a fair distribution of income. This lack of attention may partly be attributed to economic circumstances. During the 1930s, the overwhelming problem of industrial societies was mass unemployment. Although the Great Depression had its distributional features—some people were even worse off than others—the central fact was the failure of the industrial economies to provide sufficient work for labor *and* capital, for the unskilled worker *or* the business manager. Although economists could, and to some degree did, argue about the division of the spoils of society, the most striking need clearly was to increase the total accumulation of spoils. Once vast numbers of idle men and machines were put back to work, there would be ample time to consider how to distribute all the added income that would then become available.

In the post-World War II period, this added income did become available, and the industrialized nations went on an economic growth spree perhaps unprecedented in history. For a time, growth itself served to mute concerns about a "just" distribution of the proceeds of that growth. There were rich and poor certainly, but if the poor were increasingly less poor in an absolute sense—if, in an historical sense, they were actually fairly well off—then did it really matter that relative inequalities still persisted? Instead of worrying about distribution, could one not emphasize the socially comfortable fact that there was more for all?

These economic circumstances were supported, as far as the issue of income distribution went, by certain developments in economic theory. In the late nineteenth and early twentieth centuries, economists had, for the most part, made do with a general utility theory of value. This theory, with suitable additions, could guide one through the maze of deciding on an equitable income distribution. If, for example, we assume that people basically all get the same degree of satisfaction (utility) from economic goods, and that the added satisfactions from additional dollars of income tend to decline as a person's income increases (the law of diminishing marginal utility), then we have an argument that tends to favor income equality in the society. A dollar taken from the rich man and given to the poor man will generally increase the total (or average) social utility. This will be true unless the transfer so diminishes economic and productive incentives that there is less total utility for all. In either event, utilitarianism could, in principle, give you some idea of how to proceed faced with a problem of distributive justice.

Unfortunately, this approach was riddled with difficulties. How could you measure utility? How could you compare it among individuals? Anyway, what gave you the right to make a value judgment to the effect that an increase in total social utility is a "good thing"? As these questions were becoming more and more pressing, it was being discovered that as far as economic analysis went, you could actually get along quite well without using the concept of measurable utility. Supply and demand and the theory of prices could be founded on indifference-curve analysis, using only ordinal rather than cardinal measurements.[1]

This reinforced a tendency among economists to shy away from the quest for fairness as between individuals. Interpersonal comparisons were forbidden. Without a measurable marginal utility, such justification as there was for equality collapsed. Economists began limiting themselves to what they hoped was the minimal value judgment involved in saying "more is better." Welfare economics became overwhelmingly focused on economic efficiency. Efficiency, as we pointed out in Great Debate Six (p. 242), involves situations where gains for some individuals can be made without cost to other individuals. The problem of actually taking money away from some people (the rich), and giving it to others (the poor), is thus largely avoided.

THE REDISCOVERY OF INEQUALITY

In the late 1960s inequality was "rediscovered," and, rather unexpectedly, the whole range of distributional questions made a sharp comeback. It was then that "poverty" was discovered in the affluent society. There was evidence of actual malnutrition in rural Mississippi. Life in the large city ghettos was revealed to be a social disgrace. Welfare programs, once on a modest scale, began to grow at a pace that a few found reassuring, many more highly threatening. By the 1972 election campaign, the issue of income distribution—dramatically exemplified in candidate George McGovern's proposal to guarantee each citizen one thousand dollars a year—was providing a central focus for political debate.

At a somewhat deeper level, it had become clear that simple economic growth—more for everybody—did not, after all, solve the question of distribution. Equality and inequality are relative terms. Absolute poverty might be on the mend, but relative poverty was not improving much at all, perhaps to the contrary.

---

[1] In indifference-curve analysis, consumers have to tell us whether they prefer one situation to another or are indifferent as between them; they rank situations by order of preference: first, second, third, and so on. However, they do not have to tell us how much utility (for example, 5 "utils," 1.8 "utils," and so on) they get from the consumption of any set of commodities.

Furthermore, social observers were beginning to realize that the resentment of inequality could become the more intense the richer the society. In a poor society, inequality of income and wealth can sometimes be justified by the need to provide surpluses for capital accumulation and economic development. But in a rich society, more growth may not be that important (or even desirable); why, then, these continued disparities in economic well-being?

At the same time, economists and philosophers were taking a second hard look at the theoretical problem of distributional justice. If one could not get very far with the utilitarian approach, was there perhaps some other intellectually acceptable way of making sense of these questions? One fact was increasingly emphasized: a society has to make, cannot avoid making, decisions on its preferred distribution of income. Satisfactory or not, *some* criteria have to be employed.

THE CLASSICAL POSITION

The net result of these developments has been a new great debate in economics about economic justice, the outlines of which we try to suggest in the readings that follow. We begin with a brief statement of what can be called the classical position. A. C. Pigou, Alfred Marshall's successor at Cambridge University in England, puts forth the general utilitarian argument for moving in the direction of reducing the degree of income inequality. The easy cases (theoretically speaking) are: (1) where the poor are in such extreme want that providing them with added income enormously increases their welfare; and (2) where transferring income from the rich to the poor does not diminish or may even increase the total income of the society. In these cases, clearly, the utilitarian will alter the income distribution in favor of the poor.

The tough case is where the gain in utility of transferring income from rich to poor (which is promised us by the law of diminishing marginal utility) is offset by losses in the total real income available to society. Suppose, for example, that because of various disincentives arising from taxing the rich and subsidizing the poor, we must end up taking $200 from a rich man for every $100 we give to the poor man. Is this good or bad? The utilitarian answer, indicated by Pigou (p. 305), is that such transfers should take place to the "level that the direct good resulting from the transference of the marginal pound just balances the evil brought about by the consequent reduction of the dividend." If the $200 brings less marginal utility to the rich man than the marginal utility of $100 for the poor man, then the transfer should be made. Reason: there is an increase in total social utility or welfare. By contrast, if the $200 brings more added satisfaction to the rich man than $100 would to the poor man, then the transfer should not be made, the inequality should be perpetuated.

JOHN RAWLS' THEORY OF JUSTICE

There are several levels at which this utilitarian logic can be subject to scrutiny. We have already mentioned the problems of the measurability of utility and of interpersonal comparisons. An even deeper line of criticism, however, was initiated by philosopher John Rawls in his path-breaking work, *A Theory of Justice*.[2] Rawls' approach attracted wide attention at the time of its publication, and the remainder of our readings will be concerned with one or another aspect of his theory.

For Rawls, the whole criterion of total social utility (or of average utility, if done on a per capita basis) is unsatisfactory. Thus, in our previous example, he would require the rich man to give up the $200 even if his loss in utility were greater than the gain in utility of $100 for the poor man. In order to make income distribution more equal, Rawls is ready to contemplate actual losses in the average utility position of all members of society.

But what is his justification for what seems on the surface a fairly extreme stance? The central feature of Rawls' approach is that it is a variant of the social contract theory of society, usually associated with Rousseau. He conceives a hypothetical situation called the "original position" (p. 306) in which men choose the shape of the future society into which they agree to enter, their choices including the principles of justice that are to obtain in this society. An individual is supposed to make his choice rationally and with the understanding that he will have to be willing to live with the institutions he has designed. However, he makes his choice without knowing what his own particular position in life will be. A "veil of ignorance" prevents him from knowing whether he will be rich or poor, monarch or slave in the society he is designing. Hence, for example, if he permits slavery in the society, he runs the risk of turning out to be a slave, a chance that a rational individual would presumably be loathe to take.

In this original position, Rawls argues, the individual would opt for what he calls "the two principles of justice" as opposed to the utility principle. The two principles of justice are:

1. *Each person has an equal right to the most extensive scheme of equal basic liberties compatible with a similar scheme of liberties for all.*
2. *Social and economic inequalities are to meet two conditions: they must be* (a) *to the greatest expected benefit of the least advantaged members of society (the maximin equity criterion) and* (b) *attached to offices and positions open to all under conditions of fair equality of opportunity (p. 307).*

The clause that particularly interests us here is 2(a). Under this principle, an inequality of income or wealth is permitted only when it can be shown to be to the advantage of the members of society lowest down on the economic scale. The basic presumption is equality. But if it can be shown that by giving more income to one man, this actually leads directly or indirectly to a greater income for those left behind—then this degree of inequality is permitted.

The contrast with the utility principle can be shown in terms of our earlier example. If we take $200 from the rich man and (because of disincentives, administrative costs, and so on) we can give only $100 to the poor man, then the

[2] John Rawls, *A Theory of Justice* (Cambridge, Mass.: The Belknap Press of the Harvard University Press, 1971).

utilitarian will justify this transfer only if the utility of the $100 to the poor man is greater than the utility of the $200 to the rich man. If not—that is, if the transfer would cause a loss in total utility—then it is rejected. By contrast, Rawls' two principles of justice will require that the transfer be made even in this latter case. The transfer does, in fact, benefit the poor man (the "least advantaged"). Since we cannot justify the rich man's having the $200 on the ground that it is "to the greatest expected benefit of the least advantaged," he must give the money up. The poor, in Rawls' scheme of things, are not required to make sacrifices for the greater good of others. Rather, inequalities are permissible only when they lead to the positive advancement of the poor. In the basic social contract, everyone in the society will have a stake in such inequalities as persist since, by the principles of justice, these inequalities must benefit even those on the lowest rung of the economic ladder.

JUSTIFICATION FOR THE RAWLS PRINCIPLES OF JUSTICE

Proving that individuals, situated in the original position, would in fact choose the two principles of justice, is, of course, a main task for Rawls' theory. His individuals are very averse to risk. The analogy, in game theory, is to the maximin rule for choice under uncertainty. By *maximin* we mean *maximizing* the *minimum* outcome. Instead of going for the highest possible prizes, one may try to make sure that the worst possible outcome is as good as possible. Thus, if everything goes wrong, one will not be in too bad shape: one will have avoided the worst disasters that might otherwise have befallen one.

Rawls believes that a similar principle can be used in the case of justice. He argues that individuals in the original position would be concerned to avoid unacceptable outcomes, that they would examine social structures in terms of the worst possible positions in which they might find themselves, choosing that structure in which the worst position was the least bad among the alternatives. As he puts it succinctly in his book: "the two principles are those that a person would choose for the design of a society in which his enemy is to assign him his place."[3]

He further suggests that an individual would find it very difficult to live with a binding, publicly acknowledged utility principle, particularly if he ended up at the bottom of the pile. Under utilitarianism, one might find that one's good is being sacrificed to that of others. There would be no argument that this sacrifice is really for one's own ultimate good: one is simply a victim of social and economic circumstance. Rawls finds this "an extreme demand psychologically." By contrast, the two principles of justice would guarantee the low men on the totem pole that such inequalities as exist do in fact "work to their advantage" (p. 310).

By the same token, of course, his two principles make a greater psychological demand on the more fortunate members of society than does the utility principle. However, Rawls feels that this strain is easily bearable because, after all, these are the more fortunate members of society and, looking at the matter relatively, they

[3] *Op. cit.,* p. 152.

are still better off than the others. Moreover, the maximin criterion has many further advantages over the utility principle: it requires less information to apply; it is more clearly understandable; and it leads to the socially desirable view that the natural distribution of abilities and talents is a "collective asset." The naturally able and talented can gain from their good fortune but only "in ways agreeable to those less favored" (p. 311). Indeed, we can come close to an arrangement of society in which "all its members can with reason be happy with their situation" (p. 310).

CRITIQUE OF RAWLS

That Rawls' analysis is just a beginning is made very clear in the articles that follow. Klevorick shows that there are rebuttals to all the particular defenses of his principles that Rawls has advanced. Thus, for example, he questions the grounds for feeling that the better situated members of society can easily accept the strains of receiving less under the maximin principle than under the utility principle. These grounds involve an implicit assumption of the law of diminishing marginal utility of income and, also, a questionable reliance on the interdependence of the satisfactions of different persons.

Robert Nozick, in his important book, *Anarchy, State and Utopia,* also questions the situation of the better endowed members of society in a Rawlsian world. Rawls has justified redistributing income from the rich to the poor in part on the grounds that this is the price the rich must bear to ensure the social cooperation of the poor. This social cooperation is of benefit to everyone and hence the more advantaged members of the society do benefit even while they are sustaining distributional losses. But, says Nozick, can't this argument also be reversed and applied to the less well off members of society? They, too, benefit from having the social cooperation of all groups. In particular, they benefit from having the social cooperation of the better endowed members of society.

Thus, Nozick goes on, the reverse of Rawls' proposition could be put to the poor. The better off could say: In return for *our* cooperation, you will be expected to accept an arrangement wherein *we* get as much as possible; if you don't accept, we won't cooperate and we'll all lose.

In other words, the fact that social cooperation is to the benefit of all leaves the rich and the poor in a symmetrical position. According to Nozick it gives no grounds for asking the better endowed members of society to make special sacrifices. If such sacrifices are demanded, the better off, contrary to Rawls, *would* have a right to complain (p. 319).

Thurow also challenges the logic of Rawls' basic analysis. He argues that it is by no means proved that individuals, about to enter upon a social contract, will choose the two principles of justice. Whether they like maximin type solutions will in part depend on their attitudes to gambling and risk. "Empirical evidence," Thurow comments (p. 326), "would seem to point toward the viability of lotteries that do not maximize the minimum prize; people are clearly willing to bet a small part of their current prize (income) in exchange for a very small chance on a very big prize." Also, what about envy? Is it really possible to get very far in the discussion of inequalities of income and wealth without a full recognition of this pervasive human trait?

Nevertheless, Thurow is basically sympathetic to Rawls' objective in forcing an explicit discussion of the issue of economic justice, and he also is impressed by several ingredients of Rawls' solution. In particular, he likes (1) the notion of assuming equality as a natural starting-point from which deviations must be shown to be beneficial; (2) the idea of a basic minimum beneath which no individual should be allowed to fall; and, finally, (3) the implicit distinction in Rawls' theory between *individual-societal preferences* and *private-personal preferences* (p. 327). The former concern an individual's feelings about the desirable design of society; the latter concern his way of behaving within society as it is currently designed. Thurow finds no contradiction, for example, in preferring a highly equal distribution of wealth in one's ideal society, and yet eagerly searching after riches in the imperfect society that actually exists.

Indeed, Thurow actually attempts to characterize what society's current individual-societal preferences about income distribution might be. He believes that these preferences might lead to agreement on a structure that achieved "a minimum earning for those with no wealth of $5,000 a year" and "a distribution of income above this level that is no more unequal than that now in place for fully employed adult white males" (pp. 330–331). This is not a final but rather an interim sketch of society's preferences, based on the notion that we probably could agree on an income distribution better than the one currently in existence in the United States, though we might not agree on what perfect economic justice would require.

The Posner article that follows strongly suggests that Thurow has considerably overestimated the degree of agreement even on this more limited, interim target. Posner expresses great skepticism about the division between individual-societal preferences and private-personal preferences. He writes: "Imagine an individual who is grasping, ungenerous, and ruthlessly acquisitive in his personal and business dealings but who, if asked, will say that he supports a restructuring of society that would result in a drastic reduction in his relative and absolute wealth and income. Does such a person *really* prefer an egalitarian society?" (pp. 337–338). He then goes on to quarrel vehemently with every single proposal for income redistribution that Thurow has made. A basic contention is that Thurow has failed to measure the costs of his redistribution program. A minimum wage would cause unemployment, less efficient production, the shift of workers from private to less-productive public sector jobs. The tax on wealth would lead to costly efforts at tax-evasion and would also impair risk-taking entrepreneurial activities. Overall, the costs would simply be too great.

THE OKUN BUCKET

This notion of important costs in any program for redistributing society's income and wealth has already been suggested in our example whereby $200 taken from the rich man leads to only $100 going to the poor man: the redistribution has cost society a net income loss of $100. Such losses are likely to occur because the various taxes and subsidies necessary to carry out a redistribution program will normally lead to certain disincentive effects on the productive members of society. Also, there will usually be various administrative and other costs in implementing any large redistributional effort.

One over-all way of putting the question of income distribution is this: Can society come to some kind of general agreement as to how *much* of a cost it will sustain in order to move towards a somewhat greater equality of income than at present? Some observers are optimistic about the possibility of at least rough agreement on this matter. Economist Arthur Okun, in a best-selling book, *Equality and Efficiency: The Big Tradeoff,* suggests various costs he himself would have society sustain at various income levels. He believes that "somehow, everyone seems to develop a sense of where deprivation and hardship begin along the income scale."[4] However, it is doubtful that much of a consensus exists, as the Thurow-Posner debate makes clear. Also, even if such agreement did exist, it would represent a vague, general feeling on the part of the members of society rather than a clear and reasoned policy.

Indeed, after reading through all the arguments in this great debate, one is likely to come to the conclusion that the question of economic justice is still in a most unsettled and unsatisfactory state. The issue cannot be avoided: society's income *will* be distributed in one fashion or another. Yet the theoretical grounds for justifying any particular arrangement are, despite Rawls' noble effort, still extremely shaky. We have an urgent, particular problem and have not yet devised a satisfactory, agreed-upon way of approaching the problem. This, of course, suggests an agenda of necessary work for the future. It would be nice to feel that our views about equality and inequality, if not perfectly consistent, at least bear some tenuous relationship to a general philosophy of life that we can live with without feeling guilty or apologetic. To this task, social scientists in the last quarter of this century will doubtless be addressing a major effort.

[4] Arthur M. Okun, *Equality and Efficiency: The Big Tradeoff* (Washington, D.C. The Brookings Institution, 1975) p. 95.

A National Minimum Standard of Real Income

A. C. Pigou

The late A. C. Pigou was Professor of Political Economy
at the University of Cambridge, England, from 1908 to
1943.

It is desired, if possible, to establish some connection between changes in the distribution of the national dividend[1] and changes in economic welfare. . . . In considering this matter we must not forget that the economic welfare enjoyed by anybody in any period depends on the income that he consumes rather than on the income that he receives; and that, the richer a man is, the smaller proportion of his total income he is likely to consume, so that if his total income is, say, twenty times as large as that of a poorer man, his consumed income may be only, say, five times as large. Nevertheless, it is evident that any transference of income from a relatively rich man to a relatively poor man of similar temperament, since it enables more intense wants to be satisfied at the expense of less intense wants, must increase the aggregate sum of satisfaction. The old "law of diminishing utility" thus leads securely to the proposition: Any cause which increases the absolute share of real income in the hands of the poor, provided that it does not lead to a contraction in the size of the national dividend from any point of view, will, in general, increase economic welfare. . . .

When we desire to determine whether the fact and the expectation of the fact, taken together, of any given annual transference of resources from the relatively rich to the relatively poor are likely to increase the

"A National Minimum Standard of Real Income," excerpted from A. C. Pigou, *The Economics of Welfare,*
4th ed (London: Macmillan & Co., Ltd. 1962), pp. 89, 758–64. Reprinted by permission of Macmillan,
London and Basingstoke.

[1] By the term "national dividend," Pigou means what we would today refer to as "national income" or "net national product."

national dividend, all the various considerations set out in the preceding chapters must be taken into account. There is little doubt but that plans could be devised, which would enable transferences, involving a very large amount of resources, to be made with results advantageous to production. Since the generality of these transferences will also increase the real incomes of the relatively poor, they must redound to the advantage of economic welfare in a wholly unambiguous way. Transferences which diminish the national dividend, on the other hand, are liable, through various reactions which have been indicated in the course of this discussion, to diminish the real earnings of the relatively poor; and, if their amount is kept constant, they may do this to so great an extent that the earnings per year of the relatively poor *plus* the transference made to them will *ultimately* be less than their earnings alone would have been, had no transference been made. When this happens, these transferences also affect economic welfare in an unambiguous way: this time by injuring it. There remains, however, one further sort of transference, the results of which cannot be unambiguous. I refer to a system of transferences varied from year to year in such a way as to compensate for any reduction that may come about in that part of the income of the poor which accrues to them through earnings. An arrangement of this sort is implicitly introduced whenever a government establishes a minimum standard of real income, below which it refuses to allow any citizen in any circumstances to fall. For the establishment of such a minimum standard, implying, as it does, transferences to the poor of a kind that differentiate in favor of poverty, is likely to diminish the national dividend, while it will, at the same time, for an indefinitely long period, increase the aggregate real income of the poor. To determine the effect, which the establishment of this kind of minimum standard is likely to exercise upon economic welfare, involves, therefore, a balancing of conflicting considerations . . .

There is general agreement among practical philanthropists that *some* minimum standard of conditions ought to be set up at a level high enough to make impossible the occurrence to anybody of extreme want; and that whatever transference of resources from relatively rich to relatively poor persons is necessary to secure this must be made, without reference to possible injurious consequences upon the magnitude of the dividend. This policy of practical philanthropists is justified by analysis, in the sense that it can be shown to be conducive to economic welfare on the whole, if we believe the misery that results to individuals from extreme want to be indefinitely large; for, then, the good of abolishing extreme want is not commensurable with any evils that may follow should a diminution of the dividend take place. Up to this point, therefore, there is no difficulty. But our discussion cannot stop at this point. It is necessary to ask, not merely whether economic welfare will be promoted by the establishment of *any* minimum standard, but also by *what* minimum standard it will be promoted most effectively. Now, above the level of extreme want, it is generally admitted that increments of income involve finite increments of satisfaction. Hence the direct good of transference and the indirect evil resulting from a diminished dividend are both finite quantities; and the correct formal answer to our question is that economic welfare is best promoted by a minimum standard raised to such a level that the direct good resulting from the transference of the marginal pound transferred to the poor just balances the indirect evil brought about by the consequent reduction of the dividend.

To derive from this formal answer a quantitative estimate of what the minimum standard of real income established in any particular country at any particular time ought to be, it would be necessary to obtain and to analyze a mass of detailed information, much of which is not, in present circumstances, accessible to students. One practical conclusion can, however, be safely drawn. This is that, other things being equal, the minimum can be advantageously set higher, the larger is the real income per head of the community. The reason, of course, is that every increase in average income implies a diminution in the number of people unable by their own efforts to attain to any given minimum standard; and, therefore, a diminution, both absolute and proportionate, in the damage to the dividend which an external guarantee of that standard threatens to bring about. It follows that, when we have to do with a group of pioneer workers in rough and adverse natural circumstances, the minimum standard may rightly be set at a low level. But, as inventions and discoveries progress, as capital is accumulated and Nature subdued, it should be correspondingly raised. Thus it is reasonable that, while a relatively poor country makes only a low provision for its "destitute" citizens, a relatively rich country should make a somewhat better provision for all who are "necessitous.". . .

Some Reasons for the Maximin Criterion

John Rawls

John Rawls is Professor of Philosophy at Harvard
University and the author of *A Theory of Justice* (1971).

Recently the maximin criterion of distributive equity has received some
attention from economists in connection with the problem of optimal
income taxation. Unhappily I am unable to examine the merits of the
criterion from the standpoint of economic theory, although whether the
criterion is a reasonable distributive standard depends importantly on the
sort of examination that only economists can undertake.

What I shall do is to summarize briefly some of the reasons for taking
the maximin criterion seriously. I should emphasize that the maximin
equity criterion and the so-called maximin rule for choice under uncertainty are two very different things. I shall formulate the reasons for the
equity criterion so that they are completely independent from this rule.

In *A Theory of Justice* I have considered the maximin criterion as part of
a social contract theory. Here I must assume a certain familiarity with this
conception. One feature of it might be put this way: injustice exists
because basic agreements are made too late. People already know their
social positions and relative strength in bargaining, their abilities and
preferences, and these contingencies and knowledge of them cumula-
tively distort the social system. In an attempt to remedy this difficulty,
contract theory introduces the notion of the original position. The most
reasonable principles of justice are defined as those that would be unani-
mously agreed to in an appropriate initial situation that is fair between
individuals conceived as free and equal moral persons.

In order to define the original position as fair in this sense, we imagine

From John Rawls, "Some Reasons for the Maximin Criterion," *American Economic Review*, 64, No. 2 (May
1974), pp. 141–45. Reprinted by permission. Footnotes are omitted.

that everyone is deprived of certain morally irrelevant information. They do not know their place in society, their class position or social status, their place in the distribution of natural assets and abilities, their deeper aims and interests or their particular psychological makeup. Excluding this information insures that no one is advantaged or disadvantaged in the choice of principles by natural chance or social contingencies. Since all are in this sense similarly situated and no one knows how to frame principles that favor his particular condition, each will reason in the same way. Any agreement reached is unanimous and there is no need to vote.

Thus the subject of the original agreement is a conception of social justice. Also, this conception is understood to apply to the basic structure of society: that is, to its major institutions—the political constitution and the principal economic and social arrangements—and how they fit together into one system. The application of the maximin criterion to optimal income taxation is, then, perfectly in order, since an income tax is part of the basic structure. But the maximin criterion is not meant to apply to small-scale situations, say, to how a doctor should treat his patients or a university its students. For these situations different principles will presumably be necessary. Maximin is a macro not a micro principle. I should add that the criterion is unsuitable for determining the just rate of savings; it is intended to hold only within generations.

But what alternative conceptions are available in the original position? We must resort to great simplifications in order to get our bearings. We cannot consider the general case where the parties are to choose among all possible conceptions of justice; it is too difficult to specify this class of alternatives. Therefore we imagine that the parties are given a short list of conceptions between which they are to decide.

Here I can discuss only two pair-wise comparisons. These are designed to reflect the traditional aim of contract theory, namely, to provide an account of justice that is both superior to utilitarianism and a more adequate basis for a democratic society. Therefore the first choice is between a conception defined by the principle that average utility is to be maximized and a conception defined by two principles that express a democratic idea of justice. These principles read as follows:

1. Each person has an equal right to the most extensive scheme of equal basic liberties compatible with a similar scheme of liberties for all.
2. Social and economic inequalities are to meet two conditions: they must be (a) to the greatest expected benefit of the least advantaged members of society (the maximin equity criterion) and (b) attached to offices and positions open to all under conditions of fair equality of opportunity.

I assume that the first of these takes priority over the second, but this and other matters must be left aside. For simplicity I also assume that a person's utility is affected predominantly by liberties and opportunities, income and wealth and their distribution. I suppose further that everyone has normal physical needs so that the problem of special health care does not arise.

Now which of these conceptions would be chosen depends on how the persons in the original position are conceived. Contract theory stipulates that they regard themselves as having certain fundamental interests, the claims of which they must protect, if this is possible. It is in the name of these interests that they have a right to equal respect and consideration in the design of society. The religious interest is a familiar historical example; the interest in the integrity of the person is another. In the original position the parties do not know what particular form these interests take. But they do assume that they have such interests and also that the basic liberties necessary for their protection (for example, freedom of thought and liberty of conscience, freedom of the person and political liberty) are guaranteed by the first principle of justice.

Given these stipulations, the two principles of justice would be chosen. For while the principle of utility may sometimes lead to a social order securing these liberties, there is no reason why it will do so in general. And even if the principle often does, it would be pointless to run the risk of encountering circumstances when it does not. Put formally, each must suppose that the marginal utility of these fundamental interests is infinite; this requires anyone in the original position to give them priority and to adopt the two principles of justice.

This conclusion is strengthened when one adds that the parties regard themselves as having a higher-order interest in how their other interests, even fundamental ones, are regulated and shaped by social institutions. They think of themselves as beings who can choose and revise their final ends and who must preserve their liberty in these matters. A free person is not only one who has final ends which he is free to pursue or to reject, but also one whose original allegiance and continued devotion to these ends are formed under conditions that are free. Since the two principles secure these conditions, they must be chosen.

The second pair-wise comparison is far more difficult. In this case the choice is between the two principles of justice and a variant of these principles in which the utility principle has a subordinate place. To define this variant, replace the second principle by the following: social and economic inequalities are to be adjusted so as to maximize average utility consistent with fair equality of opportunity. The choice between this variant and the two principles is more delicate because the arguments from liberty can no longer be made, at least not so directly. The first principle belongs to both conceptions, and so the operation of the utility principle is hedged by basic rights as well as fair equality of opportunity.

One reason favoring the two principles of justice is this. From the standpoint of the original position, the parties will surely be very considerably risk-averse; if we ask how risk-averse, we might say not less than that of most any normal person. Of course, this is extremely vague; but if we assume that utility is estimated from the standpoint of individuals in society and represents, as the classical utilitarians believed, a quantity ascertainable independent of choices involving risk, then, given the crucial nature of the decision in the original position, the claims of the utility principle seem quite dubious. On the other hand, if we suppose that utility is measured from the original position and takes account of risk, the utility criterion may not differ much from maximin. The standard of utility approaches maximin as risk aversion increases without limit. So, either way, the original position pushes us toward maximin. However, in weighing the second pair-wise comparison, I assume that, based on considerations of risk aversion alone, there is a significant difference between the two conceptions. Thus the problem is to identify other attractive features of the maximin criterion that tip the balance of reasons in its favor.

First, much less information is needed to apply the maximin criterion. Once the least-favored group is identified, it may be relatively easy to determine which policies are to their advantage. By comparison it is much more difficult to know what maximizes average utility. We require a fairly precise way of comparing the utilities of different social groups by some meaningful standard, as well as a method of estimating the overall balance of gains and losses. In application this principle leaves so much to judgment that some may reasonably claim that the gains of one group outweigh the losses of another, while others may equally reasonably deny it. This situation gives those favored by existing inequalities an opportunity to exploit their advantage so that, as a result, inequalities are likely to be excessive, undermining the justice of the system.

A further consideration is this: a distributive criterion is to serve as a public principle. Citizens generally should be able to understand it and have some confidence that it is realized. Pattern criteria, those that require the actual distribution to exhibit certain ascertainable features, do well by the test of publicity. Of these, strict equality (equal division) is the sharpest principle. The trouble with pattern criteria is that sharpness is not the only desideratum, and they often have little else to commend them. On the other hand, the utility principle is not sharp enough: even if it were satisfied, there could be little public confidence that this is indeed the case. The maximin criterion has sufficient sharpness; at the same time it is efficient while strict equality is not.

Another ground supporting the maximin criterion is based on the strains of commitment: in the original position the parties are to favor those principles compliance with which should prove more tolerable, whatever their situation in society turns out to be. The notion of a contract implies that one cannot enter into an agreement that one will be unable to keep. By this test, also, maximin seems superior, for the principles chosen would regulate social and economic inequalities in the basic structure of society that affect people's life-prospects. These are peculiarly deep and pervasive inequalities and often hard to accept.

Looking first at the situation of the less advantaged, the utility principle asks them to view the greater advantages of others who have more as a sufficient reason for having still lower prospects of life than otherwise they could be allowed. This is an extreme demand psychologically; by contrast, the maximin criterion assures the less favored that inequalities work to their advantage. The problem with maximin would appear to lie with those who are better situated. They must accept less than what they would receive with the utility principle, but two things greatly lessen their strains of commitment: they are, after all, more fortunate and enjoy the benefits of that fact; and insofar as they value their situation relatively in comparison with others, they give up that much less. In fact, our tendency to evaluate our circumstances in relation to the circumstances of others suggests that society should be arranged so that if possible all its members can with reason be happy with their situation. The maximin criterion achieves this better than the principle of utility.

I have noted several reasons that support the maximin criterion: very considerable normal risk-aversion (given the special features of the original position), less demanding information requirements, greater suitability as a public principle, and weaker strains of commitment. Yet no one of them is clearly decisive by itself. Thus the question arises whether there is any consideration that is compelling. I want to suggest that the aspirations of free and equal personality point directly to the maximin criterion.

Since the principles of equal liberty and fair equality of opportunity are common to both alternatives in the second comparison, some form of democracy obtains when either alternative is realized. Citizens are to view themselves as free and equal persons, social institutions should be willingly complied with and recognized as just. Presumably, however, certain social and economic inequalities exist, and individuals' life-prospects are significantly affected by their family and class origins, by their natural endowments, and by chance contingencies over the course of their lives. We must ask: In the light of what principle can free and equal moral persons permit their relations to be affected by social fortune and the natural lottery? Since no one deserves his place in the distribution of talents, nor his starting place in society, desert is not an answer. Yet free and equal persons want the effects of chance to be regulated by some principle, if a reasonable principle exists.

Now when the maximin criterion is followed, the natural distribution of abilities is viewed in some respects as a collective asset. While an equal distribution might seem more in keeping with the equality of free moral persons, at least if the distribution were a matter of choice, this is not a reason for eliminating natural variations, much less for destroying unusual talents. To the contrary, natural variations are recognized as an opportunity, particularly since they are often complementary and form a basis for social ties. Institutions are allowed to exploit the full range of abilities provided the resulting inequalities are no greater than necessary to produce corresponding advantages for the less fortunate. The same constraint holds for the inequalities between social classes. Thus at first sight the distribution of natural assets and unequal life-expectations threatens the relations between free and equal moral persons. But provided the maximin criterion is satisfied, these relations may be preserved: inequalities are to everyone's advantage and those able to gain from their good fortune do so in ways agreeable to those less favored. Meeting this burden of proof reflects the value of equality.

Now the maximin criterion would conform to the precept "from each according to his abilities, to each according to his needs" if society were to impose a head tax on natural assets. In this way income inequalities could be greatly reduced if not eliminated. Of course, there are enormous practical difficulties in such a scheme; ability may be impossible to measure and individuals would have every incentive to conceal their talents. But another difficulty is the interference with liberty; greater natural talents are not a collective asset in the sense that society should compel those who have them to put them to work for the less favored. This would be a drastic infringement upon freedom. But society can say that the better endowed may improve their situations only on terms that help others. In this way inequalities are permitted in ways consistent with everyone's self-respect.

I have attempted a brief survey of the grounds for the maximin criterion. I have done this because historically it has attracted little attention, and yet it is a natural focal point between strict equality and the principle of average utility. It turns out to have a number of attractive features. But I do not wish to overemphasize this criterion: a deeper investigation covering more pair-wise comparisons may show that some other conception of justice is more reasonable. In any case, the idea that economists may find most useful in contract theory is that of the original position. This perspective can be defined in various ways and with different degrees of abstraction and some of these may prove illuminating for economic theory.

Comments on Rawls' Maximin Criterion

Alvin K. Klevorick

Alvin K. Klevorick is Associate Professor of Law and
Economics at Yale University.

I shall use John Rawls' remarks on the maximin criterion as the organizational framework for my comments. In particular, I shall focus on his more difficult comparison—the one between his two principles of justice and a variant of these in which the difference principle is replaced by the principle that "social and economic inequalities are to be adjusted so as to maximize average utility consistent with fair equality of opportunity." Rawls presents several reasons which, he believes, support the maximin criterion in this comparison. I would like to question whether, upon further examination, these arguments provide as strong a case as he suggests they do. . . .

Rawls' first argument is based upon the "very considerable normal risk aversion" individuals will display in the original position. He grants that, because of the crucial nature of the choice faced in that position, the utility criterion may not differ much from maximin, and he cites the result that the standard of utility approaches maximin as risk aversion increases without limit. Nevertheless, he writes, "I assume that, based on considerations of risk aversion alone, there is a significant difference between the two criteria." But that is all the risk aversion argument comes to: an assumption.

Second, Rawls argues that "much less information is needed to apply the maximin criterion." While maximin may require less information than average utility maximization, I think the difference is smaller than Rawls suggests. First, the same group may not be least favored under each possible arrangement so that under maximin one has the considerable task of determining the least favored group under all alternative ar-

Excerpted from Alvin K. Klevorick, "Distributional Equity—Discussion," *American Economic Review*, 64, No. 2 (May 1974), pp. 158–61. Reprinted by permission.

rangements. Second, this task requires one to measure the utility of each group and compare the utility of different groups to determine which one is the least favored under a particular arrangement. Third, the method of estimating the overall balance of gains and losses in the average utility setting is readily at hand since it has been agreed that the goal is maximization of the *average* of the utilities. Rawls states that in applications the average utility principle "leaves so much to judgment that some may reasonably claim that the gains of one group outweigh the losses of another, while others may equally reasonably deny it." It would seem that such reasonable differences of opinion could also arise under maximin in determining which is the least favored group. This suggests that a real cost under both of the two sets of principles Rawls is comparing is the cost of resolving such differences of opinion. Or does his statement that everyone reasons in the same way exclude this problem? If it does, then surely it must also apply to resolving the disputes to which he alludes in the average utilitarian context. . . .

His third argument is that maximin is more suitable as a public principle. The maximin principle is sharper than the average utilitarian principle: one would expect maximin to be understood better by citizens generally. But, while it may be difficult for the public to verify that average utility has been maximized, one should not understate the difficulty the public would have in verifying that the least favored group's position has been maximized. In particular, preliminary to any such verification would be the need for all members of the public to agree about exactly which is the least favored group. I have already questioned whether such agreement will be readily achieved.

The next reason Rawls offers in support of the maximin criterion is that it imposes weaker strains of commitment: "in the original position the parties are to favor those principles compliance with which should prove more tolerable, whatever their situation in society turns out to be." He discusses the difficult strains which face the less advantaged under the utility principle. In contrast, notes Rawls, under maximin the serious strains of commitment are faced by the better situated. Just as the less advantaged must accept less under the utility principle than they could have otherwise (for example, under maximin), so the more advantaged must settle for less under maximin than they could receive otherwise (for example, under the utility principle). Two factors are, however, supposed to lessen greatly the strains those who are better off face under maximin: (a) they are more fortunate and enjoy the benefits of that fact and (b) insofar as they value their position relative to others', they give up that much less. There would seem to be a problem with each of these supposedly mitigating factors. Argument (a) is implicitly based on the assumption of diminishing marginal utility of income. Otherwise, why should we count the dissatisfaction of the better off less than the dissatisfaction of the less well-situated? Argument (b) is based on an assumption about human behavior which, though it may be confirmed by armchair (and some careful) empiricism, introduces the very kind of strong interdependence of utility functions that Rawls excludes his individuals from having or considering in the original position. . . .

The last argument Rawls puts forth in support of the maximin criterion is the one he finds most compelling. He writes, "I want to suggest that the aspirations of free and equal personality point directly to the maximin criterion." As Rawls indicates, when his two principles are followed, the natural distribution of abilities is viewed in some ways as a collective asset. Furthermore, the maximin criterion would conform to the rule "from each according to his abilities, to each according to his needs" if society were to impose a lump-sum-tax-and-transfer program based on ability levels. Rawls finds two major problems with such a lump-sum tax scheme. First, there are considerable practical difficulties involved in operating such a program. Second, and more important, the scheme would involve "a drastic infringement with freedom"—"greater talents are not a collective asset in the sense that society should *compel* those who have them to put them to work for the less favored" (emphasis added). "But," says Rawls, "society can say that the better endowed may improve their situation only on terms that help others."

Rawls has set out here—in very cogent fashion—a fundamental tension in the postconstitutional life of the society he discusses: the tension between freedom of behavior and *ex post* equality. A preliminary question that must be confronted is how should one measure the degree of compulsion or degree of interference with liberty. Clearly, any tax system interferes with liberty to some degree; any such system involves some compulsion. But presumably tax programs which allow people to choose, for example, between market (taxable) and nonmarket (nontaxable) uses of their natural assets (for example, time and abilities) would be considered less interfering or less compulsive than tax systems which are structured so as to disallow such choices. Bypassing that preliminary question in this discussion, one can still ask why maximin provides the best resolution of the liberty-equality tension and what "best" means in this context. Why, for example, is maximin (which chooses a particular liberty-equality mix) superior to a rule which says that the better endowed may improve their own situation only if they improve the situation of the least advantaged by x percent—or by at least as much as they improve their own situation? Put another way, why does maximin provide the optimal degree of coercion in a Rawlsian world?

"Rawls' Theory"

Robert Nozick

Robert Nozick, like John Rawls whose theory he criticizes, is Professor of Philosophy at Harvard University.

We can bring our discussion of distributive justice into sharper focus by considering in some detail John Rawls' recent contribution to the subject. *A Theory of Justice* is a powerful, deep, subtle, wide-ranging, systematic work in political and moral philosophy which has not seen its like since the writings of John Stuart Mill, if then. It is a fountain of illuminating ideas, integrated together into a lovely whole. Political philosophers now must either work within Rawls' theory or explain why not. . . .

Rawls imagines rational, mutually disinterested individuals meeting in a certain situation, or abstracted from their other features not provided for in this situation. In this hypothetical situation of choice, which Rawls calls "the original position," they choose the first principles of a conception of justice that is to regulate all subsequent criticism and reform of their institutions. While making this choice, no one knows his place in society, his class position or social status, or his natural assets and abilities, his strength, intelligence, and so forth.

The principles of justice are chosen behind a veil of ignorance. This ensures that no one is advantaged or disadvantaged in the choice of principles by the outcome of natural chance or the contingency of social circumstances. Since all are similarly situated and no one is able to design principles to favor his particular condition, the principles of justice are the result of a fair agreement or bargain.

What would persons in the original position agree to?

Excerpted from Robert Nozick, *Anarchy, State and Utopia* (New York, Basic Books, Inc., 1974), pp. 183, 189–190; 192–3, 195–7.

Persons in the initial situation would choose two . . . principles: the first requires equality in the assignment of basic rights and duties, while the second holds that social and economic inequalities, for example, inequalities of wealth and authority are just only if they result in compensating benefits for everyone, and in particular for the least advantaged members of society. These principles rule out justifying institutions on the grounds that the hardships of some are offset by a greater good in the aggregate. It may be expedient but it is not just that some should have less in order that others may prosper. But there is no injustice in the greater benefits earned by a few provided that the situation of persons not so fortunate is thereby improved. The intuitive idea is that since everyone's well-being depends upon a scheme of cooperation without which no one could have a satisfactory life, the division of advantages should be such as to draw forth the willing cooperation of everyone taking part in it, including those less well situated. Yet this can be expected only if reasonable terms are proposed. The two principles mentioned seem to be a fair agreement on the basis of which those better endowed, or more fortunate in their social position, neither of which we can be said to deserve, could expect the willing cooperation of others when some workable scheme is a necessary condition of the welfare of all.

This second principle, which Rawls specifies as the difference principle, holds that the institutional structure is to be so designed that the worst-off group under it is at least as well off as the worst-off group (not necessarily the same group) would be under any alternative institutional structure. If persons in the original position follow the minimax policy in making the significant choice of principles of justice, Rawls argues, they will choose the difference principle. Our concern here is not whether persons in the position Rawls describes actually would minimax and actually would choose the particular principles Rawls specifies. Still, we should question why individuals in the original position would choose a principle that focuses upon groups, rather than individuals. Won't application of the minimax principle lead each person in the original position to favor maximizing the position of the worst-off *individual?* To be sure, this principle would reduce questions of evaluating social institutions to the issue of how the unhappiest depressive fares. Yet avoiding this by moving the focus to groups (or representative individuals) seems *ad hoc*, and is inadequately motivated for those in the individual position. Nor is it clear which groups are appropriately considered; why exclude the group of depressives or alcoholics or the representative paraplegic? . . .

No doubt, the difference principle presents terms on the basis of which those less well endowed would be willing to cooperate. (What *better* terms could they propose for themselves?) But is this a fair agreement on the basis of which those *worse* endowed could expect the *willing* cooperation of others? With regard to the existence of gains from social cooperation, the situation is symmetrical. The better endowed gain by cooperating with the worse endowed, *and* the worse endowed gain by cooperating with the better endowed. Yet the difference principle is not neutral between the better and the worse endowed. Whence the asymmetry? . . .

Rawls would have us imagine the worse-endowed persons say something like the following: "Look, better endowed: you gain by cooperating with us. If you want our cooperation you'll have to accept reasonable terms. We suggest these terms: We'll cooperate with you only if we get *as much as possible*. That is, the terms of our cooperation should give us that maximal share such that, if it was tried to give us more, we'd end up with less." How generous these proposed terms are might be seen by imagining that the better endowed make the almost symmetrical opposite proposal: "Look, worse endowed: you gain by cooperating with *us*. If you want our cooperation you'll have to accept reasonable terms. We propose these terms: We'll cooperate with you so long as *we* get as much as possible. That is, the terms of our cooperation should give us the maximal share such that, if it was tried to give us more, we'd end up with less." If these terms seem outrageous, as they are, why don't the terms proposed by those worse endowed seem the same? Why shouldn't the better endowed treat this latter proposal as beneath consideration, supposing someone to have the nerve explicitly to state it?

Rawls devotes much attention to explaining why those less well favored should not complain at receiving less. His explanation, simply put, is that because the inequality works for his advantage, someone less well favored shouldn't complain about it; he receives *more* in the unequal system than he would in an equal one. (Though he might receive still more in another unequal system that placed someone else below him.) But Rawls discusses the question of whether those *more* favored will or should find the terms satisfactory *only* in the following passage, where *A* and *B* are any two representative men with *A* being the more favored:

The difficulty is to show that A has no grounds for complaint. Perhaps he is required to have less than he might since his having more would result in some loss to B. Now what can be said to the more favored man? To begin with, it is clear that the well-being of each depends on a scheme of social cooperation without which no one could have a satisfactory life. Secondly, we can ask for the willing cooperation of everyone only if the terms of the scheme are reasonable. The difference principle, then, seems to be a fair basis on which those better endowed, or more fortunate in their social circumstances, could expect others to collaborate with them when some workable arrangement is a necessary condition of the good of all.

What Rawls imagines being said to the more favored men does *not* show that these men have no grounds for complaint, nor does it at all diminish the weight of whatever complaints they have. That the well-being of all depends on social cooperation without which no one could have a satisfactory life could also be said to the less well endowed by someone proposing any other principle, including that of maximizing the position of the best endowed. Similarly for the fact that we can ask for the willing cooperation of everyone only if the terms of the scheme are reasonable. The question is: What terms *would be* reasonable? What Rawls imagines being said thus far merely sets up his problem; it doesn't distinguish his proposed difference principle from the almost symmetrical counterproposal that we imagined the better endowed making, or from any other proposal. Thus, when Rawls continues, "The difference principle, then, seems to be a fair basis on which those best endowed, or more fortunate in their social circumstances, could expect others to collaborate with them when some workable arrangement is a necessary condition of the good of all," the presence of the "then" in his sentence is puzzling. Since the sentences which precede it are neutral between his proposal and any other proposal, the conclusion that the difference principle presents a fair basis for cooperation *cannot* follow from what precedes it in this passage. Rawls is merely repeating that it seems reasonable; hardly a convincing reply to anyone to whom it doesn't seem reasonable. Rawls has not shown that the more favored man *A* has no grounds for complaint at being required to have less in order that another *B* might have more than he otherwise would. And he can't show this, since *A does* have grounds for complaint. Doesn't he?

Toward a Definition of Economic Justice

Lester C. Thurow

Lester C. Thurow is Professor of Economics and
Management at the Massachusetts Institute of
Technology.

Modern economics springs from the search for a definition of economic
justice, but has largely abandoned that search. Thus, 19th-century
utilitarian economists, such as John Stuart Mill, spent much of their time
searching for the principles that would lead to a condition of equity. But
by the 1940s, economists reluctantly came to the conclusion that there
were no *economic* statements that could be made about equity. In this they
were in agreement with moral philosophers and other social scientists that
no ethical statements can be deduced from purely factual or purely logical
statements—the only two kinds of statements to be found in modern
economic theory. By the 1950s questions of economic equity were not
even discussed in the basic textbooks, except to note that it was necessary
for a market economy to start with a "just" distribution of economic
resources. What made any such distribution "just" was left blank or was
vaguely handed over to the political process.

For a time economists thought that progress could be made by shifting
from utility theory, with all of its technical problems of quantification, to
the analysis of choice and preference. An attempt would be made not to
quantify utility, but simply to determine whether individuals preferred
State A to State B. Individuals would rank different states of the world in
a certain order of preference, and these different rank orderings could
then be combined to make a social judgment about economic equity.
Kenneth Arrow's impossibility theorem shattered this vision. He was able

Excerpted from Lester C. Thurow, "Toward a Definition of Economic Justice *The Public Interest*, No. 31
(Spring 1973), pp. 56–80. Copyright © National Affairs, Inc., 1973. Reprinted by permission of the publisher and author.

to show that there was no method of combination—no social decision rule (e.g., majority voting)—that could in all circumstances lead to a "social ordering" without violating some seemingly mild and reasonable conditions. As a result, even the political process could not handle the question of economic equity perfectly.

Such intellectual conclusions, however, neither obviate the need to make decisions about economic equity nor stop such decisions from being made. They are in fact being made all the time. Every time taxes are levied, or public expenditures are made, decisions about economic equity are being made. Even if governments had no public expenditures programs, the problem would exist. It is unavoidable. In market economies, individual preferences determine market demands for goods and services, and as a consequence determine the market distribution of income—but individual preferences are weighted by economic resources *before* they are communicated to the market. An individual with no income or wealth may have needs and desires, but he has no economic demands. To make his personal preferences felt, he must have economic resources. If income and wealth are distributed in accordance with equity (whatever that may be), individual preferences are properly weighted, and the market can efficiently adjust to an equitable set of demands. If income and wealth are not distributed in accordance with equity, individual preferences are not properly weighted. The market quite efficiently adjusts to an inequitable distribution of purchasing power.

To have no government programs for redistributing income is simply to certify *de facto* that the existing market distribution of incomes is equitable. One way or another, we are *forced* to reveal our collective preferences about the "just" distribution of economic resources. As a result, one basic responsibility of government in a market economy is to create an equitable distribution of income and wealth if it has not been produced by the market.

While the tension between the need to make decisions about economic justice and the intellectual desire to avoid discussion of economic equity can be suppressed, it eventually breaks out. John Rawls's recent and much-discussed book, *A Theory of Justice,* is the start of such an outbreak. As is usual in such cases, both the pessimism with which the discussion was abandoned and the optimism with which the discussion is reintroduced are probably excessive. The problem of specifying economic equity is simply a difficult problem to which there is no universal answer. At the same time, there are important arguments to be understood.

There are several directions from which one can attempt to specify economic equity:

1. Reliance can be placed on process and procedures. An economic game is specified as fair or equitable when individuals agree on the rules of the game, and any outcome of that game is thus considered just.

2. Individual preferences can be the key criterion. If the outcome of an economic game is in accordance with the individual preferences of the citizens of a country, the outcome is equitable. Equity is achieved when society reaches the distribution of economic resources that generates the most agreement.

3. Merit, however defined, can be used to specify equity. Equity occurs when resources are distributed in the same manner as merit. In nineteenth-century liberal economic thinking, this would mean rewarding everyone based on his or her marginal product as determined in a free market place. The person who contributes most, gets most.

4. Equity can be related to the common good, however defined. Equity is that distribution of economic resources that maximizes the common good. Substantively, the problem then devolves into one of determining the common good.

Obviously, any actual specification of economic equity can, and probably will, have elements of all four of these facets of equity. At the same time, there are problems with using any and all of these techniques for specifying a just distribution of economic resources. To clarify some of the issues surrounding the problem, I shall outline the fundamental reasons that have led economists to abandon their search for economic equity, examine some of the practical and intellectual escapes that have been proposed, and suggest a candidate of my own for a definition of an equitable distribution of economic rewards.

THE UNDISCUSSABILITY OF ECONOMIC EQUITY

No one can deny that value judgments play an important role in specifying economic equity. Often this observation has led to the invalid conclusion, however, that economic equity is therefore undiscussable. Thus, one hears it said that there are economic statements to be made about the character of economic efficiency, but there are no economic statements to be made about the character of economic equity; there are only prejudices. But, in fact, statements about economic efficiency are not value free. They depend upon an underlying set of discussable value judgments, just as statements about equity depend upon an underlying set of discussable value judgments. In both cases, there are technical studies to be done once values are adopted.

Modern analysis of economic efficiency depends upon the acceptance of what our textbooks call Pareto optimality: State A is better than State B if at least one person is better off in A and no one is worse off. (A person is assumed to be better off in A if he prefers to be in A rather than in B.) In a weaker version of the same principle, State A is better than State B if those who are better off in State A could adequately compensate those who are worse off in State A. We move toward Pareto optimality when scarce resources are used in such a manner as to maximize potential output, which in turn maximizes potential choices. When efficiency improves, there is a larger bundle of goods and services (including leisure) that individuals can choose among. More is better.

All analysis of economic efficiency depends upon these postulates. All of these postulates are thoroughly ethical in nature. A value judgment is made that each individual is the best judge of his or her own happiness, and that more choices are always better than less. Without such value judgments, "efficiency" in modern economics ceases to have any meaning.

Paretian efficiency values were easily absorbed into economics because they seemed to be universally held. They are, after all, the values of a liberal-individualistic society. The invocation of value judgments that are universally held has been the traditional way to avoid discussing values. This occurs partly because we believe what is universally held does not need to be discussed, but also because values that are in fact universally held seem to be intuitively true and are often held to be facts rather than values. To many "more (choice) is better" is a fact and not a value.

We may all share such postulates, but this does not alter the fact that they are value judgments or elevate them beyond the realm of analysis. Take the inviolability of consumer preferences. Given the 19th-century belief in the existence of innate wants within the individual, the inviolability of consumers' preferences seemed sensible. Given modern sociology and psychology, the postulate of innate wants is no longer so plausible. We now perceive that every society or culture generates the "wants" of its population. Moreover, as our knowledge of how "wants" are generated improves, the activity of generating wants will increasingly fall within the domain of deliberate policies. Indeed, the debate as to whether our society should try to generate traditional economic "wants" or other life styles is currently under way.

As this example illustrates, various types of beliefs about matters of fact—psychological and sociological matters of fact, above all—can force alterations in values. Similarly, many economic beliefs about matters of fact can affect values. Two examples are: "Income equality is bad because it leads to less work," or, "Socialism is good because it stops an individual from acquiring economic power over other individuals." Before going to the barricades over either of these statements, a lot of hard empirical economic research and tough economic analysis must be done. Does income equality lead to less personal effort? Is economic power less concentrated under socialism? When does the adverse work effort effect set in? How should economic power be measured?

If "more is better" and the "inviolability of consumers' preferences" are both values underlying any analysis of economic efficiency, what are the values underlying the analysis of economic equity? The problem fundamentally depends upon whether you subscribe to Rousseau's belief that all men are by nature equal or the Greek belief that men are by nature unequal. It also depends on how you proceed to define these beliefs more precisely. The argument gets complicated, but it nevertheless does seem clear that a belief in the equality of men means that social and economic differences must be based on the conviction that such differences contribute to the common good. In other words, these differences must be justified as *functional*. They must be shown to lead to something else of merit that legitimates a departure from the norm of equality.

Traditionally, the American goal for economic rewards has been phrased in terms of "equal opportunity." But subscribing to equal opportunity answers only part of the problem. There is still the problem of determining (a) what economic game should be played and (b) what the structure of prizes should be. This involves two different determinations. Playing a mixed free-enterprise game does not say anything about the optimum structure of economic prizes. Markets can always be adjusted to yield almost any structure of prizes.

Nor is there any escape from such moral determinations via the route of "fair process." The "natural lottery" and "equal opportunity" are all variants of the fair process argument. But what constitutes a fair game? Do we let consumers' preferences determine the economic merit of an opera company or do we create, through education, a public demand for operatic performances? Is a fair game a game where each person has an equal chance to win? If chances of winning are to be equalized, do we handicap those born with advantages or compensate those born with disadvantages? What constitutes an equal start? Should every individual be subject to the same initial budget constraint? Consider inheritances. Is there any difference between the individual who inherits one million dollars and the individual whose athletic talents will earn him the same lifetime income?

As these questions indicate, the rules of the natural lottery are not intuitively obvious. The rules can only be specified when one knows the desired distribution of prizes to be generated. The rules cannot be used to determine the desired distribution of prizes, since lotteries or market economic games can be formulated to yield any distribution of prizes. The market may be a "fair process" to which most Americans are willing to submit, but it is necessary to stipulate some other principles to determine the equitable distribution of economic prizes within this game.

AGGREGATING PREFERENCES

The basic thrust of both nineteenth-century liberal thinking and the economics profession has been to seek specifications of economic equity in the aggregation of individual preferences, or "utility functions." Unfortunately, the process of aggregation has run into seemingly insoluble difficulties. Economists, therefore, have more recently been inclined to leave the problem to "someone else." The most recent "someone else" to attempt the isolation of a social welfare function is John Rawls. He uses a belief in process to establish both the natural equality of men and the optimum distribution of prizes. As in Rousseau, the natural equality of men comes from a social contract in which each man's signature is as necessary and important as anyone else's. But, unlike Rousseau, Rawls sees the structure of economic prizes as also being determined in the process of signing the social contract. Rules for distributing prizes are to be set on the assumption that each person, so far as he knows, has an equal chance of landing at the top or middle or bottom of the social order. Rawls argues that there is only one structure of prizes that everyone would be willing to accept: This is a prize structure that maximizes the minimum prize. In economists' terms, Rawls is asserting that every individual is (or should be) absolutely "risk averse." Everyone acts on the assumption that he will be getting the smallest prize, and thus wants to maximize the smallest prize. No one wants to take a chance on winning a larger prize. No one thinks about anything but his own prize.

Although maximizing the minimum prize seems egalitarian (Rawls believes it to be so), it need not be. Under this rule, I can undertake any project that raises my income by any amount so long as it also raises the income of the poorest group—no matter by how little. Rawls believes that the trickle-down effect is so large that it would be impossible to design economic activities that concentrate income gains among high-income groups. As an economist, I do not share this faith: The world is not divided into economic activities with no trickle-down effects and activities with substantial trickle-down effects. There are many economic activities with marginal amounts of trickle-down. To be really egalitarian, social rules would have to state that individuals must choose those economic activities with the largest trickle-down effects.

As Rawls's specification of economic equity indicates, a great many assumptions about preferences must be made to generate his desired distribution of prizes. The gambling man's preferences are illegitimate. Given that the economic lottery is a game where some prize is necessary to survive, the idea of a minimum prize makes sense (although there probably are some people who would be willing to take a chance on their own starvation); but maximizing the minimum prize is something else again. Empirical evidence would seem to point toward the viability of lotteries that do not maximize the minimum prize; people are clearly willing to bet a small part of their current prize (income) in exchange for a very small chance on a very big prize. Rawls is also forced to rule out the envious man. Suppose the worst-off man were envious. In this case, anything that lowers the income of better-off people faster than it lowers the income of the worst-off man maximizes the minimum prize. If envy were not ruled out, maximizing the minimum prize could lead to zero incomes for everyone.

The distinction between factual states and preference states creates problems for Rawls as it has for other philosophers. His golden rule is "do unto the worst-off man as he would be done unto." To some extent the worst-off man will be the man with the worst measurable economic position; but to some extent he will also be the man with the preference structure that is hardest to satisfy. To what extent should the distribution of economic prizes take into account the personal usefulness (utility) of those prizes? Should the man who is relatively inefficient in processing economic prizes—who gets less satisfaction out of his income than do others with the same income—get larger prizes because of his inefficiency?

Perhaps Rawls could convince us that the willingness to take risks, or that an interest in factors other than one's own income, is a perverse preference in the same sense that masochism is a perverse preference. But it is not obvious that this is the case. And Rawls certainly cannot persuade us that maximizing the minimum prize constitutes economic equity unless he involves something other than the process of signing a universalizable social contract.

Rawls has, however, isolated two important ingredients in a specification of economic equity. (1) *A belief in the natural equality of man (no matter how established) leads to the conclusion that deviations from economic equality must be shown to be beneficial.* The burden of proof is on those that advocate inequality. (2) If one is willing to assert that a rational man is risk averse enough to want to avoid suicide, then *some minimum economic prize is an essential ingredient in economic equity.*

FINDING THE ARCHIMEDEAN POINT

Rawls also implicitly focuses attention on another essential distinction in specifying economic equity. There is a difference between allowing individual preferences to affect the form of the social welfare function and making social welfare purely a function of individual utilities.

Individuals have different levels of preferences. They have preferences about the rules of the economic game and the distribution of prizes that it should generate; but they also have preferences about how to maximize their own utility in the current economic game—no matter how much they dislike the economic game they are forced to play. There is nothing self-contradictory, for example, in seeking to become extremely wealthy and powerful in our current economic game, yet believing that a better economic game would be one where there are no "extremely wealthy" prizes to be had. To distinguish these two levels of preferences I will call the one *individual-societal preferences* and the other *private-personal preferences.*

This distinction makes it possible to avoid some of the problems in individualistic social welfare functions. Societies can, if they wish, discuss what constitutes economic equity without worrying about individual differences in the efficiency with which people process economic goods. A preference such as envy is ruled out, not because it does not exist and not because it does not affect private personal preferences—it does—but because society chooses not to take envy into account in its social rules, even though each one of its members may be envious. In their individual-societal preferences, individuals decide to rule out the private-personal preference of envy, since collectively it can lead to absurd results.

If social welfare is a function only of private-personal utilities, it is not in general possible to specify economic equity. Using our individual-societal preferences, however, we can make economic equity a separable problem, if we so desire.

More fundamentally, the whole "utility function" approach is misconceived in a world without innate preferences. The social welfare function is the place where society is supposed to make interpersonal comparisons—yet the individualistic social welfare function lets each person determine his own importance in social welfare. In addition, how does society determine that two people are equally happy? You cannot have an individualistic social welfare function unless utilities can be added together. To compare utilities, you need some "objective" criteria of when two people are equally well off. Utilities theory has been searching for its Archimedean point for a long time without success. In a world that does not believe in innate preferences, the search is futile.

It is, however, also unnecessary. Although the Archimedean point cannot be derived from private-personal preferences, it *can* be specified on the basis of individual-societal preferences. Socially, we simply decide that individuals are economic equals—i.e., are equally "happy"—under certain circumstances. Thus, the specification might say that individuals are economic equals when they have the same income, wealth and family size. But whatever the conditions, the Archimedean point is clearly specifiable by an act of social judgment. In a similar manner, the optimum distribution of economic resources is socially specifiable even though it is not derived from any aggregation of private-personal preferences. This is because the distribution of economic resources may itself be one of the factors in determining individual utility functions. Individuals may want to live in a society where economic prizes are distributed in some specified manner—even if they live (and express their preferences accordingly) in a society with a different scheme of distribution. . . .

ECONOMIC EQUITY

Since individual-societal preferences about the structure of the economic game and its distribution of prizes are continually changing as preferences are molded by history and culture, economic equity is not a static condition. At the same time, it is possible to consider the different facets of equity and come to the conclusion that one particular distribution of economic resources is more equitable than another at some moment in time. The current distributions of income and wealth are given in Tables 1 and 2. What would constitute a more equitable set of distributions?

To be both concrete and provocative, let me suggest a set of more equitable distributions. These suggestions are not my personal "individual-societal preferences" about the optimum distribution of prizes, but are my interpretation of our society's revealed preferences, upon consideration of the four facets of equity.

While there is general social allegiance in the United States today to the fairness of the market process in determining incomes, this allegiance is not to marginal productivity payments but to marginal productivity as it is modified by wage contours, relative deprivation, interdependent preferences and so on. At the same time, there is a general perception that the

Table 1.   U.S. Distribution of Family Income in 1970[1]

Portion of Total Families by Income	Percent of Total Family Income
Lowest Fifth	5.5
Second Fifth	12.0
Third Fifth	17.4
Fourth Fifth	23.5
Highest Fifth	41.6
(Top 5 per cent)	(14.4)

[1] Median income = $9,867, mean income = $11,106.

Table 2.   U.S. Distribution of Family Wealth in 1962[1]

Percent of Total Families by Wealth	Percent of Total Family Wealth
Lowest 25.4	0.0
Next 31.5	6.6
Next 24.4	17.2
Top 18.7	76.2
(Top 7.5)	(59.1)
(Top 2.4)	(44.4)
(Top 0.5)	(25.8)

[1] Median net worth = $7,550, mean net worth = $22,588.

market does not generally meet the competitive axioms for many groups. The group that comes closest to the "natural lottery" is composed of white adult males who work full time and full year. In general, these workers do not suffer from the handicaps of race, sex, age, personal deficiencies or adverse macroeconomic policies. By examining their earnings rather than their income, the effects of inherited wealth can be eliminated. As can be seen in Table 3, the earnings for this group are more equal than the income distribution for the whole population. *Income dispersions would be reduced 40 percent if the national economic lottery yielded a structure of prizes as equal as that now generated for fully employed adult white males.*

Since adult white males who work full time and full year are the majority and backbone of the work force, the dispersion in economic rewards necessary to keep them working is certainly wide enough to keep the economy and other groups working. At least this much reduction in inequalities could occur without having to worry about adverse work effects.

I would argue that considerations of both "fair process" and the "common good" would seem to lead to a specification of this distribution as an interim equity target to which the economy should be slowly moving. The

Table 3. The Natural Lottery

Annual Earnings (in Thousands of Dollars)	Distribution of White Male Money Earnings for Those Working Full Time and Full Year in 1970[1]	Distribution of Total Money Income for All Individuals 1970[2]
0 – 1	1.7%	10.4%
1 – 2	1.3	8.3
2 – 3	1.5	6.9
3 – 4	3.0	6.8
4 – 5	4.4	6.2
5 – 6	6.8	6.7
6 – 7	8.6	7.0
7 – 8	10.5	7.8
8 – 10	19.7	13.2
10 – 15	27.9	17.7
15 – 20	11.2	6.8
25 & over	3.3	2.3

[1] Median = $9,223, mean = $10,218.

[2] Median = $6,670, mean = $7,537.

process is the market process, which is regarded as fair, and which clearly does not conflict with the common good of more growth and thus higher incomes for everyone.

An important question remains, however, as to whether public efforts should focus on restructuring market rewards or whether reliance should be placed on tax and transfer policies. My own view is that both will have to be used, but *the emphasis should lie on establishing an equitable distribution of market rewards before, rather than after, taxes and transfers.* The political unpopularity of universal tax and transfer systems, the experience of World War II, and the political popularity of minimum wage legislation all point in this direction. As the recent Social Security legislation indicates, there is a willingness to establish an adequate transfer payment income floor for those too ill or old to work; but as our experience with the Family Assistance Plan indicates, there is no willingness to do the same for those who can work. Those who *can* incur a cost *must* incur a cost.

While the distribution of earnings for fully employed white adult males may constitute an interim specification of general economic equity, it does not handle the minimum income dimension of economic equity. Using Rainwater's finding that the public basically believes that those who make a full-time effort should not have less than half of what the general population has, would lead to a minimum annual earning of approximately $5,000 for a fully employed head of a household. Such a number is also consistent with the belief that those who work should get more than those on welfare. At the moment, welfare levels for a family of four are in the neighborhood of $4,000 in most northern urban states. Five thousand dollars conveniently preserves a gap. As Table 3 indicates, however, almost 12 percent of the fully employed white male population makes less than $5,000 per year. This means there is a need for public policies to insure that no full-time worker falls below $5,000 per year.

Examination of wage contours, relative deprivation, interdependent preferences and the rest would lead to the clear understanding that tax and transfer policies are *not* the optimum instruments for establishing this floor. The preferred method would be minimum wage legislation coupled with public employer-of-last-resort programs to guarantee that everyone who wanted full-time work at the minimum wage could have it. Since fully employed workers work about 2,000 hours per year, the minimum wage would need to be about $2.50 per hour.

Obviously, achieving a minimum earning for those with no wealth of $5,000 a year, and achieving a distribution of income above this level that is no more unequal than that now in place for fully employed adult white males, has implications for the distribution of wealth. It is at this point that the tax system plays its major role. A progressive wealth and/or inheritance tax system would be necessary to hold the distribution of income from wealth within the same proportions as that of income from earnings.

Since the top 14.5 percent of the adult white fully employed males earns 28 percent of the total earnings of this group, a wealth and/or inheritance tax would need considerably to reduce the current inequalities in wealth. The wealthiest 14.5 percent of the families now have between 60 and 70 percent of total wealth. This would have to go down to about 30 percent. While a cut from 60 percent to approximately 30 percent is substantial, it is hardly confiscatory.

No one need agree with my specification of economic equity; but if there is one lesson in the state of the art of equity economics, it is that there is no way to avoid the problem of specifying economic equity. It is a problem that is not going to fade away. Our political history has been a verbal subscription to the ideal of equality coupled with the practical desire to avoid having to specify what constituted equity (i.e., an acceptable degree of inequality). As with all temporary solutions, this one now seems to be breaking down.

Economic Justice and the Economist

Richard A. Posner

Richard A. Posner is Professor of Law at the University of Chicago.

In a recent issue of *The Public Interest* (No. 31, Spring 1973), Lester Thurow, an economist at the Massachusetts Institute of Technology, argued that economic justice requires radical changes in the distribution of income and wealth in this country, and proposed specific redistributive measures. I shall argue three points here:

(1) The measures proposed by Thurow are highly questionable.

(2) There is no basis in economics for the concept of economic justice from which these measures are derived.

(3) The economist has an important role to play in a study and discussion of the distribution of income and wealth, but it is not the role that Thurow set for himself.

Thurow's specific proposals are as follows:

1. The federal minimum wage (now $1.60 an hour, with a number of exemptions) would be increased to $2.50 an hour, the level at which every fully employed worker would earn at least $5,000 a year. Presumably the exemptions in the present minimum wage law (for domestic workers, some farm workers, employees of very small businesses and a few other groups) would be eliminated.

2. The federal government would offer employment at the minimum wage to anybody who wanted to work full time and could not find a job in the market.

3. A tax on "wealth and/or inheritance" would be imposed, designed to bring about the same distribution of wealth (i.e., property) as found in the earnings of white, male, fully employed workers. Thurow considers this distribution an appropriate "interim equity goal." The brackets and rates of the tax would be set so as to reduce the wealth of the wealthiest 14.5 percent of American families, who according to Thurow now have between 60 and 70 percent of the nation's wealth, to 28.5 percent of that wealth, because this is the percentage of the annual earnings of white, male, fully employed workers that goes to the highest-paid 14.5 percent of those workers.

These proposals would, if implemented, create costly dislocations in the economy, and in the society as a whole. As of April 1970, fully 43 percent of all private nonfarm, nonsupervisory workers were earning less than $2.50 an hour, while the *median* wage of farm workers was much less than $2.50 an hour. A large number of studies of the employment effects of minimum wage laws have found, not surprisingly, that increases in the minimum wage cause unemployment.[1] And these were studies of much smaller increases than those proposed by Thurow. Moreover, the minimum wage law has always exempted the occupations in which the adverse effect on employment of imposing a minimum wage would be most serious. Thurow's proposal would eliminate these exemptions. One does not know just how many of the more than 20 million workers affected by the proposal would lose their jobs. But the number could be substantial—would almost surely be in the millions—and would be concentrated among the marginally employable, such as black teenagers and middle-aged women first entering the labor force; for we know from previous studies of the employment effects of the minimum wage that these groups are especially vulnerable.

Thurow, a labor economist, must know all this, which is presumably why he also proposes to require the federal government to offer jobs to all those who cannot find work. But he seems oblivious to the practical difficulties of implementing such a proposal. Once the Thurow proposal for a universally applicable $2.50 hourly minimum wage became effective, all sorts of people, all over the country (and especially in the South, where wages are lowest), would find themselves without work—farm workers, domestic help, dishwashers, sales clerks, soda jerks, delivery men, elevator operators, charwomen, restroom attendants and so on. They, together

[1] See, e.g., John M. Peterson and Charles T. Stewart, Jr., *Employment Effects of Minimum Wage Rates* (1969), and studies cited therein; Marvin Kosters and Finis Welch, "The Effects of Minimum Wages on the Distribution of Changes in Aggregate Employment," *American Economic Review* 62, No. 323 (1972).

with people able to obtain only part-time employment at the minimum wage, would present themselves to the nearest federal office and demand work. How would the government respond? It could buy and operate restaurants, grocery stores, fruitstands, home-maintenance services and farms in order to be able to offer workers made jobless by the minimum wage (or unable to find full-time employment at that wage) the same kind of work that they had previously done, and in the same places. This seems a highly inefficient, indeed an impracticable alternative. Then again, the government could offer these people jobs as postmen, clerks in army commissaries, orderlies in Veterans Administration hospitals, and the like. This latter alternative—a massive expansion in distinctively "public-sector" jobs—seems to be what Thurow actually has in mind. All other objections aside, the huge costs of relocating large numbers of workers from private-sector to public-sector jobs, often in different localities, seem a decisive objection.

Alternatively, the government could simply pay the employers of workers now paid less than the statutory minimum the difference between their wage and the minimum; but this approach is also open to serious practical objection. The employer of such workers would have a powerful incentive to maintain wages at the lowest possible level (or even to reduce them) in order to maximize the government's subsidy of his labor costs. Clearly, he would never raise the wage of a worker whose competitive wage was lower than the statutory minimum, so the government's subsidy would rise over time as increases in general wage levels required increases in the statutory minimum. And the incentive for employers to upgrade the skills of their working force would be reduced, since if the market wage rate of the workers rose above the statutory minimum the employers would cease to receive any subsidy. The approach would assure the continued existence of a sizable class of marginal workers.

A related but more general criticism of Thurow's proposal is that it would reduce the incentive of marginal workers to improve their skills. The worker who today earns $3,000 a year has a strong incentive to upgrade his skills to the point where he can earn $5,000. Under Thurow's proposal he would have no such incentive, because his reward would be zero.

Thurow's proposal would have other consequences. Firms that employ workers at wages less than the proposed minimum would react by (1) increasing their wages, (2) discharging workers and either curtailing output or substituting capital for labor inputs or (3) doing a little of each. Whichever course was followed, the cost of production would rise. At least part of the increase would be reflected in higher prices to consumers. And taxes would have to be raised in order to defray the costs to the federal government of employing all those made unemployable by the increase in, and extension of, the minimum wage.

At a guess, the wealth tax proposed by Professor Thurow would be even more dislocating. Assuming that the average size of wealthy families is not much different from the size of other families (actually it is slightly smaller), the 14.5 percent wealthiest American families must comprise about 30 million people. Very few of them are really wealthy: A survey conducted in 1963 showed that, as of December 31, 1962, only 6.7 percent of U.S. households had a net worth of $50,000 or more. In the $50,000–$99,000 bracket, where two thirds of these "wealthy families" fell, 23 percent of the average family's net wealth was accounted for by home and automobile ownership.[2] Most such families are not what we have in mind when we speak of "the rich," yet all of them would be forced to surrender to the government 50 percent of their net worth.[3]

A byproduct of the tax would be a change in spending patterns. Since people would not be permitted to accumulate much money, they would have an incentive to substitute expenditures on consumption for savings. An extravagant style of living would be encouraged, and the apparent inequality of income and wealth thereby increased. To encourage extravagance by the rich seems an odd way to promote economic justice.

By labeling his tax a wealth "and/or inheritance" tax, Thurow implies that the desired redistribution of wealth could perhaps be accomplished by an inheritance tax alone. But even a 100 percent inheritance tax would not achieve Thurow's purpose, since only a small fraction of the wealthiest 14.5 percent of American families owe their wealth to inheritance. The Projector and Weiss study found that, even among families with $500,000 or more in wealth, only 34 percent reported that inheritance accounted for a substantial portion of their wealth; for the $50,000–$99,000 bracket, the figure was only 12 percent. A very steep inheritance tax would also create the undesirable incentive, just noted, to substitute consumption for savings. (A corollary is that the tax would yield little revenue.)

A striking feature of Professor Thurow's program is that it contains no provisions designed to benefit the millions of people who are incapable, for whatever reason, of full-time work. The program he proposes would

[2] See Dorothy S. Projector and Gertrude S. Weiss, *Survey of Financial Characteristics of Consumers* (1966), pp. 151, 21.

[3] Thurow does not indicate how the burden of the wealth tax would be allocated among people subject to it, but he implies that it would be allocated evenly, since he indicates a concern with possible Constitutional objections to taking away more than half of a person's wealth. If the group as a whole must reduce its wealth by one half, and no member is to be forced to give up more than one half of his wealth, then obviously every member's wealth must be reduced by exactly one half.

actually make them worse off than they are now, since the higher minimum wage would, as mentioned earlier, increase the cost and hence prices of goods.

The subordination of the interests of the nonworking poor and of consumers to the interests of workers, and the preoccupation with expropriating property, place Professor Thurow's proposals in the Marxist tradition. Marxists do not want to solve specific social problems; they want to turn society upside down. His proposals would do that. And these are only "interim" proposals!

Thurow's program of redistribution is offered as the fruit of an economic analysis of the problem of the just distribution of income and wealth. However, in presenting and justifying the program, Professor Thurow is not speaking as an economist, and his proposals have no support in economic theory.

The opening pages of his essay suggest that economic theory does not yield a definition of the just distribution of income and wealth. This is true, and might well have served to end the essay, since Thurow's professional competence is as an economist. But he does not stop there, because he regards the unwillingness of the economist to define the just distribution of wealth as both a source of reproach to the profession[4] and a "cop-out," since in his view economic analysis rests ultimately on postulates concerning just distribution. . . .

Although Thurow holds that economics cannot escape from having to grapple with the problem of the just distribution of wealth, he apparently thinks it proper for the economist, in grappling with the problem, to escape from economics. His definition of the just distribution of wealth owes little to economics but much to an unspecified mélange of public opinion polls, introspection, and political hunches.

The key to his analysis is the concept of "individual-societal preference." This is an individual's preference for how the wealth and income in the society should be divided up, and is to be distinguished from the individual's "personal-private preference," which determines what goods he buys, where he works, and so on. The just distribution of income and wealth is determined by adding up people's individual-societal preferences. Unfortunately, this is difficult to do. An advantage of economic markets is that they enable preferences to be determined in a generally reliable manner. If I say that I prefer a cheap foreign import to an

---

[4] The essay begins, "Modern economics springs from the search for a definition of economic justice, but has largely abandoned that search." This is an eccentric definition of the springs of modern economics. Modern economics is rooted in the interest of Smith, Ricardo, Marshall and others in the operation of economic markets.

expensive American car, but then buy the latter, the purchase speaks louder than the words. Willingness to pay provides more credible evidence of preference than willingness to say. It also provides a means of weighting preferences by their intensity: Scarce goods are assigned to the people willing to pay the most for them. The ascertainment and weighting of preferences in the absence of markets is extraordinarily difficult. The democratic political process is the normal alternative in our society—and a growing literature documents its numerous and serious deficiencies as a method of revealing the preferences of the electorate. Its use in place of the market should be carefully circumscribed. . . .

It does not appear that Thurow looks to the democratic political process to reveal our individual-societal preferences. Plainly, the preferences revealed by that process are for a good deal less economic equality than Thurow believes just. Yet political feasibility is mentioned frequently. I note in this connection, unkindly, that Thurow was one of Senator McGovern's principal economic advisers in the 1972 Presidential campaign—not very good credentials for a political seer. The lesson Thurow draws from the 1972 campaign debacle is in any event a peculiar one: The voters were unwilling to support massive redistributions, by means of taxes and subsidies, to the nonworking poor; *therefore* they could be induced to support a more drastic redistribution of income and wealth accomplished through a combination of stiffer minimum wage laws and more extensive federal government employment with heavy wealth taxes. This view reflects a certain contempt for the thinking processes of American voters. Anyone who resents using taxes to support people who do not work should, as a matter of consistency, also resent using taxes to pay someone $5,000 a year for work worth only $1,000 or $2,000 in the market, and will view massive federal employment programs as boondoggles for the unproductive. . . .

Because "society's" preference for massive redistribution rests ultimately on the views expressed by the small minority of educated and well-to-do people who dominate the Left in this country, it is important for Thurow to reassure the reader that there is no contradiction between wanting to maximize one's personal wealth (the usual personal-private preference) and wanting to have society changed in a way that will significantly reduce that wealth. The difference between a "personal-private" and an "individual-societal" preference is clear enough in principle. But I, at least, would have difficulty identifying the authentic preference of someone whose personal-private and individual-societal preferences were not merely distinct, but opposite and indeed mutually exclusive. Imagine an individual who is grasping, ungenerous, and ruthlessly acquisitive in his personal and business dealings but who, if asked, will say that he supports a restructuring of society that would result in a drastic reduction in his relative and absolute wealth and income. Does such a person *really* prefer an egalitarian society? Do not his actions speak louder than his words? Is it not likely either that he is a hypocrite or that deep down he believes that in the restructured society his wealth and income (not necessarily pecuniary) would be greater than they are now?

Thurow's program rests on a weak foundation: the avowals, which only the credulous would take at face value, of a small and unrepresentative segment of the American people. He would be on firmer ground if he abandoned the pretense that his program is founded on people's preferences. He is telling people what they should think, not what they do think (which is again in the Marxist tradition). In any event his proposals owe nothing to economics.

The two gravest weaknesses in Thurow's essay are ones that he shares with most proponents of redistributing income and wealth, and therefore deserve special attention. They are the failure to define economic equality correctly and the failure to weigh the costs of redistribution against its benefits.

Thurow assumes that the distribution of annual money incomes among household units constitutes a reasonable measure of economic equality. It does not. Consider first the problem of the intertemporal distribution of earnings. Two workers, a carpenter and a baseball player, have the same lifetime earnings, but the first has a steady income every year while the lifetime earnings of the second are bunched in a few years. In any given year the earnings of the two will be highly unequal; and in a table of annual earnings, they will contribute to an impression of inequality. But there is no meaningful inequality between them. A related point is that a table of annual earnings will include the earnings of a young worker just starting out and a worker in his prime. The earnings of the two will be highly unequal; yet again, their lifetime earnings may be identical.

Consider next the differential investment in human capital (earning capacity). A dentist has higher lifetime earnings than a plumber. But the dentist may have borrowed money to go to college and dentistry school, and the difference between his lifetime earnings and the plumber's may be merely equal to the amount required to repay the loans with interest, plus the dentist's forgone earnings while in college and dentistry school. Differential investment in human capital may explain much of the difference between male and female earnings. If most women prefer to remain at home while their children are young, it follows that they will spend less time in the work force than men. Their lower potential lifetime earnings will induce them to invest less in their earning capacity, so their annual earnings (which include repayment of, as well as return on, investment in human capital) will be lower. Their shorter time in the work force will also lead employers to invest less in training them, with similar results.

Another important factor is uncertainty of earnings, and taste for or against risk. Suppose that a successful inventor has an average income of $100,000 a year but only one out of ten inventors is successful (the rest have zero incomes from inventing). Then the average earnings of inventors will be only $10,000 a year and this is the correct figure to use in comparing inventors' incomes with those, say, of civil servants. Suppose, in addition, that people are "risk-averse," preferring the certainty of earning $10,000 a year, for example, to a 10 percent chance of earning $100,000 a year. If so, it will be necessary to compensate people for bearing risk. Society may have to pay successful inventors $150,000 a year before inventing becomes as attractive a career as civil service. The civil servant with his $10,000 income and the successful inventor with his $150,000 income will contribute to the statistical impression of economic inequality; in fact, their incomes are not unequal in any meaningful economic sense.

Still another very important factor is attitude toward deferred income. A high school graduate must choose between continuing in school, thereby deferring the production of income for several years, or beginning to work immediately. The additional education will enable him to obtain a higher income; but the additional income, as we saw earlier, is not pure gravy—it includes the repayment, with interest, of his investment (chiefly in the form of forgone earnings during the period of education) in earning capacity. If he attaches a very high time value to money—if a dollar today is worth much more to him than a dollar tomorrow—the return on such an investment may not compensate him for the present earnings that he will have to forgo. He will prefer to begin work immediately, even though his lifetime earnings will be lower. Income inequality is thus partly a matter of choice.

Finally, money income does not adequately measure real income. Consider two families, one where both husband and wife work and earn $10,000 each, and the other where only the husband works, and earns $10,000. The real income of the first family may be lower, not higher, than the real income of the second. The wife in the second family may be staying home because her services in the home are thought to be worth more than the income she would receive in a job outside the home. Suppose she could earn $12,000 in such a job. Then her services in the home (ignoring the tax advantages of nonmarket income) must be worth at least $12,000, making the family's real income $22,000. Or consider two construction workers, one of whom receives higher wages but has a more dangerous job. His higher wage is simply compensation for the higher expected accident costs in the more dangerous job, but it contributes to the statistical impression of economic inequality.

Income to the economist is a different concept from *monetary earnings*. It includes leisure and all sorts of other nonpecuniary yields from activity that are excluded in measures of pecuniary earnings, and it excludes repayment of human capital, compensation for risk, interest or deferred earnings, and other items that the statistical aggregates count as income. It is the economic concept of income that is relevant in appraising economic equality. The economic concept is poorly approximated by the kind of measure that Thurow uses.

Thurow treats the distribution of wealth as a measure of economic equality distinct from and coequal in importance to the distribution of income. This procedure would be defensible if he defined wealth properly, but he does not. A person's wealth is the present value of all of his future earnings, pecuniary and nonpecuniary (less the costs involved in the production of those earnings). The value of a home is the present value of its imputed rental income; the value of jewelry is the present value of the nonpecuniary income, in the form of pleasure, that the jewelry yields; the value of a share of stock is the present value of its expected dividends and capital gains. These forms of wealth are included in the statistics on which Thurow relies—but the most important is excluded: human capital or earning capacity. Were it included, the distribution of wealth would not be, as Thurow asserts, much more unequal than the distribution of income.

If income and wealth were correctly measured—as an economist would measure them—we could evaluate Thurow's premise that there is serious economic inequality among people who work. He has failed to establish this premise. And he considers only one type of cost associated with altering the distribution of income and wealth: the reduced incentive to work associated with heavy income taxes. He wholly ignores the costs of the redistributive measures that *he* proposes—the extension of the minimum wage, the expansion of public employment, and the tax on wealth. All of these are costly measures. His minimum wage proposal would, by raising the price of much labor far above market levels, reduce the efficiency with which labor is used in production. Employers would substitute methods of production that were cheaper to them, given the artificially high price of labor, but more costly to the society than the methods that had been displaced. Workers would be shifted from private-sector to government jobs, in which their labor would probably be less productive (otherwise the shift would presumably have taken place already). The heavy tax on wealth would induce costly adaptations designed to reduce its impact. It would also weaken the incentive to engage in various high-risk activities—such as starting new companies—that are economically feasible only because success is highly rewarded. True, the entrepreneurial role could be taken over by the government, but the experience of the Communist countries suggests that this would be highly inefficient.

The fact that the redistribution of income and wealth along the lines proposed by Thurow would have very high costs is not a decisive objection against his proposals. But in measuring those costs, Thurow would have contributed to an understanding of the issues involved in distributive policy.

The last point suggests the essential failing of Thurow's essay. He has refused to respect the division of labor between economists and other students of society. Economics is a positive science. The economist has an important contribution to make to the debate over the appropriate distribution of income and wealth, but it is descriptive rather than normative. He can measure economic equality, or at least point out the limitations of the conventional indices; he can attempt to explain the real inequality that he finds; he can assess the distributive effects of various policies; and he can estimate the costs of various redistributive measures. Thurow does none of these things. He attempts instead to prescribe the just distribution; and this is a matter outside of his competence as an economist.

Finally, I am puzzled by the fact that nowhere in his essay does Thurow suggest a reason why a much greater equality of income and wealth would be a good thing for our society. He does not claim that society would be wealthier, or happier, or politically more stable as a result—and none of these conclusions is self-evident. He does not claim that the well-being of the people who would benefit from the redistribution is more important than that of the people who would lose from the redistribution. He takes for granted the desirability of redistributing income and wealth, and discusses only methods and tactics. While I have concentrated on what seem to me to be serious errors in his analysis, I am above all struck by his having ignored the fundamental question of what society would gain by achievement of his "interim" redistributive goals.

A Reply

Lester C. Thurow

What distribution of economic resources constitutes a just distribution of economic resources? This is the question that I attempted to answer in my original article. My basic objection to Posner's reply is that it is completely negative. If he had stated why I was wrong in my analysis and then gone on to show how the problem of economic justice should be handled, I would have enjoyed responding. The interchange between a bright legal mind and an economic mind might even have led to some progress beyond that achieved in either of the original attempts.

Nowhere in his article does Posner say that the specification of economic justice is irrelevant or unimportant. He merely maintains that "there is no basis in economics for the concept of economic justice." He implies that the current market distribution of income is all right, but he is unwilling to argue that it constitutes economic justice. I have no objection to someone exercising his comparative advantage in negative thinking, but it should be pointed out that Posner provides no help in solving the basic problem. . . .

Most of this response will be devoted to analyzing the costs of shifting from the current distribution of economic resources to the one that I suggested—but first I must clear away some of the verbal underbrush.

CHARGE 1:

"There is no basis in economics for the concept of economic justice." This contention is right, wrong and irrelevant all at the same time. There is a large

Excerpted from Lester C. Thurow, "A Reply," *The Public Interest,* No. 33 (Fall 1973), pp. 120–27. Copyright © National Affairs, Inc., 1973. Reprinted by permission of the publisher and author.

corpus of literature called welfare economics (discussed at some length in my article). In principle, social welfare functions could be used to make interpersonal comparisons and to specify economic justice. This large literature does not yield definitive deductive definitions of economic justice, but it does provide some interesting tools and insights into the problems. Paul Samuelson was given his Nobel prize partly for work in welfare economics. Kenneth Arrow was awarded his Nobel prize for his work on the difficulties of aggregating individual preferences to make social choices. Graduate schools of economics give courses in welfare economics. Posner might think that economics has nothing useful to say about economic justice, and that economists have no right to think about it, but there are obviously many people who do not agree.

Moreover, his contention would be irrelevant even if it were true. We would still be left with the problem of specifying economic justice. If the answer lies outside of economics, then we have to search wherever the answer lies.

Certainly he is right that the answer does not lie entirely within economics. That is why I went outside my "professional competence." I discussed some of the philosophical, psychological and sociological principles that have been advanced. I do not claim to have advanced degrees in all of these other fields (I do have one in philosophy), but this does not mean that I am barred from thinking about the implications of other intellectual findings on the problems of economic justice. My original article was an attempt to discuss a problem persuasively; it was not, either in content or in tone, an attempt to speak *ex cathedra* from superior professional competence.

As my original argument stated, fundamental value judgments are necessary to specify economic equity. If you are a follower of Rousseau and believe in the natural equality of man, then deviations from equality must be shown to be beneficial on some dimension. If you accept the position of classical political philosophy and believe in the natural inequality of man, then movements toward equality must be shown to be beneficial on some dimension. The article clearly stated that I took the Rousseauan position and went on to examine the various dimensions on which inequality could be justified as beneficial. I accepted many of these and did not advocate complete equality or even anything close to it. The article called for a distribution of economic resources (income and wealth) that was no more unequal than the distribution of earnings *currently* existing for adult white males—hardly a revolutionary equalization of incomes!

CHARGE 2:

"Thurow is thus incorrect in saying that efficiency 'ceases to have any meaning' unless certain 'ethical' postulates such as 'more is better' are accepted." While it is possible to define efficiency in such a manner that it does not depend upon ethical postulates, when it is defined in this manner it ceases to have any normative implications. There is no reason to want to be efficient. Let's take the Posner man who believes "that less is better and the optimum output of the economic system is zero." This man has no budget constraint. All economic goods have become free goods with zero price. There is no normative significance to wasting economic resources by being inefficient. One is wasting something with zero value. Efficiency can be defined as the condition that exists when the fewest possible resources are used to accomplish some task, but efficiency only has economic significance if there is a budget constraint in existence. The budget constraint leads one to want to be efficient. The Posner man has no need to be efficient, and thus an efficiency expert can tell him nothing of value. Economic advice on how to conserve zero-value assets has itself a zero price. Efficiency exists, but is valueless.

CHARGE 3:

"The democratic political process is the normal alternative [to the market] in our society—and a growing literature documents its numerous and serious deficiencies as a method of revealing the preferences of the electorate. Its use in place of the market should be carefully circumscribed." I will not comment on the irony of such a statement from a man who is busy accusing others of being antidemocratic. I am willing to join with Posner in swearing allegiance to market principles. Economic markets must, however, start out with something that is certified as a just distribution of economic resources if they are to yield desirable results. The distribution of economic resources is the distribution of economic votes in the marketplace. How are the economic votes to be distributed—that is the fundamental question. It is a question left unanswered by Posner, a question not answered by pledging allegiance to the market. A market economy that starts with an unjust distribution of economic resources will yield an unjust distribution of goods and services, regardless of its efficiency.

In my original article I discussed the possibility of allowing the market itself to determine economic justice. This would yield the marginal productivity distribution of economic resources, but Posner does not say whether he considers this to be a state of equity.

CHARGE 4:

"The difference between a 'personal-private' and an 'individual-societal' preference is clear enough in principle. But I, at least, would have difficulty identifying the authentic preference of someone whose personal-private and individual-societal preferences were not merely distinct, but opposite and indeed mutually exclusive."
Posner makes an elementary error in logic here, since personal-private and individual-societal preferences can never be mutually exclusive. They exist in different domains. Individual-societal preferences concern the rules of the game; private-personal preferences concern the best way to play the existing game.

Since Posner says that he understands the distinction, I am afraid that the remaining problems lie in his own personal inadequacies. There is nothing inconsistent about an individual who advocates a 50 mph speed limit on the highways to reduce accidents and to conserve energy, yet still drives at the 70 mph legal limit. This driver knows that even more accidents are caused by cars driving at very different speeds, and that any gas savings on his part will simply lower the price of gasoline and cause someone else to use up the energy he saves by driving slowly. Similarly, a belief in communism is not a belief in the efficacy of personal poverty. There is nothing inconsistent about a communist who lives in a capitalist country and who acquires an unequal income. There is no way that he can acquire an equal income. He acts within the rules of the game in the society in which he lives, but he can still attempt to change the rules through the political process. If a person is willing to vote for substantial income redistribution, then he has revealed his individual-societal preferences on that issue.

CHARGE 5:

"Thurow assumes that the distribution of annual money incomes among household units constitutes a reasonable measure of economic equality. It does not." This statement is not true since I used both the distribution of money income (a distribution dominated by the distribution of earnings and human capital) and the distribution of physical wealth to represent the current distribution of economic resources. Both are necessary since unrealized capital gains are not included in the income series and since physical wealth, as well as income, represents potential control over economic resources. Since human capital cannot be sold, only rented, in a country prohibiting slavery, its earnings are appropriately added into the income series. To mix human capital and physical capital together is to add

commodities that can be sold to a commodity that cannot be sold; the sum of these is hardly a meaningful measure of potential purchasing power.

Posner is evidently unable to live with the fact that the lowest fifth of all families have 5.5 percent of total income and the highest fifth have 41.6 percent of total income (as reported by the U.S. Census), or that the poorest 25.4 percent of all families have *no* wealth while the top 18.7 percent own 76.2 percent of all private physical assets and the top 0.5 percent own 25.8 percent of all assets (as reported by the U.S. Federal Reserve Board; for the complete distributions, see page 329 of my original article). He argues that the distribution of psychic income (happiness?) is more equal than the distribution of money income or physical wealth.

Even if this were true, the distribution of happiness is not coterminous with the distribution of economic resources. Happiness is not spendable in those efficient economic markets. It does not command purchasable economic goods and services. Economic justice has to do with the appropriate distribution of economic resources vis-à-vis economic markets. Economic justice is not the same thing as justice without the adjective "economic."

Although Posner implies that his suggested corrections would lead to a more equal distribution of economic resources, they need not do so. His human capital correction has already been included in the distribution of income. There are no direct data with which to make his proposed lifetime income correction, but it is possible to get an idea of the difference that lifetime incomes would make by comparing, within a given category of the population, the distributions of income for particular age groups with the distribution of income for all members of the category. If lifetime incomes are more equally distributed than annual incomes, the distribution of income among particular age groups should be substantially more equal than the distribution of income for the category as a whole. Table 1 compares the distribution of income for males 45 to 54 years of age with the distribution of income for all males 25 years of age and over. As the data indicate, the distribution of income among males 45 to 54 years of age is actually a bit more unequal than that for all males. This suggests that an appropriate lifetime correction might make the distribution of income more *unequal* rather than more equal. . . .

We also know that you cannot predict the actual consequences of a system of taxation without empirical studies. This is particularly the case with income tax, for it engenders two opposite economic effects. The first of these is that high taxes lead to reduced incomes, which in turn induce greater work and investment in order to recoup and to achieve standard-of-living goals—the "income effect." But high taxes, by reducing

Table 1.   U.S. Distribution of Male Income (1971)[1]

Proportion of Males by Income	Percent of Male Income	
	All Males 25 & Over	Males 45 to 54
Lowest Fifth	4.8	4.2
Second Fifth	11.8	13.1
Third Fifth	17.8	17.6
Fourth Fifth	24.8	23.7
Highest Fifth	40.8	41.4

[1] Source: Bureau of the Census, *Current Population Reports*, Consumer Income, 1971, pp. 112, 113.

net hourly earnings, also lead to more leisure and less work—the "substitution effect." Our actual experience with income taxes has been that, under a progressive rate structure up to 90 percent, the income effect equals or exceeds the substitution effect. Inasmuch as the same two effects exist for wealth taxation, wealth taxes, like our income tax, may cause *more* work and investment rather than less.

Posner suggests that random risk or luck explains much of the dispersion in the distribution of income and wealth. Luck is one of those conveniently unmeasurable variables that you can maintain explains everything without having to worry about inconvenient data. I will note, however, that if luck does explain the dispersion in income and wealth, then taxes can cause a complete equalization of incomes without any cause for worry about economic incentives. The existing income differentials do not affect economic incentives since they are completely determined by luck—not economic effort.

CHARGE 6:

"The proposals would, if implemented, create costly dislocations in the economy, and in the society as a whole." My proposals would reduce the dispersion in incomes and wealth by about 40 percent. Somehow Posner thinks that if the economic lottery *now in place* for adult white males were expanded to everyone else, the economy would collapse. Since he is an adult white male, this is self-serving at the very least. Adult white males survive that distribution now, and I suspect that the whole economy could survive the same distribution. Economic markets are a lot more robust than Posner thinks; if they weren't, they would have collapsed long ago.

We also know that free enterprise market economies can operate with such a distribution of income. If the distribution I suggest were in place, the U.S. distribution of income would be almost exactly that now existing in Japan. The world's fastest-growing free enterprise economy appears to survive such a distribution of income. There might even be a connection between Japan's higher rate of growth and its more equal distribution of income.

Let us look more closely at the $2.50 minimum wage that is supposed to cause such havoc. If Posner is right, he had better start heading for his economic bomb shelter since, as I write this reply, one house of Congress has already passed a $2.20 minimum wage. Empirical studies of the impact of the minimum wage do not agree, but let's examine the one referenced by Posner. This is a study by M. Kosters and F. Welch on "The Effects of Minimum Wages on the Distribution of Changes in Aggregate Employment" in the *American Economic Review* for June 1972. Since Posner presumably searched the economics literature for the study with the largest adverse impacts, we can take it as the outer limit of the possible effects. Let me quote from that study: "Our hypothesis is that minimum wages serve to reduce shares of normal employment and to increase shares of transitional employment for those groups of workers with low average productivity." Translated, this means that the minimum wage makes a low-productivity group more sensitive to cyclical fluctuations in employment (the business cycle), but that it does not stop the group from being fully employed if the economy is operated at full employment. Appropriate macroeconomic policies can offset the dislocations Posner fears according to his own favorite study of minimum wages.

But let's go on to the conclusions of this same study:

For adults, the overall effect of increased minimum wages is to stabilize their employment. This increased stability occurs through shifting the incidence of employment fluctuations to teenagers, and the stabilizing effect is strongest for white adult males. It also appears that increased minimum wages may have stabilized employment for non-white adult males, although the effect is apparently very small and the statistical insignificance of the elasticities precludes any strong statements.

The last phrase means that the results have not been proven in accordance with the standard statistical tests of whether a hypothesis is valid. In other words, there is no hard statistical evidence that even these limited conclusions are valid. These are hardly the fearsome effects painted by Posner. In any case, to cover the possibility that the adverse effect on teenagers did exist, even though it cannot be statistically proven, I proposed the establishment of a public employment program.

Posner's economics of a wage subsidy is so bad that I am afraid that it would flunk an Economics I examination at any college in the country. He has completely forgotten the economic markets he likes so well. Take the case where a wage subsidy is paid to the employer of a low-income worker: In terms of the economist's standard supply and demand diagrams, this causes an upward shift to the employers' demand curve for labor (see Figure 1). The size of the shift is given by the wage subsidy. Employment rises, the new minimum wage is achieved, and the employers' payments fall somewhat, so that the subsidy must be larger than the increase in the minimum wage. But a limit to the employers' reduction in wages is set by supply and demand conditions—the more horizontal (elastic) the demand curve, the less the reduction in employer wage payments. The employer would have no volitional control over wages, as stated by Posner. His wages, as always, would be controlled by supply and demand. (The reader can work out for himself what happens when the subsidy is given to the employee rather than to the employer. This causes an upward shift in the supply curve.)

In the mid-1960s the President's Commission on Automation issued a report going into great detail as to the productive things that a public employment program would do: Cleaner cities, more school assistants and

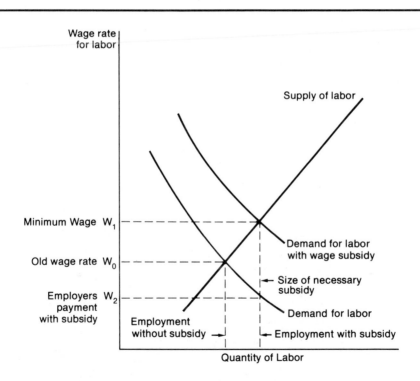

Figure 1   The Economics of a Wage Subsidy

a host of other possibilities were listed. Anyone interested in a long discussion of public employment should look at that report. If Posner thinks that there is nothing productive to be done in our society, I am sorry for him.

My original proposals were carefully tailored to minimize economic dislocations. As this section indicates, the dislocations Posner prophesies are not apt to occur. They are not even substantiated by his own references.

Where does this leave the discussion of economic justice? It is for the reader to decide whether my original contentions still stand. But whatever that decision, it is clear that Posner has not improved our understanding of how to handle the problems surrounding the just distribution of economic resources. He hasn't even tried.

GREAT DEBATE EIGHT

THE ISSUE OF MONETARISM

THE ISSUE OF
MONETARISM

F OR THE past two decades the great debate in macroeconomic theory has been about the role of money in the economy. In a sense, this is surprising because money has been a subject of study among economists since the dawn of the field. But the matter still is not clear, or at least agreed upon. The most provocative challenge has come from Professor Milton Friedman of the University of Chicago. In countless books and articles, he has argued that the prevailing orthodoxy, variously called Keynesian economics or post-Keynesian economics or eclectic Keynesian economics, has vastly understated the role of money in economic life and, by the same token, vastly overstated what the government can achie've through nonmonetary and especially fiscal policy efforts. Professor Friedman's doctrine is called *monetarism,* and this will be the subject of the following debate.

QUANTITY THEORY OF MONEY

To put the question in a proper perspective, a brief piece of history is in order. If we go back to the pre-Keynesian era (before the mid-1930s), we find that the prevailing analysis of money was centered on the *quantity theory of money.* This theory can be expressed in terms of the following equation, sometimes called the "equation of exchange":

$$M \times V = P \times Q$$

M is the stock of money in the economy (say, currency plus demand deposits), V is the income velocity of money, P is the price level and Q is the level of real national income.

The key concept here is that of the income velocity of money. It is meant to measure the number of times the average dollar bill or demand deposit circulates through the economy during a given period in exchange for final output. In particular, it is defined as:

$$V = \frac{P \times Q}{M}$$

In words, the income velocity of money is equal to money national income in a given year divided by the total of currency and demand deposits available on the average during the course of that year.

This definition raises a possible source of confusion about our quantity theory equation; namely, the equation appears to be true by virtue of the meaning of income velocity. $MV = PQ$ becomes a truism that tells us nothing whatever about the real world. This is quite correct, and what it means is that in order to get a proper theory about the role of money in the economy from this equation we have to make some further statements about its terms. And this the quantity theorists did.

They said, first, that on the whole, national income in real terms (Q) was determined by real factors—size of the labor force, amount of capital, the general level of technology and so on. These factors would alter over time but very slowly, and in any event they would not be affected by the quantity of money in any serious or enduring way. This was pre-Keynesian economics in which full employment was taken to be the norm except for various temporary frictions and adjustments.

Second, they argued that V was largely determined by institutional factors and could also be regarded as independent of changes in M. V would be influenced by such factors as the state of banking practice, and the ways in which wage payments and other disbursements of funds were made in the economy. Consider, for example, the differences in the velocity of money when a man gets his salary on a weekly basis and when he gets it on a monthly basis. If the man gets $250 in a weekly paycheck and spends it all each week, he will at any given moment of time, be holding on the average $125 in money. (If all payments are by check, this will be his average bank balance.) If, however, he is paid by the month (something over $1,000 a month), his bank balance will on the average be over $500. The income velocity of money will be four or more times as great if his paychecks are on a weekly as opposed to a monthly basis.

What the quantity theorists said was that these and other such institutional factors largely determined V. At the same time, Q was largely determined by technology and the available quantities of the factors of production. What then happened when M was altered? Clearly, the only variable left to be affected was P. And this was the main contention of the quantity theory; namely, that changes in the quantity of money produced roughly proportional changes in P (and presumably also in wages, W) throughout the economy.

In terms of Samuelson's quotation of Tobin's remarks (p. 386), this theory embodied a combination of two views of money: (a) "Money does not matter," and (b) "Money alone matters." In terms of real national income and employment, money mattered very little according to this theory. In terms of prices and wages, by contrast, the quantity of money more or less completely called the tune.

THE KEYNESIAN SYNTHESIS

Keynes was concerned with providing a synthesis of real and monetary analysis. He did not deny that institutional factors could affect the velocity of money, nor even that, under certain special circumstances (particularly when full employment had been achieved), the quantity theory might be a fair approximation to reality. But he did deny that full-employment national income could be taken as the natural state of affairs, and he also stressed the effects of M on the interest rate (r).

Keynes suggested that, in addition to the transactions' demand for money embodied in the quantity theory, people also wished to hold money for various other reasons (he spoke of a "precautionary" motive and a "speculative" motive). Now, insofar as money is being held simply to carry out our day-to-day or week-to-week transactions, then the quantity theory holds; that is, given the prevailing institutional arrangements, the amount of money we will need for our transactions will depend on the size of the money income in the economy ($P \times Q$). This is tantamount to saying that the V for transactions money is effectively given.

But the demand for liquidity will also be affected by the possibility of holding our wealth in the form of other assets: Treasury bills, bonds, stocks and so on. In particular, this demand for money will be substantially affected by the rate of interest, r. If the rate of interest is high, then this means that we are foregoing important earning opportunities by holding our wealth in the form of non-interest-bearing money. Also, a high r implies that bond prices are low; this may make it likely that bond prices are due to rise, which would be a further motive for going into bonds as opposed to money. In short, a high r will make people less willing to hold their wealth in the form of money. By reverse reasoning, a low r will increase the demand for money. Or to put it in terms of the equation of exchange: V, in Keynesian theory, will depend on the rate of interest—it is not simply given by institutional factors.

Furthermore, in a depressed state of the economy, V may become very low indeed. Keynesians have referred to this phenomenon as the *liquidity trap*. Expectations may be so pessimistic that even if the central bank keeps pumping new M into the system, everyone may simply hold this money as money and not try to invest it in bonds or other securities. In the liquidity trap, as M increases, V falls, and this is tantamount to saying that changes in M will have no effects on the economy, either on prices or on real national income.

In the general Keynesian case, however, changes in M will have some effect on the economy, and these effects will be on the real sector as well as on monetary or nominal values, such as money prices or money wages. An increase in M in the Keynesian world will generally have the effect of lowering the interest rate, and a lowered r will be expected to stimulate investment and other spending. This increased spending will, in turn, raise the level of real national income in the economy. Only when that real national income approaches its full employment capacity level will the main effect of increased M be on prices. Conversely, decreased M will tend to raise r, and this will tend to depress investment and real national income. *M* thus does affect *Q* in the Keynesian world, although its effects may be limited if there is a very depressed situation and a liquidity trap develops.

An interesting question arises: If *P* is not proportional to *M* in the Keynesian world, exactly how is *P* determined? This is a complicated matter because, ultimately, the question can be answered only in terms of the whole Keynesian system. However, it is important to note that critics of Keynes have pointed out that you cannot determine prices in the Keynesian system without assuming a given level of money wages, *W*. Friedman refers to the system's dependence on "rigidities and imperfections" (p. 368), and one of these, it is alleged, is that you can get unemployment equilibrium in the economy only if you assume that money wages are rigid, that they are held up artificially, say by union-management wage contracts that prevent wages from falling. Given that assumption, the critics say, prices will also be held up artificially high and unemployment can persist. *But,* they go on, the existence of unemployment would normally bring a progressive bidding down of money wages in the economy as unemployed workers try to secure jobs. This will lead to a fall in prices and, according to the equation of exchange, if *P* is falling, and if *M* and *V* remain constant, won't this mean a rise in *Q*? In other words, can't we really cure unemployment by a downward plunge of wages and prices and doesn't this mean that the whole Keynesian system simply rests on a few artificial rigidities?

Of course, the key phrase in the above argument is "if *M* and *V* remain constant." In a sense that is the whole issue. To see why this is so, let us show how wages and prices fit into the Keynesian system by following through on the suggestion that unemployed workers will bid down wages in order to get work. Let us imagine an economy with high unemployment and wages flexible downward. *W* is going down and *P* along with it. What effects will this have, according to Keynes?

The interesting thing is that these declines in money wages and prices would theoretically have much the same net effect as an *increase* in the money supply:

As wages and prices fall, the value of money national income falls (P X Q falls). This means that for a given quantity of money (M), less money is needed in the transactions sphere and more is available for precautionary or speculative purposes. The effect of more money available for these non-transactions' purposes will, under favorable circumstances, be a lower interest rate. This lower interest rate should have some favorable effect on investment and, by the national income multiplier, on real national income (Q). Thus, the potentially favorable effects of a general fall in wages and prices on total output and employment will come through a route similar to the effects of an increase of the money supply—via the interest rate.

And, by the same token, such favorable effects can be nullified by the liquidity trap (a falling *V*) in a seriously depressed economy. They can also be nullified if the process of *falling* (as opposed to *low*) wages and prices discourages business investment. In other words, in the Keynesian theory, the route to full employment via either monetary policy *or* general wage cuts is a highly uncertain one.

PIGOU EFFECT

There is, however, another effect of such wage-price cuts, often referred to as the *Pigou effect* (Friedman, p. 367, and Samuelson, p. 383), named after A. C. Pigou whose work we discussed in another connection in the debate on income distribution. It was, in part, this particular effect that led to the "rediscovery of money" and the spread of monetarism in the postwar period.

What Pigou said was that as wages and prices fall systematically throughout the economy, the *real* (as opposed to *nominal*) value of the money supply increases in the same proportion. Suppose we have an economy with substantial unemployment and a given stock of money, M. Wages and prices are completely flexible downward, we assume, and this means that unemployed workers will bid down wages, which will have the further consequence of lowering prices throughout our economy. Let us suppose that P falls to half its previous value. What Pigou said was that this means a doubling of the real value of the money wealth held in this economy. My individual share of the money supply (my average bank balance) is, say, $1,000. Before the fall in P, this was equivalent to a certain amount of purchasing power. *After* the halving of P, this same $1,000 is equivalent to twice as much purchasing power—$2,000 at the original P. My *real wealth* has thus been increased by the fall in W and P and there is every likelihood that I will now spend more. Thus, we would expect consumption to rise and this would have a favorable effect on real national income and employment.

It might be objected that this increase in my real wealth from $1,000 to effectively $2,000 is too small to have any major effect on my consumption, which would still depend mainly on my income. However, notice that, in our assumed economy, this process of raising the real value of M can go on indefinitely. If halving P is not sufficient, then it can be lowered to a tenth or a thousandth of its original value. In this last case, my $1,000 becomes the equivalent of $1 million in terms of purchasing power at the original prices. Surely this will have substantial effects on my consumption demand.

Now the Pigou effect we have been discussing is not so easily applicable to the real world as it might seem from this account. In our modern economy, where the problem tends to be unemployment and price *inflation* (see Great Debate Four), the notion of W and P falling to one-half their previous levels is rather fanciful. To expect them to fall to a tenth or a thousandth of their previous levels is simply delusionary. Furthermore, it is not so clear that the M in our equation would remain constant as this massive fall in W and P took place. To some extent, the supply of money in the economy depends, for any given level of bank reserves, on the demands for money in the system. Such a large contraction in the transactions' demand for money might be expected to be accompanied by at least some contraction in M. And, finally, of course, the problem of *low* versus *falling* wages and prices arises again. The process of reducing W and P by half in the present-day American economy might be so fraught with hazard that it would actually harm the goal for which the process was launched.

Nevertheless, the Pigou effect does suggest that money can enter the macroeconomic picture in more ways than the original Keynesian analysis allowed for. Consideration of such effects had something to do with the desire of some economists to upgrade the role of money far beyond what even an amended, or post-Keynesian theory might permit.

MONETARIST DOCTRINE

With this brief history in mind, we can now describe the main doctrines, empirical issues and policy questions raised by Professor Friedman and his monetarist colleagues.

Friedman presents a summary of his doctrines with wonderful economy in our first reading (pp. 363–365). The very first proposition tells much of the story: "There is a consistent though not precise relationship between the rate of growth of the quantity of money and the rate of growth of nominal income. If the quantity of money grows rapidly, so will nominal income and conversely" (p. 363). Apart from qualifications, this statement suggests that we are basically back in a sophisticated form of the quantity theory. For the monetarist, once we know what is happening to M we can fairly well determine what is happening to nominal income ($P \times Q$). The whole Keynesian income-expenditure approach to national income determination is basically abandoned in this doctrine.

This major difference with the Keynesians is, in turn, premised on a variety of more specific differences. In an introductory essay to a book on the quantity theory,[1] Friedman suggested three areas of difference between quantity theorists and Keynesians. The first concerns the "stability and importance of the demand for money." This has to do ultimately with the amount of variability of the velocity of money, V. While Friedman does not argue that V is a numerical constant, nevertheless the monetarist position is dependent on reasonably modest fluctuations in V and on a limit to the number of variables that affect V. Second, the monetarist doctrine depends on the view that the demand and supply of money are to a large degree independent. If the banking system simply adjusts the supply of money to the demands for it, then changes in the quantity of money will be a reflection of, not a cause of, changes in economic conditions. Finally, a good quantity-theorist will reject the notion that there is a "liquidity trap" and/or that the "only role of the stock of money and the demand for money is to determine the interest rate."

Given the monetarist approach to these issues—and especially the notion of a reasonably stable V—we can understand that M will largely determine $P \times Q$. But what will its specific effects on Q be? In the old-fashioned quantity theory, M merely affected P, while real national income remained happily pegged at something close to the full-employment level.

On this point, it is necessary to distinguish between the short run and the long run. In the short run, it is beyond doubt that the monetarists believe that

[1] Milton Friedman, ed., *Studies in the Quantity Theory of Money* (Chicago: University of Chicago Press, 1956).

changes in the money supply can have massive and disastrous effects on real national income and employment. Friedman attributes the "Great Contraction" (the depression of the 1930s) largely to the fact that the Federal Reserve System followed a deflationary policy, reducing the amount of money in the economy by one-third (p. 368). This implies an extremely potent role of money in its effects on real variables and, if the analysis is accepted, it would indeed be "tragic testimony to the power of monetary policy."

In the long run, however, Friedman argues that monetary policy has very little effect on real variables. Thus, he maintains that monetary policy cannot determine the long-run level of employment in the economy. In that long run, the role of M is to affect nominal quantities (like the price level) and not real quantities (like employment and real national income). This is because the initial effects of actions to alter M will be different from the long run effects. Thus, suppose the monetary authority increases the supply of money to raise the rate of employment above its "natural" level. *Initially,* this will affect Q more than P, but in the long run, wages and prices will rise in money terms and—with a largely constant V—that rise will mean a reverse in the increase of employment back to its original level.

This differentiation between immediate and long-run effects also explains why Friedman feels the central bank cannot peg the interest rate at some desired level. Suppose it increases M and brings down the interest rate. The longer-run effect will be for prices and wages to rise and a consequent rise in the interest rate back to its former level. Indeed, it is likely to overshoot the mark as expectations of inflation force the interest rate to rise above its original level. Thus, in the long run, an expansionary money supply brings (via inflation) not lower but higher interest rates than would otherwise be the case (p. 370).

All of which raises the problem of how long the short run and long run are supposed to be in the monetarist world. Friedman's short run can be fairly long—"as much as five or ten years" (p. 364)—and during this period there could, of course, be substantial departures from full-employment income. To sum up: Under monetarism, long-run real national output and employment are determined by real factors, not by M. However, M can substantially affect these factors in a short run of fairly considerable length; indeed, when M gets out of whack, it can cause major dislocations in real, as well as in money, or nominal, values in the system.

EMPIRICAL ISSUES

The resolution of the differences of opinion between the monetarists and the post-Keynesians might seem to be a simple matter of getting the "facts." However, as we suggested in our introduction to all these great debates, the facts in economics are seldom laid out in such a way that they allow decisive tests of competing theories. In the particular case of monetarism, this general difficulty is reflected in a number of more specific problems:

What are the key variables we are talking about? In our summary analysis above we used the term *money* as though it were a simple and unambiguous concept. In fact, our definition of money in terms of currency and demand deposits is only one of several definitions. Economists use the term M_1 for this particular definition. But there are also M_2, M_3, M_4, and so on, as we include various time and savings deposits as well as demand deposits and move closer to government bonds and other forms of near-money. Now it is not perfectly clear which concept (M_1, M_2 and so on) the monetarists are talking about. Nor is it completely clear that it is the size of the money stock, whatever its definition, rather than its *rate of change* that may be crucial. Thus both Samuelson (p. 388) and Heller (p. 393) raise the question of whether monetarists have played fair, or whether they change their key variables (and hence their theories) as the evidence alters.

What are the relevant leads and lags? Because economic effects are produced by causes that precede them in time, we might expect that there would be various leads and lags when we come to examine the empirical relationships between variables. Thus, in the simplest cases it might seem that if variable A is exerting a causal influence on variable B, this would be reflected in changes in A preceding changes in B by some fairly regular period of time. This problem causes difficulties (1) because it is hard to determine what the appropriate "lead" or "lag" is, and (2) because economic systems are so complex that precedence in time may have no connection with causality at all. Thus, James Tobin has constructed a theory in which the quantity of money has no influence on money income, yet this quantity is regularly predicted to change in advance of changes in money income. Indeed, this "ultra-Keynesian model" does rather better than Friedman's own in describing the historical timing of the money-money income relationship (pp. 401–402).[2]

How to distinguish cause and effect? The lag problem is one aspect of the more general problem of distinguishing cause and effect. How do we decide, when the money supply and money national income change simultaneously, how much of this represents a response of the money supply to the expanded requirements of national income and how much represents the causal impact of an expanded money supply *on* national income? How do we decide whether money is an *exogenously* determined variable (determined by forces outside the system—for example, by a policy decision of the Federal Reserve Board), or an *endogenously* determined variable (a function of other variables in the system)?

How to weigh "mountains" of evidence? Professor Friedman has done massive empirical research on the influence of money in the economy, as have a number of his colleagues. Because of the general difficulties we have cited, however, there is still more work to be done. Also, despite sophisticated modern statistical techniques, questions of judgment keep arising. Thus, the monetarist position depends heavily on some reasonable stability in V. But how much? For example, income velocity of money (M_1) in the United States varied between 1.93 in the first quarter of 1946 to 3.87 in the fourth quarter of 1962—exactly doubling in this period. Furthermore, V went down in recessions and rose in prosperities during this

---

[2] Also see James Tobin, "Money and Income: Post Hoc Ergo Propter Hoc?" *Quarterly Journal of Economics* (May 1970).

period.[3] Should this be regarded as part of the "mountains of evidence" *for* Friedman's position or as part of the evidence that Samuelson, Heller and so on raise *in opposition to* that position. At the present time, economists are divided on this matter. Probably the majority believes that the evidential verdict comes down slightly against the monetarists, but there are exceptions in universities, business and government (the Federal Reserve Board of St. Louis is a notable example), and it is clear that still further mountains of evidence will have to be excavated.

THE POLICY ISSUES

It is also clearly of great importance that this further evidence be accumulated. The reason is that the monetarist versus Keynesian or post-Keynesian debate has enormous consequences for the policies that the government should follow in the whole area of macroeconomic stability.

We have already mentioned the increased potency attributed to monetary policy by the monetarists. Even more striking, however, is the *impotence* attributed by them to fiscal policy. This is the nub of the discussion between Friedman and Heller (p. 393 and p. 399). Heller's views are in the Keynesian tradition whereby fiscal policy has a direct effect on the level of income and employment, while Friedman's position is that fiscal policy influences the *division* of national income between the public and private sector but not the overall *level* of national income, employment, prices and so on. This is a direct consequence of the theory that M basically determines $P \times Q$. All that increasing government expenditures do is to increase public Q as opposed to private Q. Being generally against expansion of the public as opposed to the private sector, Professor Friedman, of course, does not favor such a reallocation of resources.

Related to this view of the impotence of fiscal policy is the theory that the way in which fiscal actions are financed is all-important. Suppose there is a tax cut leading to an increased national debt that is financed by the Treasury selling bonds to the Federal Reserve System. This action, rather like the open-market operations of the Fed even when there is no new Federal deficit-spending involved, will lead to an increase in the money supply.[4] Although the Keynesians would attribute direct economic impacts to the tax cut itself—for example, by raising the consumption function—the monetarists argue that the really important effect is the continuing increase in the money supply that this deficit would entail. Indeed, if the deficit were financed by selling bonds to the public (with no increase in M), it would, according to the monetarists, have minimal macroeconomic effects.

[3] Lawrence S. Ritter, "The Role of Money in Keynesian Theory," reprinted in *Readings in Macroeconomics,* ed. M. G. Mueller (New York: Holt, Rinehart and Winston, 1966), p. 171.

[4] Though, as Samuelson points out (p. 384), there is a difference between Fed purchases of bonds on the open market when there is no new deficit and when these purchases are financing such a deficit. In the former case, the Fed is purchasing the bonds from the public and, although this will lead to an increase in the money supply, it will also reduce the public's holdings of government bonds; thus, to some degree, there will be an offset to the increased money supply in terms of the community's sense of monetary wealth. This offset does not occur when the bonds are newly issued to finance a new deficit.

Even in the operation of monetary policy, the monetarists are very critical of the Keynesian approach. For one thing, they regard the Keynesians as having a tendency to focus too much on the interest rate (as opposed to the money supply, or its rate of change) as the key policy variable. This criticism is a direct result of the view that the Fed cannot really peg the interest rate anyway, especially in the long run, and, indeed, that the attempt to do so may lead to perverse effects (for example, the interest rate rising when M is increased and vice versa). Even more dramatic is the question of whether the government should employ *any discretionary policy at all* in this area. Friedman's general conclusion is that both logic and historical experience suggest that discretion produces far more errors (and serious errors) than it produces triumphs. Hence he favors the establishment of a fixed rule of conduct that the government should observe, increasing the money supply by a certain percentage every year—say, 3 to 5 percent a year—and then letting the market do the rest. This rule is perhaps even more restrictive, in that it would focus the Fed's attention exclusively on a single monetary aggregate—the quantity of money—as opposed to interest rates, the tightness of credit, general market conditions and the like. Such a fixed rule, for Heller, is like locking "the steering gear into place, knowing full well of the twists and turns in the road ahead. That's an invitation to chaos" (p. 396).

So the debate goes on.

The trend of things? In the late 1960s, Meltzer, a monetarist sympathizer, found that the Fed in the person of then-chairman William McChesney Martin, Jr. was moving toward a recognition of certain key monetarist doctrines (p. 409). In 1972, however, Andrew F. Brimmer, then a member of the Board of Governors of the Federal Reserve System, spoke of the "highwater mark of monetarism in 1970" and concluded:

Taking the Federal Reserve Board as it is today, I would conclude that all elements in the system (with the exception of the Federal Reserve Bank of St. Louis) remain highly eclectic and pragmatic in their conception of the tasks of monetary management. They show no signs of being led astray by simple prescriptions offered by the monetarists as to how they should perform their jobs.[5]

Thus, monetarists and post-Keynesian eclectics even differ on the question of which side is winning out. And this is probably appropriate in a debate that challenges the very basics of the standard macroeconomic theory and policy of the last 35 to 40 years.

[5] Andrew F. Brimmer, "The Political Economy of Money: Evolution and Impact of Monetarism in the Federal Reserve System," *The American Economic Review: Papers and Proceedings,* 62, No. 2 (May 1972), p. 351.

The Key Propositions of Monetarism

Milton Friedman

Milton Friedman, the father of monetarism, is Paul
Snowden Russell Distinguished Service Professor of
Economics at the University of Chicago.

Let me summarize what I regard as the key propositions of monetarism.

1. There is a consistent though not precise relationship between the
rate of growth of the quantity of money and the rate of growth of
nominal income. If the quantity of money grows rapidly, so will nominal
income and conversely . . .

2. This relation is not obvious to the naked eye over short periods,
because it takes time for changes in monetary growth to affect income
and how long it takes is itself variable. The rate of monetary growth today
is not very closely related to the rate of income growth today. Today's
income growth depends rather on what has been happening to money
over a past period.

3. On the average, a change in the rate of monetary growth produces a
change in the rate of growth of nominal income about six to nine months
later. This is an average. Sometimes the delay is longer, sometimes shorter. But I have been astounded at how regularly an average delay of six to
nine months is found under widely different conditions. I have studied
the data not only for the United States but also for Israel, for Japan, for
India and for a number of other countries. Some of our students have
studied it for Canada and for several South American countries. Whatever country you take, you almost always get a delay of about six to nine

From *Money and Economic Development: The Horowitz Lectures of 1972* by Milton Friedman. © 1973 by
Praeger Publishers, Inc., New York. Excerpted and reprinted by permission.

months between the change in money on the one hand and the change in income on the other.

4. The changed rate of growth of nominal income typically shows up first in output and hardly at all in prices. If the rate of monetary growth is reduced, for example, then about six to nine months later, the rate of growth of nominal income and also of physical output will decline. However, the rate of price rise will be affected very little. There will be downward pressure on the rate of price rise only as a gap emerges between actual and potential output.

5. On the average, the effect on prices comes some nine to fifteen months after the effect on income and output, so the total delay between a change in monetary growth and a change in the rate of inflation, averages something like 15 to 24 months. That works both ways. A speeding up of the rate of monetary growth tends to have its effect on inflation 15 to 24 months later; a slowing down of monetary growth has its effect on inflation 15 to 24 months later. That is why it is a long road to hoe to stop an inflation that has been allowed to start. It cannot be stopped overnight. That is really the main reason why you shouldn't let one get started.

6. Even after allowance for the delay in the effect of monetary growth, the relation is far from perfect. There is many a slip 'twixt the monetary change and the income change.

7. In the short run, which may be as much as five or ten years, monetary changes affect primarily output. Over decades, on the other hand, the rate of monetary growth affects primarily prices. What happens to output over the longer period depends on real factors: the enterprise, ingenuity and industry of the people; the extent of thrift; the structure of industry and government; the nature of competitive institutions; the relations among nations and so on.

8. It follows from the propositions I have so far stated that *inflation is always and everywhere a monetary phenomenon* in the sense that it is and can be produced only by a more rapid increase in the quantity of money than in output. However, the reason for the rapid increase in the quantity of money may be very different under different circumstances. It has sometimes reflected gold discoveries, sometimes changes in banking systems, sometimes the financing of private spending, sometimes—perhaps most of the time—the financing of governmental spending.

9. Government spending may or may not be inflationary. It clearly will be inflationary if it is financed by creating money, that is, by printing currency or creating bank deposits. If it is financed by taxes or by borrowing from the public, the main effect is that the government spends the funds instead of the taxpayer or instead of the person who would otherwise have borrowed the funds. Fiscal policy is extremely important in determining what fraction of total national income is spent by government and who bears the burden of that expenditure. By itself, fiscal policy is not important for inflation. What is important is how the spending is financed.

10. A change in monetary growth affects interest rates in one direction at first but in the opposite direction later on. More rapid monetary growth at first tends to lower interest rates. But later on, as it raises spending and stimulates price inflation, it also produces a rise in the demand for loans which will tend to raise interest rates. In addition, rising prices introduce a discrepancy between real and nominal interest rates. That is why throughout the world interest rates are highest in those countries that have had the most rapid rise in the quantity of money and also in prices—countries like Brazil, Chile, Korea and Israel.

In the opposite direction, a slower rate of monetary growth at first raises interest rates but later on, as it reduces spending and price inflation, it lowers interest rates. That is why interest rates are lowest in those countries that have had the slowest rate of growth in the quantity of money—countries like Germany and Switzerland. . . .

The two-edged relationship between money and interest rates explains why monetarists insist that interest rates are a highly misleading guide to monetary policy.

Those are the key propositions of monetarism, viewed as part of positive economics. The policy implications that can be drawn from these propositions are by no means unique. Some people who accept these propositions draw the conclusion that monetary policy should be used as a sensitive fine tuning instrument to adjust the economy. Other people, like myself, draw a very different conclusion. We think that the looseness of the relationship, the ignorance about the details of the relationship, means that the most important thing is to keep monetary policy from doing harm and that that can best be done by producing a steady growth in the quantity of money.

The Role of Monetary Policy
Milton Friedman

There is wide agreement about the major goals of economic policy: high employment, stable prices, and rapid growth. There is less agreement that these goals are mutually compatible or, among those who regard them as incompatible, about the terms at which they can and should be substituted for one another. There is least agreement about the role that various instruments of policy can and should play in achieving the several goals.

My topic for tonight is the role of one such instrument—monetary policy. What can it contribute? And how should it be conducted to contribute the most? Opinion on these questions has fluctuated widely. In the first flush of enthusiasm about the newly created Federal Reserve System, many observers attributed the relative stability of the 1920s to the System's capacity for fine tuning—to apply an apt modern term. It came to be widely believed that a new era had arrived in which business cycles had been rendered obsolete by advances in monetary technology. This opinion was shared by economist and layman alike, though, of course, there were some dissonant voices. The Great Contraction destroyed this naive attitude. Opinion swung to the other extreme. Monetary policy was a string. You could pull on it to stop inflation but you could not push on it to halt recession. You could lead a horse to water but you could not make him drink. Such theory by aphorism was soon replaced by Keynes' rigorous and sophisticated analysis.

Keynes offered simultaneously an explanation for the presumed impotence of monetary policy to stem the depression, a nonmonetary interpre-

Excerpted from Milton Friedman, "The Role of Monetary Policy," *American Economic Review* 58, No. 1 (March 1968), pp. 1–17. Reprinted by permission of the author and the publisher.

tation of the depression and an alternative to monetary policy for meeting the depression, and his offering was avidly accepted. If liquidity preference is absolute or nearly so—as Keynes believed likely in times of heavy unemployment—interest rates cannot be lowered by monetary measures. If investment and consumption are little affected by interest rates—as Hansen and many of Keynes' other American disciples came to believe —lower interest rates, even if they could be achieved, would do little good. Monetary policy is twice damned. The Contraction, set in train, on this view, by a collapse of investment or by a shortage of investment opportunities or by stubborn thriftiness, could not, it was argued, have been stopped by monetary measures. But there was available an alternative—fiscal policy. Government spending could make up for insufficient private investment. Tax reductions could undermine stubborn thriftiness.

The wide acceptance of these views in the economics profession meant that for some two decades monetary policy was believed by all but a few reactionary souls to have been rendered obsolete by new economic knowledge. Money did not matter. Its only role was the minor one of keeping interest rates low, in order to hold down interest payments in the government budget, contribute to the "euthanasia of the rentier," and maybe, stimulate investment a bit to assist government spending in maintaining a high level of aggregate demand.

These views produced a widespread adoption of cheap money policies after the war. And they received a rude shock when these policies failed in country after country, when central bank after central bank was forced to give up the pretense that it could indefinitely keep "the" rate of interest at a low level. In this country, the public denouement came with the Federal Reserve-Treasury Accord in 1951, although the policy of pegging government bond prices was not formally abandoned until 1953. Inflation, stimulated by cheap money policies, not the widely heralded postwar depression, turned out to be the order of the day. The result was the beginning of a revival of belief in the potency of monetary policy.

This revival was strongly fostered among economists by the theoretical developments initiated by Haberler but named for Pigou that pointed out a channel—namely, changes in wealth—whereby changes in the real quantity of money can affect aggregate demand even if they do not alter interest rates. These theoretical developments did not undermine Keynes' argument against the potency of orthodox monetary measures when liquidity preference is absolute since under such circumstances the usual monetary operations involve simply substituting money for other assets without changing total wealth. But they did show how changes in the quantity of money produced in other ways could affect total spending even under such circumstances. And, more fundamentally, they did undermine Keynes' key theoretical proposition, namely, that even in a world of flexible prices, a position of equilibrium at full employment might not exist. Henceforth, unemployment had again to be explained by rigidities or imperfections, not as the natural outcome of a fully operative market process.

The revival of belief in the potency of monetary policy was fostered also by a re-evaluation of the role money played from 1929 to 1933. Keynes and most other economists of the time believed that the Great Contraction in the United States occurred despite aggressive expansionary policies by the monetary authorities—that they did their best but their best was not good enough. Recent studies have demonstrated that the facts are precisely the reverse: the U.S. monetary authorities followed highly deflationary policies. The quantity of money in the United States fell by one-third in the course of the contraction. And it fell not because there were no willing borrowers—not because the horse would not drink. It fell because the Federal Reserve System forced or permitted a sharp reduction in the monetary base, because it failed to exercise the responsibilities assigned to it in the Federal Reserve Act to provide liquidity to the banking system. The Great Contraction is tragic testimony to the power of monetary policy—not, as Keynes and so many of his contemporaries believed, evidence of its impotence.

In the United States the revival of belief in the potency of monetary policy was strengthened also by increasing disillusionment with fiscal policy, not so much with its potential to affect aggregate demand as with the practical and political feasibility of so using it. Expenditures turned out to respond sluggishly and with long lags to attempts to adjust them to the course of economic activity, so emphasis shifted to taxes. But here political factors entered with a vengeance to prevent prompt adjustment to presumed need, as has been so graphically illustrated in the months since I wrote the first draft of this talk. "Fine tuning" is a marvelously evocative phrase in this electronic age, but has little resemblance to what is possible in practice—not, I might add, an unmixed evil.

It is hard to realize how radical has been the change in professional opinion on the role of money. Hardly an economist today accepts views that were the common coin some two decades ago. The pendulum has swung far since then, if not all the way to the position of the late 1920s, at least much closer to that position than to the position of 1945. There are of course many differences between then and now, less in the potency attributed to monetary policy than in the roles assigned to it and the criteria by which the profession believes monetary policy should be guided. I stress nonetheless the similarity between the views that prevailed in the late twenties and those that prevail today because I fear that, now as then, the pendulum may well have swung too far, that, now as then, we are in danger of assigning to monetary policy a larger role than it can perform, in danger of asking it to accomplish tasks that it cannot achieve, and, as a result, in danger of preventing it from making the contribution that it is capable of making.

Unaccustomed as I am to denigrating the importance of money, I therefore shall, as my first task, stress what monetary policy cannot do. I shall then try to outline what it can do and how it can best make its contribution, in the present state of our knowledge—or ignorance.

WHAT MONETARY POLICY CANNOT DO

From the infinite world of negation, I have selected two limitations of monetary policy to discuss: (1) It cannot peg interest rates for more than very limited periods; (2) It cannot peg the rate of unemployment for more than very limited periods. I select these because the contrary has been or is widely believed, because they correspond to the two main unattainable tasks that are at all likely to be assigned to monetary policy, and because essentially the same theoretical analysis covers both.

PEGGING OF INTEREST RATES

History has already persuaded many of you about the first limitation. As noted earlier, the failure of cheap money policies was a major source of the reaction against simple-minded Keynesianism. In the United States, this reaction involved widespread recognition that the wartime and post-war pegging of bond prices was a mistake, that the abandonment of this policy was a desirable and inevitable step, and that it had none of the disturbing and disastrous consequences that were so freely predicted at the time.

The limitation derives from a much misunderstood feature of the relation between money and interest rates. Let the Fed set out to keep interest rates down. How will it try to do so? By buying securities. This raises their prices and lowers their yields. In the process, it also increases the quantity of reserves available to banks, hence the amount of bank credit, and, ultimately the total quantity of money. That is why central bankers in particular, and the financial community more broadly, generally believe that an increase in the quantity of money tends to lower interest rates. Academic economists accept the same conclusion, but for different reasons. They see, in their mind's eye, a negatively sloping liquidity preference schedule. How can people be induced to hold a larger quantity of money? Only by bidding down interest rates.

Both are right, up to a point. The *initial* impact of increasing the quantity of money at a faster rate than it has been increasing is to make interest rates lower for a time than they would otherwise have been. But this is only the beginning of the process not the end. The more rapid rate of monetary growth will stimulate spending, both through the impact on investment of lower market interest rates and through the impact on other spending and thereby relative prices of higher cash balances than are desired. But one man's spending is another man's income. Rising income will raise the liquidity preference schedule and the demand for loans; it may also raise prices, which would reduce the real quantity of money. These three effects will reverse the initial downward pressure on interest rates fairly promptly, say, in something less than a year. Together they will tend, after a somewhat longer interval, say, a year or two, to return interest rates to the level they would otherwise have had. Indeed, given the tendency for the economy to overreact, they are highly likely to raise interest rates temporarily beyond that level, setting in motion a cyclical adjustment process.

A fourth effect, when and if it becomes operative, will go even farther, and definitely mean that a higher rate of monetary expansion will correspond to a higher, not lower, level of interest rates than would otherwise have prevailed. Let the higher rate of monetary growth produce rising prices, and let the public come to expect that prices will continue to rise. Borrowers will then be willing to pay and lenders will then demand higher interest rates—as Irving Fisher pointed out decades ago. This price expectation effect is slow to develop and also slow to disappear. Fisher estimated that it took several decades for a full adjustment and more recent work is consistent with his estimates.

These subsequent effects explain why every attempt to keep interest rates at a low level has forced the monetary authority to engage in successively larger and larger open market purchases. They explain why, historically, high and rising nominal interest rates have been associated with rapid growth in the quantity of money, as in Brazil or Chile or in the United States in recent years, and why low and falling interest rates have been associated with slow growth in the quantity of money, as in Switzerland now or in the United States from 1929 to 1933. As an empirical matter, low interest rates are a sign that monetary policy *has been* tight—in the sense that the quantity of money has grown slowly; high interest rates are a sign that monetary policy *has been* easy—in the sense that the quantity of money has grown rapidly. The broadest facts of experience run in precisely the opposite direction from that which the financial community and academic economists have all generally taken for granted.

Paradoxically, the monetary authority could assure low nominal rates of interest—but to do so it would have to start out in what seems like the opposite direction, by engaging in a deflationary monetary policy. Similarly, it could assure high nominal interest rates by engaging in an inflationary policy and accepting a temporary movement in interest rates in the opposite direction.

These considerations not only explain why monetary policy cannot peg interest rates; they also explain why interest rates are such a misleading indicator of whether monetary policy is "tight" or "easy." For that, it is far better to look at the rate of change of the quantity of money.

EMPLOYMENT AS A CRITERION OF POLICY

The second limitation I wish to discuss goes more against the grain of current thinking. Monetary growth, it is widely held, will tend to stimulate employment; monetary contraction, to retard employment. Why, then, cannot the monetary authority adopt a target for employment or unemployment—say, 3 percent unemployment; be tight when unemployment is less than the target; be easy when unemployment is higher than the target; and in this way peg unemployment at, say, 3 percent? The reason it cannot is precisely the same as for interest rates—the difference between the immediate and the delayed consequences of such a policy.

At any moment of time, there is some level of unemployment which has the property that it is consistent with equilibrium in the structure of *real* wage rates. At that level of unemployment, real wage rates are tending on the average to rise at a "normal" secular rate, i.e., at a rate that can be indefinitely maintained so long as capital formation, technological improvements, etc., remain on their long-run trends. A lower level of unemployment is an indication that there is an excess demand for labor that will produce upward pressure on real wage rates. A higher level of unemployment is an indication that there is an excess supply of labor that will produce downward pressure on real wage rates.

Let us assume that the monetary authority tries to peg the "market" rate of unemployment at a level below the "natural" rate. For definiteness, suppose that it takes 3 percent as the target rate and that the "natural" rate is higher than 3 percent. Suppose also that we start out at a time when prices have been stable and when unemployment is higher than 3 percent. Accordingly, the authority increases the rate of monetary growth. This will be expansionary. By making nominal cash balances higher than people desire, it will tend initially to lower interest rates and in this and other ways to stimulate spending. Income and spending will start to rise.

To begin with, much or most of the rise in income will take the form of an increase in output and employment rather than in prices. People have been expecting prices to be stable, and prices and wages have been set for some time in the future on that basis. It takes time for people to adjust to a new state of demand. Producers will tend to react to the initial expansion in aggregate demand by increasing output, employees by working longer hours, and the unemployed by taking jobs now offered at former nominal wages. This much is pretty standard doctrine.

But it describes only the initial effects. Because selling prices of products typically respond to an unanticipated rise in nominal demand faster than prices of factors of production, real wages received have gone down—though real wages anticipated by employees went up, since employees implicitly evaluated the wages offered at the earlier price level. Indeed, the simultaneous fall *ex post* in real wages to employers and rise *ex ante* in real wages to employees is what enabled employment to increase. But the decline *ex post* in real wages will soon come to affect anticipations. Employees will start to reckon on rising prices of the things they buy and to demand higher nominal wages for the future. "Market" unemployment is below the "natural" level. There is an excess demand for labor so real wages will tend to rise toward their initial level.

Even though the higher rate of monetary growth continues, the rise in real wages will reverse the decline in unemployment, and then lead to a rise, which will tend to return unemployment to its former level. In order to keep unemployment at its target level of 3 percent, the monetary authority would have to raise monetary growth still more. As in the interest rate case, the "market" rate can be kept below the "natural" rate only by inflation. And, as in the interest rate case, too, only by accelerating inflation. Conversely, let the monetary authority choose a target rate of unemployment that is above the natural rate, and they will be led to produce a deflation, and an accelerating deflation at that.

To state the general conclusion still differently, the monetary authority controls nominal quantities—directly, the quantity of its own liabilities. In principle, it can use this control to peg a nominal quantity—an exchange rate, the price level, the nominal level of national income, the quantity of money by one or another definition—or to peg the rate of change in a nominal quantity—the rate of inflation or deflation, the rate of growth or decline in nominal national income, the rate of growth of the quantity of money. It cannot use its control over nominal quantities to peg a real quantity—the real rate of interest, the rate of unemployment, the level of real national income, the real quantity of money, the rate of growth of real national income or the rate of growth of the real quantity of money.

WHAT MONETARY POLICY CAN DO

Monetary policy cannot peg these real magnitudes at predetermined levels. But monetary policy can and does have important effects on these real magnitudes. The one is in no way inconsistent with the other.

My own studies of monetary history have made me extremely sympathetic to the oft-quoted, much reviled, and as widely misunderstood, comment by John Stuart Mill. "There cannot . . . ," he wrote, "be intrinsically a more insignificant thing, in the economy of society, than money; except in the character of a contrivance for sparing time and labour. It is a machine for doing quickly and commodiously, what would be done, though less quickly and commodiously, without it: and like many other kinds of machinery, it only exerts a distinct and independent influence of its own when it gets out of order."[1]

True, money is only a machine, but it is an extraordinarily efficient machine. Without it, we could not have begun to attain the astounding growth in output and level of living we have experienced in the past two centuries—any more than we could have done so without those other marvelous machines that dot our countryside and enable us, for the most part, simply to do more efficiently what could be done without them at much greater cost in labor.

But money has one feature that these other machines do not share. Because it is so pervasive, when it gets out of order, it throws a monkey wrench into the operation of all the other machines. The Great Contraction is the most dramatic example but not the only one. Every other major contraction in this country has been either produced by monetary disorder or greatly exacerbated by monetary disorder. Every major inflation has been produced by monetary expansion—mostly to meet the overriding demands of war which have forced the creation of money to supplement explicit taxation.

The first and most important lesson that history teaches about what monetary policy can do—and it is a lesson of the most profound importance—is that monetary policy can prevent money itself from being a major source of economic disturbance. This sounds like a negative

---

[1] J. S. Mill, *Principles of Political Economy,* Book III, Ashley ed. (New York, 1929), p. 488.

proposition: avoid major mistakes. In part it is. The Great Contraction might not have occurred at all, and if it had, it would have been far less severe, if the monetary authority had avoided mistakes, or if the monetary arrangements had been those of an earlier time when there was no central authority with the power to make the kinds of mistakes that the Federal Reserve System made. The past few years, to come closer to home, would have been steadier and more productive of economic well-being if the Federal Reserve had avoided drastic and erratic changes of direction, first expanding the money supply at an unduly rapid pace, then, in early 1966, stepping on the brake too hard, then, at the end of 1966, reversing itself and resuming expansion until at least November, 1967, at a more rapid pace than can long be maintained without appreciable inflation.

Even if the proposition that monetary policy can prevent money itself from being a major source of economic disturbance were a wholly negative proposition, it would be none the less important for that. As it happens, however, it is not a wholly negative proposition. The monetary machine has gotten out of order even when there has been no central authority with anything like the power now possessed by the Fed. In the United States, the 1907 episode and earlier banking panics are examples of how the monetary machine can get out of order largely on its own. There is therefore a positive and important task for the monetary authority—to suggest improvements in the machine that will reduce the chances that it will get out of order, and to use its own powers so as to keep the machine in good working order.

A second thing monetary policy can do is provide a stable background for the economy—keep the machine well oiled, to continue Mill's analogy. Accomplishing the first task will contribute to this objective, but there is more to it than that. Our economic system will work best when producers and consumers, employers and employees, can proceed with full confidence that the average level of prices will behave in a known way in the future—preferably that it will be highly stable. Under any conceivable institutional arrangements, and certainly under those that now prevail in the United States, there is only a limited amount of flexibility in prices and wages. We need to conserve this flexibility to achieve changes in relative prices and wages that are required to adjust to dynamic changes in tastes and technology. We should not dissipate it simply to achieve changes in the absolute level of prices that serve no economic function.

In today's world, if monetary policy is to provide a stable background for the economy it must do so by deliberately employing its powers to that end. I shall come later to how it can do so.

Finally, monetary policy can contribute to offsetting major disturbances in the economic system arising from other sources. If there is an independent secular exhilaration—as the post-war expansion was described by the proponents of secular stagnation—monetary policy can in principle help to hold it in check by a slower rate of monetary growth than would otherwise be desirable. If, as now, an explosive federal budget threatens unprecedented deficits, monetary policy can hold any inflationary dangers in check by a slower rate of monetary growth than would otherwise be desirable. This will temporarily mean higher interest rates than would otherwise prevail—to enable the government to borrow the sums needed to finance the deficit—but by preventing the speeding up of inflation, it may well mean both lower prices and lower nominal interest rates for the long pull. If the end of a substantial war offers the country an opportunity to shift resources from wartime to peacetime production, monetary policy can ease the transition by a higher rate of monetary growth than would otherwise be desirable—though experience is not very encouraging that it can do so without going too far.

I have put this point last, and stated it in qualified terms—as referring to major disturbances—because I believe that the potentiality of monetary policy in offsetting other forces making for instability is far more limited than is commonly believed. We simply do not know enough to be able to recognize minor disturbances when they occur or to be able to predict either what their effects will be with any precision or what monetary policy is required to offset their effects. We do not know enough to be able to achieve stated objectives by delicate, or even fairly coarse, changes in the mix of monetary and fiscal policy. In this area particularly the best is likely to be the enemy of the good. Experience suggests that the path of wisdom is to use monetary policy explicitly to offset other disturbances only when they offer a "clear and present danger."

HOW SHOULD MONETARY POLICY BE CONDUCTED?

How should monetary policy be conducted to make the contribution to our goals that it is capable of making? I shall restrict myself here to two major requirements for monetary policy that follow fairly directly from the preceding discussion.

The first requirement is that the monetary authority should guide itself by magnitudes that it can control, not by ones that it cannot control. If, as the authority has often done, it takes interest rates or the current unemployment percentage as the immediate criterion of policy, it will be like a space vehicle that has taken a fix on the wrong star. No matter how sensitive and sophisticated its guiding apparatus, the space vehicle will go astray. And so will the monetary authority. Of the various alternative magnitudes that it can control, the most appealing guides for policy are exchange rates, the price level as here defined by some index and the quantity of monetary total—currency plus adjusted demand deposits, or this total plus commercial bank time deposits, or a still broader total.

For the United States in particular, exchange rates are an undesirable guide. It might be worth requiring the bulk of the economy to adjust to the tiny percentage consisting of foreign trade if that would guarantee freedom from monetary irresponsibility—as it might under a real gold standard. But it is hardly worth doing so simply to adapt to the average of whatever policies monetary authorities in the rest of the world adopt. Far better to let the market, through floating exchange rates, adjust to world conditions the 5 percent or so of our resources devoted to international trade while reserving monetary policy to promote the effective use of the 95 percent.

Of the three guides listed, the price level is clearly the most important in its own right. Other things the same, it would be much the best of the alternatives—as so many distinguished economists have urged in the past. But other things are not the same. The link between the policy actions of the monetary authority and the price level, while unquestionably present, is more indirect than the link between the policy actions of the authority and any of the several monetary totals. Moreover, monetary action takes a longer time to affect the price level than to affect the monetary totals and both the time lag and the magnitude of effect vary with circumstances. As a result, we cannot predict at all accurately just what effect a particular monetary action will have on the price level and, equally important, just when it will have that effect. Attempting to control directly the price level is therefore likely to make monetary policy itself a source of economic disturbance because of false stops and starts. Perhaps, as our understanding of monetary phenomena advances, the situation will change. But at the present stage of our understanding, the long way around seems the surer way to our objective. Accordingly, I believe that a monetary total is the best currently available immediate guide or criterion for monetary policy—and I believe that it matters much less which particular total is chosen than that one be chosen.

A second requirement for monetary policy is that the monetary authority avoid sharp swings in policy. In the past, monetary authorities have on occasion moved in the wrong direction—as in the episode of the Great Contraction that I have stressed. More frequently, they have moved in the right direction, albeit often too late, but have erred by moving too far.

Too late and too much has been the general practice. For example, in early 1966, it was the right policy for the Federal Reserve to move in a less expansionary direction—though it should have done so at least a year earlier. But when it moved, it went too far, producing the sharpest change in the rate of monetary growth of the postwar era. Again, having gone too far, it was the right policy for the Fed to reverse course at the end of 1966. But again it went too far, not only restoring but exceeding the earlier excessive rate of monetary growth. And this episode is no exception. Time and again this has been the course followed—as in 1919 and 1920, in 1937 and 1938, in 1953 and 1954, in 1959 and 1960.

The reason for the propensity to overreact seems clear: the failure of monetary authorities to allow for the delay between their actions and the subsequent effects on the economy. They tend to determine their actions by today's conditions—but their actions will affect the economy only six or nine or twelve or fifteen months later. Hence they feel impelled to step on the brake, or the accelerator, as the case may be, too hard.

My own prescription is still that the monetary authority go all the way in avoiding such swings by adopting publicly the policy of achieving a steady rate of growth in a specified monetary total. The precise rate of growth, like the precise monetary total, is less important than the adoption of some stated and known rate. I myself have argued for a rate that would on the average achieve rough stability in the level of prices of final products, which I have estimated would call for something like a 3 to 5 percent per year rate of growth in currency plus all commercial bank deposits or a slightly lower rate of growth in currency plus demand deposits only. But it would be better to have a fixed rate that would on the average produce moderate inflation or moderate deflation, provided it was steady, than to suffer the wide and erratic perturbations we have experienced.

Short of the adoption of such a publicly stated policy of a steady rate of monetary growth, it would constitute a major improvement if the monetary authority followed the self-denying ordinance of avoiding wide swings. It is a matter of record that periods of relative stability in the rate of monetary growth have also been periods of relative stability in economic activity, both in the United States and other countries. Periods of wide swings in the rate of monetary growth have also been periods of wide swings in economic activity.

By setting itself a steady course and keeping to it, the monetary authority could make a major contribution to promoting economic stability. By making that course one of steady but moderate growth in the quantity of money, it would make a major contribution to avoidance of either inflation or deflation of prices. Other forces would still affect the economy, require change and adjustment, and disturb the even tenor of our ways. But steady monetary growth would provide a monetary climate favorable to the effective operation of those basic forces of enterprise, ingenuity, invention, hard work, and thrift that are the true springs of economic growth. That is the most that we can ask from monetary policy at our present stage of knowledge. But that much—and it is a great deal—is clearly within our reach.

Monetarism Objectively Evaluated

Paul A. Samuelson

Paul A. Samuelson, Institute Professor at the
Massachusetts Institute of Technology, was the first
American economist to be awarded the Nobel Prize.

There are fashions within science. Nowhere is the oscillating pendulum of opinion more marked in the field of economics than in the area of money. By the end of the 1930s, after the so-called Keynesian revolution, courses and textbooks continued to be devoted to money. But in fact money had almost completely dropped out of them and the emphasis had shifted to analysis of income determination in terms of such Keynesian concepts as the multiplier and the propensity to consume.

COMEBACK OF MONEY

If the market quotation for monetary theory sagged in the decade after 1936, by the early 1950s there were unmistakable signs of a comeback. It was Professor Howard S. Ellis of the University of California who coined in those years the expression, "the rediscovery of money." And the famous Accord of 1951, which gave back to the Federal Reserve its freedom to pursue an autonomous monetary policy independently of the needs and desires of President Truman's Treasury, was the objective counterpart of the reappearance of money in the theoretical models of academic scholars.

Of course, we cannot expect recovery to take place at the same time in all markets. Within Britain, the historic home of central banking, the news of the revival of money was late in coming; and even later in being believed. As recently as 1959 the prestigious Radcliffe Report, technically

Excerpted from Paul A. Samuelson, "Monetarism Objectively Evaluated" in Paul A. Samuelson, ed., *Readings in Economics*, 7th ed. (New York: McGraw-Hill, 1973), pp. 120–29. Reprinted by permission.

known as the Committee on the Working of the Monetary System, devoted upwards of 3½ million words to the subject. Yet the unanimous conclusion of this distinguished group of British academics and men of finance was, in the end, that money as such did not matter.

Often, if a stock goes down too far in *price,* in reaction it may subsequently go up too far. There is danger of this in the case of monetary theory. A crude monetarism is now stalking the land. In the present article I wish to provide a scientifically objective evaluation of the issues and a balanced history of the oscillations in monetary doctrines.

FRIEDMAN AND THE CHICAGO SCHOOL

Undoubtedly the popularity of monetarism can be traced in large part to one man, namely Professor Milton Friedman of the University of Chicago. His monumental *Monetary History of the United States, 1867–1960,* written with Mrs. Anna Schwartz, is the bible of the movement; and let me say as an infidel that it is a classic source of data and analysis to which all scholars will turn for years to come. In addition to this scholarly work, Professor Friedman has published numerous statistical studies in learned economic journals. He has testified before Congress and lectured before lay groups. His influential columns in *Newsweek* and writings for the financial press have hammered away at one simple message:

It is the rate of growth of the money supply that is the prime determinant of the state of aggregate dollar demand. If the Federal Reserve will keep the money supply growing at a steady rate—say 4 to 5 percent by one or another definition of the money supply, but the fact of steadiness being more important than the rate agreed upon—then it will be doing all a central bank can usefully do to cope with the problems of inflation, unemployment, and business instability.

Fiscal policy as such has no independent, systematic effect upon aggregate dollar demand. Increasing tax rates, *but with the understanding that money growth remains unchanged,* will have no effect *in lessening the degree of inflation; it will have no* independent *effect in increasing the level of unemployment in a period of deflation; changes in public expenditure out of the budget (it being understood that the rate of growth of the money supply is held unchanged) will also have* no lasting effects on inflationary or deflationary gaps.

In the past, budgetary deficits and budgetary surpluses have often been accompanied by central bank creation of new money or deceleration of growth of new money. Therefore, many people have wrongly inferred that fiscal deficits and surpluses have predictable *expansionary and contracting effects upon the total of aggregate spending. But this is a complete confusion.* It is the changes in the rate of growth of the money supply which alone have substantive effects. *After we have controlled or allowed for monetary changes, fiscal policy has negligible independent potency.*[1]

This is my summary of the Friedman-type monetarism. No doubt he would word things somewhat differently. And I should like to emphasize that there are many qualifications in his scientific writing which do not logically entail the *simpliste* version of monetarism outlined above. Indeed it is one of the purposes of this article to demonstrate and emphasize the point that the weight of the evidence on money, theoretical and empirical, does not imply the correctness of crude monetarism. . . .

KEYNES AND KEYNESIANS

I believe monetarism could be deemed fruitful, to the degree that it has pushed economists away from a *simpliste* Keynesian model, popular in the United States during the Great Depression and still lingering on in Britain, and made economists more willing to recognize that monetary policy is an important stabilization weapon, fully coordinate with fiscal policy as a macro-economic control instrument. However, my reading of the development of modern economic doctrine does not suggest to me that the post-Keynesian position that I myself hold, and of which Professor James Tobin of Yale and Franco Modigliani of M.I.T. are leading exponents, has been materially influenced by monetarism. Indeed, speaking for myself, the excessive claims for money as an exclusive determinant of aggregate demand would, if anything, have slowed down and delayed my appreciation of money's true quantitative and qualitative role.[2]

[1] Professor Friedman is careful to specify that fiscal policy does have important effects upon the *composition* of any given total of gross national product. Thus increases in government expenditures will pull resources out of the private sector into the public. John Kenneth Galbraith might like this but Milton Friedman does not. Also, increasing taxation relative to public expenditure, although having no independent effect on aggregate demand, will tend to lower consumption and reduce interest rates. This contrived increase in thriftiness will move the mix of full-employment output in the direction of more rapid capital formation; it will speed up the rate of growth of productivity and real output, and will increase the rate of growth of real wages. If the trend of the money supply remains unchanged, this will tend toward a lower price level in the future or a less rapidly rising one.

[2] To clarify my point, let me state my belief that Professor Friedman has been a force of the first magnitude in getting economists generally to realize the desirability of flexible exchange rates. He, and Professors Frank Knight and Henry Simons at Chicago before him, deserve an honored place in the history of economic thought in influencing economists to appreciate the merits of market pricing as against direct government interventions. But I do not believe that the positions today of the Tobins and Modiglianis of the modern scene would be very different if a Chicago School had never existed.

KEYNES VS. KEYNESIANS

Although the neglect of money is often said to be a characteristic of Keynesian economists and a heritage of the analysis in Keynes' 1936 classic *General Theory of Employment, Interest and Money*, it is doubtful that Keynes himself can be properly described as ever having believed that "money does not matter." If one writes down in the form of equations or graphs the bony structure of the *General Theory*, he sees that money enters into the liquidity-preference function in such a way that an increase in the money supply lowers interest rates, thereby inducing an increase in investment, and through multiplier mechanism causes a rise in employment and production, or, if employment is already full and output at capacity levels, causes upward pressure on the price level.

For a quarter of a century before 1936, Keynes was the principal exponent of monetary theory and the inheritor of the Cambridge tradition of Marshall and Pigou. Although the *General Theory* did represent the repudiation of some of the doctrines Keynes espoused in his 1930 *Treatise on Money*, it represented a continuation and culmination of many of those monetary doctrines. At frequent intervals in the last decade before Keynes' death in 1946, he affirmed and reaffirmed in print and private correspondence his faith that, if the long-term interest rate could be brought down low enough, monetary policy could play an effective role in curing depression and stagnation.[3]

POST-KEYNESIANISM

How is it that some Keynesians should ever have become identified with the doctrine that money does not matter? Most converts to Keynesianism became converts during the slump years of the late 1930s. Then the deep-depression polar case did seem to be the realistic case. It is a sad fact about many scholars that they learn and unlearn nothing after the age of 29, so that there exist in chairs of economics around the world many economists who still live mentally in the year 1938. For 1938, when the

---

[3] When an author writes as much as did Keynes, it is inevitable that certain of his passages might seem to contradict others. There are *some* of his paragraphs written in the 1930s that do seem to play down the quantitative potency of monetary policy in times of deep depression. And those many writers, such as Sir John Hicks, Sir Roy Harrod, Professor James Meade, and the late Oskar Lange, who have codified the *General Theory* in the form of simple equations and graphs, are able to formulate a "deep-depression" polar case in which money does not matter (either because the liquidity-preference schedule displays infinite elasticity at a "liquidity trap," or the marginal efficiency schedule of investment displays complete inelasticity to interest rate changes). But note that this is not the general case of the *General Theory*, but only a special polar case, just as the classical quantity theory of money is the special case at the opposite pole.

interest rate on Treasury Bills was often a fraction of a fraction of a fraction of a percent, even a monetarist might despair of the potency of central bank monetary policy.

As one who lived through those times, I can testify by recall how money got lost so that it could later be rediscovered. First, multiple correlation studies by people like Jan Tinbergen, of the Netherlands, who pioneered for the League of Nations macrodynamic models of the business cycle, invariably found that such variables as interest rates turned up with *zero or perversely-signed weights in their estimating equations.* Second, case studies at the Harvard Business School and elsewhere invariably registered the result that *the cost and availability of credit was not a significant determinant of business behavior and investment.* Third, large-scale questionnaire surveys, like those emanating from Oxford and associated with the names of Sir Robert Hall, Sir Hubert Henderson, Sir Roy Harrod, Charles Hitch, and Phillip Andrews, uniformly recorded answers denying the importance of interest rates and monetary conditions. Fourth, as Professor Alvin Hansen and other contemporary writers noted, the inflow to the States of billions of dollars of gold resulting from distrust of Hitler's Europe, produced almost a controlled experiment in which the reserves of the banking system were vastly expanded and yet no commensurate expansion in business activity or even in the total money supply was achieved. Finally, it was fashionable in those days for theorists to argue that interest was a negligible cost where short-term investment projects were involved, and where long-term projects were involved the irreducible uncertainties of expectations served to dwarf the importance of the interest rate as a controlling variable.

However realistic it may have been in the 1930s to denigrate the importance of money, and with hindsight I do believe that even this may have been overdone, still in the high-employment epoch that is characteristic of the post-World-War-II years there was little excuse to remain frozen in an archaic denial of money. This is not the place to sketch in detail the evolution of post-Keynesian analysis. Already in the war years, Professor Modigliani in a justly famous article had shown the logical need for placing greater emphasis upon stocks as against flows than had been done by the *General Theory* and its first commentators.

Professor Pigou, in a handsome recantation of his first rejection of the *General Theory,* supplied in the 1940s an important influence of the real money stock as it acts directly on the propensity to consume even in the absence of the interest rate effects that had been recognized in the *General Theory.* Recognition of this "Pigou effect" served to reconcile the deep cleavage between neoclassical theory and the Keynesian revolution:

theoretically a sufficiently large decline in the wage rate and the price level could, with a fixed quantum of money, restore full employment; practically no one—and certainly not Pigou—advocated such hyper-deflation as a practicable program to combat unemployment.

HOW IT WORKS

By the 1950s and 1960s a body of analysis and data had been accumulated which led to a positive, strong belief that open-market and discount operations by the central bank could have *pronounced macroeconomic effects upon investment and consumption spending in the succeeding several months and quarters.* One of the principal preoccupations of the post-Keynesian economists, which is to say of the ruling orthodoxy of American establishment economics, has been to trace out the *causal* mechanisms whereby monetary and fiscal variables produce their effects upon the total of spending and its composition.

Thus, an open-market purchase of Treasury bills by the Fed first bids up bond prices and lowers their yield; this spreads to a reduction in *yields* on competing securities, such as longer-term government bonds or corporate bonds or home mortgages. The lowering of interest costs will typically be accompanied by *a relaxation in the degree of credit rationing,* and this can be expected to *stimulate investment spending* that would otherwise not have taken place. The lowering of interest rates generally also brings about an *upward capitalization of the value of existing assets,* and this increase in the money value of wealth can be expected to have a certain *expansionary influence on consumer spending,* and in a degree on business spending for investment. As a limit upon the stimulus stemming from money creation by orthodox open-market operations, must be reckoned the fact that as the central bank pumps new money into the system it is in return taking from the system *an almost equal quantum of money substitutes* in the form of government securities. In a sense the Federal Reserve or the Bank of England is merely a dealer in second-hand assets, contriving transfer exchanges of one type of asset for another, and in the process affecting the interest rate structure that constitutes the terms of trade among them.

What needs to be stressed is the fact that one cannot expect money created by this process of central-bank open-market operations *alone,* with say the fiscal budget held always in balance, to have at all the same functional relationship to the level of the GNP and of the price index that could be the case for money created by gold mining or money created by the printing press of national governments or the Fed and used to finance public expenditures in excess of tax receipts. Not only would the creation of these last kinds of money involve a flow of production and spendable income in their very *act of being born,* but in addition the community would be *left permanently richer* in its ownership of monetary wealth. In money terms the community *feels* richer, in money terms the community *is* richer. And this can be expected to reflect itself in a higher price level or a lower rate of unemployment or both.

By contrast, money created through conventional central-bank operations quite divorced from the financing of fiscal deficits or the production of mining output does not entail an equivalent permanent increase in net wealth as viewed by people in the community. Post-Keynesians emphasize that extinguishing the outstanding interest-bearing public debt, whether by a capital levy or by open-market purchase of it, does rationally make the community *feel poorer* than would be the case if the same amount of money existed and the public debt had been unreduced. All men are mortal. Most men do not concern themselves with the wellbeing of their remote posterity. Hence, government bonds as an asset are not completely offset in their minds by the recognition of the liability of paying in perpetuity taxes to carry the interest on those bonds. Only if people live forever, foreseeing correctly the tax payments they (or the posterity as dear to them in the most remote future as is their own lifetime wellbeing) must make on account of the perpetual future interest payments on government bonds—only then would it be true to say that retirement of public debt would have no substantive effects upon the reckoning of wealth, the levels of spending, and the level of prices generally. Rejecting such a perpetual-life model as extreme and unrealistic, we must debit against an increase in money through open-market operations a partial offset in the form of retirement of some of the outstanding public debt.

Finally, to clarify the significant difference between the post-Keynesian analysis which most modern economists believe to be plausible as against the tenets of monetarism, I must point out that even when the money supply is held constant:

1. Any significant changes in thriftiness and the propensity to consume can be expected to have systematic independent effects on the money value of current output, affecting average prices or aggregate production or both.

2. Likewise an exogenous burst of investment opportunities or animal spirits on the part of business can be expected to have systematic effects on total GNP.

3. Increases in public expenditure, or reductions in tax rates—and even increases in public expenditure balanced by increases in taxation—can be expected to have systematic effects upon aggregate GNP.

All these tenets of the modern eclectic position are quite incompatible with monetarism. (Indeed that is the differentiating definition by which we distinguish the Chicago School monetarism from the post-Keynesian positions with which it has so much overlap.) The eclectic position is incompatible with monetarism, but it is not incompatible with a *sophisticated* version of the Quantity Theory of Money. For as soon as one follows the logic of neoclassical analysis (expecting that less of any kind of inventory will be held if, other things equal, the cost of holding it has gone up) and postulates that the *velocity of circulation of money is a rising function of the interest rate,* the post-Keynesian (and even the simple Keynesian) model becomes compatible with the Quantity Theory. One way of looking at Keynesian liquidity preference is as *a theory of the velocity of circulation.*

FAULTY LOGIC

When post-Keynesians study recent economic history, they find that interest rates and money do enter into their estimating equations and with the theoretically expected algebraic signs. Case studies bear out the importance for investment decisions of the cost and availability of credit. Properly phrased questionnaires to business elicit answers that point in the same direction. And plausible theories to explain how businessmen make their investment decisions and how they ought to also bear out the fact that monetary policy does matter. So there is simply no excuse for living in a 1938 dream world in which money does not matter.

The bearing of all this on monetarism is well illustrated by an incident a few years ago at an American Bankers Association symposium where leading academic economists were commenting upon Professor Friedman's writings. Professor James Tobin went to the blackboard and wrote down three sentences:

1. MONEY DOES NOT MATTER.
2. MONEY MATTERS.
3. MONEY ALONE MATTERS.

He went on to say: Professor Friedman produces evidence to prove that the first proposition, Money doesn't matter, is false: he purports to have demonstrated from this that the third proposition, Money alone matters, is true; whereas the correct logical conclusion is that the second proposition, Money does matter, is all that follows. And on that there is no quarrel among leading modern macroeconomic economists.

Power and cogency of relevant evidence. I think there is much wisdom in this. When Professor Friedman defends monetarism, as for example in a late-1968 debate at New York University with new economist Walter Heller, he refers to a mountain of evidence that supports monetarism. But how many members of the thousands in the overflow crowd attending that debate were able to appraise that evidence to see whether it supports the proposition 2, that money matters, rather than the central tenet of monetarism, that (when it comes to predictable systematic effects on aggregate demand and on inflationary or deflationary gaps) money alone matters? Sir Ronald Fisher, the greatest statistician of our age, pointed out that replication a thousandfold of an inconclusive experiment does nothing to add to its value. In terms of the language of statistics, most of the evidence compiled about money has little or no power to differentiate between propositions 2 and 3. Let me illustrate.

Anecdotes about incidents. A typical bit of historical evidence put forth to support monetarism goes like the following. "In 1919, after World War I, the U.S. Treasury wished to stabilize the interest rate. Keeping the Discount Rate constant resulted in a great increase in the money supply and in strong inflation. Then, early in 1920 on an identifiable date, the Treasury changed its policy; there followed a sharp reduction in the growth of the money supply; there followed a collapse of prices and the Recession of 1920–21. Ergo monetarism is true." But surely, for our purpose, this is a complete *non sequitur*. If we accept the chronology as given, it should indeed give pause to some witness before the Radcliffe Committee who argues that money never matters. But a whole range of mountains of evidence of this type does not tell us whether other factors—such as fiscal policy—may not also have an independent influence on the pace of inflation. Replicating a refutation does not add commensurately to its weight, so I shall forebear from giving other examples of similar reasoning.

Cyclical leads and lags. But let me mention a different kind of evidence sometimes adduced for monetarism. The rate of change of the money supply precedes by 16 months or so, on the average but with great variance, the turndowns in the business cycle. Now it is easy to show that this set of facts fits in as well with an ultra-Keynesian model as with an ultra-Friedman model. Indeed, Professor Tobin has shown that the kind of Keynesian model that only a Radcliffe Committee member could still believe in does *better* than the monetarist model in fitting those facts. And let me add that those facts on timing are not very impressive facts. Those who play seriously the game of looking for leading indicators to predict business activity find the money-change series only one of many straws to indicate the way the wind is blowing. And not one of the more useful straws. Moreover, according to the most thorough studies, those by Dr. Geoffrey Moore of the National Bureau of Economic Research and Dr. Julius Shiskin of the U.S. Census Bureau, the money-change indicator has been scoring less well in recent decades than in earlier times.

Actually, in the 50 years since Warren Persons of Harvard initiated these leads and lags studies, the stock of money always tended to be one of the laggards rather than leaders in business cycle findings. Instead of turning up in the A group of leaders, money and interest rates tended to appear in the C group of laggards. Subsequent work by Arthur F. Burns and Moore at the National Bureau tended to confirm this finding. Indeed it is only in recent years that research is beginning to show signs that Money itself turns down and up as early as, or before, general GNP does—and, ironically, I believe this is probably to be explained by the fact that the Federal Reserve has been disregarding the advice of the monetarists and has tried to do some advance forecasting so that it can lean against the winds of recession before they begin to blow very hard.

What does a monetarist do when confronted with the fact that his causal factor, money, does not empirically lead his response factor, general business? One desperate artifice is to change his focus from the *stock* of money to its *time derivative*, its *rate of growth*. It is a mathematical fact that any periodic fluctuation that behaves a bit like a sine curve will have its derivative turndown a quarter cycle before itself; so if money itself does not lag business by as much as one quarter, one cannot help but get some lead at turning points by using the rate of change of money. But by that kind of frivolous action, one could use the derivative of production, its rate of change, to predict the turning points of the stock of money: or, with recognition of noise in the data, use production's own rate of change to predict its turning points.

Dimensional traps. Obviously, we have to find the reason for using dM/dt, the rate of change of money, rather than $M,$ the stock of money, as our causal variable. One ridiculous argument for using the former is dimensional: both the level of GNP and the rate of growth of the money supply are measured in terms of dollars *per year.* Therefore, relate GNP and $dM/dt,$ not GNP and $M.$ This argument is ridiculous because the whole basis of the quantity theory of money is that $V,$ the velocity of circulation of money or its reciprocal, is the dimensional constant that exists to relate the stock of money and the flow of national product. Professor Friedman, more than any other modern economist, has sloshed through the mountains of Yugoslavia to demonstrate that every peasant holds seventeen-weeks purchasing power in his pockets. The whole demand-for-money concept is for the purpose of making hypotheses about how that number

17 will change when interest rates, branch banking or price expectations change. Moreover, there is involved a profound misunderstanding of how dimensional analysis is to be used in any science. The behavioral equation of a simple pendulum has for its very purpose the relating of two dimensionally different magnitudes—the position of the pendulum as measured in centimeters or dimensionless angular degrees and its acceleration as measured in centimeters per time squared. Nor is this a special example: Newton's universal law of gravitation, the greatest system of the world produced by man's thoughts, relates dimensionally different magnitudes in precisely the way that Dr. Friedman criticizes.

Trial by simple correlation. Let me mention one last kind of evidence that allegedly bears out the position of monetarism. Dr. Friedman, with the collaboration of Dr. David Meiselman, prepared for our Commission on Money and Credit a comparison of which does better for prediction: a simple correlation of money with GNP, or a simple correlation of some kind of Keynesian multiplicand with GNP or a related measure. They end up with a somewhat larger Pearsonian correlation coefficient for money. Ergo, monetarism is correct; Keynesianism has been defeated in a trial of honor. In my view this is simply silly. I waive the fact that the choice of variables and periods selected for the study has been subject to much criticism and debate. The post-Keynesian position which I adhere to does not believe in either of the simple theories set up as straw men, and is not particularly interested in which has the higher simple correlation coefficient. Even the St. Louis Federal Reserve Bank, a bastion of monetarism, when it came to compare either simple theory with an eclectic combination of both—which was still, in my eyes, an overly simple model and not one optimally formulated at that—they found that there was a statistically significant reduction in unexplained variance from a combination of the two simple theories . . .

CRUCIAL TESTS IN 1966–1967, 1968–1969, AND 1974–1975

Personally, as a scientist, I would cheerfully accept *any hypothesis that would deliver the goods and explain the facts.* As a fallible human being, I do not relish having to change my mind but if economists had to hang from the ceiling in order to do their job, then there would be nothing for it than to do so. But monetarism does not deliver the goods. I could make a fortune giving good predictions to large corporations and banks based on monetarism if it would work. But I have tried every version of it. And none do.

To this there are two standard answers. The first is that nothing works well. Fine tuning is an illusion. There is much "noise" in the data. No one can claim that monetarism would enable the Federal Reserve to iron out all the variation in the economy. All we can say for it is that stabilizing the growth rate of money is the best policy that the ingenuity of man can ever arrive at. All this involves what I call the chipmunk syndrome. The nimble monetarist sticks his neck out in an occasional prediction: that prediction is not always free of ambiguity, but it does seem to point qualitatively in one direction, often a direction counter to the conventional wisdom of the moment: then if subsequent events do seem to go in the indicated direction, the prediction is trumpeted to be a feather in the cap of monetarism. If, as is happening all the time, events do not particularly go in that direction—or if as happens often, events go somewhat in a direction that neither competing theory has been subjected to a test of any resolving power—the chipmunk pulls in his head, saying that there is no way of fine tuning the economy or making completely accurate predictions.

The other argument against the view that monetarism simply does not work is the assertion, "Monetarism does work. So and so at the Blank bank uses it and he beats the crowd in batting average." I believe this to be a serious and important subject for investigation. Let me therefore, because of space limitations, confine myself to a few observations based upon preliminary investigations of the matter.

1. Those analysts who use their monetarism *neat* really do *not* perform well.

2. A number of bank economists, who give great weight to the money factor but who *also* pay attention to what is happening to defense spending and inventories and a host of other factors, seem to me to have compiled an excellent record at forecasting. Not a perfect record. Who has a perfect record? And not, as far as quantitative studies known to me suggest, a better record than the best macroeconomic forecasters who do not consciously put special stress on the money factor (but who do not neglect it either!). In short, it is impossible to separate "flair" in forecasting from success attributable primarily to use of money-supply variables.

3. The years 1966–67 are often referred to as years of a crucial test in which monetarism defeated Keynesianism. I have gone over all the main forecasts used by both schools during that period and I must report that this is a misapprehension. There was *wide range* of forecasts by practitioners of both schools: there was a *wide overlap* between these two ranges. On the whole, the monetarists averaged better and *earlier* in their perception of the slowdown beginning to be seen in late 1966 in consequence of the money crunch of 1966. And one would expect this to be the case from an eclectic viewpoint since the independent variable of money received the biggest alteration in *that* period. But many of the monetarists went overboard in predicting a recession in 1967 of the National Bureau type: indeed some of the more astute monetarists warned their brethren against following the logic of the method, lest it discredit the method! And some of the largest squared errors of estimate for 1967 that I have in my files came from dogmatic monetarists who did not heed the warning from inside their own camp.

4. Again, the year 1969 is thought by some to provide a test of some power between the two theories. Yet I, who am an eclectic, have my own GNP forecast for the year nicely bracketed by the two banks that have been most successful in the past in using monetarism in their projections. And though I must admit that the last part of 1968 was stronger than those who believe in the potency of fiscal policy and the mid-1969 tax surcharge to be, I do not interpret that extra strength as being a negation of any such potency or as due solely or primarily to the behavior of money during the last 12 months. Without the tax surcharge, I believe the GNP would have surprised us by soaring even faster above predictions. Since history cannot be rerun to perform controlled experiments, I cannot prove this. But the weight of all the evidence known to me does point in this direction. In a soft science like economics, that is all even the best practitioner can say.

5. Both in 1974 and 1975 monetarism generally led to particularly bad forecasts. At President Ford's September 1974 summit, Dr. Beryl Sprinkel used monetarism to give the most erroneous of 28 economists' forecasts; the summer forecasts of the St. Louis Federal Reserve economists such as Dr. Jordan were about as bad in missing the virulence of the decline in the last one-half of 1974. Early in 1975, during February, Professor Milton Friedman was quoted as saying that the recovery could not begin until the end of 1975; but in fact it now dates as beginning in April 1975. The desperation tactics of monetarists to shorten their lags seem like the desperation tactics of those who introduced dummy variables to improve their statistical fits: Nature usually takes a bitter revenge, making such forecasters pay in future errors for the illusory improvement in fit within the samples.

Is Monetary Policy Being Oversold?

Walter W. Heller

Walter Heller, a former chairman of the President's
Council of Economic Advisers, is Regents' Professor of
Economics at the University of Minnesota.

At the outset, let's clarify what is and what isn't at issue in today's discussion of fiscal-monetary policy. The issue is *not* whether money matters—we all grant that—but whether *only* money matters, as some Friedmanites, or perhaps I should say Friedmanics, would put it. Or really, whether only money matters *much*, which is what I understand Milton Friedman to say—he is more reasonable than many of the Friedmanites.

Again, in the fiscal field, the issue is not *whether* fiscal policy matters —even some monetarists, perhaps in unguarded moments, have urged budget cuts or tax changes for stabilization reasons. The issues are *how much* it matters, and how heavily we can lean on discretionary changes in taxes and budgets to maintain steady economic growth in a dynamic economy.

Summing up the key operational issues, they are: Should money be king? Is fiscal policy worth its salt? Should flexible man yield to rigid rules?

Let me review with you the factors that say "stop, look, listen" before embracing the triple doctrine that only money matters much; that control of the money supply is the key to economic stability; and that a rigid fixed-throttle expansion of 4 or 5 percent a year is the only safe policy prescription in a world of alleged economic ignorance and human weakness and folly.

Reprinted from *Monetary vs. Fiscal Policy: A Dialogue* by Milton Friedman and Walter W. Heller. By permission of W. W. Norton & Company, Inc. Copyright © 1969 by the Graduate School of Business Administration, New York University. Excerpts from pp. 15–23, 25–28, 30–31.

One should note in passing that Professor Friedman's findings and conclusions fit into a steady process of rescuing monetary policy from the limbo into which it was put by the interest-rate peg of World War II and the late 40s—a rescue effected by the Monetary Accord of 1951 and by the subsequent steady expansion of its scope. This has been a healthy renaissance. But having been resurrected from the debilitating rate peg of the 1940s, does monetary policy now face the threat of a new peg, Milton's money-supply peg, in the years ahead? Is it doomed to go from cradle to grave in twenty years?

I exaggerate, of course, for emphasis. President Nixon, for example, has been reported as saying that he doesn't buy the fixed-throttle formula. At the same time, he has reportedly suggested that he intends to put more emphasis on money supply. So this is a particularly apt juncture for a close look at the monetarists' doctrine.

Now, turning to doubts, unresolved questions, and unconvincing evidence, I group these into eight conditions that must be satisfied—if not completely, at least more convincingly than they have been to date —before we can even consider giving money supply sovereignty, or dominance, or greater prominence in economic policy.

The first condition is this: the monetarists must make up their minds which money-supply variable they want us to accept as our guiding star—M_1; the narrow money supply, just currency and bank deposits; M_2, adding time deposits; or perhaps some other measure like the "monetary base"? And when will the monetarists decide? Perhaps Milton Friedman has decided; but if he has, his disciples do not seem to have gotten the word.

It doesn't seem too much to ask that this confusion be resolved in some satisfactory way before putting great faith in money supply as our key policy variable.

Second, I would feel more sympathetic to the money-supply doctrine if it were not so one-track-minded about money stock—measured any way you wish—as the *only* financial variable with any informational content for policy purposes.

As Gramley has noted, for example, if we look at money stock alone for 1948, it would indicate the tightest money in the post-war period.[1] Yet, the rate on Treasury bills was 1 percent, and on high-grade corporates 2¾ percent. (That does sound like ancient history.) But isn't it curious that we had tight money by the money-supply standard side by side with 1, 2,

[1] Lyle Gramley, The Informational Content of Interest Rates as Indicators of Monetary Policy," in *Proceedings*, 1968 Money and Banking Workshop, Federal Reserve Bank of Minneapolis (May 1968), p. 23.

and 3 percent interest rates? We were swamped with liquidity—so interest rates do seem to have been telling us something very important.

Or, if we look at 1967 *only* in terms of the money stock, it would appear as the easiest-money year since World War II. M_1 was up 6 percent, M_2 was up 12 percent. Yet there was a very sharp rise in interest rates. Why? Probably because of a big shift in liquidity preference as corporations strove to build up their protective liquidity cushions after their harrowing experience the previous year—their monetary dehydration in the credit crunch of 1966. Again, the behavior of interest rates is vital to proper interpretation of monetary developments and guidance of monetary policy. Interest rates are endogenous variables and cannot be used alone —but neither can money stock. Either interest rates or money stock, used alone, could seriously mislead us.

I really don't understand how the scarcity of any commodity can be gauged without referring to its price—or, more specifically, how the scarcity of money can be gauged without referring to interest rates.

Third, given the fluctuations in money velocity, that supposedly inexorable link between money and economic activity has yet to be established. We should not forget this, however sweet the siren song of the monetarists may sound. Clearly, velocity has varied over time—some might say "greatly," others "moderately." Let me sidestep a bit and say, for purposes of this discussion, "significantly." For I would remind you that the income velocity of money rose roughly 28 percent during the 1960–68 period. Had velocity been the same in 1968 as it was in 1960, nominal GNP would have been not some $860 billion, but only $675 billion.

Fourth, it would help us if the monetarists could narrow the range on *when* money matters. How long are the lags that have to be taken into account in managing monetary policy?

Fifth, I'd be happier if only I knew which of the two Friedmans to believe. Should it be the Friedman we have had in focus here—the Friedman of the close causal relationship between money supply and income, who sees changes in money balances worked off gradually, with long lags before interest rates, prices of financial and physical assets, and, eventually, investment and consumption spending are affected? Or should it be the Friedman of the "permanent-income hypothesis," who sees the demand for money as quite unresponsive to changes in current income (since current income has only a fractional weight in permanent income), with the implied result that the monetary multiplier is very large in the short run, that there is an immediate and strong response to a change in the money stock? As Tobin has noted, he can't have it both ways. But which is it to be?

Sixth, if Milton's policy prescription were made in a frictionless Fried-manesque world without price, wage, and exchange rigidities—a world of his own making—it would be more admissible. But in the imperfect world in which we actually operate, beset by all sorts of rigidities, the introduction of his fixed-throttle money-supply rule might, in fact, be destabilizing. Or it could condemn us to long periods of economic slack or inflation as the slow adjustment processes in wages and prices, given strong market power, delayed the economy's reaction to the monetary rule while policy makers stood helplessly by.

A seventh and closely related concern is that locking the money supply into a rigid rule would jeopardize the U.S. international position. It's quite clear that capital flows are interest-rate sensitive. Indeed, capital flows induced by interest-rate changes can increase alarmingly when speculators take over. Under the Friedman rule, market interest rates would be whatever they turned out to be. It would be beyond the pale for the Fed to adjust interest rates for balance-of-payments adjustment purposes. Nor is it clear that by operating in the market for forward exchange (which in any event Milton would presumably oppose) the system could altogether neutralize changes in domestic market rates.

Milton has heard all of this before, and he always has an answer —flexible exchange rates. Yet, suffice it to note that however vital they are to the workings of his money-supply peg, floating exchange rates are not just around the corner.

Eighth, and finally, if the monetarists showed some small willingness to recognize the impact of fiscal policy—which has played such a large role in the policy thinking and action underlying the great expansion of the 1960s—one might be a little more sympathetic to their views. This point is, I must admit, not so much a condition as a plea for symmetry. The "new economists," having already given important and increasing weight to monetary factors in their policy models, are still waiting for signs that the monetarists will admit fiscal factors to theirs.

The 1964 tax cut pointedly illustrates what I mean. While the "new economists" fully recognize the important role monetary policy played in facilitating the success of the tax cut, the monetarists go to elaborate lengths to "prove" that the tax cut—which came close to removing a $13 billion full-employment surplus that was overburdening and retarding the economy—had nothing to do with the 1964-65 expansion. Money-supply growth did it all. Apparently, we were just playing fiscal tid-dlywinks in Washington.

It seems to me that the cause of balanced analysis and rational policy would be served by redirecting some of the brilliance of Friedman and his followers from (a) single-minded devotion to the money-supply thesis and unceasing efforts to discredit fiscal policy and indeed all discretionary policy to (b) joint efforts to develop a more complete and satisfactory model of how the real world works; ascertain why it is working far better today than it did before active and conscious fiscal-monetary policy came into play; and determine how such policy can be improved to make it work even better in the future.

In a related asymmetry, as I've already suggested in passing, some Friedmanites fail to recognize that if fiscal policy actions like the 1964 tax cut can do no good, then fiscal policy actions like the big budget increases and deficits associated with Vietnam can also do no harm. Again, they should recognize that they can't have it both ways.

Now, one could lengthen and elaborate this list. But enough—let's just round it off this way: If Milton Friedman were saying that (as part of an active discretionary policy) we had better keep a closer eye on that important variable, money supply, in one or more of its several incarnations—I would say well and good, by all means. If the manifold doubts can be reasonably resolved, let's remedy any neglect or underemphasis of money supply as a policy indicator relative to interest rates, free reserves and the like. But let's not lock the steering gear into place, knowing full well of the twists and turns in the road ahead. That's an invitation to chaos.

Again, we need to stop, look and listen lest we let simplistic or captious criticism operate to deny us the benefits of past experience and thwart the promise of future discretionary action on the monetary and fiscal fronts.

What has been the course of the American economy during the postwar period of an increasingly active and self-conscious fiscal-monetary policy for economic stabilization? Or, for that matter, let's broaden it: what has been the course of the world's advanced industrial economies during this period? The correlation is unmistakable: the more active, informed, and self-conscious fiscal and monetary policies have become, by and large, the more fully employed and stable the affected economies have become. Casual empiricism? Perhaps—yet a powerful and persuasive observation.

Witness the conclusion of the two-and-a-half–year study for the OECD by a group of fiscal experts from eight industrial countries:

The postwar economic performance of most Western countries in respect of employment, production and growth has been vastly superior to that of the pre-war years. This, in our view, has not been accidental. Governments have increasingly accepted responsibility for the promotion and maintenance of high employment and steady economic growth. The more conscious use of economic policies has undoubtedly played a crucial role in the better performance achieved—an achievement which, from the point of view of the ultimate social objectives of policy, is of paramount importance.

Perhaps an even more telling testament to the effectiveness of active modern stabilization-policy is the change in private investment thinking and planning not only in the financial sense of sustained confidence in the future of corporate earnings and stock market values, even in the face of temporary slowdowns in the economy—but more important, in the physical sense of sustained high levels of plant and equipment investment which seem to be replacing the sickening swings that used to be the order of the day.

Why? In good part, I take it to be the result of a constantly deepening conviction in the business and financial community that alert and active fiscal-monetary policy will keep the economy operating at a higher proportion of its potential in the future than in the past; that beyond short and temporary slowdowns, or perhaps even a recession—that's not ruled out in this vast and dynamic economy of ours—lies the prospect of sustained growth in that narrow band around full employment.

Reply

Milton Friedman

I want to comment on some of the points that Walter made initially and try to answer some of the questions he raised. I think that I might very well start with a point he made before and which he repeated now. He said that he would like us to stop being asymmetrical about tax increases or tax cuts on the one hand, and expenditure decreases on the other.

I want to make it clear that I have never favored expenditure decreases as a stabilization device. I agree with Walter that it would be inconsistent, completely inconsistent, for me to argue that tax increases and decreases are ineffective in stemming inflation or promoting expansion, but that spending decreases or increases are effective. That would be a silly position and, as far as I know, I have never taken it, though maybe I've been careless in what I have written and have given a misleading impression. I have been in favor of tax decreases and expenditure decreases in 1964, in 1966 and in 1968, but not for stabilization purposes. I am in favor of expenditure decreases from a long-range point of view because I think that the U.S. federal budget is too large compared to what we're getting for it. We're not getting our money's worth out of it. And, therefore, I would like to see government spending brought down. I have not argued—at least, if I have, I will immediately admit that I should not have and I don't know of any quotation in which I have (if Walter has any, I hope he will give them to me)—that expenditure decreases are a way to achieve stabilization at a time of inflationary pressure.

Reprinted from *Monetary vs. Fiscal Policy: A Dialogue* by Milton Friedman and Walter W. Heller. By permission of W. W. Norton & Company, Inc. Copyright © 1969 by the Graduate School of Business Administration, New York University. Excerpts from pp. 73–80.

I have said something different. I have said that, from the point of view of the fiscalists, a tax increase or expenditure decrease are equivalent. And, therefore, I have often said that if you are going to adopt the policy of the fiscalist, I would rather see you adopt it through expenditure decreases than through tax increases. But I personally have never argued that that is an effective stabilization device, and I don't believe that it is.

Let me turn to some of the specific issues that Walter raised in his first discussion and see if I can clarify a few points that came up.

First of all, the question is, Why do we look only at the money stock? Why don't we also look at interest rates? Don't you have to look at both quantity and price? The answer is yes, but the interest rate is not the price of money in the sense of the money stock. The interest rate is the price of credit. The price of money is how much goods and services you have to give up to get a dollar. You can have big changes in the quantity of money without any changes in credit. Consider for a moment the 1848–58 period in the United States. We had a big increase in the quantity of money because of the discovery of gold. This increase didn't, in the first instance, impinge on the credit markets at all.

You must sharply distinguish between money in the sense of the money or credit market, and money in the sense of the quantity of money. And the price of money in that second sense is the inverse of the price level—not the interest rate. The interest rate is the price of credit. As I mentioned earlier, the tax increase we had would tend to reduce the price of credit because it reduces the demand for credit, even though it didn't affect the money supply at all.

So I do think you have to look at both price and quantity. But the price you have to look at from this point of view is the price level, not the interest rate.

Next, he said that 1967 was the easiest money year since 1962. Yet there was a big rise in interest rates. In other connections, I have argued that our researches show that a rapid increase in the quantity of money tends to lower interest rates only for a brief period—about six months. After that, it tends to raise interest rates. Conversely, a slow rate of increase in the quantity of money tends to raise interest rates only for about six months, and after that, it tends to lower them.

If you ask where in the world interest rates are higher, the answer is in Brazil, Chile, places like that where the quantity of money has been going up like mad. Interest rates in the U.S. fell dramatically from 1929 to 1933. The quantity of money declined by a third. So it's not a surprise to us that you could have the quantity of money easy in the sense of quantity, and interest rates rise or fall or do almost anything else.

Next, he asks, "Which of the Friedmans do you believe—the one who stresses permanent-income relationships or the one who stresses the close causal connection?" Well, believe both of them if you take them at what they said. The permanent-income analysis has to do with the demand for real money balances, and it was an analysis that was based on annual data covering decades. There is no Friedman who has argued that there is an immediate, mechanical, causal connection between changes in the quantity of money and changes in income.

What I have always argued is that there is a connection which is, on the average, close but which may be quite variable in an individual episode. I have emphasized that the inability to pin down the lag means that there are lots of factors about which I'm ignorant. That doesn't mean that money doesn't have a systematic influence. But it does mean that there is a good deal of variability in the influence.

The data support the view that a 1 percent change in the rate of expansion of the quantity of money tends to produce, on the average, a 2 percent change in the rate of growth of nominal income. There is a big multiplier, as the permanent income analysis would lead you to expect. And there is a cyclical relation. I'm sorry, but I really don't see any inconsistency between the position I've taken on these two points.

Next, Walter Heller asks, Which of the money supplies do you want? M_1 or M_2? Which quantity of money do you want to use? A perfectly reasonable and appropriate and proper question and I'm glad to answer it. In almost all cases, it makes no difference. The only time it makes a difference is when our silly Regulation Q gets in the way. We have a Regulation Q that pegs the maximum rate that commercial banks can pay on time deposits. Whenever you either hit that Regulation-Q limit or you come through from the other side, the two monetary totals diverge and tell you different stories, and you cannot trust either one.

At all other times, you will very seldom find that the message told to you by M_1 is much different than the message told to you by M_2.

Then there was all this talk about being locked into a rigid rule. You know, I have always found it a good rule of thumb that when somebody starts resorting to metaphors, there is something wrong with his argument.

When you start talking about cars driving along a road, and whether you want to lock the steering wheel, well that's a good image; the automatic pilot, I agree, is a good one. But metaphors or similes are to remind you of arguments; they are not a substitute for an argument.

The reason I believe that you would do better with a fixed rule, with a constant rate of increase in the quantity of money, is because I have examined U.S. experience with discretionary monetary policy. I have gone back and have asked, as I reexamine this period, "Would the U.S. have been better off or worse off if we had had a fixed rule?" I challenge anybody to go back over the monetary history of the United States and come out with any other conclusion than that for the great bulk of the time, you would have been better off with the fixed rule. You would clearly have avoided all the major mistakes.

The reason why that doesn't rigidly lock you in, in the sense in which Walter was speaking, is that I don't believe that money is all that matters. The automatic pilot is the price system. It isn't perfectly flexible, it isn't perfectly free, but it has a good deal of capacity to adjust. If you look at what happened to this country when we adjusted to post-World War II, to the enormous decline in our expenditures, and the shift in the direction of resources, you have to say that we did an extraordinarily effective job of adjusting, and that this is because there is an automatic pilot.

But if an automatic pilot is going to work, if you're going to have the market system work, it has to have some basic, stable framework, it has to have something it can count on. And the virtue of a fixed rule, of a constant rate of increase in the quantity of money, is that it would provide such a stable monetary framework. I have discussed that many times in many different ways, and I really have nothing to add.

The final thing I want to talk about is the statement that Walter made at the end of his initial talk, when he said, Look at the world economy; hasn't it been far healthier during post-World War II than it was between the Wars? Of course. It certainly has been enormously healthier. Why? Well, again, I'm sorry to have to be consistent, but in 1953, I gave a talk in Stockholm, which is also reprinted in that collection of papers, under the title of "Why the American Economy is Depression Proof."

I think that I was right, that as of that time and as of today, the American economy is depression proof. The reasons I gave at that time did not include the fact that discretionary monetary and fiscal policy was going to keep things on an even keel. I believe that the reason why the world has done so much better, the reason why we haven't had any depressions in that period, is not because of the positive virtue of the fine tuning that has been followed, but because we have avoided the major mistakes of the interwar period. Those major mistakes were the occasionally severe deflations of the money stock.

We did learn something from the Great Depression. We learned that you do not have to cut the quantity of money by a third over three or four years. We learned that you ought to have numbers on the quantity of money. If the Federal Reserve System in 1929 to 1933 had been publishing statistics on the quantity of money, I don't believe that the Great Depression could have taken the course it did. There were no numbers. And we have not since then, and we will not in the foreseeable future, permit a monetary authority to make the kind of mistake that our monetary authorities made in the 30s.

That, in my opinion, is the major reason why we have had such a different experience in post-World War II.

The Question of Evidence

James Tobin

James Tobin, a former member of the President's
Council of Economic Advisers, is Sterling Professor of
Economics at Yale.

I will concentrate on the question of evidence, which is crucial to the great debate. One kind of evidence, which has been presented at some length, is timing evidence: namely, the leads of changes in stock of money, or of changes in the rate of change of the stock of money, or of other monetary aggregates over income, or over the rate of change of income or over other measures of economic activity. A large amount of the work of Friedman and Schwartz in their *Monetary History of the U.S. 1867–1960* and in their article, "Money and Business Cycles,"[1] is concerned precisely with pinning down these timing patterns. Now I think it is clear that timing evidence—leads, lags and so on—is no evidence about causation whatsoever.

I have engaged in a little irreverent exercise which constructs two models: on the one hand, one of these British models that Paul Samuelson was referring to, an ultra-Keynesian model where money has no causal relationship to anything, and on the other hand, a Friedman-like model in which money is the driving force of the business cycle. I have then compared the timing patterns of money and the change in money relative to money income and the change in income implied by these two different worlds. As it turns out, the ultra-Keynesian world produces a

---

[1] Milton Friedman and Anna Jacobson Schwartz, *A Monetary History of the United States, 1867–1960* (Princeton, N.J.: Princeton University Press, 1963; Milton Friedman and Anna Jacobson Schwartz, "Money and Business Cycles," *Review of Economics and Statistics*, 65 (Supplement: February 1963), pp. 32–78.

Excerpted from James Tobin, "The Role of Money in National Economic Policy," in Federal Reserve Bank of Boston, *Controlling Monetary Aggregates* (Boston: Federal Reserve Bank, 1969), pp. 21–24. Reprinted by permission of the publisher.

pattern of leads and lags in business cycles that superficially looks much more like money causing income than the Friedman world in which money actually is causing income. Moreover, the ultra-Keynesian model produces patterns of leads and lags in business cycles which coincide precisely with the summary of empirical results about such timing that appears in the Friedman-Schwartz article, whereas the implications of Friedman's and Schwartz's own theory diverge considerably from their own empirical findings.

Milton Friedman has responded that he knows better than to think that timing evidence has anything to do with causation. If this is stipulated, we can regard as descriptive but irrelevant detail all those pages about timing that an unwary reader might think were there for the purpose of making some point about causation.

There is a related point about evidence, which has to do with the effects on the data of the sins of the Federal Reserve and other monetary authorities in the past. Now let me give you a ridiculous example to make the point. Don't take it too seriously. Suppose that some statistician observes that over a long period of time there is a high association, a very good fit, between gross national product and the sales of, let us say, shoes. And then suppose someone comes along and says, "That's a very good relationship. Therefore, if we want to control GNP, we ought to control production of shoes. So, henceforth, we'll make shoes grow in production precisely at 4 percent per year, and that will make GNP do the same." I don't think you would have much confidence in drawing this second conclusion and policy recommendations from the observed empirical association.

Over the years, according to the monetarists, the Federal Reserve has been acting like the producers and sellers of shoes. That is, the Fed has been supplying money on demand from the economy instead of using the money supply to control the economy. The Fed has looked at the wrong targets and the wrong indicators. As a result, the Fed has allowed the supply of money to creep up when the demand for money rose as a result of expansion in business activity, and to fall when business activity has slacked off. This criticism implies that the supply of money has, in fact, not been an exogenously controlled variable over the period of observation. It has been an endogenous variable, responding to changes in economic conditions and credit market indicators via whatever response mechanism was built into the men in this room and their predecessors.

The evidence of association between money and income reflects, to a very large degree, this response mechanism of the Federal Reserve and the monetary authorities. It cannot be used simultaneously to support the reverse conclusion: namely that what they have done is the *cause* of the changes in income and GNP. Perhaps the monetarists will be sufficiently persuasive of the Federal Reserve and of Congressional committees to bring about, in the future, a controlled experiment in which the stock of money is actually an exogenous variable.

Much evidence has been presented purporting to show the superior power of monetary variables over fiscal variables and private investment measures in explaining changes in GNP. This evidence comes in what I call pseudo-reduced-forms.

The meaning of the term *reduced-form* is this: If you think of the economy as really a complex set of equations—basic structural relationships describing business investment, demands for loans, demands for money, the consumption function and so on—conceivably you could solve such a system and relate the variables in which you are ultimately interested, such as GNP, to the truly exogenous variables including the instruments of the monetary and fiscal authorities. Such a solution of a big complicated model you would call a *reduced-form*. And then one possible way of estimating a model of the system would be not to estimate the structural equations, the building blocks of the system, but to estimate the condensed equations which relate the ultimate outputs like GNP to the ultimate causal factors. That would be reduced-form estimation.

There are a lot of difficulties in that procedure. Therefore, most builders of big and small models of the economy do not proceed in that way; but, instead, try to estimate the individual structural equations one by one. What I mean by a pseudo-reduced-form is an equation relating an ultimate variable of interest, like GNP, to the supposedly causal variables, but one which doesn't come out of any structure at all. Instead, the investigator just says, "Here are the effects and here are the causes, let's just throw them into an equation." The form and content of the equation—the list of variables and the lag structure—are not derived from any structural model. That is what we have had presented to us as the main evidence for the supposed superiority of monetary variables in explaining GNP.

When, in contrast, we try to take a *theory* of how money affects the economy, and test it in the form it is presented, we have to look at one of two things: either a demand for money equation, or some complicated set of linkage equations through which changes in the money stock affect investment demand, consumption demand, etc. As far as the demand for money equation is concerned, the crucial assumption of some monetarists is that interest rate variables are of no importance, so that there is a tight linkage between the stock of money and GNP. If real GNP and prices, current and lagged, are the only important factors in the demand for money balances, then we know that control of money stock is uniquely decisive, and we don't have to look elsewhere in the system. However, all the tests that I know in which interest rates are allowed to enter demand for money equations, indicate that interest rates have important explanatory power.

If we do not really know that the demand for money is exclusively determined by income, then things other than income may absorb changes in money supply. There is no short cut. We have to look for the effects of changes in the stock of money, and it is hard work. We have to look through the system of structural equations to see how money enters directly and indirectly into investment demand and consumption demand and so on. We have to examine long chains of causation. In those chains there could be many slips, and there could be many structural changes, innovations in markets and institutions. That is the purpose, I suppose, of the hard work involved in large econometric models, work which these other attempts to find evidence try to short-circuit completely.

Two Opposing Views

Allan H. Meltzer

Allan H. Meltzer is Maurice Falk Professor of Economics
and Social Science at Carnegie-Mellon University.

An understanding of monetary policy, of the role of money as an indicator, and of the difference between the effects of changes in credit and
money can be obtained by contrasting two frameworks. In one view,
monetary and fiscal policies are seen as the means by which the public
sector offsets instability in the economy resulting from changes that occur
in the private sector. Fluctuations in prices and output are seen as the
result primarily of real forces and changes mainly in attitude or outlook
that raise or lower investment, thereby raising or lowering the nominal
value of income, market interest rates, and the demand for money. The
task of monetary policy, in this framework, is to offset undesired changes
in interest rates caused by the unforeseen changes in investment. The task
of fiscal policy is to offset the unforeseen changes in the private expenditure and maintain expenditures at the full employment level. Monetary
policy is called "restrictive" if market rates are permitted to rise; "permis-
sive" if market rates are prevented from rising; and "coordinated" if the
balance of payments is in deficit, and market rates are permitted to rise so
as to attract an inflow of short-term capital from abroad. With this
framework, it appears reasonable to accept interest rates as the main
indicator of monetary policy. If the framework were correct, the decision
might be more tenable—although still not correct.

The alternative view—at least my view—does not deny that changes in
market interest rates are partly the result of changes in attitude or

Excerpted from Allan H. Meltzer, "The Role of Money in National Economic Policy," in Federal Reserve
Bank of Boston, *Controlling Monetary Aggregates* (Boston: Federal Reserve Bank, 1969), pp. 27–29. Reprinted by permission.

changes in technology that shift private expenditures. The difference —and it is an important difference—is a difference of emphasis and interpretation. Not only are changes in private expenditure assigned a smaller role, but many of these so-called autonomous changes are viewed as a delayed response to past monetary and fiscal policies.

The effect of a monetary or fiscal policy is not limited to the initial change in interest rates. An expansive monetary policy raises the monetary base, stocks of money and bank credit, and initially lowers market interest rates. The expansion of money increases expenditure, increases the amount of borrowing and reduces the amount of existing securities that individuals and bankers wish to hold at prevailing market interest rates. These changes in borrowing and in desired holdings of securities reverse the initial decline in interest rates; market rates rise until the stock of existing securities is reabsorbed into portfolios, and the banks offer the volume of loans that the public desires. If expansive operations continue, expenditures, borrowing, and interest rates rise to levels above those in the starting equilibrium. Later, prices rise under the impact of increases in the quantity of money, further reducing the desired holdings of bonds and other fixed coupon securities, and increasing desired borrowing. A rise in holdings of currency relative to demand deposits adds to the forces raising interest rates on the credit market.

In this interpretation, the effect of monetary (or fiscal policy) is not limited to the initial effect. The response to a maintained change in policy includes the effects on the credit market, the acceleration and deceleration of prices and ultimately, if policy makers persist, the changes in attitudes and particularly in anticipations of inflation or deflation. These changes, however, are regarded as reliable consequences of maintaining an expansive or contractive monetary policy, just as much to be expected as the initial effect.

It is the temporary changes in the level of interest rates observed on the credit market that frequently mislead monetary policy makers into believing their policy is restrictive when it is expansive. Large changes in the growth rate of money become a main source of instability precisely because the credit market and price effects dominate the initial effect of monetary policy in an economy close to full employment. Misled by the change in market interest rates—or their interpretation of the change —the Federal Reserve permits or forces the stock of money to grow at too high or too low a rate for too long a time. Excessive expansion and contraction of money becomes the main cause of the fluctuations in output and of inflation or deflation. Inappropriate public policies, not changes in private expenditures, become the main cause of instability.

A portion of the second interpretation has now been accepted by the principal spokesman of the Federal Reserve System. In his March 25th statement to the Senate Banking Committee, Chairman Martin said:

I do not mean to argue that the interest rate developments in recent years have had no relation to monetary policy. We know that, in the short run, expansive monetary policies tend to reduce interest rates and restrictive monetary policy to raise them. But in the long run, in a full employment economy, expansive monetary policies foster greater inflation and encourage borrowers to make even larger demands on the credit markets. Over the long run, therefore, expansive monetary policies may not lower interest rates; in fact, they may raise them appreciably. This is the clear lesson of history that has been reconfirmed by the experience of the past several years.

With that statement, Chairman Martin abandoned the framework that has guided Federal Reserve policy through most of its history and has been responsible for major errors in policy. Recognition that interest rates generally rise fastest under the impact of monetary expansion—that the credit market effects dominate short-term changes in interest rates—is probably the single most important step toward an understanding of the role of money that has been taken in the entire history of the Federal Reserve System.

If we develop our analysis and concentrate on improving our understanding of money and of the differences between money and credit, rather than on the issue of whether Milton Friedman is wholly right or wholly wrong, we will have more progress to report next time we meet. Thank you.

GREAT DEBATE NINE

THE PROS AND CONS OF WAGE-PRICE CONTROLS

THE PROS AND CONS OF WAGE-PRICE CONTROLS

IF WE asked an American citizen what this nation's major economic problem was in the mid-1970s, he would doubtless mention either inflation or unemployment. If he were economically sophisticated, he might answer: inflation *and* unemployment. For it is this conjunction of two economic problems, traditionally conceived as opposites, that has brought citizens (and policy-makers) near to despair in most industrialized nations in the western world.

It has also brought these nations to experiment with various forms of what are often called *incomes policies* and what we can think of more directly as *wage-price controls.* Europe has had a long history of such controls in peacetime (in wartime, of course, such controls tend to be more or less universal), and the United States made a major entry into the field in 1971. Under a conservative administration, this country instituted a wage-price freeze in August, 1971 (Phase I), a period of mandatory wage-price controls ending in January, 1973 (Phase II), a period of loose regulation until June, 1973 (Phase III), another quick freeze (Phase III½), another series of controls (Phase IV), and finally the dismantling of the whole program in April, 1974. These major moves, moreover, followed numerous efforts by the government in the 1960s to stem the inflationary tide by issuing *wage-price guideposts.* Like wage-price controls, these guideposts set standards for appropriate wage-price behavior, but adherence to them was voluntary, and public criticism was the government's major weapon for encouraging compliance.

Have these several policies been notably successful? Hardly. In the year 1974, the United States had both double-digit inflation (consumer prices rose by 11 percent over the year before) and its most serious postwar recession (unemployment went above 9 percent of the labor force in early 1975). What is unclear is whether this experience proves the futility of wage-price controls or the inadequacy of one particular example of such controls. What is also unclear is the existence of any meaningful alternative to controls. This, indeed, is what the following Great Debate is all about.

WHY SOMETHING HAS TO BE DONE

One alternative, of course, would be simply to let things go on as they have been. The basic reason why such a course is unacceptable is shown in Figure 1. This diagram depicts the behavior of prices (GNP Deflator) in this country over more than a hundred years. In the last 30 years of the nineteenth century, U.S. prices went down. In the early twentieth century, U.S. prices went up and then down (in the Great Depression). In the 40 years since the 1930s U.S. prices have gone up, and then up, and then up.

Indeed, the situation is worse than Figure 1 suggests. For there is strong evidence that the tradeoff between inflation and unemployment has worsened in recent years.[1] This worsening relationship suggests that our economy is beginning to anticipate inflation and, in that anticipation, to make moves that will only worsen the inflation. Thus, if I am a union leader engaged in wage bargaining with management, I am likely to demand a much higher wage increase if I anticipate that next year's prices will rise by 15 percent, than if I believe they will be stable or rise by only 3 or 4 percent. Insofar as these anticipations of price increases get built into the structure of the economy, then inflation will tend to accelerate. As Grayson notes succinctly (p. 437), "Expectations feed inflation."

All of which raises the possibility that inflation—at least inflation at current levels—involves a built-in tendency to acceleration. To do nothing is to court the appearance of galloping inflation and the potential social holocaust that this might entail. At inflation rates of 3 or 4 percent per year, this risk might be taken. At 10 to 15 percent per year (or in the case of Japan or Great Britain at 20 percent or above per year) the risks become greater and less acceptable. Surely, something can be done to minimize the possibilities of this kind of disaster.

INADEQUACY OF MONETARY-FISCAL REMEDIES

But what? For the salient fact is that the Keynesian revolution which remade so much of economic theory and policy making in the last few decades is essentially powerless to cope with this current problem. The basic reason is that Keynesian analysis dealt primarily with only one kind of inflation: inflation caused by an excess of aggregate demand at or fairly near the full employment level. Inflation thus became the opposite, theoretically speaking, of unemployment. If the sum of consumer, investment and government spending were inadequate to achieve full employment, then we would have unemployment but not inflation. If the sum of consumer, investment and government spending exceeded the economy's capacity at (or near) full employment, we would have inflation but very little unemployment.

In this simple world, the cures were equally simple. Faced with unemployment, increase aggregate demand either by fiscal measures (increased government spending, lowered taxes) or monetary measures (increased money supply, lowered

---

[1] Economists often portray this relationship between price inflation and unemployment in terms of the so-called Phillips curve. The worsening of the tradeoff implies an outward shifting of the Phillips curve.

Figure 1   U.S. Price Index, 1867–1973 (1929 Base)

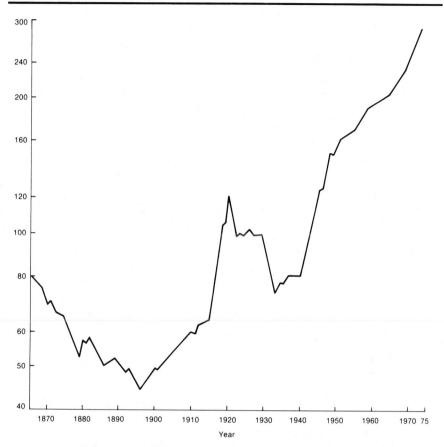

Source: Figures for this graph were pieced together by Professor Benjamin Klein of the University of California at Los Angeles from estimates made by Robert Gallman for 1874–1909, Simon Kuznets for 1910–46, and Department of Commerce for 1947–73. Diagram is Figure 1 in Robert M. Solow, "The Intelligent Citizen's Guide to Inflation," *Public Interest,* No. 38 (Winter 1975), p. 37. Copyright © National Affairs, Inc., 1975. Reprinted by permission of the publisher.

interest rates). Faced with inflation, curtail aggregate demand either by fiscal measures (reduced government spending, increased taxes) or monetary measures (lowered money supply, rising interest rates). Faced with inflation and unemployment simultaneously . . . .

There, of course, was the rub. The policy recommendations to cure one ill were the opposite of those to cure the other. Practically, what it meant was that to cure an inflation that was accompanied by unemployment, one might have to deepen the unemployment in a very serious way, perhaps throw the economy into a genuine depression. The cure might easily be worse than the disease.

Professor Friedman's monetarist doctrine (see Great Debate Eight) might seem to be potentially more optimistic than the Keynesian-rooted approach. After all, monetarists argue that, in the long run, changes in the money supply affect only nominal variables (like prices) and not real variables (like employment and GNP). This raises the possibility of curing inflation by restricting the rate of growth of the money supply and yet having no long-run negative impacts on output and unemployment. The trouble with this prescription (apart from questions about its factual base) is that Professor Friedman's long run can, as we know, be very long indeed. His short run—during which a restrictive monetary policy *would* have negative impacts on unemployment and output—could run as long as ten years. A decade of intensified unemployment might seem to be hard medicine, almost as hard as that involved in a restrictive policy along Keynesian lines.

Critics of Keynesian policy are, however, on fairly sure ground in one respect. It seems almost certain that the widespread adoption of the "new economics" in the post-World War II period has helped create our present version of the inflation-unemployment problem. It has done so by its very success in reducing the possibility of serious and prolonged recessions. Professor Robert Solow has suggested that the price level was more stable in the good old days because the economy was *less* stable.[2] When recessions were expected momentarily to arrive on the scene, businessmen might show greater resistance to wage demands and a greater readiness to cut prices, knowing that their markets might be vulnerable to tough downward competition from their rivals. Similarly, labor might lessen its wage demands in good times and be prepared to accept wage-cuts at the first sign of bad times. If business and labor widely believe that the bad times are not coming, the possibilities of downward wage-price adjustments and lessened upward wage-price adjustments may largely disappear. Success in preventing "great" depressions may thus in fact be one of the major causes of our inflation-recession dilemma. Modern monetary-fiscal policies, paradoxically, may be not part of the cure, but part of the problem!

ELEMENTS IN THE NEW INFLATION

All this is premised, of course, on the hypothesis that our current inflation is not fundamentally of the excess aggregate demand ("demand-pull") type. Certainly it is not exclusively of that kind, as the existence of major inflation and major unemployment simultaneously prove beyond doubt. What then are the new elements that can give rise to inflation in an economically depressed, or at least relatively soft, environment? Many are discussed explicitly or implicitly in the readings that follow. They include:

THE BATTLE OVER INCOME DISTRIBUTION

Ackley makes the struggle over the distribution of income the centerpiece of his description of a modern inflation (p. 426). He sees different groups in society as trying both to increase their shares of real income and also to protect their present shares of real income against erosion. Inflation, without compensating income

[2]Robert M. Solow, "The Intelligent Citizen's Guide to Inflation," *op. cit.,* p. 59.

gains, threatens each group in society. Modern means of measurement and communication have made each group especially conscious of its relative position. Furthermore, the current attitude of society is tolerant of relatively aggressive uses of market power. In this kind of situation, each group seems to itself to be acting defensively, merely trying to protect what it already has, but each group's action serves as a threat to, and therefore brings a further defensive reaction from, some other group. In a fundamental sense, this kind of struggle is self-defeating. Admittedly, certain groups may make marginal gains at the cost of other groups, but, in total, no one gains; and yet the inflation produced can be a serious problem, and a worsening problem because the need for self-defense becomes ever greater as price increases become more rapid.

POWER OF THE LABOR UNIONS

Ackley's description of the battle over income distribution depends on the exertion of market power by both business and labor. Some analysts tend to see the aggressive use of market power by labor unions as a primary cause of today's inflation. Labor unions succeed in getting wage increases that are in excess of productivity increases and, indeed, are independent of the degree of employment or unemployment in any particular labor market (Houthakker, p. 441). These wage increases are then simply passed on by business to the consumer. The unions do gain as a result of these activities: union wages are substantially higher than non-union wages for comparable work.[3] However, critics argue that these gains come at the expense not of the capitalists, but of other, unorganized laborers.[4] The consequence, they claim, is that labor as a whole does not benefit from this exercise of labor market power, but that the whole of society loses because of the great stimulus it gives to inflation.

POWER OF BIG BUSINESS

Other commentators, while acknowledging labor's role to some extent, place primary emphasis on the responsibility of business, and especially big business (Lekachman, p. 423). The concentration of economic power in the hands of a small number of large, oligopolistic firms in many industries dilutes the forces of competition and replaces them with strategies favoring higher prices, smaller outputs, greater expenditures on advertising. The oligopolistic firm need not resist a wage demand because it has the market power necessary to raise its prices and preserve or improve its profit position. Just as labor unions are able to secure wage increases even when there is considerable unemployment in that industry, so are

[3] See the study of Paul M. Ryscavage: "One of the major findings of the present study is that, in May, 1973, the usual hourly earnings of organized craftsmen were estimated to be about 20 to 25 percent more per hour than the earnings of workers who had similar characteristics, but were not members of unions." "Measuring Union-nonunion Earning Differences," *Monthly Labor Review,* 97, No. 12 (December 1974).

[4] See Harry G. Johnson and Peter Mieszkowski, "The Effects of Unionization on the Distribution of Income: A General Equilibrium Approach," *Quarterly Journal of Economics,* 84, No. 4 (November 1970), p. 560.

these oligopolists able to initiate price increases even when the sales and output in the industry are well below capacity. Proof: the automobile industry succeeded in raising its prices substantially in 1974 and 1975 despite the recession, and the particularly harsh impact of the energy crisis on automobile sales. This, the critics of business would say, is characteristic of behavior for industries dominated by a few large firms.

SHORTAGES AND RELATIVE PRICES

Inflation can also be caused by the shortages of particular commodities (Sharpe, p. 457). Indeed, one of the striking characteristics of the acceleration of U.S. inflation in 1973 and 1974 was that the market power factors—organized labor, concentrated industries—were relatively quiescent, at least domestically. Food and fuel shortages (accompanied, of course, by the cartelization of oil production under the auspices of the Organization of Petroleum Exporting Countries) led to substantial rises in the prices of particular commodities. Inflation of this kind—sometimes called *commodity* inflation, as opposed to *demand-pull* or *cost-push* inflation—does ultimately require some exercise of market power on the part of business and labor. In a purely competitive world, an increase in demand for and/or shortage of supply of a particular commodity would lead to a rise in its price *relative* to that of other commodities. This relative rise in price would normally be accomplished partly by a fall in the prices of other commodities as well as partly by a rise in the price of the commodity in short supply. In other words, particular shortages are not intrinsically inflationary. If, however, there is a resistance on the part of business and labor to any downward adjustment of prices and wages, then all this relative adjustment must take place by rising prices. Particular shortages *plus* downward rigidity of wages and prices do make for an inflationary situation. The only way in which the economy can reflect the relative abundance or shortage of different commodities is by upward movements of some prices. All change takes place on a one-way street.

THE MANY OTHER ELEMENTS INVOLVED

The above list is by no means all-inclusive. Some commentators would stress the increasing internationalization of inflation. All countries are undergoing inflation simultaneously. World prices will reflect conditions abroad as well as domestically. Others focus on the role of expectations. Inflation, simply by its continued existence, tends to foster expectations that perpetuate and worsen inflation. Traditional elements are also involved. The expansion of the money supply is certainly an important factor in the continuation of any inflation. Aggregate demand factors can also combine with institutional rigidities to create a continuing inflationary trend. If prices rise during business expansions and do not fall during contractions, then the prevailing price drift will be always upward on the average.

However, what we are trying to stress here is not all possible causes of inflation, but those that make the now old-fashioned Keynesian cure of restrictive fiscal and monetary policy difficult to apply. It is this weakness of traditional tools that has made so many nations and economists turn to controls as a possible solution.

ARE CONTROLS AN ANSWER?

The case *for* controls is really implicit in everything we have said so far. This case does not state that restrictive monetary and fiscal policies could not stop inflation, but rather that, because of the various institutional and structural features of our economy that contribute to its inflationary bias, the *cost* of such a restrictive approach would be much too high. Mild restrictions would not suffice. Heavy restrictions would be intolerable. We would be asked "to accept 6 or more percent unemployment, accept a decline in output, give up essential social programs, give up economic growth, and maybe, eventually, the rate of inflation will come down" (Sharpe, p. 457). This is simply too horrific a cure. The only sane approach is to limit inflation directly by controlling wages and prices and then to use our fiscal and monetary policy to make sure that we have high employment, reasonable growth, proper social and environmental policies and so on. Controls emerge as the only viable alternative in a difficult situation.

What kind of controls? Here there is much disagreement among those who feel that some kind of mandatory system is unavoidable. Ackley and Okun both seem to favor controls on a last-resort basis. The system would be applied only to that segment of business and labor that involved large firms and large unions. Mostly, the system would be voluntary along the lines of the guidepost approach of the 1960s. However, in "particularly flagrant or crucial cases" (Ackley, p. 433), the government could step in and prohibit particular wage or price increases. By contrast, Lekachman (p. 424) argues that it is "a delusion" to believe "that controls are required only in exceptional circumstances." He urges a much more thoroughgoing and pervasive system as part of the "normal apparatus" of government in our society.

Also there is the question of the relationship of controls to the battle over income distribution. Insofar as this battle is an important element causing inflation, the controllers will have to decide whether the government's role is to be passive—essentially, to preserve the status quo—or reformist—to use wage-price controls to secure what is believed to be a more "equitable" distribution of income. Most proponents of wage-price controls recognize that trying to apply this instrument to achieve social equity is to step on a hornet's nest; however, most probably lean towards the judicious use of the government's mandates to achieve something in this direction, at least in the long run.

The case *against* controls is many-sided. Three general lines of argument stand out:

CONTROLS DON'T WORK

This is a large part of Grayson's argument (p. 437). Controls have been tried endlessly, and always abandoned. In war, for short periods, they work somewhat, but even then imperfectly. European nations have tried them in peacetime with very little success. We have tried them and abandoned them. Business and labor will not cooperate. The public becomes restive. Controls erode. Deep inequities develop. Further dissatisfaction and erosion take place until the controls are given up (and then tried again and given up again a few years later). In short, wage-price controls are not a real alternative; they are a proven failure.

THE COSTS OF WAGE-PRICE CONTROLS ARE TOO GREAT

Even if wage-price controls could work, they would be unfair and inefficient (Lewis, p. 458). Certain groups end up being effectively controlled and others not, which causes greater inequalities than exist even at present. Controls put the economy in a strait jacket and prevent prices from serving their crucial role in the allocation of resources. Eastern bloc countries have been trying for the past several years to repair the enormous inefficiencies in their economies caused by administratively determined price systems that neglect the basic forces of supply and demand. The attempt to get around the system (by reclassifying jobs, by allowing product deterioration and so on) will tend both to defeat the controls and to make the economy less efficient overall. These costs, in total, are greater than the costs of the inflation that is being controlled.

THE PROPER ALTERNATIVE IS STRUCTURAL REFORM

The reason that monetary and fiscal measures may fail to deal with the inflation-unemployment dilemma is because of certain structural features of the economy, especially the existence of concentrated economic power in the hands of big business, big labor and, indeed, big government. Wage-price controls would at best be cosmetic tools, dealing only with symptoms. The better approach is to face the need for structural reform of the economy so that it ceases to have such a deep inflationary bias. This is the so-called procompetitive strategy (Houthakker, p. 443) It would involve a more intensive application of antitrust laws in the case of industry, and very probably the new application of these laws to labor unions. It would also involve a considerable revision of governmental legislation that, in many instances, as in the case of agricultural policy, has a built-in tendency to keep prices up.[5] Once these structural changes have been effected, the nation would have the advantages of competitive efficiency plus the ability to apply a flexible fiscal and monetary policy to cure such inflationary or deflationary forces that develop.

Of course, there is a strong rebuttal to this last point. Even some economists who might agree that structural reform is a preferable solution might say that it is politically unfeasible. Structural reform, by being more basic, is also more painful.

---

[5] A list of some government programs that actually tend to stimulate inflation might include: farm price-support programs; import quotas on meat, dairy and other farm products; "voluntary" quota agreements on steel and textiles; artificial restrictions on rates, routes and licensing in the case of truckers, railroads, airlines, inland water carriers and freight forwarders; state prorationing of oil and gas and the Connolly Hot Oil Act; resale price maintenance laws in those states that still have them, and many more.

Everyone's special interest is, or seems to be, under attack. One could take the position that structural reform is desirable but that, because it is out of the question, wage-price controls have to be instituted as the only realistic alternative.

What are the ultimate stakes in this debate? Even here there is fundamental disagreement. It is not very common to hear these days the refrain of the 1950s and early 1960s that a "little inflation is a good thing." Some restraint is clearly called for. But how much restraint and what kind? A long recession? A depression? The administrative nightmare of wage-price controls? The disruptive and divisive efforts for structural reform? It depends in a way on one's assessment of just how bad a threat inflation poses to the underlying fabric of our economic, political and social life. If you think we are on the edge of the abyss into which Germany trembled and fell in the horrendous inflation of the early 1920s, you will be prepared to take drastic steps, unpleasant though they be. If, on the other hand, you think our inflation is far from being out of control, you may consider that a change in psychology is sufficient—now that we have overcome the problem of "great depressions," we must simply focus somewhat more on moderating our inflationary tendencies.

And it is, of course, because we can never be *sure* which prognosis is correct that this debate in economics (like the others we have considered) continues, and is likely to do so in the decades ahead.

The Inevitability of Controls
Robert Lekachman

Robert Lekachman is Distinguished Professor of
Economics at City University of New York, Lehman
Campus.

The spectacle of the olympian Arthur F. Burns lobbying for national
incomes policy implies that the lengthy resistance of economists to un-
abashed public intervention into "free" market resource allocations has
just about ended, save, naturally, in Chicago, the University of Virginia
where Herbert Stein has fittingly migrated, the University of California at
Los Angeles, the Federal Reserve Bank of St. Louis, and a few other
tabernacles of the true faith.

OLD AFFECTIONS

The romance had a long run. John Stuart Mill in 1848 was insisting that
"only through the principle of competition has political economy any
pretension to the character of a science." The truth is, that even in the
face of 1974 reality, the best worked out chapters of any standard introductory text deal with price determination under competitive assumptions. It is a mark of the persistence of old affections that, when the text
discussion turns to oligopoly, the best the embarrassed authors can do is
talk about Paul Sweezy's kinked demand curve—a 1939 *jeu d'esprit*—or
von Neumann's and Morgenstern's 1944 exercise in the theory of games.

In economics, as in other branches of theology, bad doctrine is preferable to no doctrine at all. I take this prejudice to explain why economists
have resisted for so long acknowledging the significance of some of the
more important features of contemporary economic organization and
political expectations. For present purposes, I specify only three such

features. In much of American industry, law and medicine, banking and life insurance, free markets are in short supply. Need I recall that in their respective industries four corporations control 99 percent of vehicle output, 96 percent of aluminum fabrication, 80 percent of cigarette production, 72 percent of the soap and detergent market, and so on? As economists concede, the usual consequences of such market concentration include higher prices, smaller output, and more substantial marketing and advertising expenditures than those generated by competitive markets. The minimum fee schedules promulgated by bar associations and the mutually beneficial alliances among doctors, hospitals, and health insurers have similar consequences for the allocation (or misallocation) of legal and medical resources and the incomes of lawyers and doctors.

A second durable feature of American economic organization is the alliance between the oldest antitrust statutes in the universe and the continuing growth and prosperity of exceedingly large economic units which exert an embarrassing degree of power over their customers, suppliers, distributors and employees. As Thurman Arnold persuasively argued some four decades back, the major function of the Sherman and Clayton acts is the performance of occasional ceremonial exorcisms of monopoly that have the effect of reassuring the gullible public and allowing the monopolists and oligopolists to accumulate additional market power, often with the quiet connivance of federal agencies and Congress. It is food for reflection that the government won a famous victory over the oil trust—in 1911. The late Richard Hofstadter memorably dismissed antitrust as a faded passion of American reform.

Finally, American attitudes toward growth, prosperity and depression have shifted since the end of World War II and the passage of the Employment Act in 1946. The voters are now unwilling, and so also are their elected representatives, to accept depression as an act of God, a moral retribution for the fleshpots of prosperity. If depression were a politically viable policy, even oligopolists and construction unions would in time respond to shrinking markets for their products and services by trimming their definitions of acceptable prices and wages. But since the voters will not (and should not) wait for 8, 9, 10 percent unemployment to cure inflation, the course of events in concentrated markets approximates the behavior predicted by students of bilateral monopoly. Strong unions, in good or bad times, extract contract settlements substantially in excess of realized or prospective productivity improvements. Their employers pass on to the customers their higher labor costs, plus a consoling dollop of added profit. For within broad limits, oligopolists can choose between smaller sales at higher prices and larger sales at lower prices. Usually they prefer, possibly as more convenient, the first alternative. The auto industry, buffeted by declining sales and vanishing profits, raised prices *five* times on 1974 models and by a average of 9.5 percent on the 1975 chariots, a figure jawboned down to 8.5 percent by President Ford in his first weeks of office. Unorganized consumers and unorganized workers pay higher prices and collect smaller paychecks because oligopolists and the unions with which they deal possess and exert the power to extract rewards for their services higher than those that free markets would confer upon them.

One way of looking at how thing go in Galbraith's aptly named planning sector emphasizes resource misallocations. Another relates to the manifest inequities which flow from an inegalitarian distribution of economic power. And a third draws the obtrusive inference that public policy is urgently required as a corrective of misallocations and inequities alike. The characteristics of such a policy are in dispute among honest economists. In what follows, I suggest only the major requirements of an institutionalized incomes policy.

PERMANENT CONTROLS

The first necessity is commitment to a permanent statutory authority to establish criteria for wages and prices and a permanent federal agency to apply the criteria. The continuing concentration of economic power and the proliferation of conglomerates and multinational corporations as recent embodiments of that power dictate the creation of a countervailing source of power operating in the public interest. Hence, the sooner economists and politicians shed the delusion that controls are required only in exceptional circumstances, the better the prospect for economic management of higher quality than that to which the late Nixon administration accustomed us.

Controls must conform to generally acceptable standards of equity if widespread evasion is to be averted. Possibly the most dangerous aspect of the 1974 inflation is a profit surge accompanied by a 5 percent decline in the real income of typical working families. The inevitable attempt of unions to catch up can only operate as additional inflationary pressure. Since the United States is a conservative country, I daresay that a fair approximation of equity amounts to restoration of the usual shares of property and labor income, possibly by acceptance of Otto Eckstein's 5 percent price guidepost and 10 percent wage guidepost for the coming year. If and when popular opinion shifts toward the left, new standards of equity would imply less for investors and managers and more for blue and white collar workers.

Controls will fail except in the context of appropriate fiscal, monetary and employment programs. Whether the emphasis is upon equity or diminished inflation, a desirable approach to policy in 1974 and 1975 commences with devices more credible than the monitoring function to which the resurrected Cost of Living Council is presently confined. On balance, tax policy probably ought to withdraw some demand from the economy, preferably by larger levies on estates, corporate profits, and affluent taxpayers. A tougher minimum tax and the plugging of some of the more outrageous tax preferences now available to oil companies, real estate developers, foundation operatives, and expense account manipulators would simultaneously collect some needed tax revenue and reassure citizens out in Middle America who cannot employ tax lawyers and accountants.

An additional $25 billion or so of new tax revenue would allow some tax relief to low and moderate income families who have been hardest hit by inflation, fund a public job program in the $10 billion range (perhaps 1 million to 1.2 million new jobs) and still, on balance, withdraw rather more potential demand than is returned to the income stream.

Dr. Burns, a conservative on an exceedingly hot spot, supports public employment and fiscal restraint (though, as good conservatives ought, he prefers to cut spending rather than raise taxes), out of an acute realization that, as matters now stand, the Federal Reserve is the operator of the only policy in town. As the world knows, that policy has already driven the stock market into a state of acute melancholia, herded numerous enterprises to the verge of bankruptcy, and raised the specter of an acute, general liquidity crisis. No wonder Dr. Burns solicits help from Congress and the White House. In its absence, his choices are grim: he can either continue present restraints and risk financial disaster—probably, as West German Chancellor Helmut Schmidt warned, on an international scale; or he can loosen credit and remove the last constraint on runaway inflation.

Although, in a world of OPEC cartels, commuting anchovies, midwestern drought, global food shortages and faltering economic development, the sources of inflation are multiple, it is not the less true that unchecked or inadequately checked private economic power has been a persistent structural source of inflation. Since the political will and the popular sentiment to fragment private power are absent, the logic of survival requires the design of appropriate public agencies. Such is the central argument for permanent controls, administered by an agency and by officials who believe in their necessity, and recognized as a respected part of the normal apparatus of public administration in societies like ours in which powerful animals of carnivorous appetites thrash through the economic jungles.

An Incomes Policy for the 1970s

Gardner Ackley

A former chairman of the President's Council of
Economic Advisers, Gardner Ackley is Henry Carter
Adams University Professor of Political Economy at the
University of Michigan.

I believe it a safe guess that wage-price policy will assume, in the 1970s, a position of coordinate importance with employment policy, both in the United States and in most other industrialized countries which rely on reasonably free markets. Committed, as they are, to the maintenance of "full employment," these economies will remain prone to a degree of intermittent and creeping inflation which, although modest by comparison with celebrated inflations of the past, will nevertheless be exceedingly visible. Even if the costs in economic terms of such inflation may be judged tolerable, I doubt that its costs in social and political terms will permit any government simply to ignore it, or to rely on policies that appear ineffective.

Today's endemic inflationary problem is obviously no simple phenomenon. Its "causes" surely relate to fairly stable "structural" aspects of labor and product markets, the effects of which depend on the degree of resource utilization—which we can assume will usually be "high." Another important element is the dynamic mechanism through which current perceptions of price and income changes are generated from past events. But in addition to these basically economic elements, the process involves major sociopsychological and political aspects.

My vision of the type of inflationary process which now concerns us sees it as essentially the by-product of a struggle over income distribution, occurring in a society in which most sellers of goods and services possess some degree of market power over their own wages or prices (in money

Excerpted from Gardner Ackley, "An Incomes Policy for the 1970s," *The Review of Economics and Statistics*, 54, No. 3 (August 1972), pp. 218–23. © the President and Fellows of Harvard College. Reprinted by permission.

terms). The extent of each firm's or union's power at any given time is affected by structural and market factors: the manner in which that power is used is affected by perceptions of what is happening, and by political attitudes and social norms. Market power is used both in an attempt to increase real incomes, and, defensively, in an effort to protect real incomes from past and expected increases in production or purchase costs. An inflationary process can be tripped off in any of a number of ways. And, once it begins, most increases in wages and prices are basically defensive—made in an effort not to fall behind. Yet every defensive wage or price increase threatens the real incomes of other sectors, and prompts an endless chain of further defensive moves. Although some groups achieve relative gains and others experience loss of position during such a price-war spiral, the main effect is simply to raise the entire level of prices and money incomes.

In my view, this model of an inflation-generating struggle to increase or protect income shares—although here grossly oversimplified—provides a substantially meaningful description of wage and price behavior in a modern industrial economy. But what is most significant is that the problem it describes appears to have become aggravated in recent years, as the social norms regulating group behavior have for various reasons become more tolerant of—or even now encourage—an increasingly aggressive use of market power. Moreover, there is an increasing sophistication of business and union leadership, along with better and prompter measurements of relative position—i.e., the perception-generating mechanism is altering. And recent experience with inflation has substantially heightened the sensitivity of most groups to actual or potential losses of relative position. For these reasons, there is a tendency to react more quickly, more fully, and frequently preemptively. The more prompt and complete are the defensive reactions to inflation, the faster is its rate—that is, the more there is to defend against.

Few would deny, I think, that society is becoming more sensitive to the existence of "inequities" or "injustices" in the distribution of income, and is therefore more supportive—or at least more tolerant—of efforts by "underprivileged" groups to improve their relative incomes, through political or economic action or both. But when the market prices of products and productive services become weapons in a struggle over income shares, the underprivileged—who often possess little market power—are likely to lose out to the already favored groups. In the absence of new social instruments for resolving these problems, I am convinced that our society and economy remain subject to substantial inflationary pressures—particularly when at the same time we remain determined to maintain full employment—i.e., labor markets and product markets strong enough that almost every group has some considerable degree of market power.

I conclude that the inflationary consequences of a struggle over income shares can only be controlled through the institution of an "incomes policy"—a system of direct restraints (i.e., more explicit and forceful social norms) limiting efforts to advance incomes through raising wages and prices. The pattern of these direct restraints can and should be systematically integrated with tax and other measures, so as together to guide the evolution of income shares in a manner which society judges to be fair and equitable.

Belief that an incomes policy is needed of course does not mean that *other* methods for the control of inflation can or should be neglected. Perhaps the single most important thing we can do to improve our control of inflation is to make more vigorous and timely use of fiscal and monetary policies to combat surges of aggregate demand that occur when the economy is already at or close to full employment. But inflation will not disappear merely by avoiding future mistakes of demand-management policy, of the kind we made in 1966–1968. Moreover, some policy mistakes are nearly unavoidable, and we should have other means to assure that mistakes will not be disastrous.

There are many structural changes which could reduce the inflationary bias in our economy. Many of the most important would be improvements of manpower policy, designed to make the labor supply more easily shiftable from one employer, one industry, one occupation, one region, to another. We should also work to eliminate a host of private practices and government policies which grew up or were adopted in an effort to protect one or another private interest in an era when full employment was neither a policy nor a reality. Today these create strong downward rigidities of particular wages and prices and unnecessary bottlenecks and immobilities at high employment. Some provide artificial support for the market power of particular groups. Others directly and unnecessarily raise costs. Unfortunately, it is a slow and politically difficult job to achieve each of these many changes. It is important to get ahead with this job, whatever else we do. But it will not solve the immediate problem.

Beyond this, there are, of course, possibilities for major changes in basic labor legislation and institutions, which would effectively reduce the market power of labor unions, and for direct limits on the size and/or market shares of giant corporations. Even if, on balance, desirable, these changes are not going to occur in the near future. In any case, I believe that the more practicable approach is not a head-on attack on the basic sources of market power, but is rather a limitation on the exercise of that power where it specifically contributes to inflation—and, for that matter, where its use collides with other important social objectives.

Elsewhere, I have considered at some length the possibility of a permanent system of compulsory wage and price controls, and have concluded that it would inevitably create distortions and inefficiencies of resource use so serious as to make the system undesirable and probably unworkable.[1] There is not space to repeat that argument. But there are other options for the design of a system of direct restraints. One would be to return essentially to the system of wage-price "guideposts" used by the Kennedy and Johnson Administrations. As is well known, the guideposts constituted a set of definitions of patterns of wage and price behavior which, if generally followed, would be consistent with efficient resource allocation, reasonable equity and approximate stability of the overall price level. Adherence to the guideposts was voluntary; but the government was prepared to—and frequently did—publicly criticize behavior which appeared to be inconsistent with the guideposts, and commend behavior which appeared consistent. It also propagandized generally about the importance and desirability of adherence to the guideposts, and frequently held private discussions with firms and unions in which it urged their specific adherence.

Many critics—economists and others—asked how a system of purely voluntary standards and government appeals could cause *any* wage or price setter to accept a wage or price below that which would maximize net income. Is not the answer that, in collective bargaining and most industrial pricing, wage rates and prices are set not by impersonal market forces but rather by human (usually collective) decisions? The decision makers have room for judgment (or there would be no real decision). Over the relevant time horizon, they usually do not know even approximately what wage or price would maximize net income. They must and do settle questions by rule of thumb, comparison, or compromise; by considerations of equity, policy, or public appearance.

To the extent that the government's arguments for restraint made sense to any of the participants in a decision; to the extent that some of the participants preferred to avoid or minimize public criticism and to the extent that they believed the government's appeals—*and their own decisions*—would affect *other* wage and price decisions, the guideposts clearly could and would have made some difference for their own decision.

To be sure, many professional mediators reported that the guideposts

---

[1] See "The Future of Wage and Price Controls," *Atlanta Economic Review*, 22 (April 1972), pp. 24–33, and my "Statement" before the Joint Economic Committee, August 31, 1971, in *Hearings on the President's New Economic Program* (Part 2, pp. 242–56).

never appeared consciously to have entered anyone's thinking during wage bargaining which they observed in the 1960s. Interestingly, however, many unions professed to believe that the guideposts were influencing collective bargaining, and frequently and bitterly attacked the government's policy. Moreover, 3.2 percent settlements came up much more frequently than they would have by chance alone. I believe that the guideposts did have some impact on wage decisions, primarily through influencing employers' bargaining positions, rather than by directly affecting union attitudes or aggressiveness, although I do not rule that out.

So far as prices are concerned I personally know that many significant price increases were either avoided or postponed, their size or their coverage reduced, or, in a fair number of cases that came to public attention, rolled back in full or in part. When, after 1965, the rate of unemployment fell progressively below 4 percent, it was not surprising that a voluntary system was unable to prevent an acceleration of wage and price increases. But, even then, I am convinced that it made an appreciable difference. The real question, of course, is whether the guideposts made *enough* difference. Could voluntary guideposts have survived as a viable system even if there had been a less serious mistake of fiscal policy than the one actually made in 1966–1968? Before attempting to answer this question, let me first indicate some specific and, I believe remediable, weaknesses of the guidepost system of the 1960s.

(1) It seems to me undeniable that any successful stabilization system—whether described as "compulsory" or "voluntary"—demands the consent or at least the tolerance of those whose wages and prices are to be stabilized. For this consent to be forthcoming, those regulated—and the general public as well—must see the system as one that is basically fair and equitable, or, at least, that embodies sacrifices by "our side" roughly equivalent to those imposed on the "other side." Moreover, members of each group must believe that the restrictions its members accept on their freedom to do as they please will achieve something important—that slowing the rise in prices is a highly desirable objective, and that this system will be effective in achieving it.

In my view, this consent can only be secured through an active participation by the major groups in society—and particularly by the organizations of labor and business—in the process of recognizing the problem to which the policy is addressed, in planning the strategy to be used, and in formulating the basic standards. This was not the case for the guideposts. Rather, the guideposts were unilaterally promulgated by the government, with no serious effort to involve the leadership of labor, business, and public opinion in the process. I know that many individual business and labor leaders did recognize the problem, and had sympathy for the approach used. Their active participation, even in an advisory role, could have made them assume some responsibility for the success of the guideposts, and surely would have given the policy somewhat greater "legitimacy" in the eyes of others. Moreover, Congress was never asked to consider the matter, so that the guideposts drew no legitimacy from the legislative branch of our political system.

(2) Administration of the policy in the Council of Economic Advisers, with the occasional involvement of the White House, had advantages. The prestige of the Presidency—whether exerted directly by the President or reflected through an agent known to have the President's confidence —was an important asset in securing adherence by business and labor. But the President's support for the steps needed to make the policy work had to be affected by broader political considerations. For example, a time when labor support was vitally needed for passage of a crucial element in the President's legislative program was not a good time for him or his personal representative to be exerting pressures for wage restraint against a strong union.

(3) The government never made an adequate commitment of resources to the administration of the guidepost program. There were, at most, one to three staff members at the Council of Economic Advisers devoting some fraction of their time to guidepost activities, with occasional research assignments to others. It was thus impossible to anticipate more than the most obvious problems, or to provide the kinds of information and analysis needed to deal effectively with potential or actual cases of guidepost violation.

Moreover, the policy never had government-wide support. Although Presidents Kennedy and Johnson gave it their clear backing, the Secretaries or other high officials of the Departments of Labor, Commerce, Interior, and others were often indifferent or hostile, as were relevant independent agencies, such as the Conciliation and Mediation Service, and the regulatory commissions.

(4) One basic problem was that although everyone knew when important wage questions were coming up for decision, there was no way fully to anticipate major price increase decisions and to bring to bear the relevant information, persuasion, and considerations of the public interest which the government might wish the price setters to be exposed to at the time when it would do the most good. Clearly, it is far easier to prevent or

delay or modify an inappropriate price increase before rather than after it has been publicly announced. At one point businesses were requested to notify the Council in advance of major price changes. Some did, and were willing to discuss them before their announcement, but most did not. Indeed, some price changes which previously would have been publicly announced now began to be heard about only second hand.

Even if the foregoing weakness of the guidepost policy had been avoided (as they perhaps are in the proposals made below), and even if there had been no serious mistake of fiscal policy in 1966–1968, the question remains whether a purely voluntary policy could have succeeded during a prolonged period of high employment, or whether a chain reaction of increasingly serious violations of the policy would not ultimately have destroyed it.

I do not think that the answer is clear-cut. Yet, as I review the experience and the current problem, I conclude that it might be unwise to take a chance on a purely voluntary system. Even if the policy can enlist the support of a substantial majority of the public and of the leaders of labor, business, and other interests, will there not always be a number of smaller firms and unions, and at least a few reasonably important ones, whose publicized and flagrant noncooperation may progressively erode the adherence of others? I wonder if—rather than overfull employment—it was not the clear desire of the leadership of the airline mechanics in 1966 to prove that they could successfully defy the government—thereby encouraging other unions to do the same—that caused the wage guidepost to crumble. Indeed, the attempt to obtain adherence mainly through giving widespread publicity to violations may be a potentially self-destructive policy. The airline mechanics' case was inherently unimportant. It was only the union's rejection of repeated highly publicized efforts by President Johnson to secure their approximate cooperation that made the case important—and its outcome so destructive of cooperation by other unions.

Doubts about the validity of a system which lacks any means of effective enforcement against the occasional flagrant noncooperator lead me to conclude that the existence of a "big stick in the back of the closet"—seldom used, and the use of which is not entirely predictable —could mightily enhance the force of public opinion in deterring clear and deliberate violations of the standards, thereby making it easier for all others to give at least approximate adherence to the standards.

I come, thus, to my suggestions for a future system of longer-run wage and price restraints for the United States. For want of a better name I will call this system the "Stabilization Agency." It would be created by legislation and responsible directly to the Congress.

1. The authority of the Stabilization Agency would be limited to the wages, fringe benefits, salaries, and executive compensation paid by employers who engage in significant collective bargaining, and to the prices of listed basic materials and of goods and services sold by the 1,500–2,000 largest corporations. However, all retail prices, rents, personal services, and farm prices would be excluded.

2. The agency's legitimacy would derive, first, from its creation through legislation, and, second, from some formal arrangement for labor-management-public participation in the formulation and review of its basic principles and policies. A relatively small tripartite board would have the basic "legislative" responsibility for formulating the agency's wage and price standards and its procedures for intervention in particular cases. But a much larger body representing the principal interest groups and segments of public opinion would meet regularly to debate major policy statements and periodic reports on the agency's activities, and might participate in the selection of the nonpublic members of the board.

3. The executive functions would be performed by a full-time staff of several hundred professionals, headed by a single administrator (appointed by the President), rather than by the tripartite board. He would be authorized to intervene, formally or informally, publicly or privately, in the determination of all wages and prices subject to the restraints. The administrator would have legal authority to require that significant price and wage changes be reported in advance, to delay for limited periods the putting into effect of proposed changes while the agency studied them, and to require submission of relevant information from firms, unions and government agencies. Based on its analysis of any case in which it chose to intervene, the agency would have the authority to recommend specific changes of wages or prices privately to the parties or publicly to the country. It could also make appropriate recommendations on related matters to federal, state or local government agencies.

4. The agency's standards would be widely publicized, explained, and adherence to them promoted. However, the standards would not need to be so simple or numerical that they could in all cases be easily self-applied either by those making decisions or by the public in judging the propriety of those decisions.

5. As a last resort, in particularly flagrant or crucial cases, authority would be available to prohibit specific wage or price changes substantially inconsistent with the agency's standards. The administrator could apply to a special court set up for this purpose for an injunction, running for a specific period of time, up to (say) one year, against the charging by named firms of specific listed or described prices, or against the payment by named employers of specific wage rates. The request for injunction would have to demonstrate that the specific changes in prices or wages to be enjoined were clearly inconsistent with the agency's standards for wages or prices, and that other workers or employers were, in general, voluntarily observing these standards. There would be no direct compulsory arbitration; but, in effect, the agency (and the special court) could in crucial cases determine the highest wage level it would permit to be paid.

I believe that a system set up along these general lines could be reasonably effective in exercising an appropriate restraint on wage and price increases, and, assuming adequate support from fiscal and monetary, farm, import and manpower policies, in keeping inflation under reasonable control. Since the basic adherence would be voluntary, the system could not insure absolute price stability, nor should it attempt to. But, in part for the same reason, I believe that it offers enough flexibility to permit the relative wage and price changes that are essential for efficient resource allocation. Of course, it may be expected that, sooner or later, there would be a breakdown of consensus and hence of the system. After an appropriate interval, and with new names, faces and slogans, it will then have to be renegotiated.

Incomes policies attempt to assure that the income claims within their purview—along with the income claims left to other determination—add up to roughly 100 percent of the total national income generated by current aggregate production, valued in current prices. But in this process, it is almost impossible to escape questions as to the *appropriate distribution* of aggregate income: as among wages, profits, farm and professional and interest incomes, and managerial compensation—and, within wage income—the appropriate differentials among various skills, occupations, industries, and regions. This distribution is only in part affected by the standards set in a wage and price policy; but it is also significantly affected by the government's tax, regulatory, tariff, agricultural, minimum wage, social security, manpower and other policies.

Many believe that the "consent" of the great economic interest groups—which, in the long run, is the only possible basis for a successful system of inflation control—can only be secured and maintained if the system of wage-price restraints is coordinated with the other tools of government policy in order quite consciously to promote a progressive *redistribution* of income in specific directions which society approves. Indeed, to the extent that the source of existing inflationary pressure lies in a fundamental dissatisfaction with the existing income-distribution on the part of one or more powerful groups, while other groups resist any significant change in that distribution, there can probably be no real "consent" to an incomes policy unless that policy is directed not only toward the total of incomes but as well to their relative size.

Others fear that mixing up such questions with the control of inflation simply guarantees the failure of an incomes policy. An explicit policy on income shares might be avoided at the beginning of an incomes policy. But I suspect that sooner or later it cannot be escaped.

Wage-Price Controls: Con

Controls are not the Answer
C. Jackson Grayson, Jr.

C. Jackson Grayson, Jr., is Dean of the School of
Business Administration, Southern Methodist University,
and was Chairman of the Price Commission during
Phase II.

I will make one clear assertion at the outset: Wage-price controls are not
the answer to inflation.

And yet I will also make the following prediction: We will turn again in
the United States, in desperation, to some form of controls over wages
and prices—just as people have done over the centuries. And the answer
will still be the same—they may make some short-term gains, but at the
expense of the long-run welfare.

The lessons of history seem pretty clear. Centralized efforts to fight
inflation were started before Christ was born. Rome, for example, fought
inflation by various means for centuries. Finally, in A.D. 301, the emperor
Diocletian imposed the first extensive price-wage control program. His
edict (referred to as "commanded cheapness") set schedules for 76 different wage categories and for 890 different price categories (222 of which
were for food!). The penalty for an offense was death. Thirteen years
later, the program, in shambles, was abandoned. In the thirteenth century, the great Mongol, Kublai Khan, decreed maximum prices. And
Medieval Europe had a "just price" code.

Not many people are aware of it, but the United States began some
attempts at wage-price controls during its early years. The American
Puritans imposed a code of wage and price limitations in 1636; those who
violated the code were classed with "adulterers and whoremongers." The
Continental Congress set price ceilings even before the Declaration of
Independence. A few states enacted price control laws. Inflation became

From C. Jackson Grayson, Jr., "Controls are not the Answer," *Challenge* (November-December 1974), pp.
9–12. Copyright © 1974 by the International Arts and Sciences Press, Inc. Reprinted by permission of
International Arts and Sciences Press, Inc.

so severe that General George Washington complained in April 1779 that "a wagonload of money will scarcely purchase a wagonload of provisions." The attempts at control were sporadic, highly controversial, and not comprehensive. All efforts were largely abandoned by 1780.

Most modern nations have instituted wage-price controls during periods of war, but it was in Europe right after World War II that almost every nation tried some form of comprehensive peacetime controls (remembering the inflation that had torn apart European economies after World War I). Some European nations had succeeded with their "incomes policies" for a period of time. Some were started, stopped, and reinstated in another version. But none has lasted continuously.

Though specific "lessons" are difficult to transfer across international boundaries, and even difficult to use in one nation from one time to another, it might be helpful to look at a summary that I have made of European experiences with controls.

General Lessons from European Incomes Policies

1. If either labor or business does not cooperate, a wage-price controls program will not work.
2. Incomes policies do not work for long. They erode with time.
3. Getting into controls is easier than getting out.
4. Rising profits drive wage demands up.
5. Neither business nor labor is very satisfied with any given distribution of their share of income at any given time. Both will seek to improve their share.
6. Voluntary incomes policies have been limited in success and in time. The tendency is toward mandatory policies.
7. Labor nearly always believes that the government figure for estimated productivity in setting wage guidelines is low. History shows that labor is generally right.
8. A wage "drift" occurs over time as business and labor cooperate to break many of the wage guidelines.
9. Efforts to restrain business and labor through education and exhortation have very limited success.
10. It is increasingly difficult to make incomes policies work as demand increases and unemployment decreases.
11. If prices are to be controlled, then so must wages be. The only exception is France, which has had a limited price control program but no wage control program.
12. Cost of living escalators accelerate inflation.
13. Less productive labor groups eventually demand comparability in wages with the more highly productive labor sectors, thereby eroding the wage guideline.
14. Expectations feed inflation.
15. Increasingly interdependent world trade can intrude upon and upset a nation's incomes policies.

These experiences were summarized succinctly by Lloyd Ulman and Robert Flanagan in their book, *Wage Restraint—A Study of Incomes Policies in Western Europe:* "Incomes policy, to generalize from the experience of the countries in this account, has not been very successful." My conclusions about the accomplishments of the Price Commission do not vary from that. Perhaps we did obtain some short-range impact on price-wage levels, but they were gained under special conditions (slack in the economy, followed by productivity gains from a highly stimulated economy, and cooperation of business and labor) and at the cost of some long-term negative results.

As a result of my sixteen months as a price controller, I can list seven ways that controls interfere (negatively) with the market system and hasten its metamorphosis into a centralized economy.

First, wage-price controls lead to distortions in the economic system, which can be minimized only in the short run. The longer controls are in effect, the harder it is to discern real from artificial signals. No matter how cleverly any group designs a control system, distortions and inequities will appear. It happened in European control programs; it started to happen in Phase II.

For instance, lumber controls were beginning to lead to artificial middlemen, black markets and sawmill shutdowns. Companies trapped with low base-period profit margins were beginning to consider selling out to those with higher base period margins, sending their capital overseas, or reducing their operations. Elsewhere, instances of false job upgrading —actually "raises" in disguise—were reported on a scattered but increasing basis. To keep away from profit-margin controls, some companies were considering dropping products where costs, and thus prices, had increased. And shortages of certain products (such as molasses and fertilizer) were appearing because artificially suppressed domestic prices had allowed higher world prices to pull domestic supplies abroad.

Exceptions and special regulations can handle some of these distortions, but the task grows more difficult as each correction breeds the need for another.

Second, during a period of controls, the public forgets that not all wage-price increases are inflationary. In a freely competitive economy, wage and price increases occur because of real consumer demand shifts and supply shortages. The resulting wage and price increases signal to businesses, "make more," or to labor, "move here," or to the public, "use less."

Controls interfere with this signaling mechanism. An artificially suppressed price can eventually cause shortages; natural gas is an example. Similar examples can be found in the labor market, where suppressed wages do not attract labor to areas in which there are shortages of skills or workers. But with wage-price controls in place, the public believes that all increases are inflationary—almost antisocial—and the clamor is for no increases, or at least very small ones.

"You can eliminate the middleman, but not his function"—this old business saying applies equally to our economic system. We live in a world of scarce resources, and, as much as some would like to repeal the laws of supply and demand, it cannot be done. Some system must allocate resources, we hope to the most efficient use for society. If wage-price controls, other government regulatory rules, or business-labor monopolies prohibit the price system from performing its natural function, then another rationing system (such as central planning and control) must be used. You can eliminate the price system, but not its function.

Third, during a control period, the public forgets what profits are all about. Even before the recent wage-price controls, the public believed profits were "too high," though they actually declined from 6.2 percent of GNP in 1966 to 3.6 percent in 1970, and increased only to 4.3 percent in the boom year of 1972. And with profit increases raised to the top of the news during the recovery of 1972 and early 1973, the negative public sentiment against profits increased. Why? The control system itself heightened the public's negative attitude toward profit at a time when capital regeneration, the fuel of the capitalist engine, was already alarmingly low.

Fourth, wage-price controls provide a convenient stone for those who have economic or political axes to grind, particularly those interested in promoting a centralized economic system. For example, in 1972 Ralph Nader argued that the control system should be used to prohibit automobile companies from raising their prices to reflect style changes. Others argued that price increases should not be given to companies that employ insufficient numbers of minorities or pollute the environment. Nor should wage increases go to uncooperative unions. And so on.

Fifth, wage-price controls can easily become a security blanket against the cold winds of free-market uncertainties. They tell people what the limits are; they help employers fight unions; and they provide union leaders with excuses to placate demands for "more" from their rank and file. The controlled become dependent on the controllers and want regulations continued in preference to the competition of a dynamic market. At the same time, the controllers themselves can become so enamored of their task that they don't want to let go.

The public begins to fear what will happen when controls are ended and seeks continuance. Witness the fears of moving from Phase II to Phase III, and the public (and congressional) pressure for the freeze to replace Phase III. Even Wall Street seemed terrified at the thought of returning to supply and demand in the market. It is much easier to get into controls than to get out.

Sixth, under controls, business and labor leaders begin to pay more attention to the regulatory body than to the dynamics of the marketplace. They inevitably come to the same conclusion, summed up by one executive: "We know that all of our sophisticated analysis and planning can be wiped out in the blink of a Washington controller's eye."

Seventh, and most dangerous, wage-price controls misguide the public. They draw attention away from the fundamental factors that affect inflation—fiscal and monetary policies, tax rates, import-export policies, productivity, competitive restrictions and the like. The danger is that attention will become permanently focused on the symptom-treating control mechanism rather than on the underlying problems.

In summary, perhaps the most dramatic way I can underscore my views is to point out the recent example of Britain, where years of successive stop-go economic policies and various types of controls (including guideposts) have led that nation to where it is today, economically and politically in a crisis state with one of the lowest income growth rates of modern nations and raging inflation.

Controls are not the answer.

Are Controls the Answer?
Hendrik S. Houthakker

Hendrik S. Houthakker, a former member of the
President's Council of Economic Advisers, is Professor of
Economics at Harvard University.

We shall not know for many months if the introduction of direct controls over wages and prices in late 1971 was followed by a significant slowdown in the trend of price and wage increases . . . . Even if attained, the modest reduction in the inflation rate officially set as a goal provides only weak justification for this drastic departure from our generally successful economic traditions. There is some indication that the Pay Board and Price Commission will serve less as a means of curtailing inflation than as watchdogs over big business and big labor. . . .

There is indeed a case for better supervision of the labor unions. In the last few years we have come closer to the situation already reached in the United Kingdom (prior to the recent legislation), where the unions could obtain wage increases not only regardless of productivity, but also regardless of the state of the labor market. Our labor laws appear to be inadequate to deal with this problem, which has greatly complicated the preservation of full employment. The power of the unions may therefore have to be constrained in other ways. Although the Pay Board and the Construction Industry Stabilization Committee have so far demonstrated only limited effectiveness in dealing with excessive wage increases, they may learn in due course. Perhaps the introduction of an official link between unemployment and wage changes (an institutionalized Phillips curve) would lead to better results.

However this may be, systematic government intervention in collective bargaining may be necessary pending a general restoration of competition

Excerpted from Hendrik S. Houthakker, "Are Controls the Answer?" from *The Review of Economics and Statistics*, 54, No. 3 (August 1972), pp. 231–34. © the President and Fellows of Harvard College. Reprinted by permission.

in the labor markets and elsewhere. The great danger of regulatory bodies, as experience in other areas suggests, is that they will come under the control of the sector they are supposed to regulate. The departure of the labor members of the Pay Board does not necessarily remove this danger; it may indicate, on the contrary, that they were satisfied the Pay Board would be responsive to the unions even without their overt participation. Any tendency on the part of the Pay Board to favor organized over nonorganized labor will no doubt make union membership more attractive and thus make the unions even more powerful. While this result may be partly offset by employers substituting nonunion for union labor, discriminatory wage controls are not likely to improve the working of the labor market.

For somewhat different reasons much the same is true if the Price Commission concentrates on big business. The danger here is not so much that large firms will have undue influence over the commission; for one thing there are far more large firms than large unions, and their interests are more diverse. The danger is on the contrary that the Price Commission will reduce the profit margins of the more efficient firms (who are usually among the larger ones) to such an extent that marginal firms (who are often small) will be squeezed; even if the latter can avoid bankruptcy, they will then have difficulty attracting capital. In view of the increasing emphasis on profit controls, this danger is by no means theoretical. Many economists believe that price controls should be confined to large firms, and recent political trends also favor this emphasis. There may well be more immediate effect on prices if firms with large profits are forced to roll back their prices, but their less profitable competitors will, by the same token, see their market share or their profits (and probably both) vanish. Those who want to use controls as an instrument against big business will thus have gained a Pyrrhic victory at best.

Presumably not all qualified observers will agree with my assessment of the short-term results of price-wage controls as modest at best, and of the long-term results as harmful. Only time will tell. But unless my fears are groundless, continued controls do not appear to be the answer to inflation, at least from an economic point of view. Let us therefore consider alternatives.

One alternative that does not need much attention is the milder "incomes policy" practiced in the United States during the middle 1960s and also widely adopted abroad. While much less disruptive than direct controls, this milder approach has not had any lasting results.

There is considerably greater promise in what may be called a "procompetitive strategy," under which the government attempts to make the factor and product markets more responsive to overall fiscal and monetary policy. Such a strategy would involve legislative reforms in the areas of labor, antitrust, transportation, energy and agriculture, in addition to liberalization of import restrictions.

The advantages of competition for the efficient allocation of resources have, of course, long been recognized, but its benefits for economic stability are no less important. In markets where competition is restricted, prices tend to be not only too high, but also too sticky. In competitive markets prices respond more promptly to changes in supply and demand, and this is especially important for the success of anti-inflationary policies. Although aggregate demand was curtailed significantly between late 1968 and early 1970, prices and wages were not affected as much as similar experiences (most recently in the late 1950s) suggested. Wages continued to rise despite considerable unemployment, and prices followed suit, despite a fall in profits. As far as the labor markets are concerned there is admittedly little direct evidence of a change in structure which would have made them less responsive to unemployment. Nevertheless better response could have been obtained by policies aimed at racial discrimination, apprenticeship requirements, hiring halls, product boycotts and other restrictive practices. Such measures were especially needed in the construction and transportation industries, where wage increases were largest.

In several important product markets measures could have been taken to let declining demand show up in lower prices rather than in lower output. Some of these measures relate to imports, which are often the most potent source of competition in oligopolistic markets. Thus, if so-called voluntary quotas on steel exports from Japan and Europe had not been negotiated in 1968 the behavior of steel prices would have been quite different. Similarly, the adoption of the Cabinet Task Force report on oil imports would have had a major impact on petroleum prices. The substantial increase in dairy support prices in March 1971 was contrary to anti-inflationary policy. So were the readiness of the Interstate Commerce Commission to grant general freight rate increases, and the efforts of the Civil Aeronautics Board to prevent overcapacity from depressing domestic air fares; these in turn encouraged the carriers to agree to the large wage increases demanded by the unions involved. Many more cases could be cited (including a few where competition was promoted and prices fell as a result, notably in international aviation), but on balance they would not change the conclusion that the government has generally been prepared to help politically powerful sectors in keeping prices up. This was one reason why the losses of output and employment implicit in the anti-inflationary policy followed up to mid-1971 were largely in vain. In fact the perverse response of these protected markets to the decline in aggregate demand may have aggravated these losses.

The principal lesson from this experience is that a procompetitive strategy is politically costly since it tends to offend powerful and well-organized interest groups. However, a strategy of controls cannot succeed either unless it hurts somewhere. As was pointed out earlier, the controls have not so far inflicted much pain, but neither have they done much to reduce inflation. The political advantage of controls is that the pain can be directed to the less vocal sectors. This is presumably why the wage boards have been willing to give preferential treatment to certain unions and why little or nothing has been done to restrain farm prices. It remains to be seen whether this selective approach will yield the desired results.

There is still another alternative: to let inflation take its course, thus avoiding the costs inherent in an effective procompetitive or controls strategy. The many studies of the effects of inflation suggest that the U.S. economy has developed fairly good adjustment mechanisms for the rather mild inflation we have experienced until now. Wages and prices go upward in tandem; long-term interest rates fully reflect the rate of change of prices; most transfer payments are adjusted periodically. For most Americans who own any property at all their main asset is a house, whose value rises at least as fast as the general price level, and their main liability is a mortgage contracted long ago and fixed in money terms; they clearly stand to gain by inflation. Of course there are flies in this ointment. The gains of homeowners are matched by the losses of thrift institutions, but expedients have been found to take care of this. More seriously, inflation through the Pigou effect leads to a rise in personal savings,[1] and this complicates the attainment of full employment. Moreover it is conceivable, though by no means certain, that inflation has a tendency to accelerate if left alone.

Of the three options before us—controls, competition, and benign neglect—my own preference as an economist and citizen is clearly for the second, the only one that is consistent with established economic analysis.

---

[1] This is the most likely explanation of the high savings rates that have surprised so many observers of the economy. These rates are not surprising if savings are viewed as the planned accumulation of assets, and if the desired money value of assets is related to money income.

The sudden switch to controls one year ago resulted from an unwillingness to bear the short-term political costs inherent in a more constructive approach. But in economic policy the hard choices cannot be avoided, and the consequences of controls, even if they reach their primary objective, may not be very appealing either. We must all hope that the present policy will work, but at the same time we must remain on the alert for indications that it will ultimately do more harm than good.

U.S. Abandons Controls with Inflation Thriving and No Extra Answers

Interview with Hendrik S. Houthakker and Arthur M. Okun by Soma Golden

Question: First, I'd like each of you to take a moment to sketch out your view of wage-price controls as a policy alternative in this country. Are you in brief a pro, or con, controls man and why?

Houthakker: I have not been an enthusiast for controls. I criticized them when they were first adopted, and I must say that nothing that has happened since then has convinced me that I was wrong. I believe they have been a failure and that they were bound to be a failure. So I feel that if we want to do something about inflation we have to find something other than controls.

Okun: It's been 30 months since August 1971, and you can divide that into two halves. In the first, we had a marked deceleration of inflation. It's only the second half that has looked bad. The fact is that by late 1972 we were down to a 3 percent inflation rate. My own view is that Phase 1 and Phase 2 did make a significant contribution toward that deceleration—riding a tide that was probably moving in that direction anyway, but helping it along.

I think that what has happened since then has reflected a number of factors, one of them that we have the kind of inflation that controls cannot do that much about, in the food and fuel areas.

I don't view myself as an enthusiast for controls but I think that some type of government wage-price effort of a direct sort, probably demanding mandatory powers, ought to be one of the tools that's available in trying to hold down inflation.

Q: Dr. Okun, were you an enthusiast of the first freeze?

Okun: I would never have recommended the kind of plunging in with a total freeze and drawing lines between pickles and cucumbers and professional football salaries that we had. Indeed, I think we were confronted with that partly because we operated with such an unwillingness to tiptoe into the area, to use government powers on anything. When we finally decided to do something, the only alternative was going all the way.

Houthakker: I feel that we had considerable slack in the economy in 1971, and this by itself would have taken care of a lot of inflationary pressure. When the slack disappeared, the controls suddenly didn't work any more. Now I attribute this to the fact that the price behavior was determined by the amount of slack in the economy, and not by the controls.

Okun: It is awfully hard to explain why the slack suddenly took hold in late 1971 without invoking controls as part of the answer.

Houthakker: Well, controls can have a temporary effect, but as President Lincoln might have said: "You can hold all prices down some of the time and some prices down all of the time, but you can't hold down all prices all of the time."

Okun: We can agree on that.

Q: Let's shift towards January 1973, and Phase 3. Would you say that we should have gotten out of the controls business then as the super boom developed?

Houthakker: Well, in testimony before the Joint Economic Committee in November 1972, my answer was that the controls should be phased out on an industry-by-industry basis, having regard to the state of the market in each industry.

Okun: I think we never should have gotten into areas where controls were creating genuine shortages. The crusade on lumber prices was one of the most absurd spinning of wheels in Phase 2.

Q: Can we read out of this that we got ourselves into too much of a detailed controls system—too many forms to file, too many little rules that each businessman had to keep up with?

Houthakker: No, I would put it the other way around. I think what was done during the last two-and-a-half years was to run a price controls system without adequate allocation mechanisms. When you control prices, you deeply affect the whole economy, and this I think was not fully realized.

As far as I can see, the controls effort starting in 1971 was largely a cosmetic exercise. It was an appearance of action without much substance to it.

If I had been asked in 1971, as a technician, 'What does it take to have an effective controls mechanism?' then I would have said you need a bureaucracy of a quarter of a million people, just to take a figure out of thin air. It would also mean a complete change in the nature of our economy and that is the main reason why I would have opposed it. But my feeling was that the effort that was made with 3,000 to 5,000 people really wasn't promising, as I think the results have shown.

Q: Prof. Houthakker, you left the Council of Economic Advisers one month before the 1971 controls hit. Your advice was not asked on this subject?

Houthakker: No, it was not. No. Of course there were various earlier efforts. There was something called the Inflation Alert in which I myself was much involved. I never quite understood what it was meant to do, but it was another of these cosmetic efforts.

Q: Are you saying that we got ourselves into a very detailed controls system at the same time we were reluctant to build a bureaucracy?

Okun: I think that is exactly it. We set up inconsistent objectives. Either you decide to do what you can do with a very small bureaucracy, which I think is to pick the rotten apples out of the barrel rather than to try to define the shape of the ideal apple, or else you move to the much more detailed set of rules and regulations such as what marked World War II and Korea and then you have the big bureaucracy. My preference would have been the first.

Q: Would the first have done much for the kind of inflation that we had with the worst inflation in the food and commodity sector? Were there many rotten apples to pick from? Was there a big company or a big union or any such visible villain in this?

Okun: No, I don't think any reasonable set of controls would have changed the story much in 1973.

Figure A   Price Inflation. Percentage Increase in the Consumer Price Index over Same Month in Previous Year.

The controls program approached—but failed to attain—its target of cutting price inflation to 2–3 percent by the end of 1972, but failed miserably in its stated aim of lowering the rate to 2.5 percent by the end of 1973.

Source: Department of Labor

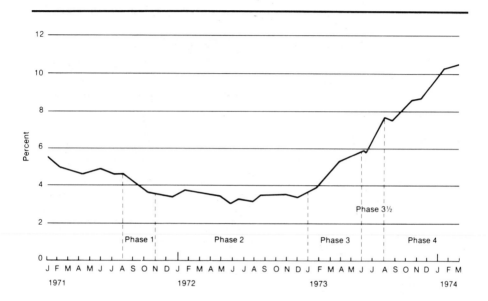

Q: Let's take another tack. The Cost of Living Council, since last summer, has been trying to spread out the post-freeze price bulge, in the hope that maybe if the economy slowed, some price increases might not even go into effect. Has that strategy been helpful?

Houthakker: No, I would say the strategy has indeed caused some very serious dislocations. I think delaying price increases was one of the major reasons why the whole controls system got into discredit—trying to control prices without controlling quantities.

Okun: The economy has areas where prices can really be read as equating supply and demand and doing a pretty sensitive job of calling the signals, and others where there is just a great deal more fuzziness. I see the opportunities for government action to alter the price of automobiles and prevent it from rising as having much more potential and much less danger of disallocation than efforts to try to fix the price of soybeans, for example.

Q: In this discussion so far we have almost ignored the wage side. Can we all agree that Cost of Living Council director John T. Dunlop is a magician on that and that the wage side has been much less of a problem than the price side?

Okun: I think the magic in 1972 was setting the standard of 5.5 percent. Basically, people believed that that was a fair wage increase, was what other people were getting and was a reasonable increase in real wages.

One of the key factors in what happened to wages in 1973 was that the biggest price increases took place in areas that don't hire a lot of labor —farms and the oil industry—and there is no way workers in other industries can benefit from those price gains. In effect, the ability of other employers to pay has not been boosted by these particular price increases.

Houthakker: I am not at all sure that we are really better off for having delayed wage acceleration in 1973, if that is what really happened. In other words, we may just have postponed these troubles to a time when they might be more difficult to solve.

Q: Where do we go from here? The controls may be over, the controls legislation may end, but inflation isn't over by any means. Don't we need some sort of anti-inflation effort that goes beyond fiscal and monetary policy?

Houthakker: Oh yes, we do. We need structural reform, which is essentially a matter of making competition more effective and increasing supply. This is something that was tried in a few areas with generally rather little success. There have been various efforts by the Council of Economic Advisors, Democrats and Republicans, to deregulate the transportation industry, to liberalize farm policy, to beef up the antitrust laws. There are quite a number of other areas, in the energy field, for example, that have seen similar things, too.

Fiscal and monetary policy is a relatively simple thing compared to much more scattered structural policies. Also, structural policy runs into much more political opposition. By now, very few members of Congress really object to fiscal-monetary policy, but when you touch the Interstate Commerce Commission, then you are touching some raw nerves.

Q: Dr. Okun, do you also feel that we must move on structural things or is that like pledging allegiance to apple pie and motherhood? Economists have been calling for these things for 15 years at least.

Okun: Yes, and everybody has been saying we have to lick inflation and we haven't either. So it seems to me that we have got to try some things that we haven't tried before, and this is one promising approach. I'd be pretty eclectic about it, and I think it ought to be sold much more as an anti-inflation package. You might get some consumer enthusiasm to countervail the producer interests that make this such a tough political problem.

Q: Wouldn't we need somebody who is in charge of doing that? Can the Council of Economic Advisors do it, or do we need what some people call a new "watchdog agency?"

Okun: Quite apart from whether any controls authority is retained, the end of the Cost of Living Council would be very undesirable in my opinion. I think the Cost of Living Council has the mechanism of being a watchdog agency and I don't think the job ought to be put on the back of the Council of Economic Advisors.

Houthakker: I believe there is a need of some reorganization of the economic policy-making mechanism. The one thing that I regret about Congress's unwillingness to extend the controls program is that John T. Dunlop was in there with a proposal for a watchdog agency, and, in fact, the Cost of Living Council would have become a watchdog agency which it really hasn't been until now. But that went down the drain with everything else.

There are two agencies in Washington that could do it—well, three perhaps. The Council of Economic Advisors is one, the Office of Management and the Budget is another, and to some extent the Justice Department.

Apart from that, we all know that departments like agriculture, interior, commerce—these are all client agencies. They speak for their clients. They will oppose any effort to improve these things.

Q: What kind of jobs would you see for this watchdog agency other than fighting within the government against inflation? Would it be useful for it to have public hearings, for example, if a union or a business seemed to step out of line in either way—on wages or prices?

Houthakker: I would say that the main purpose would be to stimulate competition by other means, not by appealing to the public responsibility of businessmen or labor leaders.

I am not saying you should never appeal to public responsibility, but on the whole I believe it is not a very fruitful approach. For one thing, it tends to be too concentrated in a few industries. It always boils down to metals—steel, copper, aluminum, these are the ones that get 90 percent of the attention, and maybe a little bit on rubber tires and shoes and then you've just about had it.

By that time you have accounted for maybe 4 percent of the economy. If you want to control inflation by this kind of approach, then you have to worry about the undertakers in Omaha who raise their burial fees by 20 percent without anyone ever knowing about it.

Q: Do you agree with that, Dr. Okun?

Okun: No. I think there is more hope of what I call picking the rotten apple out of the barrel. When I put the list (of key industries) together, it accounts for more like 15 percent of industrial wholesale prices than 4 percent. But I think the real impact of these prices is that a lot of them are associated with key collective bargaining settlements in industry.

On that score, I regard Congress's seeming unwillingness to extend controls legislation—even in a very weak form—as the result of a very effective lobbying effort by business and labor combined.

Q: Instead of controls, some have suggested the wide use of indexing[1] or escalator clauses to protect people and to induce the Government to slow things down without as much pain from unemployment. Are we naked to inflation without controls unless we follow the indexing route?

Okun: We are not quite naked to inflation, but we would be with a comprehensive indexing system. So far as I can see, a fully indexed economy means any disturbance on any price has no upper limit. If we had had complete indexing in the past 15 months, our inflation rate would be double and triple what it is today.

Houthakker: I am not much in favor of indexing either, though I believe it could overcome some equity problems. In fact, when I was a member of the council, we had a session with the labor union economists in late 1970 where we made some delicate remarks about the possibility of 100 percent cost of living clauses. But they evidently didn't feel they could sell it to their members.

Q: Do you remember why?

Okun: Yes. People want to believe in money, both business and labor. They don't want to have the yardstick stretched.

[1 By *indexing* is meant tying all contracts in the economy to some price index—say, the consumer price index—so that inflation has no redistributional effects, as between creditor and debtor, etc. The disadvantage, as Okun points out, is that this virtually guarantees a more rapid rate of inflation. RTG]

Q: Professor Houthakker, what was the logic behind the C.E.A.'s indexing proposal? Did you think that it would help slow inflation if you could get labor to buy it?

Houthakker: Yes, but it was primarily a way of eliminating what we saw as an emerging bias against organized labor. As far as we could see, union wages were falling behind . . . That's why we thought it would appeal to them, but it didn't.

There was another aspect of this proposal—we did see a price deceleration ahead. We were worried about the fact that labor would try to get large recoupments of price increases that were already slowing.

Okun: Talking about the kinds of schemes that are not politically feasible at the moment, I've got a variation on indexing that I think is better than

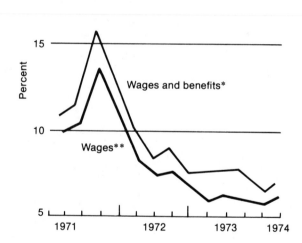

Figure B   Wage settlements

First-year changes in wage rates alone and in wages plus benefits. Major collective bargaining settlements, private nonfarm economy.
The controls program was fairly successful in achieving its objective of reducing wage settlements to a 5.5 percent annual increase, or 6.2 percent, including benefits.

*Wage and benefit figures cover agreements for 5,000 workers or more.

**Wage figures cover agreements for 1,000 workers or more.

Source: Department of Labor

simply letting wages rise to chase prices. If labor were willing to accept cost-of-living adjustments, I think that could better be done through tax credits than the sort of pay jumps that put direct upward pressure on employers' costs and thus on prices.

Q: Have you tried out this idea on labor?

Okun: Yes, with very unenthusiastic responses.

Q: What should happen at the end of this month to the controls legislation?

Houthakker: Abolish it, with the exception of a watchdog agency—but one without the power to roll back wages and prices. The agency might hold hearings, but not on particular wage and price decisions. In fact, it would probably serve as a watchdog over regulatory commissions, which I think is most necessary of all.

Okun: I'd like a continuation of some statutory control or authority that would permit wage or price decisions to be overturned after some due process. Still, I think we'll be out of the controls business for a while. Then, after its bad reputation wears off, we'll be back into it. This has been the history of a lot of European countries.

I'm always reminded of the P. T. Barnum story that it's easy to put a lion and a lamb in the same cage as long as you have a large reserve supply of lambs. I think that's the story with the lamb of controls and the lions of business, labor and excessive fiscal and monetary enthusiasm —you need a big supply of lambs.

Q: Then, we're stuck, as are most other industrialized countries that have tried to pursue full-employment policies. . . .

Houthakker: No, no, there's still another route which we haven't talked about and that is a somewhat tighter monetary policy. I believe that the present inflation not only in the United States but especially in other countries is due to a very large extent to unduly accommodating monetary policies caused by too much worry about interest rates.

I think we should aim for a little more slack in the economy. But slack isn't just the unemployment rate; I would say it has three main components—unemployment, capacity utilization and inventories.

Okun: Unemployment is generally a good indicator of overall utilization, but in 1973 for the first time in the postwar generation we really had very different signals from capacity and inventory on the one hand and unemployment rates on the other. I think we will be alert to those very different signals in the future.

Q: It seems as if, starting in 1973, there has been a whole bag of problems that nobody and no controller could deal with—they weren't the problems of a controller . . .

Okun: Not a wage controller, and not a price controller, and not a money controller, or a tax and spending controller is my view. Let me replay fiscal and monetary policy with perfect hindsight over the last two years and I don't think I could save you more than a couple of points on the rate of inflation. Let me replay agricultural policy and energy policy, however, and I'll give you five points.

Houthakker: I would give fiscal and monetary policy more blame for the problem and agriculture less.

Q: In the sum then, what is your view of the success or failure of controls or incomes policy? Does it help only when you don't need it?

Okun: No, my view is that at most controls buys you a couple of points of growth before you run into the problem of excess demand, of inevitable inflation.

But if it buys you those few points, I'm willing to pay the price of having the Government's scope increased, and I think that's really what it comes back to in looking at how different people evaluate controls.

Houthakker: I don't have strong feelings on the grounds of principle on this. If I could be convinced that it did have an effect I would talk quite differently about it. But this I think is really the issue—did it make a difference or not? I'm not convinced.

The Great Debate on Wage-Price Controls
David Lewis and Myron E. Sharpe

David Lewis is leader of the New Democratic Party in Canada. Myron E. Sharpe is editor and publisher of *Challenge: The Magazine of Economic Affairs.* Pierre Burton is a well-known Canadian author and television personality.

Mr. Burton: Mr. Sharpe, you have four minutes for the affirmative.

Mr. Sharpe: Mr. Chairman, Mr. Lewis: The other day I found a nursery rhyme that says:

> For every evil under the sun
> There is a remedy or there is none.
> If there be one, seek till you find it;
> If there be none, never mind it.

We face the most serious economic crisis since the 1930s. The economy is out of control. Our rampant inflation tells the story. If we judged by the dismal performance of our governments, we would have to conclude there is no remedy—and never mind it. But there *is* a remedy. Wage-price controls can stop inflation immediately. Unless we are willing to use controls, we may find ourselves on the road to disaster.

To understand why wage-price controls are necessary—even inevitable—we have to understand the nature of the present inflation. Actually, there are three types of inflation. The first is caused by too much overall demand in relation to supply. Contrary to popular opinion, we don't have this type. In fact, we have too little overall demand. The proof is that we are in a recession and we have a rising rate of unemployment.

The second type of inflation is caused by the leapfrog of wages and prices, the well-known wage-price spiral. Businesses raise their prices. To

Excerpted from the Global Television Network/Pierre Burton broadcast of "The Great Debate," November 14, 1974, Canada. Reprinted by permission of Pierre Burton, The Great Debate, Toronto and Global Television Network.

catch up, labor demands higher wages. Businesses raise their prices again. The process can go on indefinitely.

The third type of inflation is caused by shortages. We're most familiar with those in farm products and petroleum. But we're also short on steel, lumber and a host of other things.

We have, then, two types of inflation. Wage-price controls are precisely what we need to deal with them. Controls effect an immediate halt to the rise in *all* prices. They stop the wage-price spiral. And what's more, they give us breathing space to apply other policies designed to cope with shortages and to increase employment.

To repeat, we not only need to stop inflation; we also need to stimulate production and employment at the same time. We can't possibly do this if we rely exclusively on monetary and fiscal policies, as our governments are now doing. President Ford's economic advisers wrongly assume that we have excess demand inflation. They busily go about restricting the supply of money and credit and cutting—or trying to cut—federal expenditures. These actions can only make matters worse. They do nothing to alleviate shortages and they do nothing to arrest the wage-price spiral. Ford's advisers ask us to accept six or more percent unemployment, accept a decline in output, give up essential social programs, give up economic growth, and maybe, eventually, the rate of inflation will come down.

I don't believe the public will tolerate a cure that is worse than the disease, nor should it. These tradition-bound economists say that wage-price controls won't work. This simply isn't true. They worked well in World War II. And more recently, they worked well in the United States during our Phases I and II. It was only when controls were relaxed that they stopped working.

No doubt circumstances, rather than wisdom, will bring us around to accepting wage-price controls in the United States. I think the same is true for Canada. But it will be much more helpful all around if we work cooperatively. Because if the rest of the world goes to hell, I doubt if Canada can enter heaven alone.

Mr. Burton: Thank you, Mr. Sharpe. Well within the time limit. Would you start the clock, please, six minutes for the negative. David Lewis.

Mr. Lewis: Mr. Chairman: Undoubtedly inflation is a very serious problem facing the entire world, but I'm surprised that anyone would suggest that one area of control would solve the problem. I certainly agree with Mr. Sharpe in opposing very strongly any attempt deliberately to slow down the economy and to create unemployment. Our government did that in 1969 and 1970 and we're still suffering from it. What Mr. Sharpe is really suggesting is a completely planned economy, and if you did that, if the resolution said that, I might be on his side. The reason I say controls won't work is not because I am a traditional economist. I'm not an economist at all, and for that I don't apologize, having read and listened to economists for a long time. I say controls won't work because you cannot control prices in a vacuum. Will you control the farmer's prices? We now have in Canada a situation where the beef producers are crying because the farmer is getting too little for his steers, for his cows, and yet the beef in the stores has not gone down very much in price. Are you going to control the farmer's price? And if you control it, will you control it at the present level? And can you control it if the cost of grain goes up and the cost of feeding the calf goes up? At what point do you do the controlling?

And can you control the quality of the article that is being sold? Can you control how much sugar is put in a chocolate bar or how many nuts are put into it? Can you control the size of these things? You can't unless you have an overall planned economy, with the state controlling not only prices and wages—and I'll come to wages in a moment—but also imports and exports and foreign exchange, so that the local capitalists and the multinationals in Canada don't take their capital out of this country and take it somewhere where they can make more profit. You can't control prices in a vacuum. And I'm surprised that any economist of Mr. Sharpe's reputation should suggest that.

As far as wage control is concerned, I think it's totally inequitable. There is no suggestion in the resolution that we'll control profits or dividends or interest or lawyers' fees, doctors' fees, architects' fees, engineers' fees or capital gains. All the people with access to very large incomes won't be controlled. But the worker in the factory, in the mine, or in the office, who gets a wage or a salary: him we shall control. I find that totally unacceptable, totally inequitable.

What you do when you control these things in the present system and in the present situation is to enshrine all the inequities, all the inequalities, all the differences that make our society less than it ought to be. And therefore I reject price and wage controls because they are not workable.

Mr. Sharpe says they worked during the war. They worked during the war to some extent, but only because, in addition to control of wages and prices, there was control of resource allocation, control of production allocation, control of the entire economy to serve the war. When you have overall controls, you might fit these things in. But even during the war, there was a breach of wage control. The powerful union and employer who were willing were able to do it. All you have to do, to take a very simple example, is reclassify all the mechanics B and make them mechanics A, and their salaries will go up. Reclassify the mechanics C and make them mechanics B, and their salaries go up. That kind of thing is available to the organized workers in strong unions. It is not available to the unorganized, nor the low-paid worker. They are really stuck with controls; they are really lodged in their low wages; they can't do anything about it. I say that we cannot accept a program which results in this kind of inequity and, indeed, makes it a firm part of the economic and social structure.

Finally, I think we have to ask ourselves, when one talks as Mr. Sharpe does about wage and price controls only in this present situation—we have to ask ourselves: for how long? Mr. Sharpe suggests to us with an innocence that doesn't become him that the controls didn't work after they were taken off. I imagine that is so. But if you talk about controls for a limited period, they'll come off at some point, and the ceiling will go to the sky. That is why I say you cannot talk about these controls without considering the entire society and the entire system in which we function. Those are the reasons I oppose them, because it's the present society that we are talking about.

Mr. Burton: Thank you, Mr. Lewis. Mr. Sharpe, I owe you two minutes for rebuttal.

Mr. Sharpe: Mr. Lewis, I believe that you are exaggerating the difficulties of wage-price controls. Perhaps they are more difficult to apply in Canada, so I should be addressing myself primarily to the United States.

First of all, I don't think that anybody in his right mind would advocate wage-price controls alone without other measures to go along with them. I do advocate other measures to go along with them. I think that we must take whatever action is necessary to increase supplies and to increase employment, and I think that wage-price controls are an ideal technique that can give us the time in which to take these measures. The examples of World War II and of our Phases I and II in the United States in 1971 and 1972 prove that if there is an economic emergency—and I do believe that there is now an economic emergency—the public will accept wage-price controls.

You say that wage-price controls are inequitable. Wage-price controls do not have to be inequitable because they do not have to be inflexible. Usually they start with a freeze to give the public a chance to get over its inflationary psychosis. But after that initial freeze, adjustments can be made for various purposes—to correct inequities, to provide economic incentives where necessary and to smooth out difficulties which arise in the freeze period. But we need that breathing space, and if we don't have it, I'm afraid we have no alternative but a serious economic disaster.

Mr. Burton: You'll have more time in a moment, Mr. Sharpe. I've got a question for you now that we're into the more inflammable part of our debate. How do you keep the chocolate bar people from reducing the number of nuts, let alone the amount of chocolate? And this is only a symbol of what Mr. Lewis is talking about.

Mr. Sharpe: This exemplifies one of the difficulties of wage and price controls. Nobody, not even the most ardent proponent of wage-price controls, argues that there are no difficulties. It is a very difficult thing to do. The question is how much more difficult are the alternatives. The number of nuts in chocolate bars is not one of our major economic problems. Nevertheless, the quality of goods and services can be defined and made an intrinsic part of the controls. I don't say that wage-price controls can do a perfect job and that we will have no inflation whatsoever, because there are forces that inevitably push prices upward. But we've got to do something sensible to stop their going up at the rate of eleven-plus percent as they are now.

Mr. Burton: Let me ask a question of David Lewis. The last depression we had came about because things slowed down to the point that money didn't move. We look back on that depression now and we say that if we'd primed the pump in some way—and of course when the war came that's exactly what happened—then the depression would have been over. Now this depression, if it can be called such, comes about because things are moving too fast. Mr. Sharpe's point is that if you slow things down, and give yourself a breathing space, you've got a chance then to stop the inflationary spiral. What about that?

Mr. Lewis: I understand his point. He says nobody in his right mind proposes wage and price controls alone. I just came through an election where precisely that was proposed. . . . I don't think the inflation is a result of the economy's moving too fast and that he's going to succeed in slowing it down. When Mr. Sharpe writes a book about planning generally and plans the entire economy, I'll take a look at it and I'm sure I'll learn from it. But what he is proposing is to slow things down, and yet he doesn't want to slow them down. He wants to increase employment as I do, he wants to increase production as I do, and he wants to freeze prices and wages at the same time. I just tell him he's talking out of his hat. You can't increase production, you can't increase employment and at the same time freeze prices and wages. It just can't be done.

Mr. Burton: The point is, in World War II it was done, production was increased.

Mr. Lewis: That was an entirely different situation for several reasons. First, you started from a price bottom rather than a price top, or almost bottom. Prices hadn't caught up very far from their depression level. Wages hadn't gone up very far from their depression level. And furthermore, you didn't really control prices and wages alone.

You know the controls we had in Ottawa. We had dollar-a-year men controlling the production of steel, of grains, of everything in the country. Now, I happen to be a democratic socialist and believe it's right to have much more collective planning and control of the entire economy, of which price and wages are a part. But you can't do it now. You can, in my opinion, have some selective price controls in the situation where the consumer is being gouged, or where the farmer is getting a price for his beef which makes him go bankrupt—while the beef in the supermarket has gone down very little in price. There is something wrong there that the government can do something about, and I'm all in favor of stopping the gouging of the consumer. But I don't see the logic in the proposal Mr. Sharpe makes.

Mr. Burton: Mr. Sharpe.

Mr. Sharpe: Mr. Lewis, you say there are some people in Canada who advocate wage-price controls alone. Perhaps I overestimated the economic sophistication of some Canadians. But I'd like, as an economist, to reply to a comment of Mr. Burton's. I do not advocate holding economic activity down. What I advocate is holding prices down so that we can give ourselves a chance to expand production and to expand employment. And here is where I come in as an economist. The techniques that we've been using in the postwar period are called monetary and fiscal policies. When inflation takes place, as it is at present, the administration—such as the Ford administration—tries to restrict money and credit and to restrict government spending in order to bring prices down. But at the same time it's also bringing about an increase in unemployment and a decrease in production. The public eventually gets tired of this. It can't stand the rising unemployment and it can't stand the declining production, and the politician gets the hint. He switches gears and expands money, credit and government spending and then we have more inflation. Soon the public reaches the point where it can't stand that, and we switch gears back again. We've been doing this during the whole post-war period. By "we," I mean the United States, Canada and the other industrial countries.

Mr. Lewis: Let's be clear. I don't accept using monetary and fiscal policy as it has been done. I agree with you, Mr. Sharpe, that this on-again, off-again business is disastrous for a country, for an economy and for the people. I'm particularly interested in the fact that it's disastrous for the people. But that's not what we are debating, that's not what the resolution is talking about, and I'm an old debater. If you want me to make a statement to the effect that, instead of using blunt instruments of fiscal and monetary policy, we ought to use explicit instruments, we ought to do something about building homes, we ought to reduce mortgage interest rates to a level where the average Canadian could conceivably buy a house or rent a unit without destroying himself—if you want to debate that kind of thing, we'll perhaps be on the same side. I'm not sure; I don't know how far you would go. I know how far I would go in trying to plan the economy—with errors of course, there are always mistakes—but trying to plan the economy for the welfare of the people. Trying to control resources, trying to allocate them. But in order to do that you can't really have price and wage controls. You've got to have import controls to make sure that you're not importing inflation. You've got to have export controls to make sure that things Canadians need are not leaving the country. You've got to have foreign exchange controls to make sure that the capital isn't leaving the country. If you're talking about an entire system of controls, then you're issuing an entirely different challenge to the Canadian people. They have to choose between the kind of society they have now and the kind of society I'd like to see.

Mr. Burton: Mr. Sharpe, if you were president of your country at this point, what would you do differently from what is being done now to handle the inflationary problem?

Mr. Sharpe: Practically everything.

Mr. Burton: What kind of price and wage controls would you institute?

Mr. Sharpe: To begin with, I would face the fact that we have an economic emergency and I wouldn't try to fool anybody by saying that the predictions show that in six months or a year or two years we'll be out of it and everything will be all right. We are in a serious emergency, and emergencies mean that we need to experiment, that we need to use appropriate techniques, that the techniques of the economists of the nineteenth century and the early part of the twentieth century are just inadequate to meet the problems that we have today. Now the problem often is described by that horrendous word stagflation and you simply can't beat stagflation—which means that you have a recession and inflation at the same time—without precise techniques. I believe that the public is willing to experiment and I believe that wage-price controls are one among an arsenal of measures that have to be used. I think Mr. Lewis and I would really be in substantial agreement, and I should hope he would be my vice-president if he were a U.S. citizen, because—

Mr. Lewis: Not on your life. I am far too fond of this country.

Mr. Sharpe: I would like to see various measures which Mr. Lewis spoke about implemented. I think we shall have to implement them. I think that circumstances are going to force us to learn if the economists don't force us to learn.

Mr. Lewis: I've been saying, Mr. Sharpe, for a good many decades now, let alone years, that we are going in a direction where the nineteenth-century economic remedies are inadequate, in fact are disastrous. But when you stop to think for a moment—even though I'm not an economist I know a little about economic theory and economic practice—when you stop to think for a moment why this time, as against past situations, you have both rising unemployment and rising prices, why you have both a reduction in overall demand and rising prices, you will find that the cause is the immense power that is exercised by the large corporations. The fact is that they set prices unrelated, or not necessarily related, to the marketplace. Now, you want to solve this by saying to the worker that his wages are going to be frozen. You say you are going to have the freeze first. How long a freeze? A friend of mine suggested a sixty-day freeze and then changed it to a ninety-day freeze and then said it was going to be a flexible freeze. How long is your freeze going to be? How flexible is it going to be? How are you going to have a freeze that is flexible, and what are you going to freeze? Are you going to freeze a collective agreement that has a provision for an increase ten days from now?

Mr. Burton: We'd better give Mr. Sharpe a chance to answer. How long are you going to freeze?

Mr. Sharpe: I would say the answer to that is that you have to freeze long enough to give the Wage and Price Control Board enough time to find office space, install telephones, and buy some desks and chairs.

Mr. Lewis: You're a typical economist. The first thing you think about is office space and a telephone.

Mr. Sharpe: And you have to give the public a chance to get over its inflationary expectations. It doesn't matter if it's sixty days or ninety days. The point is, during that time, you develop a program and you decide how you're going to apply that program to large businesses, to labor unions, to small businesses, to farmers. The length of the freeze is really not an essential question. It's what you do afterward that matters. If you take controls off immediately, then prices are going to shoot right up. You have to adopt other measures to increase production and to increase employment.

Mr. Lewis: What do you do if you have what you had during one of your freezes in the states? Farmers shipped their beef across the border into Canada. Our farmers didn't like it, but yours could get a higher price. What do you do when you have to have export controls?

Mr. Sharpe: You have people who know more about freezes.

Mr. Lewis: You have to have export controls.

Mr. Sharpe: I quite agree.

. . .

Mr. Burton: Time to sum up the debate. We give forty-five seconds each. Will you start, Mr. Sharpe, for the affirmative.

Mr. Sharpe: There is an anecdote that John Kenneth Galbraith tells which goes as follows. Somebody recommended to him, when he was a price controller in World War II, that he fix a price of $5 for everything because it would make things much simpler. I made a calculation, and that price would now be $14.97. But, of course, wage and price controls don't mean fixing an inflexible price or an inflexible wage for everything and everybody. There must be fairness; there must be adjustments. Profits and fees should be part of the control package as should a catch-up for wages that have fallen behind increases in the cost of living. I believe Mr. Lewis exaggerates the difficulties. Controls succeeded in World War II. People accepted emergency measures. We have an emergency now, and we must act accordingly.

Mr. Burton: David Lewis for the negative.

Mr. Lewis: I haven't any doubt that we need new techniques. I have believed that all my adult life. We need new techniques to run our economy and we need a new system of values in our society that give priority to the lives and future of people. I have no doubt about that. But I object to the suggestion that I have exaggerated anything. I haven't. If I had had time, I could tell you a much more horrendous story about these suggestions about control. I exaggerated nothing. The fact is that price and wage controls in isolation are unworkable and unfair, and that's why I reject them.